KOULÈV

ADVENTURES
of an
AMERICAN SNAKE HUNTER:
BOOK ONE

PRAISE FOR KOULÈV : ADVENTURES OF AN AMERICAN SNAKE HUNTER, BOOK ONE

Long ago I met Dennis Cathcart by accident, literally and figuratively. He and a friend saw me and a friend get into a serious auto accident deep in the Florida Everglades. We began sharing life adventures involving reptiles almost immediately. Dennis had many real-life experiences in the West Indies by the time I met him. His storytelling captivated me just as his book will captivate you. Dennis was an early mentor at the time without knowing it. If you want a book to take you from weird, to almost unbelievable life adventures, this is the book for you. I'm in more than one of those surreal adventures myself!

— Tom Crutchfield,
Homestead, Florida,
Tom Crutchfield - *A Life Lived Among Venomous Snakes & Dangerous Reptiles*

Mr. Cathcart's honest portrayal of my father, his work and what it meant to not only Costa Rica, but the region, is excellent. While I was not alive during that time and only had my father with me for a short time after that, what I read gave me a greater understanding of a man, who even with his faults, made the world a better place while with us. I will always be grateful to Mr. Cathcart for sharing his experiences.

— Lt. Col. Herschel H. Flowers Jr.,
US Army CBRN School, Fort Leonard Wood, Missouri

The author, Dennis Cathcart, has done a magnificent job with this book, sharing his lifetime of passion and drive for adventure. It is sure to bring enjoyment and excitement to every reptile enthusiast from amateur hobbyists to professionals alike. A walk back in time, starting in the epic days when South Florida was the center of the exotic reptile trade. Then it's on to adventures in the Caribbean, Costa Rica, and beyond, detailing history-making events. The book is just plain enjoyable.

— Jack Facente,
AGRITOXINS Venom Lab, St. Cloud, Florida. Board Member, King Cobra Conservancy
https://www.thekingcobra.org/

A pleasant walk down memory lane. When Dennis and I became friends, we formed a bond over a shared interest in collecting and studying reptiles. This went on for many years. Our travels together led us through most of the Caribbean, Mexico, Haiti and Florida...and some of the best times of my life. It's a great read.

— Ed Chapman,
Reptile Research Support, Inc., Homestead, Florida

Meeting Dennis at the World Bromeliad Conference in 1994, I appreciated his abundant knowledge and sincerity; fortunately, we became good friends. Having enjoyed his writing style in his quarterly Cargo Report, my thought was always that a book of his adventures would be a super read—and it is!

— Stephen Littlefield,
Underhill Studio: https://www.stephenlittlefield.com/

KOULÈV

ADVENTURES
of an
AMERICAN SNAKE HUNTER:
BOOK ONE

Book One in the Adventures in Paradise Series.
Strange but true stories of exotic adventures
in search of reptiles
in Florida, the West Indies, Mexico, and Central America.

Dennis Cathcart

The Amicorum Group LLC, Sarasota, Florida

ISBN 978-1-956374-01-8

BISAC codes:
BIO023000   BIOGRAPHY & AUTOBIOGRAPHY / Adventurers & Explorers
NAT028000   NATURE / Animals / Reptiles & Amphibians
TRV007000   TRAVEL / Caribbean & West Indies

Edited by Mark Mathes, https://reedsy.com/mark-mathes/
Book design by Nancy Koucky, www.nrkdesigns.com
Photography by the author unless otherwise noted

Koulèv: Adventures of an American Snake Hunter, Book One
is by published by The Amicorum Group, LLC, Sarasota, Florida
For more information contact: TheAmicorumGroup@gmail.com
https://denniscathcart.com/

I dedicate this book to my grandchildren:
Daniel, Isabel, Kayleigh, and Khloe,
and to young people with a lifetime ahead to explore our amazing world.
May you always find joy in discovery
and keep your youthful enthusiasm and curiosity.
And may our world always hold places to explore
and mysteries to be solved.

TABLE OF CONTENTS

DENNIS CATHCART

"Where the heck is Dennis?" teachers at Edgewood Elementary in the 1950s would exclaim, when they discovered that, once again, he'd slipped off the recess field into the woods to look for snakes! His dad constructed a sturdy snake cage, which his teachers allowed him to keep outside the classroom window, to not discourage his curiosity. A high school summer job with a wild animal importer cemented his resolve to become an explorer and animal collector. He went on to work in a venom production laboratory in Costa Rica, then spent the next ten years traveling through 13 countries in the Caribbean, across Mexican deserts, Central American jungles, the Venezuelan cloud forests, and the Lost World. He became a noted collector of reptile specimens for zoos, institutions, and private collectors. Then, in 1976, he gave up snakes. Some colleagues were shocked, others happy, all were surprised. His adventures continued, around the world, when exotic plants became his new passion. This story is of the ten years he followed his first love: snakes. Passionate, danger-filled years, surrounded by beauty, steeped in adventure, that echoed with laughter, into worlds few are privileged to see.

DICK BARTLETT
FOREWORD

Time has flown. The years have gone. All that's left are memories. Too seldom are memories such as these put to the printed page, and often when they are chronologed they are, compared with reality, often a bit on the dull side. Not so, these.

Dennis' recollections, his memories, and his ability to document, have allowed him to chronicle past times in vivid detail. As I read *Adventures of an American Snake Hunter*, I found myself swept inextricably into times and travels long gone. Although travel certainly is an important part of this book, you are reading far more than a travelogue. This book is not just about exploring wild places although that is an important part. This book is about relationships earned and friendships honed and how a young man from a small town in Florida took the swashbuckling nature adventure stories he read as a kid as a template for his own life.

I met Dennis in the late 1960s. He and his wife lived about a half-hour's drive from my home in St. Petersburg. On our first visit I found he had a room-sized collection of snakes, most of them venomous, which I found perfectly normal and wholly understandable. We'd trade off on evening visits once or twice a week, the only invitation on either end needed was: We've got a pot of coffee on. Come on over!

Dennis and I ventured into the field on many occasions—short trips at first—and I found him to be a steady field companion. A field companion is an individual who shares your interest in arcane beetles, snakes, orchids (although his own interests may put orchids first and beetles last, the composition is the same), and he is eager to get wet, mud-covered dirty and very tired while looking for these creatures. A good field companion shares that last half bag of potato chips (even if begrudgingly), will insist that you take the last can of cold soda (depending, of course, on flavor), and cheerfully bears his share of expenses without quibbling. He (or she) thinks nothing about crawling into storm drains during a downpour or doing a crazy balancing act across a sliding hillside of talus on a day so hot your ears shrivel. Meals from 7-Elevens are nourishing enough, and it makes sense to rent a motel room for the night even though you'll be driving roadways until 4 am and heading home before 9.

These are the tales Dennis is sharing, although some have been awakened grudgingly from a vault I had thought permanently sealed.

I hope you enjoy these memories, stories from a man who has always felt that life is indeed what you make it, and who, I am sure, will continue to do so.

— Dick Bartlett, of Gainesville, Florida, is the prime photographer and the author or co-author of some 60 books on reptile care and reptile/amphibian field guides in the New World. He has been an avid traveler in South America and Mexico; was a columnist for NOAH (Northern Ohio Association of Herpetologists) and *Reptiles* magazine for 15 years, currently writes an online blog for Kingsnake.com and is a contributor for SnakeSnap.com.

ABOUT THIS BOOK

This book is not about snakes. It's about my life, a Florida boy who becomes infatuated with snakes and grows into a man in their pursuit. It's my journey through the 1950s and '60s that leads to myriad, often death-defying, adventures. Often, I venture alone, at times with fascinating people to exotic locales in thirteen countries in the Caribbean, North America, Central America and South America. Life lessons abound. My appreciation for nature grows and expands as the world around me changes. As I mature, my views evolve. So, this book is about my life, and yes, snakes and other creatures, draw plenty of admiration.

Events in this story happened over fifty years ago when the world was manifestly different than today. Yet to be invented were cell phones, personal computers, and digital cameras. Travel was easier, affordable, safer, and there was less regulation. In 1966, at eighteen years old, I set out alone with my Ford Bronco from Florida for a ten-day trip to Mexico with $150 in my pocket. It would be foolhardy and insanely dangerous today. Times were blessedly simpler, I think saner, certainly more fun, in my opinion, better.

The land was largely unspoiled; South Florida was dotted with small towns and modest-sized cities separated by wilderness. Today, both the Atlantic and Gulf coasts and the Keys are one contiguous mega-city. Many unique habitats are lost forever, along with their fauna and flora. Others are fragmented and reduced, while many more are threatened. According to LandScope.org, "During the mid-20th century, Florida lost more than seven million acres of forest and herbaceous wetlands to development." Since then, it has only accelerated. As of 2021, 133 animal species of all types (insects, to fish, birds, reptiles, and mammals) are listed as endangered by the state* or federal authorities. This includes 20 reptiles (such as the indigo snake and American Crocodile), and four amphibians (such as Frosted Flatwoods Salamander). The majority of these are endangered by habitat loss. *Source: "Florida's Endangered and Threatened Species" (2021) Florida Fish and Wildlife Conservation Commission.

I and other characters in the book shared a love and appreciation for animals. In the 1960s and early 1970s, few restrictions limited collecting and importing them, especially reptiles. Most of us in the hobby then were doing nothing illegal, immoral, or unethical, and we acted in as careful and conservative a manner as were dictated by norms of the time.

Times have changed. People and governments, now more aware of the value of herptiles, seek to protect and/or regulate them as their habitats shrink. Most field collectors are on board with these changes and work within evolving rules. In some cases, they helped formulate them. Husbandry, rare then, has become a conservation tool and a major source of specimens in captivity today.

What was then a benign activity is now considered by some—even many—to be unacceptable, offensive, and is sometimes illegal. Looking back, it's easy to see issues not so obvious then. What this book hopes to accomplish is to provide an unblinking look into the history of reptile collecting as witnessed through my eyes. The joy of being in the field, of discovery, our challenges, and adventures. Although it is from a single person's viewpoint, the book covers many aspects of the hobby and business, and exposes the good, bad, and ugly sides of the animal trade, including reptiles. Whether you applaud or condemn the practice, I hope you will learn from these accounts, about a time long past, but which is part of the history of the hobby of herpetoculture.

Snake hunters were different then. Often pioneers. We were fewer, often loners, private people pursuing our interests while limiting our exposure to a public that viewed us as quirky at best, or weird. And yet, back then, most all of us lacked the tattoos, piercings, and other trappings of the freak-show that the reptile world now seems to attract. Meeting others in the hobby then was largely by accident while in the field, or by association with other herpers. Many of us spent years in proximity, yet never met. Now, everybody knows everyone. We did not have the internet or reptile expos. There were wild animal importers, and darn few of them. Word of mouth was the way our fame or infamy spread. Despite this relative isolation, few eras in herp history have produced more or better herpetologists, herpetoculturists, or more fervent reptile protagonists and conservationists.

As a living fossil of sorts, my "snake years" were largely before the modern era of herpetoculture. We collected, kept, and traded wild species before reptile keeping grew into the huge, profitable, widespread, mainstream hobby that it is today. Immense expositions sprang up in many cities throughout the US and

Europe. The granddaddy of them all is the National Reptile Breeders' Expo in Daytona Beach, Florida. Here, hundreds of vendors sell their wares to thousands of eager buyers from around the world. Rare species to be sure, more than 90 percent captive-bred, but all the rage are the aberrant or "designer" snakes and lizards, with exceptional colors, rarely if ever found in nature.

These specialty animals include albinos, amelanistic (lacking Black pigment), anerythristic (lacking red pigment), piebald (normal pattern interrupted by large areas of white) and many, many more. Special breeding, for example with Corn Snakes (Red Ratsnakes), has resulted in dozens of morphs, given fancy names for the trade: Creamsicle, Lavender Ghost, Motley Blue and so many more. And Ball Bythons—over two dozen morphs! The trend has spread to lizards, turtles, amphibians and beyond. I do not regret my exodus from reptiles before this new wave of popularity and modern morphs. I still love seeing animals in their natural habitats and in their natural colors. The new-age reptiles remind me of the fancy $5 cups of coffee at Starbucks. I prefer a $1 cup of black-no-sugar joe from 7-Eleven.

⁓

Regarding nomenclature, reptile names in this book were current during the era of the story. Many binomials (technical names) have changed, and will continue to do so, with the advent of DNA research. I use a common, non-technical, name when they are generally known. In conformance with a growing nomenclatural trend, I have adopted the practice of capitalizing common names of animals and plants when a name is specific to a species. This convention has been adopted by several societies and organizations as a means to reduce ambiguity when proper common names are written. Among them: the American Fisheries Society (AFS), the International Ornithological Congress (IOC), the Society for the Study of Amphibians and Reptiles (SSAR), and the Herpetologists' League.

I have compiled tables of reptile and amphibian names that have changed since the time span of this book, to names current as of 2021. (Snake nomenclature data verified by Peter Uetz of The Reptile Database (http://www.reptile-database.org/). For other animals, a table is provided to reference the binomial when only the common name is given in the text. Tables are found in the Appendix.

What's real and what's not? I will stress that the events represented in this story are real and true to the best of my recollection. Everything (in Book One) happened fifty years ago or longer. Some events may be out of sequence for the purposes of clarity or combined for brevity or because I can't remember exactly when they took place. All characters are real, and their real names are used—except when I could not recall them. In those cases, I used a pseudonym to make the story more coherent. With certain exceptions, conversations are representative, based on my recollection of what was said, and are not intended to be verbatim quotes. Some characters in this book who are still with us may disagree with words I attribute to them. They might assume that their memory is sharper than mine!

Out of respect for privacy, in this book I do not mention my former wife's name. She and I persisted in marriage for seventeen years, seven years beyond the ending of this story. Our lives diverged and I continued down familiar pathways, eventually finding a new partner in Linda, who has been with me almost forty years at this publication.

Life continues to take Linda and me on many adventures around the world, some of which I hope to publish onto the pages of other books. Life, karma, or angels have blessed me beyond all reasonable expectations. I hope to show my gratitude by sharing my experiences with you for years to come.

All direct quotes, unless otherwise credited, are based on the author's recollections of events, on personal notes and conversations with the parties in question.

Photos in this book are by the author, unless otherwise noted. Quality may be poor in some cases (or terrible!), but they reflect the times and topic as accurately as possible. Some news articles, certificates and other printed matter are not legible in the reduction necessary to fit in this book. These items and additional photos can be viewed in clearer context on the author's website: https://denniscathcart.com/.

ACKNOWLEDGMENTS

This is my first book; therefore, I have many to thank. First, my Lord and Savior, Jesus Christ, who answered prayers, and saw fit to send His angels to my rescue more times than I deserve. My parents, whose optimistic outlook on life inspired me. My mother, Lynn, loved me unconditionally and knew when it was time to let me go. My father, Oswald "Jack" Cathcart Jr., led by example, loved all of nature, and did his best to instill within me the faith, empathy, self-reliance, and sense of adventure that has served me so well. My teachers, elementary through high school, who kept up the pressure on a reluctant student, seeing potential, despite my resistance. I thank you, Linda, my wife, partner, and travel companion of four decades, for your constant encouragement. You joined me after the years covered in this tome but heard my stories often enough that you could have written this book without me.

To my field companions and mentors: Ed Chapman, Dick and Patti Bartlett and Lew Ober, all dear friends without whom many of my adventures would not have happened. A salute to US Army Major Herschel H. Flowers, from whom I learned about life, venomous snakes and honor, and his son Lt. Col. Herschel H. Flowers Jr. who so generously shared his family archives for this book. I thank Jack Facente for his personal story of his service in Vietnam. For technical assistance and/or information: P. Uetz, P. Freed, R. Aguilar, & J. Hošek, (editors) (2021) The Reptile Database, http://www.reptile-database. org/, and Kim Weismantle and the Old Davie School Historical Museum, (http://www.olddavieschool.org/).

Old friends too numerous to name, who have stood by me, for years, encouraging me to write my stories, I owe much. Without them I am not sure if this book would have come to fruition. Not least, every person mentioned in this book had an influence on my life. They are my story. They shaped, in large part, who I am. This sentiment goes equally for those who helped me, those who stood in my way, and those who simply populated the incredible worlds that I had the privilege to explore.

As a novice writer, I thank the members of the Sarasota Writers Group, (https://fwasarasota.blogspot.com/), for their support, encouragement and for selflessly sharing invaluable experience and knowhow. Peter Frickel, http://peterfrickel.com/, for guidance and inspiration. To Anne Perry Moore: You gave me a dose of reality with your first edit. To Mark Mathes, https://reedsy.com/mark-mathes/ my main editor, I thank you for your great editing and much needed coaching. I appreciate my friend Ken Marks of Gainesville, Florida, for his additional copy editing and technical advice. Nancy R. Koucky, https://nrkdesigns.com/, for her layout and design work. Stephen Littlefield, Underhill Studio: https://www.stephenlittlefield.com/, longtime steadfast friend, artist, and native Floridian, who painted this awesome cover. Once again, my wife Linda, for reading and re-reading my manuscript. I am grateful to all these folks, and more.

PROLOGUE
BOOK ONE

My story begins at a time when South Florida was a tranquil, tropical wonderland. When many roads were still dirt. When the world was still full of wonder and mystery. A time, post-WWII when opportunities seemed limitless. These were the times, and this was the place, now largely memory, where I grew up and fell in love with the natural world. When I started exploring the Everglades, it came to the doorstep of Ft. Lauderdale and Miami. I went on to investigate the Bahamas, then an archipelago of solitude and unspoiled beauty before the invasion of mega-resorts.

Mexico was my first big expedition, traveling solo when such a journey was seen as an adventure, not a foolhardy mission that could end as a fatal enterprise. I found friendly people and the vastness of pristine deserts, mountains, and jungles, and plenty of reptiles. I never feared the danger.

I explored Haiti next, in a time when the island was steeped in mystery, superstition, and danger. We encountered exotic wildlife, primitive culture, brutal Tonton Macoute, and strange Voodoo. A potent and addictive gumbo that led to many returns.

I witnessed history while wandering Central America when the region was rife with turmoil and civil war. My travels crossed paths with President Lyndon Johnson. During a life-changing sojourn in the earthly paradise of Costa Rica, I attended the ceremonial handover of an American antivenom program with the awarding of the US Legion of Merit Award to a US Army Major and witnessed the awesome destructive force of a volcanic eruption.

I'm blessed to have been at the right places at the right times to meet and share experiences with some of the herpetological world's most noted and intriguing characters. A wealth of episodes that shaped my future and left lasting memories—and a few scars.

In between, life happens. I learn to balance domestic obligations of marriage and work, with my all-consuming drive to explore. A utility strike comes as a personal financial blow, but I use the windfall of time for a bold Bahamian journey, crossing the Gulf Stream, solo, by boat. After a successful hunt for boas, I leave my boat in Bimini, and fly on to Andros Island—the largest in the Bahamas. Finding new species comes at the price of injury but results in a successful journey.

After an extraordinary Haitian trip with an English herpetologist, I embark on what was planned as a short, exploratory trip to the Exumas to seek rock iguanas. When I'm marooned on a waterless desert island, the ordeal nearly costs my life. The few-day trip runs into weeks yet opens new doors.

And this is not half of it. Many more adventures with reptiles followed. In further adventures (Book Two) I observe in the wild, capture, import, and handle some of the world's rarest reptiles. There are trials and tribulations, troublesome regulations, logistics, and double-dealing. The drama of lost trust. A snakebite that nearly ends it all.

Travel to the jungles of Venezuela opens new doors and sets my course to irreversible change. New discoveries, new friends, and a new life direction.

Join me as our Adventures in Paradise continue across Central and South America, Southeast Asia, Australia, and Africa for forty more years, with all the danger, intrigue, beauty, and discovery—but in the botanical world. Meet new travel companions, including my wife Linda, and come along as we defy all reason and face risk and peril to bring back some of the world's most exotic flora.

I am an irredeemable wanderer.
Bits of my body and soul lie scattered on every beach,
each mountain, jungle, and desert
that I have trod.

The moccasin, tipped from the muslin sack, lay motionless in the mud for a long moment, a heap of black and brown coils. Surveying its surroundings with an unblinking stare, she flicked her tongue, straightened gradually, sliding silently, tentatively, into the swamp. Sweat dripped from my temples, blood rushing in my ears, the only sound. I drank in the gravity of the moment, then turned away from my first love, a decade as a reptile collector. End of an era. All specimens sold, given away or released...I was free. I stood at the threshold of an unfamiliar road promising new adventures, wondering would they, could they, compare to my years as a snake hunter? I'd known beauty, tranquility, islands, deserts, jungles, the thrill of discovery—and danger. Oh yes, danger is addictive, that supercharged feeling as adrenaline courses through your veins, increasing strength, erasing fear. Heady stuff. But I'd known loneliness too, and terror. I know what it's like to be run over, shot at, left to die on a waterless, uninhabited island, to get lost, stung, and bitten by venomous creatures, jailed, and deceived. Having survived, I wouldn't change a thing. In 1976, at twenty-eight years old I faced my biggest challenge: change. But, let me take you back to the beginning....

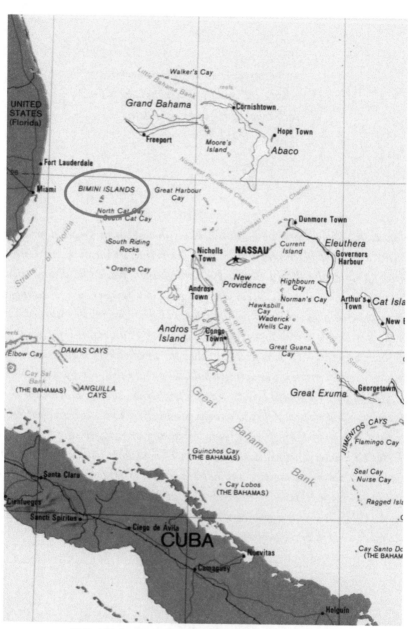

United States Central Intelligence Agency. The Bahamas.
[Washington, D.C.: Central Intelligence Agency, 1986] Map.
https://www.loc.gov/item/2005631594/

PART ONE:
Youth and the Dawn of My Age of Reptiles

Growing up in the wonderland that was 1950s and '60s South Florida, moving to Davie on the edge of the Everglades, finding buddies to explore and hunt snakes with. School's a challenge, I skip often. Kennedy's assassination is a reality check. I work at an animal farm, start a business, join a herpetological society, and meet important friends. Boyhood ends with a crash that changes everything. Then: My first trip overseas.

Fort Lauderdale Beach, 1955. (State Archives of Florida/Barron)

CHAPTER 1:
Boy Meets Snake

Whether an obsession or fascination, snakes are a part of my earliest recollections. My childhood was ordinary for the era. Blessed by happy, optimistic parents and a glorious place to grow up, I flourished. South Florida, in the post-war years, was an earthly paradise for a kid who loved the outdoors. A safe world, clean and green. My folks settled on the woodsy outskirts of Ft. Lauderdale in the late 1940s.

Our modest house was a castle for me. Backed up to 25 wooded acres with oaks, pines, and cabbage palms where none of the neighborhood kids ventured. "An old witch lives in there." I believed that for a while, feared the unknown. My dad loved the outdoors. As a boy, he rode horses and explored the hills and forests of his native New England. He'd take me for walks in the woodland. We found rabbits, raccoons, opossums, and squirrels, but no witches.

I reasoned. "She must only come out at night."

My father, in his gentle way, with simple wisdom, explained. "There's nothing in darkness that isn't there in the light."

Dad hung the moon. I trusted his every word. They strengthened me, and I began exploring the forest on my own to test the limits of my newfound courage. With each step I grew bolder. My friends listened wide-eyed when I told of things I'd seen, but few joined me. I claimed the wooded lot as my private domain, and learned each tree, rock, and meadow.

Snakes were common on our walks. Dad wasn't fearful of them (or anything else). "Most are harmless. Don't mess with them and they won't bother you."

3

Unlike most of my friends, I never developed a fear of snakes. I grew bolder, played outside in the evening breeze after supper, and avoided the dark wood. Until that one day, or I should say, night, I followed a familiar trail. No flashlight, moonlight illuminating the sugar sand path. Deeper and deeper. Tree limbs and palm fronds cast sinister moon shadows. My heart beating fast, I walked on and returned without running.

I told my dad where I'd been, and he said he was proud but cautioned. "There're rattlesnakes in there."

Confused, I questioned his earlier statement. The darkness and light thing. "How come we've never seen one in the daylight?"

"Just be careful, okay?" Kids are so literal. I hoped I hadn't hurt his feelings.

Though I never saw a rattler in the woodlot behind our house, I became intrigued by snakes. The first I can remember catching was a Red Ratsnake, *Elaphe guttata,* in our backyard, where they were frequent visitors. Tan with reddish blotches outlined in black, a lovely creature. I begged my dad to build a cage. His eyes said he wasn't keen on the idea. I was six years old; he knew I couldn't keep the snake alive for long. Still, he constructed a sturdy wooden box with hardware cloth on the front and hinged top.

My parents hoped my fascination was a passing phase. It wasn't. Instead, it sparked a passion spanning two decades, filled with adventure, travel, exotic animals, and wild places. But I'm getting ahead of myself.

∽

"Red" grew docile with handling. Kids from our street and the next showed up to see him. I became the center of attention. Imagine my shock in front of Donny, Mikey, and Paul when he bit the back of my hand. Blood poured from my tender skin. The boys bolted, and I ran to my mom. Upset with me for having a snake in the first place, she washed my wound.

When the bleeding stopped, tiny tooth marks in the outline of his jaws remained. Shock forced my tears until I realized the bite was painless. That removed my fear, made me braver in the eyes of my pals. Try as I might, I could convince none of them to hold Red. I was okay with that and enjoyed my notoriety.

A few weeks passed, and my father asked, "What are you feeding Red?"

"What? Gosh, nothing, I mean, what does he eat?"

Not the right answer. "It's time to let Red go home."

"No! Not that. I love him, Dad."

"We can't keep him forever without food."

Crushed, but I understood. Like walking to the gallows, we crossed the backyard. Tears welled as I nudged Red and watched him crawl into the brush.

I survived the crisis, and a few weeks later Dad brought home a Florida Box Turtle, *Terrapene carolina bauri*, in an old pail. "You can keep her for a while."

I picked her up, and then she pulled in her head and feet and closed her shell. Box turtles have a hinged plastron that seals tight. I set her inside the cage, closed the lid, walked away. Her head poked out, slowly at first, next the feet. Soon she was crawling around, exploring her new home.

She refused melon, lettuce, bread, and grass for an entire week. Leftover worms from a Saturday fishing trip changed everything. She gobbled them. We found she loved canned dog food and learned to take bits from my fingers.

I kept Myrtle's enclosure clean, and water dish full, Dad made sure. After a month came the dreaded question. "Are you ready to take Myrtle home? She needs sunshine and room to roam. You've done a good job caring for her, but she's not happy living in a box."

He let me think and enjoy her for a while longer. On the weekend we headed out to the Everglades. We released her on the same dirt road through a swamp where he'd found her. We watched as she rambled along between sawgrass in the shallow water until she disappeared. Now I understood. The lesson was respect for living things. Dad was pleased, I felt proud.

With my promise to set them free after a week or two, Dad let me keep snakes. Most thrived in captivity. Others tried nonstop to escape, rubbing their noses raw. I learned how to care for them, so they'd stay healthy and content. Most importantly, how to enjoy and turn them loose before they got stressed. As I became more responsible, Dad bought me a baby iguana.

Author with his father in Conch Key, circa 1956

CHAPTER 2:
Trouble in Paradise

O ur family left for Florida when I was a month old. Dad pulling our house trailer behind a 1946 Buick Roadmaster convertible. First stop, New Port Richey on Florida's West Coast. A few months later we head south to settle in Hacienda Village, beside New River in the Everglades outside of Ft. Lauderdale. Lauderdale's population is 20,000. They embrace the climate, wilderness, fabulous beaches, and friendly folks.

Mom and Dad brim with post-war optimism. They find work, prosper, and in 1951 buy a vacant lot to build a house in suburban Edgewood. Mom keeps our home filled with love and kindness and the smell of fresh-baked cookies. Dad's laughter brings joy. His simple goodness, honor, belief in hard work and sweat give refuge. Their faith, strength, values, and appreciation for what we have shaped my life's outlook.

We enjoy the Eden of South Florida. When I hear "Mr. Sandman," I recall our little wooden boat, fishing, and collecting coconuts from islands in the Intracoastal Waterway. Fun pulling tourists out of sand at the beach with Dad's WWII surplus Jeep. Mom fussing when I'd leave tadpoles in my pants pocket. The rides to Miami in our convertible to eat chicken-in-a-basket served by girls on roller skates. The smell of popcorn recalls Dad taking me and my friends to the drive-in movies in the back of his dump truck. Good times. Carefree times.

My half-brother Ron, nine years older than me, leaves home when I'm in second grade. His leaving signals things are not as rosy as I see them. So much I don't, can't, or won't see.

Divorce splits our household in 1956. Kids never understand. Mom loves the suburban life, Dad longs for the country. She drinks, he doesn't. Nightlife suits her. He's an early riser. My older brother joins the service. I live with Mom. Dad rents a house nearby.

Before it happened, I never wanted to grow up. Now I can't wait. At first, little changes. After school, I explore the woods, build tree houses, and underground forts. Snake hunting is part of my daily routine. I visit when Dad is home. Most days he works until after dark, driving a dump truck. Mom tries her best, but she understands how I miss being around my dad.

⌒⌒

A half-mile away, a tropical wonderland beckons. Forest, swamp, and abandoned rock quarries filled with limpid blue water, ripe to explore. Rumors are rattlesnakes and moccasins live in there. With less supervision now, I slip over after school.

Ants to sugar, boys from far and wide come to swim and jump from a rope swing hung from a gigantic oak. My father forbids me to enter the crystal waters without him. Dangerous, sheer-sided, 20-foot-deep. A hangout for teenagers from nearby Naval Air Junior High. They don't tolerate younger kids. We keep watch until they leave, then invade the swimming hole.

Physical size matters. Big for my age, most of the neighborhood boys look up to me. I enjoy it. They expect me to push the limits, lead the way. But when I explore the dim, swampy, mysterious woods, they bail. A pathway, cut by surveyors, runs straight through the deepest part of the swamp. Used by mosquito control, we dub it skeeter-man trail. To traverse means wading in water from knee to waist-deep. It calls me. I can't resist. Nervous the first time. After that, it's easy.

The other boys listen wide-eyed when I relate tales of things I found. I bring out souvenirs; colorful mushrooms on rotted limbs, leaves from unfamiliar trees. I explore the swamp end to end. The first time I persuade my best buddy to come in with me, we see an Eastern Diamondback Rattlesnake. My first. I'm nervous. Donny, terrified, never returns. I can't stay away.

One Sunday, Dad and I are shooting bottles with a .22 rifle at a roadside trash dump near the rock pit. A fun and common pastime. I spot a three-foot rattler and call out. He comes over and prepares to shoot it. "Don't Dad, please."

He doesn't. The snake crawls into palmettos. Mesmerized by its bright black-and-white diamond pattern and its rattles, I must have one. The serpent casts its spell. I can think of little else. A few months pass, alone, looking for snakes, I see another at the dumpsite.

Nervous but determined, I find a stick and try to pull it from the tangle of trash. When touched it coils, rattling loud in a fearsome display. A robust four-footer. I chicken out but realize it's no longer if—but when.

∽

My school, Edgewood Elementary, sits in the same forest as the rock pit, next to the Ft. Lauderdale Airport, the old WWII Ft. Lauderdale Naval Air Station. The teachers support my interest in reptiles, introduce me to reptile books in the library. By fourth grade, they allow me to keep a snake cage outside my classroom window. With no air conditioning, one entire wall has glass windows, kept open most days. I often catch garter snakes and ratsnakes on the playground. When I find something new, the teacher lets me show the class.

My passion earns attention from the students. Teachers respect and see value in self-expression. This affirms as normal, a curiosity that others thought quirky.

Without a doubt, my love of nature comes from my father. My hero. An imposing six-foot-three, strong and virtuous. And a mature 34 when I was born. He loves horses, farm animals and wildlife. Saturdays when I ride with him in his truck, he tells stories of when he was young. How he was a cowboy and mined gold in Arizona. Dad seldom mentions the war. When he does, his stories center on the islands, the natives, the jungles.

During the week he hauls road fill. On weekends, topsoil. Sometimes he drops me at the quarry to hunt for snakes while he delivers his loads. Two older Black men run a dragline and front-end loader at the muck pit. He asks them to keep an eye on me. I soon disappear into the woods surrounding the pit, climbing spoil piles, turning over any object that might hide a snake. Out of sight, but I keep an ear tuned for my dad's truck. I'm careful not to get in the way of heavy equipment. A sweltering day, I soon look for something to drink.

At their flatbed, I take the tin cup and get water from an Igloo cooler. Joe, the stocky equipment operator says, "Boy, yo' daddy's gonna whup you."

I'm puzzled, panicked. "Why, what did I do?"

"Drinkin' out that keg, that's what." I don't understand I've crossed a Jim Crow line.

No sooner spoken when my dad drives into the pit and walks to their truck. "Hey Joe, Art." He picks up the same cup, takes a drink. "Denny's not giving you any trouble, is he?"

"No suh, he's a fine boy."

He treated everyone the same, fair and kind. I know little of any such social taboos and never saw prejudice in my father. Never.

Dad bought a piece of land in the rural town of Davie in western Broward County. Working weekends for several months, he and a few men built our house. I help put up fence and a barn, handing up tongue and groove lumber dad used for the roof. In 1958, at ten years old, I moved in with him. It changed my world.

CHAPTER 3:

Davie

"First Settlement in the Everglades" was Davie's promotional slogan. Originally called Zona, when settled in 1909, and first populated by returning workers from the Panama Canal Zone. Back then, the Glades extended to downtown Fort Lauderdale. North and South New River Canals formed Davie's borders.

Only Pond Apple Slough remains of the cypress forests and tepid swamps. To the east, New River transforms. Docks and seawalls line its shores, its name changes to the Tarpon River. Bridges span, and tunnels pass beneath its dark, brackish waters. In the wet season, water from Florida's swampy interior decreases salinity. Myriad canals form the islands of Las Olas, with yachts berthed behind homes of the well to do. It meets the Intracoastal Waterway, here called the Stranahan River. Through Port Everglades, the lifeblood of the "River of Grass" spills wasted into the Atlantic. No longer flowing south into Florida Bay.

Today, Davie's cypress woods are long gone, Sawgrass prairies drained, everything's changed. Intensive development covers the woods and fields where I rode horses and hunted snakes. In the late 1950s—early '60s era, Davie defined a classic rural town. Two feed stores, a drugstore, Anderson's General Store and Klein's Hardware. A firehouse that burned to the ground. Tom's Bar and the Horse and Hounds, and Primrose grocery, where I got my first after-school job at 13. Not much else, except the rodeo grounds. No traffic lights. The county sheriff covered policing.

Dad names our place J bar D Ranch, for Jack and Dennis. West of town, where ranches, groves, and farms dominate, neighbors are few. Ours is a sandy lane off Kirkland Road. Beyond us, where a wooden bridge crosses the canal into Gulfstream Farms, the tar-and-slag-pebble pavement ends. It continues another mile as a dirt road, ending in a sod field. So far out, Dad liked to say, "We won't get yesterday's paper till tomorrow."

What's a farm without livestock? Dad built a chicken yard and coup with a double row of nest boxes. Ducks, geese, and turkeys run free. I was born for this. In no time I wore a straw hat, ran barefoot with duck poop between my toes. Rode horses, milked goats, made forts of hay bales in our barn.

Best of all, this was "Snake Town." Snakes, omnipresent in woods, fields, canals, and swamps around us, visit our barnyard often. A shelf in the barn holds several nice cages. I helped Dad build them.

What could beat living in Davie, the snakiest place imaginable? Our little farm, animals, plenty of room. What else could I want? Well, friends for one. Snakes to the rescue. Two boys, Adrian known as "Sonny" and Ronny Bird live a quarter-mile away. Our closest neighbors. Lifelong snake collectors, my interest in snakes opens their door. Kindred spirits, immediate best buddies, the Three Musketeers. We become inseparable. Life is grand.

Mr. Bird runs a bookkeeping service from home and raises Toggenburg dairy goats and rabbits for meat. Their family is better off than most on nearby farms and ranches. How thrilling to watch *Bonanza,* the only color television show in 1959, on their color TV. The boys keep critters, badgers, magpies, and coyotes from the west. Tropical South American birds, exotic anteaters, Ocelots. Walk-in enclosures with gangly spider monkeys have branches to climb. Smaller cages for gentle Woollys and semi-tame Capuchins, which they call "organ grinders."

To stock their private zoo, we became skilled at trapping wild animals alive. Raccoons, Striped and Spotted Skunks, otters, and Bobcats. Water-filled pits made of concrete blocks hold turtles. A canal alongside rural Kirkland Road, our hunting ground.

After school, we'd strike out, buckets, nets, cloth sacks in hand, for the hunt.

Author at 11 years old, with horse Big Red ca 1959.
Dad's 1949 Chevy pickup in background.

Snake cages in author's family barn, early 1960s.

Clearing Water Hyacinths with a dragline in 1960s. (State Archives of Florida/LaHart)

CHAPTER 4:
The Canal

Most people see a ditch beside Kirkland Road, to us it's the center of our lives. Its iced-tea-colored water is the blood in our veins. Waist deep, 15 feet wide. Our world, where we escape notice of passing drivers, wade the shallows, searching for creatures to net or catch. A source of adventure and refuge, our private domain.

A county dragline comes to remove Water Hyacinths once a year. It operates from the west bank, opposite the road, flattening the tangle of Elderberries and Castor Beans. From tons of aquatic vegetation and mud scooped and deposited, dozens of creatures pour forth. Fish, prawns, turtles, and sirens, an eel-like, slimy salamander with two front and no back legs.

A dragline by the canal when we arrive from school is a sure bet, we'll skip the next day.

It's an exciting time. We show up early with buckets and bags. Sometimes the operator tries to chase us off, but we persist. Once convinced we'll stay clear, he pays us no mind. We toss fish, sirens, eels, large turtles back into the water. We keep any snake and turtles smaller than our hands. What we can't catch may crawl into the matted weeds and die. We're on a mission far too important to let school interfere!

Friendly operators wait while we collect if a load has many animals. Sometimes they're playful and drop the bucket in a puddle of muck and splatter us. Good fun, no one gets hurt. We go home with our animal treasures, joyous and as tired and dirty as coal miners.

❦

On the banks we set traps for skunks, raccoons, and opossums. At night, we search with flashlights for mud turtles, watersnakes, and frogs. A freshly cleaned canal, stark and lifeless, means no collecting until weeds return.

Our friend Dale lives on Gulfstream Farms. His father's a cowboy on the expansive Angus ranch. The bridge to the farm has iron pipes set inches apart that can support a truck, but cattle won't cross. Dangerous for horses, we ford beside the span and enter through a barbed wire gate.

Dale's father is a hard man, hardworking, lean, and stern. They live in ranch housing, small and plain. Their yard, notched into a pasture, has no trees, but room for a clothesline in back and pickups and horse trailers on the grass in front. Dale invites none of us boys inside, though I don't know why. He's the first to show for a hunting trip.

❦

As kids, we're not above doing dumb things. We joust on our bicycles, pelting one another with handfuls of sandspurs. It's not unusual for someone to get pushed into the canal on the half-mile walk to the school bus stop. In 1960, when I was 13, we discovered a way to shoot each other with fence staples! A stout rubber band between thumb and forefinger can launch a staple with the force of a bullet. It stings like the dickens, and we'd end up with welts and bruises on our arms and backsides.

One day, we discover a group of boys, strangers, in *our* canal by the Gulfstream Farms bridge. We confront them, they're frightened. "Get out of here. Don't come back."

The oldest of them is defiant. "You can't make us leave."

Ronny answers by shooting him with a fence staple. Instead of leaving a welt, it sticks in his forearm! It breaks the skin; he pulls it out and screams. We panic and run. He's not hurt, not badly anyway, but it scares them. Us too, enough to avoid the canal for a week.

CHAPTER 5:
Branching Out

Road collecting is the easiest way to catch snakes in numbers and types not found near our farm. Often, I ask my father to take me and the boys out cruising. Despite rising at 4 am and working the entire day, he never complains. His best-dad-in-Davie reputation is well deserved.

We pile in his 1949 Chevy pickup for a ride along the edge of the Everglades, where snakes cross the roads each evening. Many get hit and killed. We stand in the truck bed, lean on the cab, and bang on the top when we spot a snake. Dad stops, we jump out, catch it in the headlights. Innocent fun for me and my buddies.

Ronny is my age, a few months older, Sonny four years older. At 16, he quit school and his parents bought him a car. Now we can night hunt whenever we want. This changes everything. A choice destination is Krome Avenue Extension, west of Miami. It crosses miles of swamp between US 27 and 41. At twilight, Florida Banded Watersnakes, *Natrix sipedon pictiventris*, crawl in the dozens along the 20-mile stretch. We drive slowly and if there's traffic, stay off on the shoulder, take turns sitting on a fender.

One evening we see a young, three-inch box turtle, and a moccasin. While Sonny and Ronny catch the Cottonmouth, I run 50 yards back to the turtle. It's in the middle of the southbound lane and a tractor-trailer is coming fast. I wait on the roadside. The driver eases over to give me a wide berth. My heart sinks when I'm sure he'll hit the tiny creature.

The semi is halfway across the center line as it sails past in a gust of wind. A wheel grazes the front of the teeny turtle's shell. Imagine pinching a watermelon seed. The little guy rockets from the road, striking my shin, and ricochets into the Sawgrass. I see stars, pull up my pants leg to show a red welt. I hobble over to Sonny and Ronny; they fall to the ground laughing. By the time I get home, I've got a fist-sized bruise the color of a plum.

⌒⌒

A summer's day in 1962, we set out to visit Thompson's Wild Animal Farm. A 75-mile trip one-way from Davie up narrow US 27 to rural Clewiston, known as Florida's Sweetest Town. Located alongside the highway, south of Lake Okeechobee, it's in the heart of snake country. Thompson's farm looks abandoned in a sea of sugar cane. Rundown buildings and a ramshackle house. Worn out tractors and equipment poke out of head-high weeds.

L.E. Thompson is legendary in the reptile world. He's run ads in magazines advertising reptiles and wild animals since the 1940s. A proud "Georgia Cracker," though he's been here most of his life. He leads us past rows of wire-bottomed cages standing on two-foot wooden legs. Wild animals of many kinds, their droppings forming stalagmites under the pens. *Does he ever clean them?* The stench is nauseating. "Everything's for sale."

I wander from the group to a pit made of stuccoed concrete blocks. A three-foot Eastern Garter Snake, *Thamnophis sirtalis sirtalis*, is the biggest I've seen. A common, non-venomous species. The moment I pick it up, it bites me on the end of my left thumb.

In an instant it works its jaws past my first knuckle as I struggle to coax it to release me. Its needle-sharp teeth in my tender skin are excruciating. In moments it has my digit swallowed to the hilt. I'm 14, too old to cry, but dang, it hurts! Despite staying silent out of fear of getting into trouble, they notice my predicament. Mr. Thompson calls out. "Come here, boy."

No way can we pull it off without shredding my flesh. He shows me to a water trough and has me submerge both hand and snake. After a minute or two of intense pain, it pulls off to keep from drowning. Thumb bloodied, ego bruised, hurting, I try not to show it. My friends are trying not to laugh.

"That's what you get messing around." The gruff Mr. Thompson's brow furrowed between his bushy eyebrows.

Old South Bar-B-Q Ranch on U.S. 27 in Clewiston. (State Archives of Florida)

There's plenty of hunting closer to home. McArthur Dairy in North Broward County is a favorite location. Drained swampland, by the early '60s it's turned to near-desert. White sugar sand, sparse clumps of grass, cacti, and old cypress logs. We roll them to find a treasure trove of reptiles. Red Ratsnakes, Scarlet Kingsnakes, glass lizards and six-foot-plus Eastern Coachwhips. This fast serpent, *Masticophis flagellum flagellum*, is the Ferrari of the snake world, with sleek tan body, black head and neck.

We unload at the Birds' place and discover a cloth sack, knotted, but empty. Whatever was inside escaped from a hole in the corner. At least we have nothing venomous. The search is on, under seats, the dash, we remove everything in the car—nothing. On the backseat Ronny picks up a small pillow. Underneath is the big coachwhip. It plants a solid bite on Ronny's nose. He staggers in shock, blood dripping on his shirt. His snout swells. Sonny asks, "Is that your nose or are you eating a bell pepper?" We laugh ourselves silly.

CHAPTER 6:
Indigo Blues

Indigo snakes, glossy blue-black giants to eight feet long, as big around as our arms are common in Davie. Fresh caught, *Drymarchon corais couperi,* hiss loud, inflate their reddish necks, look fierce. They never bite, and once handled, become docile. Indigos often soak up warmth on pavement during cooler days of winter. Many get hit. Our hearts break each time we encounter these magnificent creatures lying dead on the road.

Convinced, if anyone hits such a large, outstanding snake, (*Drymarchon* means "Lord of the Forest") they must have done so on purpose. We devise a plan, in our boyish minds, to make the culprits pay. With a recently run-over indigo, we set a trap. Into holes chiseled in the pavement, we insert upright 16-penny nails, then arrange the dead, normal-looking creature along the spikes in a natural position. We hide in the bushes, waiting for the killer to strike. It looks alive. Several vehicles swerve to avoid it. With so little traffic on our rural byway, boredom overcomes us when no one takes the bait.

Hours later, we find the indigo missing. We remove the remaining nails and wonder what became of it. Did vultures eat it? That evening, I hear my grandmother telling my father she got stranded with a flat tire on Kirkland Road. A ranch hand from Gulfstream Farms came by and helped her. It's as though someone dumped ice water on me! I'm freezing and sweating at the same time. My grandma, under five feet tall, sits on cushions to drive her big Buick. She's half-blind for sure and likely never saw the snake. The next morning at the bus stop we swear a pact to never tell what we did and to never do it again!

CHAPTER 7:
Family, Old and New

My father, remarrying in 1960, changed everything in my little world. I now have a stepbrother, Tex. A year younger than me, we share a room and a mutual love of horses. He loathes snakes so he doesn't run with me and my friends. Church-going, he studies hard in school, stays home, helps his mom with chores. As my opposite, we learn each other's boundaries and get along okay.

When Dad's aging parents move in, things changed again for everyone. Grandma takes charge of cooking, running the house and gardening. Grandpa, a gruff sort, doesn't say much to us boys. He controls our only TV. Our viewing options are: *Gunsmoke, Paladin, Wagon Train. Lawrence Welk, Mitch Miller*, and *Ed Sullivan. Little Rascals* Saturdays, if we behave.

I regret not getting to know my granddad well before he passed in 1961. His was a colorful life. Born in 1881, around the turn of the last century, he went West. Along the way, a chance meeting with William "Buffalo Bill" Cody set off a chain of events. He accepted a job at Cody's TE Ranch in a period 1904 to 1906, when Cody was trying to establish a dude ranch. Though those efforts failed, Grandpa's hard work earned his respect. That led to a position in the famed Buffalo Bill's Wild West Show for its final European tour. He lined up food, lodging, and space for a veritable tent city. Supplies and equipment for hundreds of men and horses.

He returned home to New York after the tour. In 1908, the 101 Ranch brought their Wild West Show to Madison Square Garden. He joined the company, returning with them to the newly formed state of Oklahoma. The 101 was the largest in the United States, over 110,000 acres. Founded by Confederate Colonel George Washington Miller in 1893. It became a major part of the oil boom.

The 101 shows featured Will Rogers. Other western luminaries were trick shooters Lillian Smith and Pawnee Bill. Later, an aging Buffalo Bill joined their show. After his stint at the 101, my grandfather left the West behind for good, entered the family pharmaceutical business, married in 1910. In 1916, the 101-spectacular returned to New York City. He took my dad as a small child to meet Buffalo Bill, Tom Mix, and famed cowboy Bill Pickett. He wasn't old enough to recall; his father told him the story.

Time is quick to slip our grasp. So many questions go unasked, stories untold. It's sad when we don't know to ask until there's no one left to answer. The scientific side of my brain can't accept that heredity shapes a person's direction in life. But I cannot deny the influence of family history.

CHAPTER 8:
Feeling the Bite

Despite changing family dynamics, my animal collection grows. Behind the barn becomes my little zoo, with cages under a shade tree. My stepbrother Tex has no interest, never ventures there. My religious stepmother has me headed straight to hell for keeping snakes. Dad struggles to keep the peace, respect her, and support my interests.

One day Sonny and Ronny help me bring an old horse watering trough home. Six feet across, 30 inches deep. I pour concrete over the rusted out bottom. An island of brick, filled with gravel, leaves a moat around that I seal with blue paint. Voila! A snake pit. Perfect for watersnakes, garters, and species that don't climb.

With my ability to keep my charges alive and healthy established, Dad's concern now is with my keeping venomous snakes. He allows me to handle them, knows I'm careful, trusts me, but still worries.

While feeding poultry, goats, and taking my horse to pasture before school, I find a big Eastern Garter Snake in the barnyard. As I take it to my pit, it bites me.

It chews with gusto in a sensitive place, the web of flesh between my middle and left index finger. I remember the encounter at Thompson's, and plunge hand and snake into a nearby turtle bucket, with green, slimy water. When it lets go, copious blood flows for a few seconds. Rinsed off, only faint marks from its minute teeth are visible on my skin.

At school, my hand swells and by the time I arrive home, it's aching. The size of a baseball. My stepmom Irene takes me to the doctor, who gives me painful tetanus and penicillin shots. The worst is coming. On the way back, she lectures me on my "punishment from God." My evening isn't the best.

Non-venomous snakebites are constant. To say I've had hundreds is no exaggeration, nor am I crazy. Any reptile enthusiast will attest, handlers are bitten often unless they take exceptional steps. Few do. A wild snake picked up fears for its life, may strike out, bite. They have four rows of minuscule teeth in their upper jaws, two on the bottom, used for holding and swallowing food whole. Bites of small species, if not painless, are no worse than a pinprick. The forearms, a frequent target, have few nerve endings. Fingertips are another story.

I've learned their behavior patterns. I must state, handling venomous snakes requires due caution every time. Any lapse in vigilance can lead to grave results.

Species, like indigos and Eastern Hog-nosed Snakes, *Heterodon platirhinos*, are bluffers. They hiss, inflate their bodies, flatten their necks, or play dead. They may strike with mouths closed, rarely bite. At worst, they emit a hard-to-wash-off, foul-smelling fluid. After a few moments of handling, they become docile.

Ratsnakes recoil, tense up, lunge and bite with fury. They too settle and abandon their defensive behavior. Bites, not painful unless on a finger, bleed a moment, leave no permanent marks. They're predictable, so getting bit is easy to avoid.

Snake pit
made from water trough,
early 1960s.

A few nervous species bite, strike over and over, rattle their tails and never become placid. They make difficult, unhappy captives. Black Racers and coachwhips are examples.

Others are sneaky, insidious. They appear docile when first captured, then bite without warning. Kingsnakes fall into this category.

My junior high classmates know I collect snakes. Darlene, a girl who lives a few miles away in Davie, calls. "I caught a Corn Snake. Why don't you come out?"

I don a clean shirt, a splash of Dad's Old Spice, saddle my horse and ride to her house.

"Door's open." She hands me a knotted pillowcase.

Her mom serves sweet tea. I untie the sack. The snake's a two-footer, grayish with red saddles outlined in black. I check it over, impressing her with my knowledge of this harmless species when it strikes out and snags my eyelid! It hurts like the dickens. Blood splatters my shirt. I'm mortified. Darlene looks to the ceiling, mouth pulled to one corner, and flashes the "Oh brother" look. Her mother gets a washcloth.

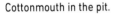

Because of my buddies, the Bird boys, I want to keep wildlife. We have the usual farm animals along with rabbits and guinea pigs as pets. They're not exotic enough. A Nine-banded Armadillo makes a great pet, friendly and

Cottonmouth in the pit.

playful. Let loose, he pokes around in the dirt and stays nearby. He grows fat as a watermelon on dry dog food moistened with water. One night a rat chews his tail, and he bleeds to death. Devastated, I hold a barnyard funeral.

My favorite is a Coatimundi pup I hand raised. A large raccoon relative with a long tail and white snout. She runs free for an hour a few times a week and returns to her cage on command. With age she becomes mischievous, scratching into feed sacks, knocking things off barn shelves. She resists going back to her enclosure. I persuade her with an egg.

No eggs in the henhouse, so I pick up a glass egg from a nest box. The Coati jumps onto my lap, sniffs it, and attacks. She bites my left bicep, leaving three deep gashes and a piece of bicep hanging loose. An ugly wound that leaves me covered in blood. I get the animal in the cage and run for the house. Irene drives me to the hospital. I'm dreading what's coming—the sermon, not the stitches. Once sewn up, I have a drain in my arm for 10 days. She saves the lecture until my father arrives from work.

He listens but balks when she says, "I knew this was coming" and "It was God's will." It's no laughing matter and ends with my agreeing to never again let my Coati run free.

CHAPTER 9:
Two Peas, Different Pods

Me and Tex are two boys cut from different cloth. He knows he'll be a lawyer one day while my focus is on my next snake-hunting trip. Opposites, but we have our share of fun.

We love "plinking," and take rifles and ride our horses to the woods or anyplace there's a trash dump to shoot bottles and cans. Never birds or other animals. Dad taught us gun safety, and to keep the guns clean. Mine is a 1911 model Winchester pump-action .22 caliber short rifle he'd bought before WWII in Arizona. I have it today.

Next to riding and shooting, swimming is our favorite pastime. Davie's downtown is an hour's horseback ride. A tall Australian Pine beside the new concrete span connecting Orange Drive to Griffin Road has a dangling rope. The city kids in town are the rough crowd. They smoke, swear, drink beer and don't want outsiders "from the sticks." They warn us, "Stay the hell out of our swimmin' hole."

We jump in without hesitation. They say nothing, our boldness worries them. We swim, roughhouse, swing from the rope, hurling ourselves into the dark river, scramble up the exposed tree roots, do it again. Carefree days.

A few of the townies leap off the higher, dangerous old wooden humpback bridge a block west. Prohibited, but no one pays attention. When manatees pass under, the boys jump on their backs, straddle them. If successful, they get bucked off in an instant. A swish of their broad tails tosses them in the air.

That's what they want. It's illegal, but the sea cows don't seem to care, they glide away as if nothing happened.

A passion is snorkeling the coral reefs along Dania Beach. A 100-yard swim to the first reef, 10 feet to the bottom, we see a few corals and fish. As time goes by, we paddle to the deeper second reef. Part of the Great Florida Reef, it ranks as one of the largest barrier reefs in the world, extending southwest to the Dry Tortugas, it dazzles with an array of fish in every size, shape, and color. Small sharks cruise between Elkhorn Coral and sea fans. Rocks riddled with caves hide giant Green Moray Eels. Twenty-foot here, crystalline, we stay at the surface, but sometimes dive for a closer look. I came up with a nosebleed once. Never considered sharks! Without flotation, oblivious to danger, we snorkel a quarter-mile offshore. We try collecting tropical fish to sell to a pet shop in Fort Lauderdale but abandon the idea when we can't master delivering them alive.

Despite the dangers, we have few actual problems. My memories of those days are vivid. A song we'd hear on the radio, "Cindy's Birthday," is a place marker for 1962, whisking me back to those carefree days my brother Tex, and I shared and loved. I can feel the surge of the waves, feel the sun on my back, smell the salty air.

Too rough to reef dive one day, so we snorkel the shallows inshore where it's knee-deep. We follow an octopus until a small stingray attracts my attention. While swimming above it, a wave tosses me over, I put my hand out to catch myself—right on top of the ray. I stand up, yelping in pain, the stinger protruding from the base of my thumb. I dare not try to pull it out. Scared, we run to a more populous part of the beach to find an adult for help.

"Pour vinegar on the stinger," a lady suggests.

We leave in Sonny's car, headed for a store to buy vinegar. If it helps, I can't tell. By the time we reach home, the wound is throbbing, aching, near unbearable.

Irene takes me to the doctor. Over two hours have passed, still hurting, burning, but the worst spasms have subsided. The doctor's pulling out the half-inch-long barbed spine reignites the stabbing pain. He squeezes the wound to "get the venom out," applies a Band-Aid, sends me home. The lecture afterward is worse than the sting, at least this time Tex is on my side.

CHAPTER 10:
In the Middle

In 1960 I start junior high school and sense early on that I don't fit or conform. The proverbial square peg in a round hole. My affinity for reptiles—snakes especially—may have something to do with it. But not to a great extent. I love being on the farm, out in the woods, hunting with my friends, helping Dad with his truck, enjoying my animals or a book.

Sonny quit school, they held Ronny back a year, so only Dale and I take the bus. In eighth grade, occasionally I ride my horse to the schoolhouse, stay over with my mom. October 1962, the Cuban Missile Crisis makes life in South Florida strange. Highways are blocked to move military equipment. We practiced duck and cover in elementary, hiding under our desks. Now we're kinda big for that. The Birds built a fallout shelter in the late '50s, expand it in '62, digging a pond for fill to bury it with sand. Weird times.

I'm marching a path apart from most of my fellow Rogers students. The exceptional teachers give me latitude, and let me develop my way. Nonconformity isn't always a negative quality. Though it can make life more complex.

My buddy Jeff lives in my old neighborhood and still looks up to me. He took a job across from Rogers Junior High at Mrs. Fann's Rabbit Farm. After classes he cleans cages, rakes earthworms, and counts them into little boxes for fish bait. She needs extra help, and he thinks of me. Good for me, but not for him. Man-sized, I work circles around Jeff, build pens, sort rabbits, and take on heavy tasks he cannot.

Many students, most faculty members, know of my focus on reptiles.

One day Mrs. Fann, a slight Chinese woman, comes to the school in a panic, looking for me. A huge Eastern Diamondback Rattlesnake, *Crotalus adamanteus*, got into a rabbit pen and is eating baby bunnies. The dean takes me out of class to help her. I catch the impressive beast and put it in a barrel. I'm her hero. Word spreads fast. Jealous guys talk trash, a few girls show interest in me for the first time. Everyone looks at me differently, for a while at least. I carry on, but Jeff, poor guy, gets swept to the wayside.

CHAPTER 11:
Wild Cargo

Every herpetologist, snake hunter, or reptile hobbyist knows Wild Cargo. The Hollywood, Florida compound is Mecca for animal enthusiasts. It's operated by Ralph Curtis, a professional fireman. His perfect work schedule allows the freedom to run a business on the side. He has mammals and birds from South America, Africa, and Asia. But his specialty is reptiles, along with related books and technical papers.

The reptile house is a candy store for herptile fanciers. From exotic lizards to venomous snakes, tortoises to pythons, he has them displayed in clean, well-lighted glass front cages. Each specimen is vibrant and healthy.

Ralph believes in his work and sharing his knowledge with others. He's accessible. Customers are free to walk through the aisles of cases and outdoor pens. Trusted clients can handle specimens. My first visit to Wild Cargo is in 1963, at 15. I save my money and ask Dad to drive me. Then I learn he'll buy snakes.

Davie is the snakiest place in Florida. We have what Ralph wants most— in abundance: Red Ratsnakes, Eastern Indigos, and Scarlet Kings. Before long, I'm riding the 12 miles on my bike with specimens to trade. Sometimes I catch Eastern Diamondback Rattlesnakes, carry them in sacks in my bicycle basket. On the rough ride, they rattle the entire way, startling anyone I pass.

I spend the day, volunteer to help clean cages or do other minor tasks. It's a thrill to be around the animals and interesting visitors. Ralph trusts me— even with venomous snakes, after showing up with big rattlers. A few specimens are off-limits. Such is the case for the rare *Varanus brevicauda,* the Pygmy Monitor lizard from Australia. He doesn't want me or anyone else to handle them.

They're so cute! In a weak moment, alone in the room, I open the top of their pen. I pick one up with care, hold it in my left hand and stroke it under the chin. It bites me with the grip of a pair of pliers. He has my right index finger in his mouth, across my fingernail. I lay him in the cage and hope he'll let go. He won't. Every time I move, he squeezes harder. This goes on until Ralph returns.

His eyes show his disappointment. He leads me to a sink. Under running water, it continues to hold. He wraps the lizard in a towel, so it can't see us, and after ten minutes, it releases its grip. I apologize. The weekly visits come to a temporary halt. My losing Ralph's trust is the hardest lesson.

CHAPTER 12:
Epiphany

Only brainiacs get into Nova High in Davie and Tex is in the inaugural class. He believes "Tex" isn't a proper handle for a lawyer and changes his name to Robert, "Bob." In Nova's 11-month program, he'll graduate the same time as me, despite being a year younger. I go on to Stranahan. My displeasure with school continues. I ignore most of my classwork, but devour every library book on animal collectors. I read biographies of Clifford Pope, Raymond Ditmars, Frank Buck. Explorers Percy Fawcett, Thor Heyerdahl, Martin Johnson, and William Bartram are my heroes. They lived the adventurous life I want.

Old books of exploration with sketchy details leave me hungry for more. I revel in maps, search for places I've read about with strange names. I imagine traveling to them, by plane or ship, as my father did to the Pacific during the war. The librarian saves titles for me she thinks I'll enjoy, that no one else reads. I know I am blessed.

I struggle through sophomore year, skip often, spur of the moment. The bus driver is on to me. If she suspects I'm hiding under the bridge, she'll look for me. The dean sent a note to my dad; I forged his signature, caught hell at both ends.

June 5, 1963, me, and Tex gain a little sister. Patricia "Trish" becomes the bond that unites our family. Many petty issues fall to the wayside or become diminished. She is a blessing in many ways, someone new to love and cherish who needs our attention. School's out for the summer on June 6; I've been feeling poorly for a couple of days and on Friday my dad takes me to a doctor. They send me to the hospital.

"Malaria, it's rare in Florida," says the doctor. On a collecting trip to Lake Okeechobee two weekends ago, sugarcane burned, Jamaican cane cutters swarmed the fields in hellish conditions, cutting, and loading cane onto wagons. Mosquitoes were thick, as usual. "That's likely where you picked it up," he says. "Malaria is officially wiped out here, but people can still carry it in."

So lucky me, I'm exiled to my bedroom, away from family and my snake hunting buddies, for the first three weeks of summer vacation. I read every *Outdoor Life*, *Popular Mechanics* and *National Geographic* magazine that they can find for me. At the brink of going stir crazy, I'm set free, and finally get to meet my little sister.

What they say is true, we never forget. Friday, November 22, 1963, in geography class at Stranahan High, two hours till school's out, the intercom crackles. "President Kennedy's been shot in Dallas, Texas." A great sadness descends. The somber mood remains for weeks. Mom weeps, Dad's prayerful. I apply myself for a change and improve my grades.

At 16 I'm driving. I take an after-school job at Jaxson's Ice Cream Parlor. Weekends, I work at an animal import company. Both are in Dania. Most Davie teenagers are into cars. Sonny loses interest in snakes and starts building a stock car to race. We get old clunkers for a few dollars, pitch in, help each other fix them. The real wrecks we chop for beach buggies. Nicer vehicles are souped-up and painted as hot rods for cruising, the all-American pastime for teens. We live for those Friday and Saturday evenings to cruise through town.

The author and his 1957 Ford Fairlane 500 Club Victoria, in 1964.

Music blaring on WQAM; Sam Cook, Dion, Elvis, Del Shannon, The Drifters, Roy Orbison, Rick Nelson, nothing since can compare. Then we'd converge at the drive-in theater.

In 1964, with a $50 loan from my mother, I buy a 1957 Ford for $150. A classic body style—Fairlane 500 Club Victoria—but with an automatic transmission, small 292 engine, and a plain interior. With Sonny and Joel's help, we have the block bored to 312 (5.1 liters) and put in a manual tranny with a Hurst floor shifter. With dual four-barreled carburetors and lake pipes, it rumbles. A five-coat, black paint job with polished chrome makes it sparkle. My friend Bill's father is a disabled WWII vet and does upholstery. He fixes me up with metal flake red and white tuck and roll seat covers, door panels, and headliner. It's sharp, a head-turner on the cruising circuit. My buddies and I spend many a joyful day working on each other's cars.

Snakes are on the back burner. But not for long. My work with Blue Ribbon Pet Farm reignites my passion. In summer 1965 I sell my beloved '57 and get a '53 Ford station wagon. A V-8 flat head, brute of a car—perfect for snake hunting.

When I join the South Florida Herpetological Society in Miami, it changes everything. My world expands beyond school and Davie. Relationships form with scientists, professors, and respected businessmen. Lew Ober, a Miami Dade College professor, is a lizard specialist. He becomes a lifelong friend. I cherish the happy hours spent in his laboratory, his live collections, skeletons, and preserved specimens. In times to come, we'll collaborate on Caribbean reptiles and an expedition to Venezuela.

Ed Chapman, consummate herpeticulturist, indeed a herpetologist, is an expert, but secretive reptile hobbyist. Our friendship begins at a meeting and leads to Everglades collecting trips. It's an honor when he invites me to see his extensive, immaculate, first-class collection. Over time, we'll team up to explore the islands, forming an enduring, if sometimes strained, relationship.

A few teenage members of the Herp Society will make herpetology a career. Jack Facente is on fire with reptiles. He lives with his parents in Hialeah and keeps an impressive snake collection in a backyard shed. Jack's passion is the vicious, difficult, eastern South American Garden Tree Boa, *Corallus hortulanus*. With a black diamond pattern, they're slender, muscular, with fiddle-shaped heads. Large eyes have vertical slit pupils and a row of heat-sensing pits above their labial (lip) scales. Night hunters, they'll strike at any warm, moving object.

Jack Facente extracting
venom from an
Eastern Coral Snake
at AGRITOXINS, 2010.
(Courtesy of Jack Facente)

Birds and bats are primary prey. Though harmless, their long, needle-sharp teeth can deliver a painful bite. Many herpers prefer handling venomous snakes to tree boas. That may explain Jack's chosen profession.

Jack worked at the Miami Serpentarium for the famed Bill Haast, then left Miami in 1972 to continue his career in herpetology. He started Reptile World Serpentarium in St. Cloud, Florida with business partner George VanHorn. He later went on to form AGRITOXINS, a venom lab to collaborate with VanHorn and Carl Barden of Medtoxin, a business designed specifically to produce coral snake venom for the Pfizer Antivenom Project. Not least, he incorporated the non-profit King Cobra Conservancy, conceived by Naia Haast, Bill Haast's daughter. Their mission: Saving remaining king cobra populations, promoting education and habitat preservation.

Louis "Louie" Porras is a native of Costa Rica and moved to Miami with his family when he was seven. Over many years of keeping, collecting, and breeding reptiles, he's become an author and scientist and lived as a true herpetologist. We built a trusting friendship.

I'm learning. Life is a series of choices. We partner with people and things that set our life's course. The decisions we make, no matter how early or insignificant, are what define us.

CHAPTER 13:

Terrytown

It's hard to imagine life before cell phones and computers. I don't know how such technology might have changed my direction if it were around back then. I'm glad it wasn't.

I'm predisposed to be an explorer. Of that I'm convinced. A true natural-born nature lover and adventurer. My parents rarely know where I am. My teachers can't keep me in class. At every chance I slip away to the woods, swamps, and wild places where I belong.

Teachers at Stranahan, from appearances, give boys from Davie more leeway. They understand we come a long way to school, live on farms, rise early to do chores. We have responsibilities other students don't. We're exempt from a no-jeans dress code. Faculty treats us as more mature. For sure, we are different. Some say we Davie boys have an honorary BA—Bad Ass degree. A mostly undeserved reputation that serves us well. There's a built-in automatic respect from the real troublemakers. The guys with a cigarette pack rolled in their shirt sleeves, the ones we called "hoods".

Among my friends, only Sonny smokes, but rarely. Nobody in our group drinks. No one, not even the bad guys at school, uses drugs. Not a single guy I know has been in Dutch with the law. Our notoriety may be a myth, but why mess with a good thing? Davie boys don't back down from a fight, and maybe that's why we're rarely challenged.

The school library remains my haunt. I read *Kon Tiki*, twice. *I Married Adventure,* Osa Johnson's tale of adventures in the South Pacific. *Serengeti Shall*

Flood control levees and canals
in Everglades of western Broward County.
(Photo: State Archives of Florida/Johnson)

Not Die by Bernhard and Michael Grzimek. My favorite is *The Wildest Game* by Peter Ryhiner, a modern-day animal collector. Ivan T. Sanderson's *Caribbean Treasure* inspires my dreams of Haiti. William Beebe's *High Jungle* foreshadows future travel and exploration in Venezuela. When reading stories of lives lived in adventure, it arouses a yearning to emulate them. Who's saying I can't? I believe I can.

I'm known to skip classes for the occasional day of snake hunting in the Glades. I drop my girlfriend at school, and head for the swamps. Terrytown, an isolated truck stop, is my jump-off point. A 35-mile trip out SR 84, then north on US 27 between Andytown and South Bay.

From there a 20-mile drive west on levee roads leads to the Miami Canal. A hidden, narrow ditch is a favorite place to hunt kingsnakes and moccasins. I leave my '53 Ford wagon on the road. It's isolated, other vehicles are rare. A 100-yard walk through sawgrass, I climb into shin-deep water between three-foot sides straight-cut into limestone. Wax Myrtles form a tunnel-like canopy over the five-foot-wide trench. At six-foot-two, I must stoop over to wade.

My snake stick is a golf club shank with a piece of brass rod bent in an "L" welded on the end. Perfect for handling venomous snakes and strong enough to flip small objects. Others prefer traditional hook-shaped sticks. They're safer to use and prevent a snake from sliding.

It doesn't take long to find a huge Cottonmouth, *Agkistrodon piscivorus*. A fat three-footer in a coil on the waist-high bank. I pin his head, pick him up, tuck his body under my arm to control him while I shake a sack open, drop him inside, twist and knot it.

I bag another big one and several smaller and call it a day. The wild Everglades stretch on for miles, no sounds except for birds, wind, and sloshing of my feet. The sweet smells of the swamp, the solitude, the excitement, sure beats being in school.

Satisfied with my day's catch, driving back, I realize the risks I've taken. The danger of being out here solo. These big moccasins could deliver a fatal bite. There's no one to help. Nobody knows where I am. It's foolish. *This is my last time.* A vow soon forgotten. It isn't long before another such foray flirts with disaster.

A bridge made of rough timbers provides many hiding places for snakes. I see several Yellow Ratsnakes from the embankment. To reach them, I'll climb over the edge to access cross braces between pilings. The deck is 12 feet above overgrown hyacinths that hide the water.

My unbleached muslin sacks, made special for snake hunting, are double-seamed. Two inches sewn across each corner to grasp when used for venomous species. I lie on my stomach, hang my legs over, wrap them around the first piling and slide to the cross member. After bagging the three Yellows within grasp, I clamber to the next, right arm bloody from several bites. The braces are in an X shape, crossing them isn't easy. The last post has loose bark. I position myself to pull it off and grab any snakes before they fall.

I stand on the X-brace six feet over the Water-Hyacinth-choked canal. A gentle tug, and the entire section falls free. To my shock, I find an enormous Yellowjacket nest. As they swarm, I let go, crash through the hyacinths into the water below to escape. It's deep, and my boots make swimming impossible. Trapped below in tangled roots, I thrash and claw my way up to get air.

In my struggle, I touch bottom, can stand with my nose above the surface. Smothered in hyacinths, I fight panic and labor through the tangle towards shore. Covered in stinking mud, roots, bugs, and spiders, I reach the shallows at the bridge abutment out of breath.

The Yellowjackets, forgotten in the drama, attack with a vengeance. A sharp sting on the neck announces their return and sends me packing. I scramble from under the bridge to the bank and up the steep incline through tall grass and shrubs. Three snakes hanging from my belt, soaking wet clothes, sodden boots, I'm a lumbering, easy target. Two more hit me before I make the gravel road and run to the car. I get in, roll up the windows, soaked, scratched, bleeding, hurting from Yellowjacket stings, and lucky to be alive. No doubt saved by angels.

CHAPTER 14:
Blue Ribbon Days

Since August 1964, on weekends and summers, I've worked for John Marolf at Blue Ribbon Pet Farm in Dania. I approached him for a reptile handler job when I visited as a buyer. Theirs were South American species, and most of them in sorry condition.

"We don't import many. They're not good sellers." *Yeah, no wonder.*

"I could clean them up if you wish." I'm eager to volunteer.

Impressed with my enthusiasm, he hires me part-time. I start on the snakes, but my duties expand each day. There is plenty of work. A steady stream of imported wildlife pours in which we reship to zoos and collectors in the US and foreign countries.

John Marolf, in his 60s (born April 1900), is a gruff sort, with a sense of humor. He loves animals. I suspect, in this tough and dirty business, he's become detached. It's hardened his heart to their suffering. There's trauma, even when things go right. Wild-caught fauna still dominates the trade, often come in sick, injured, terrified. Losses are staggering. Unscrupulous collectors and dealers cause untold cruelty.

John is an expert on the birds and mammals he imports. He keeps his farm clean, but it's ragged. The farm is on rented land alongside US 1, bordered by the Dania Cut-Off Canal, a mile from the Ft. Lauderdale Airport, nestled in tropical woods extending to mangroves along the Intracoastal. Blue Ribbon's office is in the same building with the rarest and most delicate specimens. The noise level is deafening with the raucous squeaks, squawks, and earsplitting whistles.

Sam, an old Black man, has worked here for years preparing food trays for the incredible array of exotic fauna with love and care. I like Sam. He's my friend. We spend time together. I learn from him.

I'd bet no zoo offers better nutrition for their captives. John has compiled a file of detailed recipes. Sam prepares each from memory, adding those he himself has created. Each creature has his favorite, perhaps because of color, or aroma. Variety in their daily diet is important. Sam makes trays with grapes, melons, and vegetables cut in pieces for tropical birds. To some, he adds diced horse meat, raw and cooked, or dry dog food soaked in water. Monkeys are most particular, often needing special diets, including insects. The big powerful cats eat raw flesh on the bone while other animals crave fish.

Sam knows each creature's preference, knows their names, and habits, and draws great pride from caring for them.

⌘

I treat the farm as my personal zoo. Animals in my charge get the best of care. My work also involves preparing shipments. John teaches me to make wooden packing crates. For mammals and birds, we pack items to eat, drink, and hold on to during transit. Naphtha heaters when sending North. We build the containers beveled on one side to allow airflow when stacked.

Most days, I clean cages and distribute food trays. My duties run from changing paper in the reptile tanks to cleaning a cage full of African Lions.

Picking up leftover bones after their repast requires entering the enclosure—a concrete slab with a tin roof and heavy chain-link sidewalls. My number one job is to be sure I'm not on the lion's menu. For months, I've entered the cage to pick up bones, hose and scrub the slab. Captive born at a zoo in Trinidad, our juvenile lions are now adult size. I carry a washtub for the waste, and bang on it to scare them away if they threaten. Past the cute stage, they roar and snarl, and John is having difficulty finding a buyer. They consume fifty pounds of meat per feeding, charge the tubs when I enter. I drop them and run. It's scary and dangerous. Then there's the smell....

We import hundreds of monkeys, keeping rare, sensitive ones indoors. Many we house in walk-in enclosures. Squirrel Monkeys, a leading seller for John, form troops led by the largest dominant male. These alpha males have massive canine teeth, incredible strength, and keep other males in line and away from females, mothers with tiny, helpless babies, and youngsters.

There's terror enough to go around for us and the monkeys when we enter their enclosure. I capture the ones John selects for shipment, using a sturdy nylon net. They scream, jumping 10 feet across the enclosure, often spraying urine. The alpha male barks, wide-eyed, and threatens with teeth bared, but doesn't attack.

Larger, stronger species bite hard and can cause significant damage. We wear heavy leather gauntlets. Spider monkeys are docile, but boxing them is no picnic. Their long limbs, fingers, and prehensile tails grip everything in sight.

Night Monkeys, Sakis, Red-faced Uakari, elfin marmosets, and tamarins need a gentle touch. The hardest for me to ship are the Woollys. Freshly imported youngsters reach out of their crates as we open them. Arms outstretched, longing for someone to cradle them. When we do, they cling, cooing, snuggling, holding on tight for security. It takes a heart of stone not to fall in love with these helpless creatures. Mine breaks when I arrive at work and find them gone. It's tough.

Giant serpents we place in a huge walk-in pen at the rear of the property. Each week I pressure clean and disinfect after first removing any snakes or objects. A log leads to a sturdy shelf where most of the boas stay. Green Anacondas, *Eunectes murinus*, sprawl on the cool cement. A thin, 14-footer has coiled up in a galvanized washtub used as a water trough. I know this one, it's ill-tempered. I lift the tub to carry it out without disturbing him.

The anaconda strikes out of the water. Its long, sharp teeth pierce my belly through my flannel shirt, which gets stuck in its mouth. I set the basin on the floor, grab the snake behind the head. The snake struggles as I extract the cloth with my left hand while holding his neck in my right. When I inspect the injury, several teeth remain embedded in my skin. I pluck them out and wash the wound. There are big welts, a little blood, but no actual damage. I'll pull other teeth out over the coming months.

～⌢～

Bites by exotic creatures are part of the job. To feed, we open cages to place fresh containers in and take old ones out. Most wild animals keep away or stay hidden in wooden boxes provided. Others attack their food and anyone near it.

A Tayra, *Eira barbara,* nails me one day. It's a giant weasel relative, the size of an otter. It darts out of its hiding box and grabs the large muscle of my lower left arm. I jerk back, and the Tayra holds on, shaking furiously, before dropping off and running into its cage. After securing the door, I go in, bleeding, to see Mr. Marolf.

John displays his lack of sensitivity. "It's nothing." He puts on Mercurochrome and bandages it. "You'll be okay."

I *was* okay. But with a few large punctures, shallow gashes, and an ugly bruise for days. After it healed, a Greater Grison, *Galictis vittata,* got hold of me in the same spot. It's another species of South American weasel that resembles a badger.

⌒⌒

At least once a week a shipment comes in from Colombia: monkeys, other small animals, birds, and snakes. We always get a crate or two of baby Green Iguanas, six to eight-inch hatchlings, 200 per box. We unpack the lizards, placing them 50 to a wire cage. Half of each consignment dies in transit or soon after arrival. It's difficult keeping them fed and healthy.

The thick woods around the animal compound crawl with them, every size imaginable. Escapees, I assume. Then, while observing another worker unpack an iguana shipment, I see him toss a squirming handful of the creatures into the bushes out of disgust or pity. When the unpacking task falls to me, I can't deny being tempted to follow suit. Still, we have more baby iguanas than we can sell. And they keep coming.

Sometimes specimens we receive are so uncommon that zoologists come to study them. An Argentinian shipment has an ultra-rare Pampas Cat and two pairs of Maned Wolves. The New York Zoological Society sends a photographer. John gains fame and recognition. He's celebrated as among the first to import these unusual animals.

Rheas arrive from Argentina, South American equals of the Australian Emu. John brings me along to deliver four in a zoo shipment to Miami Internatiional Airport. Packed one per large, corrugated carton with screen windows for fresh air. The bottoms have extra layers of cardboard and shredded paper. We drop them off at cargo and leave for the farm.

John's wife Jeanette is in a panic when we arrive. "The airfreight agent called. The Rheas have escaped! They're running around the airport, causing flight delays."

The return trip to Miami takes more than an hour. Security and freight agents are frantic. Two got loose, they've caught one, the other they chased into a field off the runway. We catch it with the help of 20 people shouting and waving their arms to keep it cornered.

Rheas are grazers, eat grassy vegetation. This results in a lot of wet poop. When the agents picked them up to load, the poop-soaked bottoms fell through, and the Rheas ran for it.

CHAPTER 15:
Wrangling Cobras

Charles P. "Bill" Chase is an animal importer a cut above typical. Honest and dignified, he cultivates the best reputable sources and clientele. My friend Louie Porras works weekends at Mr. Chase's nondescript warehouse near Miami International Airport. Wall-to-wall and floor-to-ceiling cages and pens hold exotic creatures. Birds call and whistle in a cacophony of noise. Out back a menagerie of mammals, small cats, rare monkeys, anteaters, and other oddities. Hot, smelling of feed, bedding, and waste—familiar to me from my job at Blue Ribbon.

His compound is a hub of the zoological trade. Prominent importers, exporters, zoo managers, and private collectors visit. He's befriended Tony Gomez, an exiled exporter from Cuba. His company, Tropifauna, specializes in hummingbirds. When he fled Castro, Mr. Chase provided space for his birds. He ships them to zoos around the world.

Australian reptiles are a specialty. Rare, expensive, next to impossible to get. He has them—legal imports. Famous for his pythons: Children's, Black-headed, Diamond, Amethystine, among others. Unusual species of monitors, giant Blue Tongue Skinks, and Shingle Backs. He has Bearded Dragons and Frilled Lizards. A collector's dream, off-limits to regular visitors. As with Blue Ribbon, his animal business requires attention 24/7.

Mr. Chase, a hard man to read, has an aristocratic air. He's friendly, but I'm sure he sees me as beneath his station. I admire him and his reputation.

Louie is visiting Costa Rica when I stop by during spring break, 1965, to see what's new. Two King Cobras, *Ophiophagus hannah*, have arrived from Thailand. Mr. Chase is angry. They're loose in wooden crates. It's an unusual occurrence. "Thank God they weren't damaged in shipment. Imagine if they escaped!" Such dangerous serpents should be double-bagged inside secure boxes for shipping.

I overhear him discussing with an employee how to transfer them into cages. He doesn't relish handling large cobras. "Is there any way I can help?" I'm eager to win points.

My love of venomous snakes clouds my judgment, leaves me bold beyond logic but no less cautious. Bill Chase is not an impulsive man. He studies me as if seeing me for the first time, hesitates a moment. "Yes."

This will be interesting. I've handled small cobras at Blue Ribbon. Here is an opportunity to prove myself. Mr. Chase shows me a wire enclosure on the concrete floor. Eight feet high, six wide and four deep, with a tree limb from the floor to an upper corner.

"One goes in here. The other over there." He points to a pen of the same size in a row of several. His hired help, Cuban men, fear snakes. They disinfect the cages with a bleach solution.

Mr. Chase makes hiding places for the nervous animals. He cuts holes in the shape of a horseshoe in two bottomless cardboard boxes. A hide helps keep them calm and will be easy to remove with no bottom. Into each cage goes a hide box and a bowl of water. I set a crate in, nails removed, top left in place, back out. I use a stick to flip off the loose board, then push the door shut.

Nothing happens. After five minutes, I nudge and bump the case. Still not stirring. We move on to the other.

We repeat the technique, but when I knock the lid off, the snake surges out like water from a fire hose. It startles us. The huge cobra is a 10-footer, thick as my wrist, stands waist-high. With its hood spread, its eyes follow our every movement.

Wow, what an experience! We catch our breath, hearts racing, there's nervous laughter, we're speechless. The first is just as large but calm, and is now lying half out of its crate, checking out its enclosure.

An appreciative Mr. Chase gives me the couple of inexpensive specimens I've picked out to buy. "Glad you were here. I don't think I could have handled the snakes alone."

My chest swells. "Happy to help any time."

He takes my name and phone info. On the way home I'm aglow, enjoying the sense of being equal, needed, useful. Not a kid. Can't deny my jealousy over Louie working for an animal dealer who knows and appreciates reptiles. John only sees dollar signs.

⌘

My stepmom disapproves of my keeping snakes and related activities. A week goes by and a guy phones and asks for Davey. "Sorry, no one here by that name."

"He gave me this number; said he could help me with a snake."

She doesn't tell me, claims she "thought it was a wrong number." I guess she felt guilty and mentions it the next day.

"It has to be Mr. Chase." I call him.

"Davey, thanks for calling." He's confusing my name with my hometown; Davie. No harm done. "Can you give me a hand boxing those two cobras? Louis is not back from his trip."

Those snakes were a handful getting out of a box. Imagine putting them into one. A bite means certain death. There are no known survivors of King Cobra envenomation.

"Sure." Nervous, I know I'm foolish for inserting myself into this situation.

To capture the kings, I bring my gear. I have two snake stick styles and a metal stand with a hoop that holds a deep cloth sack attached with clothespins. This set up works for big rattlesnakes. Will it serve for a ten-foot cobra?

I fluff up a bunch of packing wool and stuff it in the receptacle. My hope is for the snake to hide in the shredded wood fiber and not seek to escape.

We tackle the placid animal first. He's hidden as I enter the enclosure with the rack. Space is tight, no escaping in a hurry. Sweat beads pop out on my forehead. I try not to show fear in front of Mr. Chase. The mighty cobra lies in a loose coil when I remove its hiding box and toss it behind me. It looks good, fatter than when it arrived. Neither has eaten since arrival, but they drank and rehydrated.

I slip my hook under his middle and lift. He's heavy at the end of my stick. I raise him to the ceiling before his head clears the top of the stand. Praying he'll stay calm, I lower his upper body in, then pick up his tail with my hand. He slides to the bottom, burying himself in the wood wool. In a quick motion, I unclip the sack, twist it, and tie it with a cord.

One down, the worst to go.

Mr. Chase paces. "This won't work for the other. He's more alert. We should find another way."

I know it's far too dangerous to enter his cage. "I agree, but I have an idea. Let's find a small carton, cut a hole. Lay a sack on the floor, box in the opening. Remove his hideaway. When the snake goes in, I'll pull the sack up over the box. What do you think?"

Mr. Chase shrugs, palms upward. "What else can we do?"

We find a container that fits in the bag, seal it with tape, cut a tennis ball-sized entrance in the side. The nervous snake remains concealed while I place it in the cage. When I lift his hide box, the feisty creature springs to attention. It strikes a defensive posture, rises to waist high, hood spread, his loud hiss unnerving. We back off, retire to the office, give him a chance to go into the other carton.

As Mr. Chase works at his desk, I sit quietly, scanning his walls. They tell a story. Crowded with pictures, plaques, framed permits, and objects collected over years of travel. Photos of him with animals and famous people I don't know. A man in his 50s or 60s, the display is a testament to his long history in the animal business.

When the second cobra is inside, without hesitation, I step in and close the door behind me. I take hold of the sack on both sides, pull up, but jerk the box off the ground. My heart stops. A quick bounce and it slides to the bottom of the sack before the startled creature can escape.

Mr. Chase has been holding his breath. He smiles and claps. "Yes, yes!"

"We did it!" Cold sweat, like melted ice, trickles from my temples. I exhale deep.

"I hate to ask, but I've got a White-lipped Forest Cobra I need to bag."

My adrenaline is peaking, surging, junkyard dog strong. "Sure, what the heck, I'm here."

Naja melanoleuca is a wary species with a reputation for being difficult. With powerful venom, they're aggressive, and they climb. An eight-footer, they grow to 10. The dangerous creature is glossy black with faint lighter bands. Head and neck are cream colored with a black collar. In the same row of walk-in cages, there's a tree branch across the top.

He's the right size for "tailing." This involves lifting the snake's upper body with a hook while picking up the tail end by hand. Off balance, as it tries to hold on to keep from falling, the handler can move it wherever needed.

That's my plan. I have much to learn. The White-lipped has other ideas.

I enter the cage and arrange the rack. No sign of aggression. I slide the hook gently under his body, 30 inches behind his head, and lift. When I grasp his rear half, he turns and wraps his neck around my stick, climbing instead of hanging on for balance. He advances up, gaining ground. In a battle of strength and wits, he's winning. At less than a foot from my hand, I'm forced to drop the stick and exit the enclosure.

Mr. Chase is unimpressed. "What now?"

"Holy crap, that's one strong snake!" My mind is spinning.

I brought a fish-landing net frame with a cloth sack attached in case I needed it for the Kings. Handy for catching large rattlers. Safer for me, and the snakes. I put a big clump of wood wool inside to give him a place to hide. My simple plan is to hold the pouch in front and herd it in with the stick. Then twist it to prevent escape. Speed is essential.

When I return, the White-lipped is in a corner. Rack removed, I step in, prepared for battle. Net sack pressed against the far wall and floor; I give the cobra a gentle nudge with the hook. He jerks alert, rises, spreads his hood, ready to fight. Then he drops and slithers in with no further prodding. Piece of cake!

Yeah, it looked easy. Both of us know it was pure luck. No game, stakes are deadly. He knocks $20 off what I buy. We're square. It was never about the money, it was something I needed to do. It's the last time I work for Mr. Chase. No reason. Louie came back from Costa Rica, and it works out that way.

CHAPTER 16:
Road Trip

Things are moving fast, with my job and a new reptile business. I have adult-size responsibilities and struggle to keep up my grades and my obligations. Time for friends is a memory. I'm in a rush to grow up. I'm not there yet.

Summer of '65, before our senior year, me and high school chum Jim Stafford head out to North Florida. Considered young adults, were eager to stretch our wings with a coming-of-age road trip. We pack my '53 Ford station wagon with wooden snake boxes, nets, collecting sticks, and plenty of cloth sacks. We're far from flush but shouldn't need much. We'll bunk in the car. Gas is 30¢ a gallon. A hamburger costs 15¢, a Coke is a dime.

We can take care of ourselves and stay out of trouble. Our parents may worry, but don't stand in the way of our summer plans. Simpler, saner times, but the world is changing. Civil rights protests are in the news. "Eve of Destruction" and "We Gotta Get Out of This Place," reflect the expanding Vietnam War. The Beach Boys' cheerful tunes, Beatles, and Supremes fill our ears. We promise to phone home collect when we arrive. We'll sleep in parking lots or roadside parks. There are few worries of any harm coming to us.

We plan to meet Ross Allen at his renowned Reptile Institute in Silver Springs east of Ocala. He replied to a written offer to trade snakes from southern Florida. "Sure, bring them with you."

Up historic old US 27, two lanes, jammed with trucks hauling goods south and produce north. Through Everglades wilderness, sugarcane fields, farms, ranches. For a pair of teenage boys, it's the road to adventure. Memories flood as we pull into Thompson's Wild Animal Farm in Clewiston. The place a garter snake swallowed my thumb. We enter the decrepit barn and find ol' Lester "L.E." Thompson, in bib overalls, butchering a hog. Hung from a rafter over a pile of guts and a pool of blood right in front of the pits and cages. He's not happy with the interruption. Jim's first visit, he looks ready to bolt.

"Got any Everglades Rats?" This special snake we want for Ross Allen is uncommon, bright orange, and named in his honor, *Elaphe obsoleta rossalleni*.

He pauses, bloody knife in hand. "Have a look."

We pass filthy animal cages. Nothing's changed, might even smell worse. Jim's face is pale green. *Is he going to vomit?* A wire pen with a tree growing inside has dozens of Red and Yellow Ratsnakes in coils or stretched along its branches. I yell. "Looks to be a few."

"Two bucks each." Jim bags them while I pay, and we hit the highway.

Lester, 50 then, seemed old to us. I don't recall ever seeing him after that day. A local Clewiston youth robbed and murdered him in 1982, hacking him to death with a cane machete. The killer stole his pickup, painted it black, removed the bed. The sheriff found it parked beside his trailer, with the original license tag still on it.

⌒⌒

Continuing north, we explore every dirt road and deserted farm. We flip old roofing tin, rotting lumber, and roll logs, amassing an excellent collection of snakes and other reptiles. Beyond Lake Okeechobee, we ride the sand ridge through orange groves and cypress swamps, to Clermont, and the Florida Citrus Tower. The attraction includes a roadside zoo with wild animals and snakes. It only serves to whet our enthusiasm to get to Silver Springs. Finally, oranges yield to horse farms and the deep Ocala National Forest. It's dark by the time we reach Silver Springs east of Ocala. We pull into the springs parking lot by to sleep, but excitement keeps us awake.

Ross Allen, despite his fame as a herpetologist and showman, is down to earth, affable. "Welcome to the Reptile Institute!" We enjoy a personal tour. A legendary figure, he was in Tarzan movies, on TV, and I saw him once on a family visit to Silver Springs. That meeting added fuel to the fire burning within me for serpents.

Ross Allen with "Big George" gator
at his Reptile Institute in
Silver Springs, August 1965.
(State Archives of Florida/Mozert)

On Loop Road
in the Everglades during
our 1965 Road Trip.

The author dipping turtles
and newts along Loop Road, 1965.

He lets Jim and me handle exotic snakes and regales us with stories of his heyday in the reptile world. It's a dream fulfilled. He trades Gray Ratsnakes, a Canebrake Rattler, and other North Florida species for the ones we brought. "Thanks for the Everglades Ratsnakes, we always need them for exhibit."

For a few, he pays cash. We keep the racers, garters, and moccasins he doesn't want. With our newfound wealth, we enjoy the famous springs, ride a glass-bottom boat on the Silver River, eat snacks. Boyhood fun at its best.

⌒

Gulf Hammock beckons, a deep wilderness along the upper Gulf of Mexico. Everywhere are signs reading No Camping or No Overnight Parking. Near Yankeetown on the Withlacoochee River, we stop at a Highway Patrol station to ask if they can recommend a place to camp.

"You're welcome to stay here, in the lot out back."

"Thanks." Instead, we drive off into the night.

No traffic in the late hour. We speed through the darkness on straight, desolate US 19. Jim yells, "Stop, stop, stop!"

We're well past a mud turtle, *Kinosternon subrubrum steindachneri*, on the road's edge when the heavy station wagon draws to a halt. Flashlight in hand, he jumps out, runs back.

In the deep-woods blackness, the rear-view mirror is useless. I lean out the window and use the centerline to guide me backing up, slowing when I think I'm about where Jim should be. I plan to pass him so he can see in the headlights. Instead, his door, half-open, hits him edge on, right on the backside while he's bending over to pick up the turtle. The force sends him sprawling in the grass. *Oh my God, I've killed him.* I run to his side. He's groaning, trying to stand. I burst out laughing. Jim's okay, has a bruised butt, tries to be mad. No use. He joins the laughter.

Bone tired, bleary-eyed, it's now past midnight. With no better prospect for a place to sleep, we return to the State Troopers' office.

We park in a dark corner of the lot behind the building. Rear seat removed for the trip, we have the whole back of the wagon to stretch out. We move equipment and specimen boxes to the roof, sacks of snakes to the front floorboard. While Jim arranges our sleeping bags, I go inside, tell the duty officer we'll be camping here. Then things become interesting.

A Great Horned Owl stands in the lighted lot. I approach. Fifty feet, 30, at 10, it's staring, not moving. I call in a low tone, to not startle the bird. He doesn't hear. I shout louder. "Jim!"

I ease closer. Two feet tall at his pointed ear-tufts, he looks bigger, majestic, in the middle of the parking lot. Near enough to touch, it still hasn't moved, I reach out. Startled, he takes flight, his wings beating fast, silent. His feathers brush me as he passes. The close encounter is exciting, exhilarating, and Jim sleeps through it.

Before going to the car, I visit a restroom behind the station. The door closes, I flip the switch—no lights. Streetlights shine enough light through a window, high on the wall, to use the facilities. The floor is a puddle of water. *How did that get here?* Ugh, never mind. It smells musty, but not terrible. *I sure wish I could see.* When I go to leave—the doorknob turns but the door won't open. *Kee-rap, now what?*

I jump to grab the window bars, pull myself up to call Jim. My voice wavers under the strain. No use, he's sound asleep. I pound my fists on the concrete station wall, yelling as loud as I can—no one hears. Exhausted, I squat in a dry corner, hang my head to rest, at a loss for what to do.

In the night I hear someone outside. It must be 2 am, I spring to my feet and yell. "Hey, hey, I'm stuck in here," bang on the door.

He tries the doorknob. "How long have you been in there?"

"A couple hours."

"I'll be right back." Fifteen minutes pass. *Where is he?* Then a knock. "The station chief has the key, I called him at home, said he'd be here, in an hour."

It seems longer. When they get the door open, it's after 3 am. The grumpy-looking trooper glares, says nothing.

"Thank you, officer." I head for the car.

I climb over the tailgate and stretch out for an abbreviated night's sleep. Our night from hell over—so I thought. With first light, Jim awakens, rested. I'm groggy and tell him of the drama he missed.

He's laughing at my misfortune when, wide-eyed, he stops. "Don't move."

"What? Why, what's wrong?"

He points with his chin towards the front seat. "Holy crap! Where did he come from?"

A robust, two-foot Cottonmouth, lying across the backrest. Dangerous, noted for their irritability, *Agkistrodon piscivorus* can deliver a serious or fatal bite.

We're lucky the snake is in full view. We know it escaped from a sack, but can't say how many others may have been in with it. Venomous snakes should be in a wooden box. In the excitement at Silver Springs, at least one got left out. We back out, recapture the escapee, and locate an empty bag with a rip in the side. Whatever it held is now running free.

For the next half hour we play "find the pit viper," look under the seats, dash, and remove every object. We give up the hunt, not knowing if it's the only loose snake. We're jumpy for a few hours, and poke at each other whenever the opportunity arises.

CHAPTER 17:
The Biz

My passion for reptiles and working for John Marolf fuels my dreams of starting a business. I'm selling and trading on a small scale under the name Tropical Reptile Ranch. I branch out with a classified ad in *Outdoor Life* magazine.

Blue Ribbon gets shipments of reptiles they don't expect or want. Their first thought is to get rid of them before they die. They'll unload them cheap. It means easy profit for me. Part goes to local dealers, and the rest I sell with ease through the mail. The quick sales encourage me.

Their client, Tokyo Aquarium, persists in requesting Florida reptiles. John does not trade in native fauna. I offer to supply them. He refuses. No time for such trivia. Their constant requests aggravate John, he grumbles in disdain, "I should let you handle them."

Taken as a green light, I make contact, claiming referral from Blue Ribbon. It might be a stretch. They send an extensive want-list of Florida snakes and turtles. Nervous but excited, I remit my reptile availability. In response, they place a $1,000 order. It's crazy money for me.

Wow, things move fast! Ed, Sonny, and Ronny help with collecting. Every available moment I spend hunting for specimens. It's a grand feeling, but an enormous responsibility.

Familiar with handling and shipping animals from working at Blue Ribbon, I take great care packing. Japan Airlines accepts the cargo freight collect from Miami. Paperwork is daunting. Now, I must wait.

Three weeks pass, and a packet arrives by certified mail. Photographs of snakes, turtles, and lizards lined up, dead. The casualties are devastating. I packed them with attention to detail, what happened? They will not pay for the lost animals, but say, "Most arrived in excellent condition." They ask for replacements and include a check and a fresh desideratum.

It's tough showing the letter to my dad. The deaths upset him. "You must be more careful packing them if you plan to continue." But he says how he's proud of me.

I post my apology by airmail and work to gather the next shipment.

Ever larger shipments to Japan follow. My techniques improve. The first losses were from freezing. When shipped in heated compartments, any loss became minimal. The client wants exotic species, which I buy from other dealers. I import directly. Consignments arrive from Colombia with many types of South American reptiles. Without my asking, they ship monkeys, Coatimundi, Tamanduas, and Kinkajous. I'm becoming a full-fledged animal dealer. I build cages and hunt for new clientele. Aside from me, this pleases no one.

CHAPTER 18:
The Visitor

A client met through my magazine ad writes asking if I'd be willing to take him snake collecting. Bob from Shavehead Lake, Michigan, arrives for a brief visit in late summer of '65. I arrange for him to stay in a cottage next door to an old hotel built by the Everglades Land Sales Company in 1911. Old Mr. Huss cuts my hair in his front porch barbershop and manages the boarding house, along with the rental cottages.

An auspicious sign: When I arrive in the morning to pick Bob up, we catch a young indigo on the steps of his apartment. "I told you Davie was a snaky place."

We begin on Flamingo Road, fabled hunting grounds for rare Scarlet Kingsnakes, *Lampropeltis triangulum doliata*. Several turn up along a row of Australian Pines. Then Loop Road for Florida Kings, on to South Bay for Everglades Ratsnakes, each high on his want list. We find them and more.

Our next jaunt is out the levees from Terrytown to search the Sawgrass prairies for Water Moccasins. Before long we find a large one in tall Johnson Grass along the Miami Canal.

Bob is a complete novice. "Watch what I do, stay back on my left side."

As we approach, the Cottonmouth is crawling away. When stretched out, I grab its tail, sling the dangerous creature to my right into the open. I pin it and bag it—piece o' cake.

"Okay, next one is yours."

Not far ahead, a three-footer lies coiled two yards up from the canal bank.

This should be a simple catch. Bob creeps closer with me on his left. The snake sees us and heads for the canal. He grabs its tail and slings it left. It wraps around my waist, then falls to my feet.

"What the hell?" I jump back.

"I guess I panicked."

"Yeah, I suppose so. We got lucky on that one. Let's go."

The roadside canals in Davie are productive. On Bob's last evening we walk a ditch bank in town and spot a fat Florida Green Watersnake, *Natrix cyclopion floridana*. I catch it and climb to the road. Bob holds the bag. As I drop the big gal in, she bites me on the right index finger, ripping an L-shaped gash requiring three stitches. A rare serious bite from an otherwise harmless species. My pride hurts more than my finger.

CHAPTER 19:
The Pro

As my name spreads in the trade, people seek me out. Most want to buy. Others look to join a collecting trip. One fellow, Daryl, has a recent zoology degree with graduate studies in herpetology. I'm awestruck, it's a privilege to take him. He laments the lack of jobs in the field, claims to have applied to most prestigious zoos and many lesser ones. His current plan elicits an eye roll. He intends to work at Miami Serpentarium. He'll find out there's a long line waiting for a chance to work for Bill Haast, a man who prefers to work solo.

Daryl is quick to name snakes, despite having seen very few species outside of books. He wears glasses with thick lenses, "Coke-bottle bottoms" as we often referred to them as kids. They must work great because, as I drive, he calls out names for every mangled specimen we pass squashed on the pavement. His use of the term DOR, for *dead on the road,* now common herp vernacular, was the first I'd heard.

Nothing's outside Daryl's knowledge. He spews details on each DOR we find. It extends beyond reptiles. Scraps of rubber from blown tires become *"Sintheticus rubercus goodyeari."*

When he said it, I laughed, it was funny. I laugh the next dozen times. After the fiftieth, I want to kill him.

After Daryl's two-day visit, I never see him.

CHAPTER 20:
The Crash

Like a pinball, life has me crashing into one experience after another en route to my destiny. Despite the chaos, 1965 has been a banner year. I've experienced more than I could have imagined. A few things are becoming obvious. University is off the table. My grades are passing but won't get me into college. Not a topic of discussion and not in my plans. I'm ready to begin life's journey, work, be on my own, set my course. Dad has shown me how little we need to achieve happiness. What's central is outlook, determination. To understand what is important to ourselves versus other's expectations. Be a decent human being. Have faith, trust.

For wanting to be an explorer with a life of adventure in wild places, I have forsaken other options. Is it fantasy or could it be my future? I have no real plan for how to carry out my aspirations. Organic so far, I've just done it. Military service is a possibility. My dad, grandfather, and older brother served. Not sure yet. Fortunate to have enjoyed wonderful experiences, a loving family, many blessings, I don't want to fail. Have I enough of what is necessary to succeed in my chosen field? Is this teenage angst? Who knows, it's not my nature to worry.

As a Stranahan senior, I try harder. I credit my interest in snakes for giving me an edge, opening doors. Being different can be painful. I wish others to like and accept me, but not to join the herd. I'll settle for respect. With school, working for Blue Ribbon, and running a business, life is getting more stressful by the day. There's a danger of spreading myself too thin. We pray, hope, and believe nothing will go wrong...but it often does. 1965 ends with a bang.

I've got a date. After school chores include bringing the horses from pasture, feeding the animals, locking the pens and chicken coop. I groom my horse Big Red while he eats his sweet feed, using the curry comb to make his coat shine. His name fits. He's a sorrel and stands 17 hands tall at the withers. He's content. I'm content. The fragrance of hay, wood shavings in the paddock mud, sweaty leather of his halter, and leg liniment is soothing to man and beast. I shower, come back to saddle Red. He loves an evening ride.

My friend lives in an old farmhouse on Griffin Road, a five-mile jaunt in the cool, fall breeze. Twilight when I arrive, after visiting a while with her mom, while her dad watches TV, I help my date into the saddle. I climb on behind her and we saunter towards town to the Rexall for a soda.

Gone only minutes when two boys in a '55 Chevy run off the roadway. We're hit.

The impact sends us flying, tumbling to the ground. Big Red lay struggling, both hind legs broken, bloody. I land face first in the grass and spring to my feet, adrenaline coursing. My unconscious girlfriend lies scraped, bleeding on the roadside. I stumble over to her, pain surging through my left leg. She comes to but is in shock, crying, screaming. I try to calm her. The boys responsible stop and run back. When another car pulls over, they flee the scene, leaving behind their smashed windshield, glass from a headlight, chrome, and a trail of oily water.

Everything's a blur. The panicked passerby is speaking, but I can't understand. A sheriff's cruiser arrives, siren wailing, lights flashing. The deputy's face goes pale seeing the carnage. My companion is sitting. While he checks her, I turn to my injured horse. Red is thrashing in pain, nostrils flared, eyes wide with terror. His squeals and groans are excruciating. No way can he survive his grave injuries.

I call out. "Shoot him, please, he's in agony."

The deputy looks panicked, uncertain, ignores my pleas and Red's painful screams. He stands frozen, doesn't act. I reach for his gun. He snaps out of his trance, shoves me, I tumble, land on my backside. I stand up, now demanding, "Shoot him. Shoot him, dammit."

I kneel by Red. Cars and pickups continue to stop. A rancher I recognize steps in and speaks with the deputy, hand on his shoulder, leaning in close. The officer nods. He draws his pistol, motions for people to stand back, then comes toward me and my struggling horse.

I lay my torn, bloodied shirt over Red's face, covering his eyes to calm him, pat his neck, speak to him. "It's all right, Red. It's okay, fella."

He lays his head, stops fighting. When I step away, the deputy holds the gun within a few inches of Red's forehead and fires one shot. Everyone flinches. Red falls silent, motionless. Eyes welling, my heart breaking. He's family. So many blissful years we've shared. I go to comfort my girlfriend, now more traumatized, sobbing.

We're a quarter-mile from her house. Her father hears the sirens and comes running. As the ambulance arrives, he climbs in back with his daughter. We don't speak. As they speed away, I stand beside the road, trying to explain what happened to the deputy. Onlookers, neighbors, and strangers gather. I hobble over to Red and try to remove my twisted, broken saddle. No longer of use, but I want it.

The rancher helps me. "I'll contact your father. About your horse, I know someone...."

"Do what it takes." My eyes are fixed on Red, my shirt covering his face, now soaked with his blood and mine. The acrid fumes of gunpowder mixed with the metallic smell of blood linger.

A second ambulance comes.

At the hospital it's x-rays, then surgery. The impact smashed my ankle, requiring a steel pin. Other injuries are superficial. I awake in my room under the influence of sodium pentothal. There's music, the Beach Boys, "I Get Around," but no radio. I have the profound sense of being alive because of divine intervention. Saved by angels.

When the fog clears, I see my father. "How's my girlfriend?"

"She's okay, only scrapes. They checked her over and sent her home."

"I'm sorry, Dad." The gravity of things weighs on me.

"It's not your fault. Those boys are in big trouble. You're safe, that's what matters."

The ordeal keeps me hospitalized a few days, on crutches for six weeks. They took Red to a slaughterhouse. The thought haunts me. I never knew his age. With me seven years, he was mature when Dad bought him. I hoped he'd die in his sleep. I wanted him to live forever.

Something must give. My leg in a cast, unable to care for my animals or go collecting. I'm missing a week of school and weeks of work. The Tokyo Aquarium arrangement has run its natural course. With few customers, mammal imports dwindle. Besides, dealing with the vet and feed bills, the mess, the labor. I no longer want it.

The accident isn't to blame for everything, but a catalyst for many changes. The close of an era. End of innocence. It will knock me out of eligibility for the service. More significantly, the relationship with my girlfriend enters a different plane. I put her in harm's way and owe her a higher form of allegiance. She expects it, her family expects it. I guess I do too, but my father cautions me. He can see me falling into a deeper commitment.

"Be careful, son."

I am. I won't go off the deep end, but it set the stage.

CHAPTER 21:

New Horizons - Bimini

While recovering from my broken ankle, I whittle my animal collection to a manageable few. I'm back to work at Blue Ribbon. Missed over a month. When I got hurt, John was in a panic. Now they've learned to do without me. I can show up, or not. He's okay with it. Truth told, the job is getting old. I yearn for change. Graduation's a few months away and I won't be hanging on much longer. Then, a breath of fresh air.

"Want to go to Bimini?"

Ed Chapman and I have become tight friends, sharing good times on forays in the Everglades catching snakes. He is 9 years my senior, and gives advice, well intended, if questionable. It excites me, inspires me. When he speaks of his experiences in Bimini, his eyes tell me how great it must be. I have read accounts of collecting in the Bahamas, and Ed has shown me his specimens from the island. I yearn to go with him on such a trip.

Zero hesitation. "Shoot yeah!"

Late '65, my leg is returning to normal. Ed needs six Bimini Boas, *Epicrates striatus fosteri* for a zoo trade. I'm an extra pair of hands to flip rocks. Flattered that he trusts me. I know he's doing me a favor. For me it's a chance of a lifetime, a dream come true. He works and I'm in school, so the plan is to travel on a Saturday, return on Sunday.

Ed springs the $35 each for tickets on Chalk's Flying Service at the Miami Seaplane Base on Watson Island. They stow our small shared overnight bag holding collecting sacks and a single change of clothes. The seaplane is a Grumman G-73 Mallard built in the late 1940s. Aboard with five fellow passengers, we taxi the ramp into Biscayne Bay. The Atlantic is a straight shot through Government Cut.

The pilot throttles up the twin nine-cylinder, Pratt & Whitney R-1340 Wasps. A deafening roar. The plane bounces and shakes. I notice a light spray in the cabin. We bounce, skipping, as a child skips a stone, up, up, airborne. A day of firsts starts with my first airplane flight.

Too noisy for conversation on the 50-mile hop. A thousand feet below, I watch white-tipped waves curl and move—to where, I do not know. Will I see a whale? Everything is new.

"Fasten your seat belts for arrival, folks, extinguish any smokes."

We bank to port, circle the harbor to warn any boatmen. The pilot throttles back, water comes up fast. Boats flash by the windows as we skim to a soft landing. As before, I detect a faint mist of seawater on my skin. Engines change pitch as we plow through the waves, and roar again as we climb the ramp. "Welcome to Bimini, the Bahamas."

I step from the plane onto Bahamian soil, my first time outside of the United States. An officer greets passengers in his snappy white jacket and pith helmet. His black trousers have a bold red stripe on the leg. He directs us to the Kings Highway gate without asking for identification. The seaplane ramp is near the southern tip of North Bimini. We pass the famed End of the World

Chalk's Flying Service's Grumman G-73 Mallard landing
in Bimini Harbour, 1965.

Saloon, hangout of Adam Clayton Powell Jr. and other notables. Then Brown's Dock, made famous in Hemingway's *Islands in the Stream.*

Here's my opportunity to explore an exotic land, and we're on a mission. Time is precious. We must hurry to begin our search for the boas. A few doors north is a shuttle boat with no schedule. Nobody is there.

The old wooden ferryboat with a canvas top and open sides sits forlorn, floor awash in seawater. Ed, concocting a story, convinces the dockmaster of our urgent need to get to South Bimini. He sends two guys. One guy mans a hand-operated bilge pump, the other fires up the inboard engine. Neither shows any motivation.

We cross the harbor and inlet in a few minutes. Water so transparent, sailboats appear to hover over the white bottom. I've never known so many hues of green. The air crisp, clean save for a hard-to-define salty smell, mixed with the ferry's diesel exhaust—far from unpleasant. A wall of mangroves frames South Bimini. The excitement is intoxicating.

Dropped at the pier, a derelict-looking, blue-painted school bus to shuttle passengers to the airstrip has no driver. "No one's ever here. Not sure the damn thing runs."

We head out, walking the two miles to the airport. The junior guy gets to carry the suitcase. November, but the island's interior is hot on the narrow road through the dense coppice. Gumbo Limbo and Poisonwood grow cheek to jowl, blocking any chance of a breeze. Between pavement and trees is a thick border of thorny shrubs.

I pepper Ed with questions. "Hold your horses." Easy for him to say, he's been here before, knows what to expect. He's excited, more than I've seen him before on a collecting trip.

"Snake!" Ed runs towards a Bimini Racer, *Alsophis vudii picticeps,* crossing the road. He stops short when it slithers into the bush. I charge in but give up after a few feet. I come out scratched and bleeding. Ed stifles a laugh. I have much to learn.

Ameiva auberi richmondi, fast-moving, striped Bimini Racerunners, dart into the thicket. We arrive at a clearing where the runway begins. Limestone boulders line the roadway. Each has a Bimini Curly Tail, *Leiocephalus carinatus coryi,* standing sentinel. Exotic-looking lizards, their tails curl upwards in scorpion fashion. Their thick bodies, patterned in brown and white, have twin yellowish dorsolateral stripes (stripes running along the sides of their back).

The single-room concrete-block airport terminal, painted pink, flies a Bahamian flag from a staff. No one stirring; a few private planes parked, tied to the tarmac. Two men inside sit before oscillating fans in the sweltering building.

A Coke machine beckons, Ed grumbles. "Look at this, 25¢ a can. Robbery." They're 10¢ in Florida. He tells the guys. "We're here for snakes."

"Mon, take dem all."

The other guy asks, "What you do wit' dem?"

"We study them." I note how Ed handles questions.

The men claim they see chicken snakes in the mornings after a rain. Neither moves from in front of the fan. We investigate a pump house behind the terminal. Nothing here, so we stash our bag inside and forge into the bush. Nobody lives on this end of the island.

"This is snake country. Check under any rock bigger than this." Ed holds his hands, making a foot-wide circle.

A grid subdivides the thick coppice north of the runway. Divided into lots long ago, but now abandoned. The overgrown cuts are easier walking than through the forest. We turn rocks, returning each to its place. Beginner's luck in force, I find a tiny brown snake coiled beneath a stone. A Bimini Ground Boa, *Tropidophis canus curtus.* My first ever exotic reptile capture!

"Nice one." Ed is beaming.

It goes into a bag hung through my belt. We continued flipping stones with renewed energy. Ed finds two more *Tropidophis* 10 minutes apart. He calls out and I run to where he's standing over a flat rock. "Look at this." He raises it.

Beneath, a Bahamian Tarantula the size of the palm of my hand, stands with its front legs raised in a defensive posture. Though *Cyrtopholis bonhotei* is not as big as many species, it's the biggest spider I've seen wild. Ed breaks a dried twig, pins it, and picks it up with care as it displays large, black fangs.

"They can deliver a nasty bite." He tosses the creature into the bushes. It stands a moment, then runs, rustling the dry leaves.

"Ever been bit?"

"Nah, I'm careful. Not like they don't try."

We take no tarantulas because they need special handling. The next half hour our only finds are a few Bimini Blind Snakes, *Typhlops biminiensis.* Curiosities only, they are not something we wish to keep.

"Damn! I missed an *Alsophis* under a piece of rotten plywood."

"Not to worry, there'll be more."

By noon we collect an *Alsophis,* another *Tropidophis,* but no boas. He's growing anxious. "Let's go to another place we call the tarpaper shack."

No trails, he knows the small island in intimate detail. Soon we arrive at what resembles an old chicken coop. Concealed in the dense coppice, eight by six feet, a few posts set in limestone with a poultry wire covering. No floor, it has a tin roof. Once covered with tarpaper, which now lies scattered on the ground. The coast is nearby, and we can smell the mangrove roots at low tide, but it is too dense to see. Even this structure is invisible a few feet away.

Ed inspects every nook and cranny, finding nothing. We shift to fallen scraps of tarpaper lying buried in leaves. A foot-square piece yields a yard-long Bimini Boa, which he puts in a sack before I can look at it. Over the next several minutes, we turn three more. Pure elation! My first *Epicrates.* With four between us, he relaxes, smiling, laughing.

We pause in the shade to examine the boas. They have a striking dark blackish-brown dorsal color broken by grayish-white chevrons. Sides gray, with a complex pattern of connected black diamonds. Unlike any other snake I had caught, a true exotic. It grows over six feet. Population estimates are in the thousands. How can this little island support them?

It's late afternoon, and Ed needs two more. Nearby, the metal cover from a five-gallon bucket lies concealed in dense thorny brush. I think of passing it by, but, *What if?* On my knees on the sharp limestone, I struggle to reach the lid. With my fingertips, I flip it. To my shock, there's a large boa coiled beneath, and she tries to escape. I plow into the bushes, ignoring spiky twigs and spines to catch her. It takes a few moments to extract her from the tangle. She turns out to be the largest of the trip.

That same metal top yields snakes on nearly every future visit.

By day's end, we capture seven *Epicrates,* four *Tropidophis,* and a few *Alsophis.* A splendid hunt by any measure. We head for the airport terminal to pick up our bag. We get lucky, a plane has arrived, we catch a ride to the ferry landing. Turns out, the bus works.

In twilight, we navigate to North Bimini. A sky splashed with sunset colors silhouettes tall coconut palms. Alice Town's lights twinkle on the harbor surface. Famished, nothing to eat since Miami. On Kings Highway, a narrow gravel road lined with small shops and tall coconut palms, we slip into the Red Lion Pub. We're dirty, smelly, scratched from crawling the bush. We conceal our satchel full of sacks of snakes under our table. If they knew....

"Marie" by the Bachelors is playing on a jukebox. Dinner is pigeon peas and rice with fried fish. Delightful. Afterward, we walk towards Bailey Town. This, the poorer section of Bimini, is where most of its 500 people live. We get a hotel room, 35 shillings in Bahamian currency, pay in full with a US $5 bill. How great to take a shower. We lay on the beds, talking of the many things we've done in a single day, till we drift off to sleep.

No time for collecting Sunday, so we stroll the town and breakfast on fried eggs over grits and corned beef. We end at the seaplane ramp for the morning flight to Miami. No one's at the Customs shack, so we check out the colorful fish in the crystal water from a dock. Conch shells piled on the shore are extending the land into the harbor. Coconut palm fronds sway in the gentle breeze. I gaze across the bay and its hundred shades of blues and greens to South Bimini and wonder if I'll return someday.

Then the drone of the Chalk's flight. We watch as it circles the anchorage, landing with a foaming wake, spray billowing from the prop wash. Moments later it's ashore, and we board. We take off to the north and circle over East Bimini. I strain to glimpse where we walked on the South Island before we head west over the Gulf Stream.

I'll return many times over the next 10 years, but this was my unforgettable first. Things I can't yet know lay ahead. A wealth of adventures in the Bahamas and countries around the world await.

Wading on storm-flooded South Bimini.

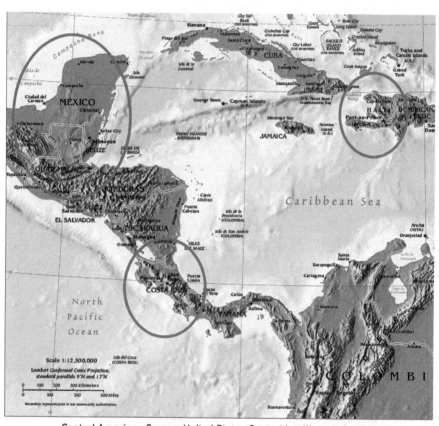

Central America - Source: United States Central Intelligence Agency

PART TWO:
Coming of Age

Graduation, independence, and the beginning of the life of adventure that I seek. Things happen fast with my first trip to Mexico, solo, then marriage, and my first big Haiti adventure. I move to Florida's West Coast, then return to Haiti, alone this time. A long-anticipated trip through Central America leads to a life-changing sojourn in pristine Costa Rica. A one-in-a-million occurrence in the Everglades leaves us stunned. While branching out to the Bahamas Out Islands, I turn 21 on Eleuthera.

Port Everglades in the 1960s. (State Archives of Florida, Florida Memory)

CHAPTER 22:
On My Own

However short, the Bimini trip renewed my spirit. With new determination, I focus on achieving my goals—whatever they may be. I'm not sure, aside from being an explorer, collector, and having an adventurous life. But how? Confusion reigns. So far, so good, but I must tighten up, concentrate on graduation. Learn who will help me, who could hold me back.

I leave Blue Ribbon at the end of 1965. It's been a hell of an education. I am grateful, but it's time for a change. My interests have grown from selling to keeping and studying reptiles, field collecting in faraway places. My father chose his path. His example makes me believe I can achieve whatever I set as my goal. Success is up to me to make it happen.

Things are changing fast. Soon to graduate, I search for proper employment. Without a doubt, I'm in for a dose of reality. Work instead of school means scant time to pursue activities I love. If I give up my animal business, less money. I apply to Florida Power and Light. Outdoors, moving each day appeals to me. I remember, as a kid, seeing FPL crews fishing in Davie canals on their lunch break. For such a dream job, no wonder there's a waiting list.

I turn my attention to Port Everglades. Florida's deepest harbor is filled with ships and shipping-related industries. I'd taken every woodworking and metal shop class in school but lack an advanced education. Forest Products is an industrial lumber company. Five acres of warehouses, mill, and outdoor stacks of exotic timbers. Wood, hard work, and heavy equipment have its appeal. They hire me on the spot for $1.25 per hour, pending graduation in a few weeks. A much-needed steady income until I find something more suitable. I have no illusion of making this my career.

At six-foot-two, 230 pounds, few believe I'm 17 when I report for duty. I thrive with the responsibilities, the thrill of learning to run the massive machines. Who knew it involved so many skills? I master stacking lumber, bundling orders, unloading rail cars. Most important, learn to fit in, in the hardscrabble world. "Go along to get along," they say. Learn to work with and earn the respect of others who lack the range of options I have. I get tough, muscles hard, become an exemplary employee, meet the expectations of my bosses by being a dependable, safe worker. Injuries come easy in this industry and can lead to loss of employment or worse.

Teamwork is new to me, but essential. The gigantic Hyster straddle carriers that can lift entire loads of lumber, weigh eight tons, can lift 20. A careless move can get a person killed. The mill, where craftsmen make moldings, is earsplitting with the whine, whistles, and groans of saws and planers. The smell of wood shavings is intoxicating. Mill men sharpen our switchblade knives to a razor's edge, to cut the twine we use for bundling lumber. At lunch we eat our sandwiches, pull splinters, sitting on huge wooden beams in a timber shed. Their ends, painted in colors to indicate species, bear cryptic marks in yellow crayon. I wonder from what jungles they might have come. The men swap bawdy stories. I blush. They swear like sailors. Ship stacks, visible over metal warehouse roofs, billow smoke and steam. We can hear their horns blow in the harbor. At day's end, lines of salt encrust my shirt. I feel like a man.

The week of my 18th birthday, Florida Power and Light calls me for an interview. They're hiring, the economy is growing, older employees retiring. The job is mine, starting October 10. My first thought is to trade my old '53 Ford station wagon. 1966 is the Ford Bronco's inaugural year. Convinced I need one, with my FPL employment confirmation in hand, I visit the dealership. A teal roadster with a canvas top and removable doors catches my eye. The basic model is $2,100 with only a driver's seat.

The salesman checks the papers, studies me a moment. "You sure I can't interest you in a Lincoln? Keep this job, son, and you'll never have trouble buying a car, a house, or much else."

My chest swells with pride. My trade-in has no value. He sells me the Bronco with no down payment. I sell the wagon to a neighboring rancher in Davie for $75. Minus the rear seat which replaces the single bucket. A machine shop splits the tire rims, welding in a 3-inch-wide band of steel. With mud tread tires, the truck has unbeatable traction. The consummate snake-hunting buggy.

The next step is the boldest. I rent a 50-year-old farmhouse in a sod field on Griffin Road. Dreams of doing a trip call for careful timing. I plan to leave Forest Products, set up my home, and travel—someplace—before my position starts at FPL.

I dread telling management of my job offer. They counter with a ten-cent raise to $1.35 if I stay. The power company is starting me at $1.50 an hour. They're disappointed. It's difficult to find younger lads for such hard labor. They understand, my leaving is not over salary, and wish me success. Fine people, I owe them. My coworkers, Frank, Ben, and Wildman, sad to see me go, are encouraging. Most of them have worked here since before I was born.

At eighteen, brought up right, taught to be self-reliant and confident, I move from home to start a life on my own. There's no drama. I'm not going far. My father, while not cheerful over my move, supports my decision. It comes as no surprise. Except for living under a different roof, our relationship won't change. Many things—everything else—will.

CHAPTER 23:
The Kid's Lost His Mind!

Bimini whets my appetite—adventure in a foreign land for a $35 plane ticket. I burn for bolder journeys. Jungles call, their siren songs haunting my thoughts and dreams since grade school. I must go. Only where, with limited time and money? Mexico? Yes! Tropical forests, and mountains, and deserts—things I yearn to see. Nothing can hold me back.

August's a whirlwind, the FPL job, moving out, buying a Bronco. After a two-week notice at Forest Products, I'm free to travel. Not for long. My new position starts in three weeks. If I aim to make a trip, the window is closing fast. With map and pencil, I work out a route, stay up late to calculate distance and drive times. Difficult before computers and interstate highways. The result, 4,600 miles—doable in ten days if everything goes right.

Gasoline costs 30¢ per gallon. I figure $100 will suffice. Fifty bucks for food and I plan to camp out. I seek a companion. No one, not Sonny, Jim, or Ed, shows interest, so I'll travel on my own. They think I've taken leave of my senses. Perhaps so. Dad has concerns despite his confidence in my abilities. He reminds me of his brush with Mexican "banditos."

When he came of age, as his father had, he traveled west seeking adventure. He mined gold in Arizona, met wooly characters like the Apache who wore a pair of six-shooters and carried a live rattlesnake in his shirt. He told of an old woman at a desert trading post selling him a rifle and pistol after she first used the handgun to shoot a row of bottles out the back door, of a gunfight he saw in a mining town, and finally in Mexico to have boots made he and two friends got ambushed by bandits riding horseback. They outran them in their car. Yes, I recall the story.

"Holy cow, Dad, that was the 1930s. Things have changed." *Haven't they?* The family farm is no longer mine to use as an animal compound. I intend to cut back to only reptiles and move them to a building at my rented home. For now, the snakes stay at Dad's. A friend promises to check on them. Sonny will take the mammals for safekeeping.

As I say goodbye to my girlfriend, I hear her dad tell her mom, "The kid's lost his mind."

CHAPTER 24:
Mexico Solo, '66

With a water keg, camping supplies, provisions, and collecting gear, I set out on a Friday in September. Map and notes beside me, cash stashed in various places as I have no credit cards. I drive near nonstop except for gas and restroom breaks to Texas. Sunday morning, I phone from Laredo, but the family has left for church. Eighteen years old, by myself, I enter Mexico with my new Ford Bronco. The country open before me, ripe for exploring.

Too excited to be nervous, I barrel south, crossing desert scrublands and rocky hills. Past cacti, yuccas, agaves, and Ocotillo. Roadrunners dart across, as I move a few horned lizards from traffic lanes. Eager to explore, I waste little time and push on to reach the tropics. In Sabinas Hidalgo, Nuevo León, I stop for lunch. Purple and gray mountains form the horizon, I can't wait to experience them up close. Monterrey is bigger than I expect. I slow to soak in the colors of the barrios, the savory aromas of strange foods, the music, the signs in Spanish. People are genial, I'm surprised how many speak English. My Español is nonexistent, my surroundings dictate my needs. At a *gasolinera*, they figure I need gas, at a restaurant, food. Easy.

In Cumbres de Monterrey, roads wind between spectacular sheer cliffs. My first time driving in mountains. DOR snakes increase, but reptile collecting is difficult. I seek rural routes with few people, to check out and to spend the night. Motels are out of the question, my canvas doors, and top leave the truck vulnerable. In off-road, out of sight spots, I sleep in peace, in the seat, or on the ground beneath heaven's starry blanket. Young and eager, any discomfort is a small price to pay for this exciting experience.

At 18, I don't recognize poverty or danger around me. With my rural upbringing, a chicken walking through an eatery isn't a shock. Friendly people are what I notice. Nonstop beauty of the countryside at every turn delights my eyes. There's much to learn. I will. I've come for adventure, not to look for social problems.

Subtly aware that I'm living my dream, I'm drawn trance-like ever southward. Tall Sierra Madre Oriental pine and oak forests yield to rainforest with palms, cycads, and philodendrons. Between Ciudad Victoria and Antonio Morales, near El Cielo, trees become laden with epiphytes, the likes of which I've never seen. Immersed in cloud forest, I walk, my clothes wet from dripping foliage. Rugged rock formations, shrouded in mist, bear orchids, bromeliads, ferns—it's mind-boggling, surreal. Raucous squawks and maniacal laughing by Maroon-fronted Parrots fill my ears. Throaty barks of trogons, buzzing of Blue-throated Sapphire Hummingbirds, my head is on a swivel. Vermilion Flycatchers, Green Jays, brilliant-hued butterflies—each is new to me. Is this paradise? The cool brume and sweet musk of decay, bracing.

A serpentine trail through the foothills leads to the natural wonder of El Nacimiento, birthplace of Río Mante. Crystal water springs forth from caverns under the jungle-covered Sierra Guatemala. The smooth stones in the chill lagoon soothe my feet. I relish the silence.

The road climbs into forest gloom where tree canopies are shadows in the *neblina*. No sounds but for tires singing on wet pavement. Fog lifts. Resplendent in sunlight, leaves sparkle, bejeweled with moisture. Over the crest, the route descends to a tropical valley. Coconut palms, papayas, and bananas grow near small villages. The passage, from Laguna del Mante to Ciudad Valles, is through Jaguar country. Cloud shrouded elevations rife with rivers, thundering waterfalls. Aquamarine waters recall memories of rock pits at home. I draw in the sweet atmosphere of unspoiled wilderness and feel unbounded freedom.

Bright green Crevice Swifts, and vivid blue and orange *Sceloporus minor* on canyon walls. Racers, whipsnakes, and garters, of types unknown to me, elude my grasp. On a limb over a stream, a Mexican Parrot Snake, *Leptophis mexicanus*, is a reminder I've reached the tropics.

Animals I recognize from captivity are a joy to see wild. Evening brings family groups of Coatis, tails held high. Cacomistles, low and sleek with bushy, black-banded tails, scamper at lightning speed. Too often I find slow-moving

Tamanduas, the Lesser Anteater, hit on the roads. By day, spiny iguanas, boa constrictors, horned lizards, I must pinch myself to prove it's real. Reptile collecting, my reason for coming, is beyond my dreams. Cat-eyed snakes, Baird's Ratsnakes, Nightsnakes, Black Tail, and Totonacan Rattlesnakes, *Crotalus totonacus*, and a variety of wonderful treefrogs. I forge south to Tamazunchale, in San Luis Potosi.

What a dream! The colonial center has a colorful, domed cathedral, San Juan Bautista, but outside of town, it's rural. The indigenous Tenek tribe of Huastec dwells in stick-walled huts with palm-thatched roofs. I want to live here! A *National Geographic* magazine come to life. Peaceful, nested in tropical forest between the towering ridges—heaven on Earth. I explore along a river, collect a spectacular Cribo, *Drymarchon melanurus erebennus*, but can't tarry. I head south towards Pachuca.

Mexican food is unfamiliar. My mom fixed canned tamales a few times, and chili con carne—I never ate a taco until now—it's great. I order what someone else has or take what they serve. A delicious other world has opened!

My long odyssey leaves little time to linger. I exit the Sierra Madre Oriental for the Mexican Plateau. On the treeless rolling hills of the Altiplano, fewer reptiles mean less reason to stop. With better roads I travel fast and far towards distant peaks. I pass into Mexico City for the sights—a colossal mistake. A terrifying maze of streets and traffic such as I have never experienced. Crowds, street vendors, blaring horns, mouthwatering aromas, and putrid odors. I get through as quickly as possible and when I do, it's dark.

People noticing my Bronco is a source of pride. Perhaps it's the first one they've seen here. At a Pemex station on the outskirts of Mexico City, a rancher in a pickup asks if I'd sell it. He speaks English, is friendly, looks over every inch of the vehicle, asking pointed questions. His intensity leaves me uneasy, so I wait till he departs and then search for a place to stay.

It's bone-chilling high in the mountains. Without other options, I pull off beside a cultivated field. No lights anywhere in sight. It seems a suitable spot. The ground is soggy. I lay on the seat shivering, in jeans and a flannel shirt, covered by my sleeping bag. My muddy boots are wet, uncomfortable, but I dare not remove them. It's an endless night.

The sun is up and bright when I awake. Workers in the field watch as I brush my teeth. It feels awkward. I guess I'll wait to pee. Hungry, but with nothing much left. Breakfast is a piece of hard bread with peanut butter and a cup of water. As I prepare to move on, I notice a man skinning a dead Bullsnake. I go to check as he takes a bundle of fresh skins from a burlap sack. Must be at least ten. As best I can tell, he intends to make leather out of them for belts and wants to sell the one he's wearing.

It's chilly in the morning air, my stomach gnawing, I try to leave but my tires spin in the slippery mud, so I lock the front hubs in four-wheel drive. It churns the soft red clay but climbs the embankment with ease. At the edge of the pavement, I unlock the wheels and roll onto the highway. A Mexican driver blows his horn, shouting, pointing. I don't understand, think something is wrong with the truck and stop on the shoulder. The man pulls alongside. In English he admonishes me for tracking the roadway with gooey clods.

"Señor, you've made a mess. You should clean it!"

I'm shocked by his ranting and embarrassed. The front bumper holds a wagon jack and a shovel. He watches me scrape up the muddy clumps and insists I dig it out of the wide rims. The Mexican stranger stays till I finish, thanks me, and we both go on our way.

He's right, I suppose. The guy has pride in his town and dislikes when someone messes it up for no reason. I understand and hope he doesn't think I have no respect for his homeland. Nothing is further from the truth. I'm falling in love with Mexico.

The high-plains route to the border is a monotonous 700 endless miles to Nuevo Laredo. Lizards abound, a few snakes DOR, but no live ones. It's hypnotic, mind-numbing as my mud tires drone on the asphalt, like a swarm of angry bees. Five days planned inside Mexico are now six with another to go, so I press on into the night. Travel after dark is ill-advised. Mexican roads can hold unpleasant surprises, are often unlined, hard to see. Rockfalls, cattle, bottomless potholes, washouts. Worse are the nighttime drivers who, for reasons unknown, drive without lights. Yes, it's true! They fly, devil may care, through the darkness. Trucks and coaches whiz past, as unseen shadows, a startling, unnerving mystery to me. No wonder horrible crashes are so common, why buses sail off cliffs. I don't care if they have a death wish so long as I'm not included in their plans.

No border issues with my reptiles. I head straight to a burger joint for a taste of American fare. I sit, savor the commonplace things we take for granted. The smells of familiar foods. Sounds of my native tongue. The carefree safety. Music is the Beach Boys' "God Only Knows," The Cyrkle's "Turn Down Day" and Roger Williams' version of "Born Free." I miss the adrenaline-fueled thrills of discovering places unknown. The mystery of not knowing what's coming next, the magnificent scenery, and yes, the danger. I'm hooked for life. Before leaving Laredo, I call my dad. I'm thankful the trip was trouble-free, nothing serious happened, I know doing this solo was naïve, foolish. But I loved it, and without a doubt, I'll be back.

CHAPTER 25:
Don't Fix It If It Ain't Broke

I'm on pilgrimage today, hoping to meet C.C. McClung, famous, eccentric, larger than life. Homeward bound from Mexico, I stop by his Snake Farm in LaPlace, Louisiana, a long-hoped-for visit. A roadside attraction in the swamp west of New Orleans, visiting is a dream held since junior high. Many are the mail-order snakes I'd bought from this legendary animal importer. Alas, C.C. is in Texas. I will not have the honor of meeting him.

Impossible to miss. Garish signs line roadsides for miles in every direction. They lure tourists like buzzards to roadkill. An entrance a blind man could see screams "sideshow." It's everything I imagined and more. Snakes galore, animals from South America, Africa, and Asia. Thrilled to be here at last, but my missing Mr. McClung is a bitter disappointment. I leave empty-handed, intending to return, but never again visit this American classic.

With the Bahamas and Mexico under my belt, it boosts my status among my peers in Davie. I can't deny the extra dose of respect feels good. Working for FPL, life is grand. The exotic animal business is ongoing but shrinking according to plan. Except for the snakes. Evenings I drive the rural roads, weekends ply the Everglades to collect. Never busier, never happier, never freer.

Bubbles come in all shapes and sizes, but have one thing in common; they burst. My world will soon change in a big way. My girlfriend and I dated through high school. Despite having no interest in reptiles, many of our dates were road collecting trips. To her credit, she does not pretend to enjoy them. My different lifestyle, the excitement, adventure, and now travel, fascinates her.

If not that, what? Cautioned by family and friends, I ignore advice, however sage, or well intentioned. Secure in a new career, carrying a sense of obligation, I diverge on an irreversible path. We make our move, marry in the spring of 1967.

It's a Southern wedding at Davie Baptist Church, with cake and fried chicken in the crepe-paper decorated reception hall. Soup cans tied behind the Bronco, we drive off with wishes for health, happiness, success, and good luck, knowing well we'd need it. Taking responsibility for another's welfare means concentrating on earning a living. If that were the only thing!

Reality takes a hefty bite. What in hell were we thinking? Perhaps we weren't. With commitment comes sacrifice, give-and-take, and adapting to newfound proximity. Did I mention sacrifice? I pick it up fast. Change is difficult but necessary. It's the old "Be careful what you wish for" adage. I may have overestimated how mature I was. Still, I forge on, try to be a dutiful husband, while maintaining the lifestyle I love. It ain't gonna be easy.

We learn about lean times, hard work. Minimum wage bumps to $1 per hour in February. At FPL I earn $1.50, we have no right to complain. Take-home pay is $42, a week after tax. Doesn't sound like much? That's because it's not. I reconsider giving up selling animals.

The house on the 20-acre sod-field that I thought was perfect, turns out it needs a few adjustments. I do them myself. In short order it looks spiffy. The barn, fitted with shelving, accommodates reptile cages. Outside pens hold tortoises. In the shade, I build a place for the few remaining monkeys and other mammals. This part of my business and life I won't miss when it's gone. I'll sell them off at the first opportunity and increase the reptiles.

CHAPTER 26:
Bimini by Boat

Much needed cash from reptile sales makes it easier for me to invest time in their pursuit. Thing is, the time is no longer only mine to use as I see fit. I am learning how things work.

A select group of clientele buys most of my specimens, and extras sell easily to other dealers. Trouble is, I've had no recent imports or trips. Both of these things will soon change.

Ed buys a 17-foot Cobia, a brilliant move. The seaworthy craft has a deep-vee hull and a 75-horse Evinrude outboard, making it suitable to cross the Gulf Stream to Bimini. He calls me for the maiden voyage. He trusts me. I'm always willing. Daylight on Saturday, gassed up, supplies aboard, we strike out of Miami's Government Cut. A straight shot, 53 miles, our estimate of a three-hour trip on target.

Sea conditions perfect, it's the first of many crossings. No Customs check for us. We beach on the west shore, South Island, and enter the bush. Things go off the rails. We come back to discover the boat breached in the surf. It threatens to capsize and sink, pummeled by waves. We struggle, get battered and bruised pulling it offshore, but save it. A close call and a hard lesson.

We move to Bimini's south side, wedge into the mangroves, and walk their stilt roots to shore. After a day of collecting, we wash up at the spigot by a radio beacon. A successful hunt. To celebrate we'll change clothes, motor to North Bimini for a meal at the Red Lion Pub. Late afternoon we return, and to our shock find the boat high and dry.

Who thinks of tides in the Bahamas? It sits level, supported by mangrove roots. Try as we may, it's not moving until the tide rises. At sundown, mosquitoes arrive in droves. The big, salt marsh kind that crunch when we smack 'em.

Ed is slapping, cursing, I shout. "Don't kill them, Ed!"

"What? Why?"

"A thousand will come to their funeral." I force a laugh, Ed groans.

On the brink of losing every drop of our blood, we're forced to take shelter in our sleeping bags to escape the onslaught. Thank God we have them.

Bundled up, no breeze on the lee side of the island, heat is brutal, the air sticky. Even the smallest opening to breathe lets in mosquitoes. We have a hellish night.

At 2 am, both still awake, we hear splashing on the hull. Another hour, the boat rocks. Desperate to escape our torment, we struggle, pushing, rocking side to side. After an eternity, it pulls free. We back out. Ed lowers the motor and cranks it, churning the grassy bottom.

He revs the engine full throttle, cuts a sweeping arc, the angle keeps the prop off the seabed. He banks the other way, repeating the move until reaching deeper water. In pitch darkness, it's a miracle we avoid hitting the many coral heads that flourish in the inshore shallows. Offshore away from the mosquitoes, we anchor, rest a few hours in the cooling breeze.

The trip is a smashing success; we are eager to return and do. In fair weather and foul, determination blinds us to danger. How great to cross between North and South Bimini at will. No more ferries. We sleep aboard, docked, or anchored offshore. Trips come with increasing frequency. So do our adventures.

Despite hardships, Bimini is in our blood. A lot of our blood is in Bimini.

CHAPTER 27:
Mexico '67

Bimini trips every few weeks are outstanding but saturate the market for *Epicrates,* and don't help things at home. An exquisite snake, but demand has limits. Most I trade for other exotic reptiles to get much needed variety. By the summer of '67, I have thoughts of another Mexico run. My first left me thirsting for more. Married now, trip planning carries other complications. It'd be great if my bride came along, but I doubt she'll be willing, so I don't ask. Instead, I reach out to friends.

Ed can't get off work. No one else shows interest in heading off into the wilds of Mexico. I'm disappointed. "Too busy. Too risky. Can't afford it." I talk it over with my spouse. She surprises me, volunteers to join me. Bottom line, she doesn't want me going alone, and she knows I will. Married only months, a splendid opportunity for bonding. Right?

I'm new at FPL, nervous sweat pops out when I approach supervision to ask off the week of July the 4th. They agree. Wow! Less daunting than I thought.

"What if I'm a few days late?"

"Don't be."

I know what to expect. Planning is easier. My wife coming complicates a few things. Safety and lodging, for starters. We plan not to stay in hotels unless for security or weather. Over her family's strenuous objections, we head west.

New this trip: an 8-track tape player. In remote places, finding music is difficult on the factory AM radio. With the extra reptile money, we splurged.

A good supply of tapes, country to the Beatles, Beach Boys, and oldies collections. We bring more food, a lantern, folding chairs.

As before, we cross the border at Laredo, following a nonstop drive to Texas. South near Sabinas Hidalgo, we stop to photograph huge barrel cacti and dig up a small one. northern Sierra Madre Oriental has spectacular scenic spots I remember and wish to share. I want to explore new locations too. Turns out, there's no shortage of picture-postcard sights.

Must be tarantula breeding season, they're out in force. We see many from South Texas throughout eastern Mexico. Amazing creatures, several types for sure, but I have no way of knowing if any are dangerous. Creeped out, my wife won't get out to look at them. To avoid mutiny, I pass up collecting any.

No big fan of hiking and climbing, she prefers staying with the vehicle while I explore. She's brought books to read, listens to music, naps. This works out well for me and eliminates the worry of someone bothering our stuff. In the mountainous corridor north of Tamazunchale is a DOR Terciopelo, *Bothrops atrox asper,* the largest and most dangerous venomous snake in Mexico. I pull over to search a steep trail into a mountain forest. The strenuous climb feels good after hours of driving. Gone a half hour, I come to a cliff overlooking the road. As I peer over the ledge, a truck pulls up behind the Bronco. Two men approach, one on each side. My stomach tightens in the grip of panic. Blood drains from my face.

"Hey! Hey, what do you want?"

They don't hear. I'm 150 feet above, so I yell louder. They stop, stare up at me. Snake stick in hand, I wave my arms like a wild man. They might think I have a rifle. They return to their vehicle and drive elsewhere. I race, scrambling, tumbling, arrive roadside winded, panting.

"Are you okay? What did those guys say?"

"Not sure. I couldn't understand them. Could be they thought we had car trouble?"

"Yeah, maybe." *I have darker thoughts.* "Guess we'll never know."

A year after our visit, a Florida couple got ambushed near there. Bandits felled a tree across the roadway to rob them and shot them when they tried to turn back. I drive on without letting on how worried I was. If it frightened her, she didn't show it.

Tamazunchale, San Luis Potosi, is a welcoming paradise resplendent with tropical wet forest. I fell in love with its charm on the last trip and want to share.

Enormous trees draped with epiphytes, and cascades of *Monstera* shade the byway. As enchanting as I remember it. Azure waters in pristine rivers. Huastec Indian villages tucked in to jungle have stick walled huts with thatched roofs.

Pulled to the shoulder of the mountain roadway, motor off, we enjoy calls of tropical birds. A low roar of river rapids drifts from the valley. Iridescent butterflies dance over a puddle. We sit, absorbing the serenity when a young man walks by dressed in white shorts and shirt.

"Buenos días." I'm not expecting a reply.

He stops, comes over, and speaks, but I can't grasp what he's saying. *"Lo siento amigo, no comprendo."* Sorry, my friend, I don't understand.

He continues speaking, so in English I explain what we are doing. I offer a cup of Kool-Aid from our thermos. He accepts, takes a sip. His nose wrinkles, lips pucker, he draws his chin in as though he'd sucked a lemon. We laugh, and he laughs. I pick up a sack.

"Culebra. No venenosa." Snake, not venomous.

As I untie and open it, curious, not fearful, he leans over to peek. He becomes animated, eyes wide, he's telling me something and pointing to the woods. I hold my hands palm up, furrow my brow, and shrug my shoulders in the universal "I can't understand" gesture. He tugs at my shirt sleeve, making it obvious he wants me to follow.

I glance at my wife. She waves her hand. "Go ahead, I'll be okay."

She passes me an empty sack and I grab a snake stick. Across the way we descend a steep jungle path. He is quick, sure-footed. I slide in the clay, trying to gain footing. The trail levels out by a river flowing swift and noisy over boulders. The youth keeps his rapid pace. After 10 minutes, I notice an Indian village on the far shore.

"Su pueblo?" I'm hoping for a break.

"Sí." He continues walking.

The path curves away from the water. He stops, points. On the ground is a fat Mexican Boa, *Boa imperator*. This species comes within a hundred miles of the US border. Its range extends through Central America, into northern South America. Known to have several color phases, this form is nicest. Tan, reddish saddles, its face bright peach, a chocolate bar through the eye.

My hands tremble with excitement as I pick the handsome creature up, gripping it a foot behind its head, and on the lower third of his body. Thick as my upper arm and heavy, it tenses its muscles but doesn't resist. As I carry it along the trail and struggle up the steep incline to the road, the serpent stays calm.

I'm winded from the hike, breathing hard. "Check this out!" My bride admires it from a distance. She tolerates my love of snakes but does not share it. I'm okay with that.

As I point out interesting characteristics, without warning, the snake strikes with mouth agape towards my face. By a miracle, it misses. This species can be ill-tempered, unpredictable. I was fortunate. Though not venomous, boas have gaping mouths with up to a hundred needle-sharp, rear-pointing teeth. Such a bite could disfigure. At the least, would be unpleasant.

"That was close." I slide my hand up, grip its neck, and take control.

"*Muchas gracias*." I give the young fellow a US dollar for leading me to the snake. We shake hands.

My partner playing the 8-track piques the Mexican lad's curiosity. I have an idea. "Pop in Herb Alpert, key to 'The Lonely Bull'."

The trumpet blares. *"El toro."* His smile broadens as he listens a few moments more, accepts a drink of water and we part ways.

Snakes are out. Our evening collecting the curvy, jungle-shrouded mountain roads is a dream. Pulled off by a bridge to check a potential camping spot, I survey a stream by flashlight. I follow the rocky shore and shine the light towards distant movement. A Jaguar! He crosses the shallow river, looks my way, doesn't run, and fades into tall grass on the opposite side.

I rush to the truck, shouting my amazing discovery and coax my wife to follow. We track to the spot where the big cat crossed. Long gone, his paw prints linger in the mud. Still exciting.

The truck bed is filling: snakes, cacti and rocks. Near Poza Rica, Veracruz, we catch a Spiny Iguana, *Ctenosaura acanthura*, with an unusual blotched green and black pattern. In the coastal lowlands, a Giant Musk Turtle, *Staurotypus triporcatus*. We turn inland, crossing the Trans-Mexican Volcanic Belt. Our catch includes horned lizards, and a Black-tailed Rattlesnake, *Crotalus molossus*. Snowy Volcán Orizaba emerges, then vanishes on the southern horizon. In Puebla we stay the night in a pleasant hotel, enjoy a delicious meal. She wants to visit Mexico City. I hoped to bypass it. I warn her, it will not be what she thinks.

As before, traffic is horrendous. But she's amazed by the buildings and colorful plazas. We stop at a nice marketplace to explore, have fun eating, buying a few souvenirs. I realize the trip has focused on what I wanted. She deserves to see more than forest and desert. Now, we have no time left.

We take the direct route to the border, up the middle, with little interesting scenery. Once in Laredo, we declare our specimens. No concern over importing reptiles from Mexico. An agent opens the tailgate to inspect and notices a cactus in a box. "No cacti allowed." They give no explanation but order me to unload the entire vehicle. They keep every plant. Our trouble, the spines in our fingers and clothes, dirt in everything—is for naught. The episode ends my interest in plants for the next several years.

We're back in the US a day early, despite having driven farther than on the first excursion. My knowing the roads helped, and driving with a purpose, we saw more in less time. On our way home, we drive to the Rio Grande Valley to visit a reptile collector with a roadside zoo. A mere speck in the desert. A wood building plastered with signs and a gravel parking lot out front. As I step from the Bronco, I spot an Indian arrowhead. Then two more.

Mr. Johnson sizes us up when we enter. A man in his 60s, barrel-chested, bearded, and grizzled from the sun. The shop holds Mexican and Texas oddities. Air-conditioned, the room is far from cool against the desert heat. He has animal skulls and bones, fossils, and cactus skeletons. A display of minerals has an old mining sign warning, "We Shoot Trespassers." He has a few clean cages with good-looking reptiles.

I fish the flint projectiles out of my pocket. "Look what I found in your parking lot."

"I throw them out for the tourists. It gets them excited." He looks into my eyes.

I resist asking if I should put them back. No sense making this more awkward than it is. I scratch "hunt for more arrowheads" off my must-do list when we leave.

"Come with me." He walks out the rear door.

A rag-tag collection of sheds, cages, and outdoor pens line the fences. Hand-painted signs give names of animals. Ringtail Cats and Coatimundi— both raccoon relatives. Coyotes, Ocelots, Tamanduas, a kind of arboreal anteater, and Coendu, a prehensile-tailed porcupine.

Best are the reptiles, lots of them. Collared and Leopard Lizards. There's an enclosure with metal walls filled with hundreds of Texas Horned Lizards. He has a few Desert Iguanas and Alligator Lizards. On shelves in a tin-roofed shed, aquariums hold several kinds of small snakes. Most animals appear healthy. But why so many of each?

He leads me to a row of pits dug into the hard, reddish clay. Each at least six feet deep and as wide, with smooth sides. "Need rattlesnakes?"

Holy crap. Western Diamondback Rattlers, *Crotalus atrox,* cover the bottom, in layers, one atop another. A few are alert, rattling, others are skinny, lay quiet. The smell of death is shocking. *What on Earth is he doing with so many rattlesnakes?*

The next ghastly hellhole is full of Texas Tortoises, *Gopherus berlandieri.* This smaller, eight-inch cousin of the Florida species, *Gopherus polyphemus,* has black dorsal scutes with yellowish centers. Many dozens of them in layers. Some appear to be dead, overturned, not moving. Worse than the rattlesnake pit.

No sign of drinking water for the animals. It's depressing. Thankfully, the sun drove my wife indoors, out of the heat, before she saw them. Back inside, I ask if two large Lindheimer's Ratsnakes are for sale. A relative of our Yellow Ratsnake, with a strong pattern of dark brown to black blotches over tan.

"Five bucks each."

They appear healthy, so I buy both to sell in Florida. We talk about Mexico awhile.

"Did you visit Puebla?"

"We passed through there. Why?"

"That's the best place for rattlesnakes. You must have stopped in Tamazunchale?"

"Yes, we caught a nice boa there. And saw a Jaguar."

"I used to hunt them." He points to a skin hanging on his crowded wall. Shocking, but not surprising. "Now they're protected." He bends over and pulls up his pants leg. "Feel my calf. Hard as a rock from climbing in those mountains."

Two days later, my spouse's face brightens, relieved, happy to be home in Florida from our first trip out of the country. Our last together for a long while. I'm already thinking of where to travel next. She prefers familiar people and places. Camping, and catching snakes is not her thing. As much as she's content without it, I need that wild side.

CHAPTER 28:
Jacques from Haiti

Jacques Durocher sells American Flamingoes from Haiti. He catches them. He sells them. Sells them only to a few of Miami's secretive animal dealers. No matter how hidden, how close they guard them, sources and contacts always leak out. Thus, Ed meets Jacques in Miami.

He comes to Florida when his fishing trawler needs maintenance. An entrepreneur, he buys, takes back, and offers articles hard to get in Haiti. Haiti is a poor country, the poorest nation in the Western Hemisphere. Poverty afflicts most. Even among the moneyed, certain goods are unavailable. That's where Jacques gets involved.

Toys, hardware, tools—he brings everything. Fishing tackle, auto parts, the list of needs is long. Ed helps source goods, storing them at his house for his next visit. Prohibited items Jacques smuggles, nothing objectionable on moral grounds. Shotguns and ammunition for hunting waterfowl are popular amongst the affluent. Ownership is lawful, but buying one, or even ammo, is impossible in Haiti. Jacques does well catering to the wants of the wealthy.

Legal items, packed in metal trash cans, he imports to Port-au-Prince with documentation, though he's not above fudging paperwork to avoid excessive duties. The trash cans escape notice. He turns them for a tidy profit. Shotguns and ammo, sealed in waterproof containers, he sinks offshore before docking. Later, retrieved with scuba gear, he slips them in on his fishing boat. He's cunning and successful.

Ed has long wanted snakes from Haiti, for several years writing to oil and other companies in Haiti with US ties, seeking a source. A few offered information about where they had seen snakes or the coveted Rhino Iguanas. Now, with Jacques in his debt, this is his opening. Jacques, sensing a potentially profitable venture, sends out word he wants snakes. After a month, he makes contact.

"Good news and bad news." He has snakes. He has lots of them. Delivery of a hundred plus to Port-au-Prince in a 55-gallon steel drum came sealed. He removed the lid only to find rotting snake soup.

It's a disaster. Jacques is livid, what can he do? The rural villagers know nothing of snakes and care even less. Was he not plain they must stay alive and healthy? The news sickens Ed, but he sees an opportunity.

Jacques agrees to take Ed to northern Haiti, from where the snakes came. His supplier kept the exact location secret. Ed's prior inquiries put focus on the town of Limbe. After a fruitless hunt, they turn to the people in the village. A few men return bearing snakes. Jacques pays, sets a return for the following day. Others set out to comb the woods. The catch for two days is 24. They thank the hunters, pay up and head for Port-au-Prince. Ed packs the animals in a suitcase and flies to Miami. No papers, no hassle.

Ed wants more. Jacques isn't eager. Such trips take too much time for not enough money. Ed brings a fellow herper from Florida, who, to Ed's chagrin, finds a lady friend in Cap-Haïtien and forgoes collecting. Jacques, no fan of snakes, is more of a bird-man. He prefers trading in flamingoes. To catch the wary birds, he ventures in a small boat deep into saline lakes and coastal lagoons where they roost, In the dark of moonless nights, he dips, silent, into the water, moves close, grabs them by the legs. With luck, he gets two before the colony spooks and flies. It's a poor method, prone to failure and danger.

Jacques saw the movie *Hatari!* where in a scene, John Wayne, Red Buttons, and a group of rough and tumble African animal collectors use a cannon net to capture a troupe of monkeys. He wants one, but there's a worldwide prohibition. Only those with legitimate scientific needs can buy them. To keep him indebted, Ed agrees to help acquire the equipment.

Prominent Haitian government friends, no doubt his clients, help Jacques get a permit. In addition, another permit for mist nets and birdlime, both also prohibited items. He'll use them to catch small birds to sell in Miami. Ed arranges for the restricted devices through his animal dealer contacts. They cost a handsome sum. A few months pass, Jacques tells us, disaster struck.

"On a night with no moon, we entered a flamingo lagoon. Our boat, made special, has a flat bottom for the shallow salt flats. It's large enough to carry four men, the cannon, and a huge net. In silence we go, using poles instead of paddles, to not scare the birds. We get into position, set the net, prime the charge, and fire."

"Did you catch many?"

"There was a deafening boom. After that, it's a blur."

Ed and I are wide-eyed. "What happened?"

"The recoil blasted the cannon through the bottom of the boat. It sank like a stone. The four of us fell into the water. The net never got off the deck."

"Holy cow, did anyone get hurt?"

"No, we made it to shore. The flamingoes flew. We found the sunken boat and the net in the morning. We lost the cannon, deep in the oozing mud."

The powerful explosive force to launch the heavy net needs solid ground. Their firing it from a boat was an expensive mistake.

With Jacques indebted by special favors, hopes are for him to export more snakes from Haiti. He opened Haiti's door, but there were limits to his largess. The "You scratch my back and I'll scratch yours" relationship produces few snakes. As the alliance becomes more one-sided, Ed ponders going to Haiti without Jacques' help.

Ed is aware Jacques is a busy man. "Let's travel up to Limbe, spend a few days, set up a collecting base, gain the people's confidence."

Jacques balks at investing the time. This was Ed's plan from the start. He seizes the opportunity to arrange an independent trip. Jacques never suspects. On a weekend Bimini run, Ed asks if I'd be willing to go to Haiti with him.

"Willing? Who do I have to kill?"

My excitement is intoxicating. The past year is dizzying with trips to Bimini and Mexico, getting married, back to Mexico. And now Haiti? I've seen Ed's Haitian Boas and I've become friends with Jacques. His open invitation to visit Port-au-Prince has kept me intrigued.

I'm aware Ed isn't inviting me along to be a nice guy. A proven field collector, he needs my help. He has few others he can trust. I might be too loyal. Without a doubt, he exploits my eagerness. Involvement in this enterprise banishes any thoughts of caution. This is my destiny.

CHAPTER 29:
Best Laid Plans

I t doesn't take long for the guys at FPL to tag me, "Snake Man." My pending travel to the wilds of Haiti only confirms my dubious mental stability in their eyes. Neither Ed nor I have time to spare. We figure six vacation days and two weekends for the trip. We'll leave on a Friday.

Planning for our future, I petition for a job in Bradenton on Florida's West Coast between Sarasota and St. Pete. Advancement with FPL takes longer in Ft. Lauderdale. The position comes with a pay raise to near $100 per week, big money for me. My jaw drops in shock when the supervisor tells me I won the bid and I'm dismayed to learn I must report only days after returning from Haiti. With a move across the state, it will be impossible.

We bid on jobs to advance. Highest seniority wins. Most we don't expect to get, but I got lucky. Or did I? I've never been to Bradenton and have no friends or family near there. I love living in South Florida. It's a dilemma. I can't bear to think of passing on the Haiti trip or declining the job. I humble myself, phone my supervisor-to-be in the new yard. He agrees to delay my start date a few weeks.

We drive over on the weekend and find it way bigger than rural Davie. Still, it's small compared to Ft. Lauderdale. We put a deposit on a two-bedroom duplex. Rent is affordable, work is close, and there is room for the reptiles.

What to do with my animals? Monkeys and other creatures with fur or feathers need permanent homes. I make an offer to an orange grove, tourist-style businesses near Davie. A package deal. They take them all, none for what they are worth, but I have little choice. Thinning the reptile collection is easy, many collectors are looking for rare specimens. I donate my exotic lizards to Professor Ober. Ed helps find buyers for rarer reptiles. He knows everyone in the trade, Hank Molt, Ray Van Nostrand, and every zoo with a reptile house. I reduce to the few dozen choicest snakes, no mammals. Friends will look in on them while I'm gone.

It's my first major trip apart since our wedding, saying goodbye isn't easy. My wife being by herself worries me. She's nervous about my going off to the mysterious island of Hispaniola. She has much to do preparing for our move, putting things in order, saying our farewells—all without my help. I should save my vacation days for moving. I can't dare ask for unpaid leave. So be it. We'll manage. My burden is heavy. The moment we step aboard the airplane to Haiti, everything else ceases to exist.

Word famous Iron Market,
Port-au-Prince, Haiti – 1967.

Vendors outside
of the Iron Market.

Workmen pulling/
pushing heavy
cart by hand,
Port-au-Prince,
Haiti

CHAPTER 30:
Pearl of the Antilles

A day of firsts. First trip aboard a jet airliner, first time in Haiti. My head is swimming with anticipation, trying to build an image of what's coming. Ed's stories of his fast Haitian visit were shy on details. It's fair to say, I can't wait. This is a seminal moment for me. My youthful dreams of exploration are becoming reality. Bimini and Mexico were great, but this opportunity is big! I'll leave Haiti addicted to the adrenaline rush of adventure.

I prepared amid the turmoil of planning a career move and relocation to a distant city. No doubt I'll need things I didn't bring; brought things I won't need. But I don't know. Much is unknown, including for Ed. When he traveled with Jacques, logistics, language, transportation, lodging was not a concern. We'll be on our own.

Air France flies a regular 700-mile route from Miami to Port-au-Prince. On the flight, we talk little, and arrive in no time. The rush of deplaning going through Immigration and Baggage Claim is a blur. We breeze through Customs, walk past without having either of our suitcases checked. Ed prepared by packing one smaller suitcase inside of each of our two larger ones. He expects a successful collecting trip.

Outside the terminal is a wall of tropical heat. A mob of porters swarms around us. Taxi drivers shout for our business in French, a few calling "Hey, mister," in English. As we scan the sea of black faces looking for Jacques, he arrives, parting the crowd with his Land Rover. Our luggage tossed in back, we climb in, relieved to be free of the throng.

"Welcome to Haiti. How was the flight? You're lucky, it's cool today. We had a storm this morning." Sweat is trickling from my temples. Ed mops his brow, quizzes Jacques about details to prepare for our trip to the north of the island. I'm trying to listen, but the sights drain my attention. Shanties line the Boulevard Jean-Jacques Dessalines from the airport. Barefoot travelers walking livestock, skinny horses, and donkeys pulling wagons. They pay no mind as the Land Rover swerves in and out between them around crater-sized potholes. En route to Pétion-Ville, we cross Port-au-Prince's teeming heart. Everything I know of Haiti comes from the two men in the front seat. Neither spoke much of what to expect.

The world-famous Iron Market looms, twin metal giants each more than a block long. An elaborate steel archway with four towering minarets connects the two. Manufactured in France in the 1890s, as a train depot for Egypt, it ended up instead in Haiti. Once red with green trim, its bright paint since replaced by rust. Merchants crowd an enormous courtyard between them. Their wares baking in the sun and withering heat.

The Land Rover inches through the multitude. Street vendors shout and thrust fruit and prepared food into the car. "Better roll up the windows."

Between colonial structures of concrete and stone, with ornate architecture, are shacks of wood, tin, and cardboard hovels. Neglected, faded, paint peeling, windows boarded. Lean-to shanties fill sidewalks. Everything looks dilapidated. The city teems with people. Many wear ragged clothes, no shoes, bear loads on their heads. Automobiles share streets with pack animals and wooden-wheeled pushcarts.

A nauseating mix of smells hangs in the air. Smoke from charcoal fires, the stench of raw sewage in trash-choked, open ditches. Garbage fills alleys, piles burn in the street. Men and women peeing openly in the gutters.

What I at first take as a lack of humanity is instead my ignorance of true poverty. It's an intense experience.

Jacques drives by the presidential palace. Built in 1920, a magnificent white edifice with three domed wings and columns that frame an entrance portico. In front, a manicured lawn, with white brick and black iron fence. Royal palms, bottoms painted white, line the Avenue de la République sidewalk. A stark contrast to the rest of the city.

In a park across from the executive mansion is *Le Marron Inconnu*. The bronze statue, of an unknown escaped slave on one knee, stands on a granite base.

The other leg, outstretched, bears a shackle and broken chain. Back arched, he's blowing a conch shell to sound rebellion. In his other hand is a machete. Jacques, a light-skinned mulatto, is proud and moved. Flowers, now fading, still lie in heaps around the pedestal from its recent dedication. We stand in silence. The powerful monument leaves me with a new appreciation for the Haitian people.

We need a travel permit to cross the island and so we stop by the Ministry of Interior. A small fee paid, documents signed, they hand us an envelope bearing an old-time red wax seal. We are to present it to the minister's office in Cap-Haïtien—the following evening. How was it possible? Those are the rules. We'll have to make an early start.

Pétion-Ville, Jacques' hometown, is a commune. In Haiti that translates to something akin to a town with an independent government. Three hundred fifty feet above the hot valley, it's cooler by a few degrees. The Massif de la Selle range extends west from the Dominican Republic. It includes Pic la Selle, at 8,793 feet, Haiti's highest point. We stop at a small hotel arranged for us. Our room is tiny, with plain furnishings, but clean, and adequate for our needs.

After checking in, our gracious host takes us on a tour. "I will take you to the Rhum Barbancourt Castle and distillery, it's close by." An anachronism of gentility in a sea of poverty. Attendants dressed in black coats, white gloves, offer samples of flavored rums. Ed nor I drink, but we sip a few to be polite, enjoy the tours, then leave.

Many of Haiti's wealthy class live in Pétion-Ville. Fine homes with high walls lined with broken glass or barbed wire on top. Cobblestone streets, well-kept, marked with street names. Neat rows of shops, no crowds. The few dogs we see look good by comparison to the living skeletons of Port-au-Prince. This is a world apart.

We follow the mountain road up to a pine forest to gain a panoramic view. In the valley below, buildings and shacks stretch to the horizon. It shows the dramatic contrast between Haiti's rich and poor.

Jacques takes us to a man named Pierre-Paul, whom Ed hired last time as a translator. Country folk speak Haitian Creole. A complex language, with roots in the French spoken here since the 1700s, with elements of Spanish, Portuguese, English, and words of African origin. He seems bright, friendly, a good choice. Jacques confirms his availability and arranges a pick-up time.

Last stop is a Hertz. Jacques' Land Rover is perfect. He'd never let us use it, so we don't ask. We follow him back to the hotel in our rented Volkswagen.

Our extra suitcases and our clothes for the trip home we leave with Jacques for safekeeping. He exchanges $100 for gourdes, the local currency. At his recommendation, we brought only US coins to buy snakes. Several rolls each of nickels, dimes, and quarters. Pierre-Paul knows to phone when we return in six days to turn in the car. We say our goodbyes, we'll leave at dawn.

Jacques provides an old Shell roadmap and written instructions to lead us out of town. In our room we spread it out on a bed. We find our route north along the coast of the Gulf of Gonâve and through the Massif du Nord to Cap-Haïtien. Turns out, it may as well have read "Terra Incognita" as few of the roads shown really exist. Even towns are absent from the locations indicated. Either incorrect designations or they never existed.

We pack our Volkswagen with clothes, collecting supplies and food from home. When we pick up Pierre-Paul, he volunteers to drive. Ed and I laugh out loud. He and I will switch off driving duties.

Tall, nicely groomed, his pleasant personality serves him well. He guides tourists from the occasional cruise ship around shops and the Iron Market. His English is self-taught and fluent. Young men like Pierre-Paul, working for tips, make a good living. Better than those selling the bright paintings and wood carvings in the marketplace.

CHAPTER 31:
The Road to Adventure

Pierre-Paul has never traveled outside of Port-au-Prince, except with Ed. It doesn't prevent him from giving us non-stop advice. At the first of several checkpoints, we show our travel papers, identifications, and proceed.

As we continue north, the countryside becomes more rural. Villages of thatched or tin-roofed huts are fewer, the road muddier. We weave around huge potholes with water of unknown depth. People walk, bearing loads on their heads, or lead donkeys with pack saddles made of straw. Sad-looking, bony horses pull rickety wagons. Poverty surrounds.

Pont-Sondé checkpoint is halfway along the 160-mile trip from Port-au-Prince to Cap-Haïtien. A guard, sitting in a chair by a wall, is short, stocky, has no shirt, only shorts. With a rifle slung over his shoulder, he approaches, asks for papers in Creole. He eyeballs us as he speaks.

Pierre-Paul translates. "He says, 'Get out of the car.'"

The sentry acts as though he wants something, so Pierre-Paul tries to engage him. Though agitated by the guard's prickly demeanor, we can't show it. Ed is impatient, knows how far we must travel.

White visitors are rare in rural Haiti. Looked upon with envy and suspicion, those who might wish to do us harm may fear repercussions. The sentinel goes back to his chair and makes a note in a book drawn from atop the wall. He nods to a policeman who raises the gate pole, allowing passage. Though nothing happened, we leave feeling uneasy.

Pierre-Paul
with author in
Furcy, Haiti, 1967.
(Photo: Ed Chapman)

Road north
checkpoint, Haiti.

Artibonite River Bridge
at Pont-Sondé.
(Photo: National Archives
of Haiti,
ex. UF Digital Library
of the Caribbean)

"He is a bad man." We ask what Pierre-Paul means. He repeats. "A bad man."

We cross the Artibonite River past the checkpoint. Longest on the island of Hispaniola, its waters the color of coffee with milk, irrigate the fertile central valley. The metal bridge, imported from France in 1880, clanks and rattles but is still sturdy. Pedestrians and vendors selling goods pack the span, reducing travel to a single narrow lane.

Over the next 20 miles, terrain changes from swampy to dry, the roadway from packed clay to rock. The VW bounces along, jarring our teeth. Dust chokes, forcing us to roll the windows up, despite the heat. The few primitive villages scattered across the dry plains have *bomas* (livestock enclosures) around stick and mud huts, recalling Africa more than the Caribbean.

Thorny *Euphorbia lactea,* called *rakèt,* is an African native planted before WWII as a source of latex. Insurance against losing access to southeast Asian rubber. Cactus-like, candelabra-shaped, the plants grow lush in central Haiti's semi-arid climate and poor soil. They are now used to form impenetrable living fences.

To us, this place is quaint, *National Geographic* scenic. Bare-chested men in shorts and bare-breasted women in skirts have ebony skins made darker by the tropical sun. The scene is eye-opening for a Florida boy. As a kid, when Dad told stories of WWII, most were of places he went, native peoples and animals he saw. Taken by the splendor of the islands and jungles, he lamented the war's destruction. In New Guinea, the allied soldiers befriended the natives they called "Fuzzy-Wuzzies." I longed to see such wild locales and characters. Now, in this strange and exotic land, my wishes are coming true.

Two boys, one carrying a big, dark-gray iguana, run when I pull over, the VW bouncing over roadside ruts. Ed yells, "Stop them, Pierre-Paul."

He shouts to them in Creole: "We want to see the iguana." They wait at a safe distance, nervous.

They have a Rhinoceros Iguana, *Cyclura cornuta,* a hulking three-foot beast with a horn on its snout, trussed up and immobile. Much desired by zoos and collectors, Ed declares, "I need it. See if they will sell it."

"They eat them," says Pierre-Paul. It doesn't surprise me. "Show them US coins."

Ed digs in his pocket. The boys gaze at two quarters in his hand. Pierre-Paul tells them the value. *"Twa goud."* Their faces wide-eyed with temptation—but they don't accept the offer.

Pushed for time, reluctantly we drive on, and a few miles south of Gonaïves we have a flat. A crowd gathers to watch as we change it. We're their entertainment. I hear several words spoken often and try to guess their meaning.

"What does *blanc* mean, Pierre-Paul?"

"It means white. Your skin." I'm taken aback.

"Wow! I thought it might be a greeting. I repeated it back to them." He laughs out loud, Ed joins him. "So how do you say hello?"

"Hello. It's the same. Or you can use *bonjour* in French."

We push on to the outskirts of Gonaïves to find the approach to town lined with tire repair shops. Small shacks, four poles with a tin roof or thatch, and piles of old tires. Several men are at each, waiting in the shade for business, homemade tools at the ready. With the flat out of the trunk, no need to explain, there's a hole as big as my thumb. As we consider our options, the man removes the tire from the rim. On a tree stump worktable, a helper holds it open while he scrubs the spot with an abrasive stone. He cuts a patch from another ruined tire and grinds the edges. With glue and a vulcanizing tool heated with gunpowder, he melts on the patch. He makes a similar repair to the tube, assembles them.

While his assistant inflates the tire with a bicycle pump, Pierre-Paul negotiates the price. He balks at the repairman's price for the work, arguing on our behalf.

"How much?" The smell of gunpowder still hangs in the sticky heat.

"Five, but I said two. He is trying to exploit your white skin."

Work aside, he saved us from buying a new tire. God knows what it might cost, assuming we could find a replacement. "How's three?" I get out three one-dollar bills.

"No US money!" Pierre-Paul, waving his hand in a stop motion.

"How many gourdes equal three dollars?"

"Fifteen—that's way too much. Pay him three gourdes."

It's equal to sixty cents in US currency. Now I'm sure we're cheating the repairman. I have so much to learn.

Gonaïves, a coastal city on the northeast shore of the Gulf of Gonâve, has a somber air. Bare concrete block buildings and shacks made of roofing metal line dirt streets. It smells of charcoal smoke and decay. Everything is brown and gray. Ed and I hope for lunch, but keep driving.

Village outside Gonaïves, Haiti.

Horses with straw saddles on
road north, Haiti, 1967.

Ladies with citrus,
near Limbe, Haiti.

Roadside market,
central Haiti.

The gate's up at a checkpoint north of town. We slow, then continue. The terrain grows hilly, the blue and purple haze of mountains looms in the distance. Dry scrub yields to scattered forest, road conditions deteriorate. The car bumps and bangs over sharp rocks and washouts, often scraping bottom. We cross our fingers for our tires to hold together.

Startled looks leave little doubt white folk are rare in these parts. At every stop the curious surround us, not threatening, but unnerving. Our tight schedule demands we press on past places we'd love to explore for reptiles. "On the way back," we say.

Then it happens, the wheel is tugging. Another flat. The road is narrow. Ed jumps out to check. There's still air in it. "Let's find a wider spot."

We pull off at the Les Trois Rivières bridge. By the rocky, limpid river, in the shade of a tree where the level ground looks the perfect place. As I stop, Pierre-Paul shouts. *"Fimye, fimye!"*

"What? What's happening?" I look over at Ed, thinking the worst, not knowing what the worst might be. There are people. Topless ladies in the shallow river doing laundry. Clothes lay strewn on rocks, drying in the breeze and sun.

Pierre-Paul, panicking, shouts. "Shit mon, shit! Go, go, go!" In a frenzy, waving his hands in the back seat.

Then the stink hits. Turns out any nice, shaded place is suitable to squat and "take care of business" out of the heat. We pull ahead 50 feet and get out. Lucky for us, the flat tire remains clean.

We ask Pierre-Paul to change it while we have a look around. He's shocked, indignant at our asking, but he does it. Ed wanders up a hillside, I check by the river's edge. Butterflies in many hues take up minerals and sun their wings on the bank. Ed returns, he'd missed catching a Haitian Green Vine Snake. The women washing clothes pay no mind, but children gather.

Plaisance is near, and tire shops easy to find. A clean, colorful town, unlike those we've seen in the flatlands. We pick up a stalk of bananas from a roadside vendor and eat our fill.

Ed drives, hurrying through dramatic scenery. The route curves and twists up the mountain through lush vegetation. We climb higher, wet forests beg us to investigate, but we must continue. Soon we descend to the Limbe River valley and our goal, the village of Limbe. I can barely contain my excitement, anxious to see a snake, but a little disappointed that the place is so ordinary

Ed stops at the same spot as on his trip with Jacques. No traffic on the dirt roadway. Nothing distinguishes this location from any other. Only a few people are stirring. Ed instructs Pierre-Paul to ask a passing woman if she knows the man who catches snakes.

He calls out and she comes over, craning her neck, looking into our car. She carries on talking to Pierre-Paul until Ed interrupts him. "What's she saying?"

"She doesn't know him."

"I'm trying to pick up a few words. "Pierre-Paul, how do you say 'snake' in Creole?""

"*Koulèv*," he says.

An older fellow sits on a log under a thatched-roof meeting place for men of the village. He says he remembers when Ed was here the last time and agrees to tell his friends we are here to buy snakes. We bid good evening and drive towards Cap-Haïtien.

Ed heads for the interior minister's office without delay, but it's closed. We missed our deadline to deliver the sealed letter. Next, to find Hôtel Roi Christophe. Pierre-Paul asks directions. This is his second time to visit Cap-Haïtien, and his eyes are wide open. Cobblestone streets are not cluttered with vendors or trash; buildings are painted bright colors. Trees and palms grow on roadsides lined with sidewalks. Sure, the town has poorer sections, but is not as shocking as parts of Port-au-Prince.

"There's the hotel." Ed points to an iron fence. He turns in the drive; an attendant opens the ornate gate. It is a world apart. Lush tropical vegetation surrounds villas with red roofs. Open porticoes are decorated with Haitian art. Black and white checkerboard tile floors polished to a shine spill out to the terraces. A porter dressed in a flowery shirt greets us.

I stand slack-jawed. "Holy cow, Ed, who's gonna pay for this?"

He smiles. "Just wait."

The receptionist speaks English and remembers Ed, as he asks for a room for three. "Do you prefer separate accommodation for your driver?" She looks at Pierre-Paul.

Before he can decline, she says, "There's no extra charge."

"Sure," Ed signs. The porter leads us to our rooms.

"So, how much is this place?" I am gazing at wooden ceilings, painting on the walls.

"Is six dollars too much? Oh, and that includes meals."

Too much? Yeah, too much to comprehend. Our room is immaculate, nice furnishings, a window overlooks a garden in back. We can see the Caribbean through the trees in front.

For dinner we enjoy *Diri ak Djon Djon*, a dish of rare mushrooms found in the Massif du Nord, with black rice, and a side of spiced plantains. The mushrooms are black which when cooked with the rice releases the black color into the rice. They serve us overlooking the pool deck in the evening breeze. *I bet Pierre-Paul never ate such a fine meal.* A band plays "Yellowbird" on steel drums, bongo, and guitar. We've seen no other guests.

CHAPTER 32:
Limbe, Day One

Even in Florida, we often forget the array of tropical fruits waiting to delight our pallets. I'm reluctant to admit, I've never been much of a fruit eater. This morning, a sumptuous platter of treats arouses my appetite. Colorful slices of pineapple, soursop, lychee, and mango drip with ripe sweetness. Their fragrance mingles with the aroma of strong coffee and fresh French bread. On fine china, with fluffy linen napkins to dab the syrup from our chins, a fructose feast.

At the minister's office, to surrender our letter, Pierre-Paul explains our delay. The minister puts it in a drawer and inquires about the reason for our visit. "Tourists, sightseeing." He's pleased and bids a pleasant stay. Nothing said of being a day overdue.

Relieved, we visit a market to buy a loaf of bread, fresh bananas, oranges, before the rough 20-mile drive back to Limbe.

Word is out. Several men and boys await to hail us to the spot we stopped yesterday. As they gather round, a boy runs to fetch the guy Ed bought snakes from on his first trip. The assembled lookers press in, I hear the familiar "*blanc, blanc.*"

A slim fellow shows up, five feet tall, wearing a ragged white shirt, shorts, and no shoes. Ed beams. "That's him." Shakes his hand and asks Pierre-Paul to get his name.

"His name is Felix."

He's smiling and strikes me as a cheerful guy.

Snake on a stick, Limbe, Haiti.

Man with boa,
Limbe, Haiti.

Boas lashed to sticks. Limbe, Haiti.

"Tell him we'll be in Limbe coming and going, today, and tomorrow, to buy any healthy snakes he finds." Pierre-Paul translates Ed's message to Felix.

The crowd grows. No one is making a move. "They won't leave until we do," Ed speaks from his experience last time. We drive a few miles from the village to explore. Ask a few other guys, but they're not interested in collecting. Pierre-Paul waits by the VW while we walk along a stream, a group of boys follows. When we return, 10 people have gathered.

Another stop, another flock. They dog us, watch our every move, including when we need to pee. No such thing as privacy here. We do as they do and turn our backs. Our being white makes everything of interest to them. A few things are harder to get accustomed to than others. Still, it's a marvelous place, and Haiti's people make it unique.

∽

The gathering for our noon return is atwitter. Excitement is palpable. Ed kneels to inspect three snakes Felix brought. My God, they are beauties. Haitian Boas, *Epicrates striatus striatus*, in shades of red and gray, iridescent in the sunlight. Tied around their necks with strips of bark and coiled on branches. It's efficient but could cause injury.

Ed is trying to untie a snake. The twine is way too snug, pulled into its flesh. I slip my pocketknife under, cut it loose. We free and inspect the other two, they're okay. Pierre-Paul fears snakes but must stay close so he can translate. We ask Felix not to tie them so tight but are careful not to discourage him.

Of those gathered, only Felix has specimens. Pierre-Paul says, "No one believed we'd come back. They laughed at him before we returned."

Now they see us paying him. Last time Jacques used Haitian gourdes. Ed, with a handful of US coins, gives him three dimes for the boas. Felix studies them, pokes Ed's hand, pointing to the nickels. He wants 15¢ for each; we agree. This pleases him, we're over the moon.

We leave with a promise to return in the late afternoon, stopping to hunt along a limestone cliff towards Cap-Haïtien. It's perfect snake habitat, but we find nothing.

∽

A larger group awaits at day's end. We'd proven dependable. Several have boas tied to sticks or balled at the ends of strands of twine. They don't have sacks; one guy brings a gourd.

The Calabash Tree, *Crescentia cujete,* produces hard-shelled gourds. In common use for storing and transporting everything from grains to water. They serve as rural Haitian Tupperware. Inside is a long, slender snake with a green body, pointed head, black, and parallel yellow lines through its eye.

"Wow, *Uromacer oxyrhynchus!*" Ed takes it from my grip.

"*Koulèv Vèt.*" The collector says. Green Snake.

The Haitian equal of familiar vine snakes in the genus *Oxybelis* of Central and South America. Rear-fanged, with mild venom, not considered dangerous to people. They posture, threaten with mouths agape, but seldom bite.

Felix brings the most snakes this afternoon. Tied, but much looser this time, he learns fast. Other men have them bound tight, near death. Ed, furious, curses and rants as we cut them loose. One has severe injuries, its skin torn open. Ed tosses it into the bush. The crowd reacts with a gasp, shock on their faces. The guy who brought the snake is wide-eyed, angry. To defuse the issue, I pay the man. Pierre-Paul explains we will not take or pay for injured snakes.

The mood tense, people talk in low tones among themselves. Despite paying for the damaged snake, a few women yell, point fingers. It's uncomfortable, probably good that we are leaving for the day. We load to head for Cap-Haïtien, promising an early return tomorrow. Pierre-Paul, nervous, has sweat beading on his upper lip. With a deathly fear of snakes, he balks at riding in the car with them.

"Okay, we'll see you here in the morning." He gets over his trepidation real fast.

Back at the hotel, we check the specimens. Outstanding, over a dozen, and despite rough handling, all are healthy. We separate them, two of equal size per sack, and slide them under a bed so as not to frighten the maid who cleans the room. Snakes find little love anywhere, but in Haiti, they're a fixture in the practice of Vodou. We're bouncing off the walls with excitement. "Told you it was fantastic." Ed has a twinkle in his eyes.

CHAPTER 33:
Limbe, Day Two

Few people await on Monday morning as we enter Limbe. None have snakes. We move on to give them a chance to collect, returning at noon to a gathering. They step back as we pull to the side. A man steps forward and dumps a heavy sack on the road. Three large turtles fall out and run. Onlookers scatter. Me and Ed each grab one, and the guy who brought them gets the other.

Haitian Sliders, *Pseudemys terrapen decorata,* a rare species. Once widespread, with capture for food and habitat loss, their population crashed. He caught these to eat but thought we might buy them. Love to, but they're far too large to take them to Florida. But, if we can get them for a good price, we will set them free.

Pierre-Paul asks how much he wants. "*Senkant goud.*" Ten dollars.

He could live two months on that. We laugh, half the crowd laughs, but they don't understand why we were laughing. We offer a dollar each. The guy gets mad, returns them to the burlap sack, and drags it as he leaves. A shame, we hate to see them killed for food.

A few others have boas. We buy them, and wait. Everyone else waits with us. Boys play with a homemade top, spinning it on a split log. I scan the silent faces, waiting for something to break up their day. In ragged clothes, impoverished, they appear healthy and content. They buzz with excitement when another guy shows up with a single snake. We bag it and prepare to leave. Then the turtle man returns and accepts the three-dollar offer. We load them in the car to take and release and hope the other men go collect.

Snake hunters, in Limbe, Haiti.

Ed Chapman hunting for boas in a hollow tree.

We'd prefer to avoid putting them in the Limbe River, as we assume that's where he caught them. Instead, we drive over to the Rivière de Port Margot. A few miles west, it may increase their prospects for survival. Away from visible huts or villages, we dump the sack on the rocky shore. A quarter-mile wide, and quiet, it looks to be suitable turtle habitat. We leave feeling good over the rescue and hope they don't end up in someone else's stew pot.

In Limbe Felix has arrived, is waiting with two boys in tow. He has several boas, including a six-footer. In gourds the youngsters have a pair of *Uromacer oxyrhynchus*, at least four feet long and active. How they got them into the gourd, I couldn't guess. Then a third snake, another species, similar but different. Smaller and slimmer, with tan body and green head. Ed comes for a closer look. "This is *Uromacer frenatus.*"

The second gourd has a species new to me. Slender built, it resembles the *Alsophis* we find in the Bahamas. It's *Hypsirhynchus ferox*, the Hispaniolan Hog-nosed Racer.

Still early, so we announce we will stay a couple more hours. We hope to see Haitian Boas in habitat, but so far have had no luck. We ask Felix if he'd take us on a hunt, assuring we'll pay him for any snakes, whoever collects them. He seems reluctant but agrees.

Pierre-Paul is less than thrilled when we tell him we need him along to translate. He prefers to stay by the vehicle. We follow between huts, struck by their simplicity. Windows with no glass or screen, dirt floors, few furnishings, no plumbing. Then into the woods beyond, on a labyrinth of trails, we walk nonstop for a half hour. When we lag, he waits. In a grove of trees beside a rocky creek, we watch as he climbs with ease, to scan limbs until 15 feet off the ground he sees something in a knothole. He probes with a broken twig until, moments later, a snake's head emerges. He grasps it by the neck, keeps a gentle, steady pull, and out comes a three-foot boa. We put it in a sack and congratulate him.

Pierre-Paul, less amused, grumbles about having mud on his nice shoes. Nervous around snakes and spiders, he jumps if a branch pokes him. This tickles Ed and me no end.

Felix climbs a few more trees but finds nothing else. A group of youths and men follow us, their constant croaking of *"blanc, blanc, blanc,"* sounds like a chorus of frogs. They watch us, they watch Felix, but none of them make a move to help look for snakes. We spot a colorful lizard, *Leiocephalus personatus*.

Rainbow hued with a curly tail, red sides, green legs, and a dorsal crest of pointed scales. Ed and I try catching several without success. Felix, intent on bigger prey, has no interest. Two lads, amused by our ineptness, join the hunt.

We pay a nickel for each. By the time we get to our car, they've captured several, making more money than Felix. This won't do, so we give Felix 50¢ for taking us with him and 15¢ for the snake. He's pleased, and we're happy.

Our audience awaits. Our presence is entertainment for the village. There are no more snakes, so Pierre-Paul asks if anyone else is coming. No one knows. We thank Felix, saying we hope to come again. I pull out a dirty tee-shirt from the VW and hand it to him. Twice his size, he beams. The throng pushes in close with hands outstretched.

Despite their poverty, we've seen no begging. Impressive. They have pride, are self-reliant, but now they all want one. As the mob closes in, we jump into the car.

Pierre-Paul is crying out. "Go, go!"

He's more nervous than we are. It's a lesson for us. We must be sure anything we give is in direct payment for something received, at least in public.

Ed with a rainbow *Leiocephalus* lizard. Note nickels in his hand

CHAPTER 34:
Limbe, Last Day

Drizzling. Raindrops leave concentric circles on the blue pool. The weather matches our mood, and breakfast is silent. Today is our last in northern Haiti. Pierre-Paul too has a long face. This has been a unique experience for him, a chance to get to know a nicer part of his country. We hang back, load the VW, wait for conditions to improve, fearing the worst. We needn't have. The rain stops before we reach Limbe.

Fifty people await—its an intimidating sight. Poor, dressed in tattered clothes, rags, most men carry machetes. What do they think of our coming into their lives? Calling, shouting, pressing in, nigh blocking our getting out of the car. Over the commotion, Ed yells to Pierre-Paul. "Tell them to stay calm, stand back."

At the edge of the dirt road, two boas lay tied with twine to stakes. A young man new to us waits by them. Others thrust sticks, snakes bound, coiled into balls at the end. They know today is their last chance to sell.

Pierre-Paul waves his arms. "*Tout moun! Fè plas!*" Everyone! Make room! It's chaos.

I set to work untying and cutting loose the bound serpents. Ed inspects the boas, pointing out flaws we wish not to find next time. He pays as he bags them. I lose count in the frenzy.

Aggressive men push to the front. We buy theirs, then a boy brings forth a calabash. When I pull the grass stopper, instead of a snake, a huge tarantula pops out onto my hand. Startled, I jerk back, both gourd and spider go flying.

Men and boys with snakes tied to sticks in Limbe, Haiti, 1967.

People gather round as the author examines snakes. Limbe, Haiti, 1967.
(Photo: Ed Chapman)

The crowd scatters and breaks into laughter. As the kid runs after the enormous spider, Ed and I laugh. I'm not used to handling them and didn't expect to find one in a gourd. We agree to keep it, if he sells us the gourd, five cents each.

Another youth has one we assume holds tarantulas, but he insists it doesn't. Ed pulls the stopper; a treefrog streaks over his shoulder. The boy scrambles to catch it. Full of three-inch *Hyla dominicensis,* the Dominican Treefrog, no doubt brought by the rains. Not on our want list. We pay 20¢ for the lot.

As we load, Felix arrives. He carries a burlap coffee sack stenciled "La Perle des Antilles." Ed takes it, unties, and dumps the contents. Everyone scatters, then regroups in a tight circle. The scene is surreal. A couple months ago, this trip was unimaginable. Now I'm kneeling over a pile of snakes on a Haitian roadway surrounded by a throng of people. I sense this as a turning point. My life's path has altered—toward my dreams.

Ten healthy boas. We put them in clean sacks and thank Felix for his collecting prowess. Next he produces a small container of woven fiber used to carry food—a Haitian lunch box. He hands it to Ed. What he pulls out is unusual, three feet long, slender in the extreme, with an oversized head. Muscular, it coils tight around his hand. A snake of legend, *Epicrates gracilis.* Maybe the rarest serpent in Hispaniola. Dubbed "Vine Boa" for its shape, it is coffee colored with dark brown dorsal saddles and lateral spots. Ed instructs me, "Give him a dollar. Maybe he can find more next time if we give him incentive."

Was it a mistake? Can he understand why one is worth more? Yes, he does. He beams, happy for the extra money and to have his efforts recognized.

We express thanks to the villagers, bid farewell, making sure it's known we will not return. They stand watching, barefoot, tattered. We wave, shout, "*Bonjour.*" Smiling, waving, many call out. Good folks, none have more than basics for survival, but they are rich in spirit, strong. People worth admiring. Grateful, our hearts heavy, we turn towards Port-au-Prince.

CHAPTER 35:
The Road Home

Our mood is festive, reflecting on our successful journey, scarcely noticing the bone-jarring ride as we descend towards the Haitian lowlands. Beside the waterfall—Saut-d'Eau—said to be a sacred spot to the *lwa, Danbala,* we stop for a stretch and the last vista of the lush mountain forests. Bromeliads and orchids cloak tree limbs. Air is moist, sweet. A pair of wary Hispaniolan Parrots, *Amazona ventralis,* watch our every move. Hunters stalk this large green parrot, a stunner with gray cheeks and red belly. The grandeur of this rare, unspoiled spot gives substance to Haiti's nickname, "La Perle des Antilles," once an earthly paradise. A perfect place to say goodbye to the Northern Mountains.

Before leaving, we release the tarantula, deciding not to carry it to Florida. Ed pulls the straw plug and lays the gourd on its side by a tree. The spider probes with two legs out of the hole. After a minute she springs out, climbs the trunk, and disappears.

Late afternoon, with the sun sinking, we discuss whether to continue to Port-au-Prince this evening. Wary of driving Haitian roads at night, we locate a place to stay in Gonaïves.

By the Gulf of Gonâve shore, a hotel looks okay. Pierre-Paul goes to check. Three dollars is more than it's worth, but we stay. For dinner we eat—chicken—the seafood smells dicey. We return to find two guys looking into the windows of our VW. We approach and confront them.

They show stern faces, wear military-style trousers and civilian shirts. One speaks in Creole. "We're checking for stolen vehicles."

Saut-d'Eau, Haiti's largest waterfall, said to be sacred to *Danbala*,
the white serpent *lwa*.

Gonaïves, Haiti

They do not ask for papers or identification. It leaves the impression they're casing it to break in, so we remove everything. Pierre-Paul declares, "They are Tonton Macoute." That's the feared secret militia of President Papa Doc Duvalier.

After his election in 1958, Papa Doc unleashed a reign of terror, pursuing his political enemies or anyone he perceived as a threat. He formed the Tonton Macoute to protect himself from any enemy, including the police and military. Only after declaring himself President for Life, did the nightmare end. The Tonton are above the law and work behind the scenes.

Our first brush with the Tonton is unsettling. It does nothing to improve the somber air of Gonaïves. On later trips, we'll know the fear they specialize in doling out.

Haiti has low crime for a nation so impoverished and overpopulated. Papa Doc wields unchallenged power, has zero tolerance for most infractions. Punishments are swift and severe. Jacques says our white skin buys protection, including from the authorities. To cause us harm may carry repercussions. We're lucky, most are not willing to take the risk. Tonton Macoute brutes have no such reservations.

In the morning we find a tire flat, change it and go for repairs south of town. Time is flying; after it is fixed, we drive with purpose towards Pont-Sondé. For thirty brutal miles we choke on dust, finally crossing the Artibonite River through throngs of vendors and pedestrians. At the checkpoint gate we stop, see the same short, heavyset guard sitting, his chair tipped against the wall. He comes over, puts both hands on the windowsill, looks Ed in the eyes.

He gives instructions, speaking Creole. Pierre-Paul translates. "We must get out."

The sentry asks for papers, makes a note in a book, then demands we take everything from the auto. We place the sacks of snakes in the gravel road on the car's shady side.

We try not to show our aggravation. Is his delay for sport or is he fishing for a bribe? We sense something amiss. No way is this a legit stop. The surly guard reaches over and grabs a sack, flinches, shrinks back. "Ayayay! What the hell's in those sacks?"

We struggle not to laugh at the arrogant little bastard.

Pierre-Paul speaks up, earning his keep in grand fashion. "The snakes are for President Duvalier's private zoo." A total bare-faced lie.

Skeptical, the guard presses for details. Pierre-Paul sticks to the story, elaborating. "The paper we had last week [our travel papers] was our orders to collect specimens." He glares, maintaining unblinking eye contact.

We don't understand his words but pick out *koulèv*, (snake in Haitian Creole). Ed picks up a bag and is untying the knot. The guard steps back. "Load your things and leave."

I drive awhile then ask, "What did you tell that guy?"

"I told him the snakes were for the president's private zoo."

"No way! Did you say that?" I look at Ed. He's chortling.

"Yes." For the rest of the trip, he's the hero.

Late afternoon, tired, filthy, we drop Pierre-Paul near his home and give him part of his pay, with instructions to meet us in the morning. At the hotel, we unload our stuff in the same room. The reptiles need water. We put two inches in the tub and allow each to drink. After we clean up, we walk around the neighborhood and find a place for dinner. Pétion-Ville is nice, but boring compared to Cap-Haïtien.

In the evening we phone Jacques, tell him we've returned, that it was a good safe trip. We go over our plans for tomorrow, to drive up to Furcy to hunt giant treefrogs.

CHAPTER 36:
Zombie Frogs

Jacques divulged rumors of giant treefrogs that inhabit Furcy, high in the Massif de la Selle. We plan to investigate. The route beyond Pétion-Ville is steep and winding, climbing towards Kenscoff. At the crest of the mountains, a hand-painted sign marks the cutoff to Furcy. Road turns to trail. Fog descends. Giant pines take on eerie shapes. Going is slow.

A man in rubber boots, carrying a shovel, confirms our arrival in Furcy. The occasional hut is nothing I'd call a village. This must be the spot. We describe the creature we seek to Pierre-Paul but aren't sure he understands. The few men he asks don't know the giant treefrog, *krapo pyebwa jeyan*, as he describes it.

"I'll watch the car," Pierre-Paul volunteers.

Jacques told Ed the behemoths "live in banana trees." We slip between strands of a barbed wire fence and slide down on a steep muddy slope into a grove. Soaked to the skin in no time by dew-laden foliage, we search for the monster anuran. Treefrogs are nocturnal, so we must find where they hide from the light. We pull back the moisture-filled outer sheaths on the banana plants, an inviting hiding place for amphibians. I capture my first giant. Slimy and cold, with enormous hands and long fingers ending in discs. *Hyla vasta*, may be the world's largest, big as my open hand. Excited, I call out to Ed, but he has found his own.

In short order, we collect a half dozen of them and notice something strange. Our eyes are on fire, watering, our noses run like faucets. Ed is first to say, "Don't touch your face!"

Revenge of the toxic treefrogs. Most species are moist and cool. These guys are sticky and leave our hands covered with viscous white foam. Desperate to wipe our burning eyes, using the sleeve of our shirts, is a mistake. Our discomfort forces collecting to a halt, and we clamber half-blinded up to the fence.

"Don't touch us or the sacks," Ed warns Pierre-Paul as we stagger to the car. He stares in disbelief at our puffy, swollen eyes, our tear-stained cheeks, and pouring red noses.

We need a place to wash, and we locate a stream. No soap, only sand and water to scrub our hands and arms to remove the sticky, toxic slime. "You're one ugly S.O.B.," Ed says.

"Yeah, you've got room to talk." I laugh and agree that we look ridiculous. When our conditions worsen, I say, "What if our throats swell? This could be serious."

After an hour, the effects subside, but our eyes stay sensitive a while longer. It ends our monster frog hunt.

The fog lifts, revealing the ethereal splendor of this mountaintop forest. Its fleeting, tall pines and broad-leaf trees, veiled in mist, appear and disappear. Shafts of light illuminate native Poinsettia growing head high, cloaking the trail in red. Coffee is planted beneath the forest canopy. Verdant vegetable gardens, leaves glistening with dew, tended with care by timid people who walk away if we approach.

Later research into why these treefrogs are so toxic turns up something startling. Voodoo practitioners use *Hyla vasta*, our noxious giants, in zombification. To create a zombie from a living person! In Haiti, belief in *zonbi*, ("zombies" in Haitian Creole), is real. Haitian law prohibits the practice but protects the rights of zombies. Skeptics should check it out, they'd be as shocked as me. We got off with swollen eyes. I guess we're lucky.

CHAPTER 37:
Iron Market

We fly to Miami on Friday, but first want to buy souvenirs, so Pierre-Paul suggests the Iron Market. "I will take you; I know everyone." Pierre-Paul is ready in the morning. At the Iron Market, he sees a friend and asks him to watch our car. He leads us through the teeming mass of humanity into the bowels of the rusted behemoth. A medieval scene, the heat, the din, the darkness. We pass vegetables, fruit, grains, and beans in neat stacks on the ground. Fish, without refrigeration, in crates and piles on the concrete floor. The smell is revolting. Live chickens hang by their legs, awaiting slaughter. Cauldrons of water boiling to remove feathers.

The meat department is a horror show. Fresh butchered and half-rotted flesh lay in heaps, the floors slippery with blood and juices. Bloody carcasses of goats and pigs lie in mounds and hang from hooks. Their guts fill tubs, blood in pails, heads lined up on tables. They waste nothing. Flies are so thick we could choke. The stench and the gore are overpowering. I fight a wave of nausea.

The dry goods section smells of cotton, straw, and leather. There are coils of rope and twine, clothing, cloth, and homemade sandals with soles cut from tires. Some vendors sell simple household wares, such as basic soap, herbs, and potions. Others have piles of aluminum pots and pans, and every shape and size of woven baskets. Everything needed for daily life is on display. They are necessities, few items for vanity or luxury.

We reach a row of booths where artists labor on wooden carvings. Paintings show colorful culture and tradition, minus the pain of poverty.

Outside the Iron Market, Port-au-Prince, Haiti.

Wharf at Port-au-Prince, Haiti. Like looking back a century.

Boats along wharf
Port-au-Prince, Haiti.

Craftsmen cut shapes from oil drum lids with a hammer and chisel. They work barefoot among sharp scraps of metal. We leave with our things, this time we walk outside in the sun.

We drive past the harbor, where rustic wooden sloops and sailing vessels line the wharf. It's how I imagine a port scene looked in the 1800s: Sweaty, bare-chested workers and nicely dressed people who might be there to pick up cargo or arrange passage. Watermelon-sized ballast stones brought from the mountains stacked next to logs and piles of fruit. Cargo in barrels, crates, and pallets tied with ropes, covered with canvas tarps. Destined for where I do not know. I can't help but wonder.

∽

At the Hertz office, while Pierre-Paul calls Jacques for a ride on their phone, Ed and I remove our souvenirs. The agent complains of the car being so dirty. He checks the tires, including the spare—misses the gaping hole, now repaired. We had turned it to the bottom, out of view. Jacques arrives, we take Pierre-Paul home and thank him. We are sincere. His eyes are misty. He knows that the past week he wasn't only working for us, he was one of us. We shared our food, fun, adventures, and camaraderie. He excelled. We pay the agreed-on fee of five dollars per day and add an extra twenty. It's an enormous sum in Haiti. If we return, we'll want him again.

Jacques is full of questions. Our trip's success surprises him. We regale him with tales of our exploits. Then we tell of our difficulties with the checkpoint at Pont-Sondé.

I give my opinion. "It was a shakedown, he's a thug." Ed agrees.

Jacques scoffs. He thinks we misunderstood.

The United States occupied Haiti from 1915 to 1934. Old wounds run deep. US involvement in neighboring Dominican Republic's civil war ignited old fears and animosities among a few Haitians. The last American forces pulled out a year ago, in September 1966.

Jacques pulls a sack from beneath his Land Rover seat. Ed unties the knot and finds a two-foot-long Ford's Boa, *Epicrates fordii*. At first glance, the creature resembles a Red Ratsnake from Florida. Gray with reddish saddles. A jewel, one of the rarest of Hispaniolan snakes. "I've asked the collector for more," Jacques says. "It might take a while."

❧

We pack our specimens into three of the four suitcases, clothes, and souvenirs in the other. A large wood carving won't fit, so I wrap it. Getting cardboard and string proves more difficult to get than the carvings. It's Friday. We thank Jacques for his help on the drive to the airport. "Let us know if you need anything," Ed tells Jacques as he shakes his hand.

No one questions what's in our luggage. Little more than an hour after we arrive, we're in the air on our way to Miami. I ask Ed, "What's the procedure at Miami Customs?"

"Don't worry, I'll do the talking. Last time they didn't check."

We breeze through Immigration and head to Baggage Claim. Ed chooses a woman Customs agent. We set the bags on the belt. "What countries did you visit?" she asks.

"Haiti."

"Got any liquor?"

"No, only snakes." Ed pops the latches on the first suitcase, opens the lid.

"Snakes? Get out of here with those!" She calls across to an Agriculture officer. "You guys want to see any snakes from Haiti?"

The reply was fast, an emphatic, "No!" Our bags on a cart, we push them out the door. By appearances, the world is normal. For me, nothing will be the same.

CHAPTER 38:
Losing Faith

Ed knows I'm eager to get home to my wife in Davie. "Take off," he says. "I'll unpack the snakes, water them. You can come over in a few days and we'll divide the catch." Sounds good to me, so I leave.

Nice to see the farmhouse. Dang, I'm going to miss it. My wife squeezes me, she has worried but now she's relieved, happy I'm safe. It was tough on her, being out in the country by herself. I feel guilty. She was here alone, afraid, dealing with things while I'm off doing what I love. I console her and give her the few trinkets I bought. She tells me what she's been working on, the things left to do before moving. A daunting task, but we'll manage.

When I return to Ed's, he has the snakes in clean sacks. When we divide the catch, we flip for first choice and then alternate. I call "tails" and win the toss. To aid sorting, we dump a few sacks at a time into his bathroom tub to look them over and make our choices. The bathroom is typical, with tiled walls, tub, sink and toilet. Spotlessly clean, I can't imagine his wife is any too happy with our trashing it up with snakes, frogs, and lizards. Fortunately, she doesn't stick around while we're doing this, and we clean up as best we can.

We go through the all the snakes, and I get the sense there seems to be fewer than we collected in Haiti. It sets my teeth on edge. We didn't count them in Haiti. I can't be sure. Still, it leaves me with a feeling something is amiss. With a move pending, I'd prefer to avoid making an issue. I choose a few to take and leave the rest with Ed to sell. We've agreed to split the profits the same as the trip expenses, 50/50.

Without doubt, Ed is more aggressive with regards to splitting the catch than I am, and usually that suits me. He knows it. Still, there was one snake with extra-bright red markings that I remember from Haiti that I would love to have—but it's not here, so I ask.

"I don't remember it." He casts his eyes to the floor, waffles, changes the subject. "Did I tell you about Jan's friend?"

Jan's his wife. "No, what happened?"

"When you left, I watered the specimens in the bathtub. A Dominican Treefrog must have gotten loose."

"Yeah, and?"

"Sunday, Jan has a friend over for a visit. Mari, you've met her, a little Cuban gal."

"Okay."

"They're looking at photos. Mari reaches to turn on a lamp beside the sofa. The treefrog was inside the lampshade. It leaped onto the back of her hand. She screamed, jerked her arm, broke the lamp. Pictures and her tea ended up on the carpet."

"Holy crap, what did Jan say?"

"She saw the frog. It isn't over, there's more hell to pay."

"Wow! Sorry, man." *Karma's a bitch. It's comeuppance for squirreling away part of the catch. I hope Jan cuts him off for a month.*

I take my leave on a handshake. "This weekend I move to Bradenton."

"I hate you're moving. I'll stay in touch, keep you abreast of what I get for the snakes."

Ed shares proceeds of our trip in dribs and drabs, I soon lose track. Months pass, I don't often ask. I should have. Sure, I may get stuck, but not duped. There's a difference. Yes, it's complicated. I appreciate the fantastic experience. What's that worth? Still....

CHAPTER 39:
Big Changes

The Bradenton move is hard. Not the trips hauling personal items and reptiles, it's leaving the tropical paradise where I grew up that's soul rending. Our home, on a 20-acre sod field, is given up for a half-duplex with neighbors we haven't met. Nothing will be the same.

"The Letter" by the Box Tops is the last tune I hear on WQAM as it fades out going north past Moore Haven. Ties to Davie cut, I never move back. The rest of my family leaves in the next few years. My new position and our getting settled leaves scant time for reptiles. I lose touch with most of my South Florida herp friends. None enjoy writing letters. Still, it doesn't take long for my nickname "Snake Man" to catch up with me at FPL's Bradenton Service Center.

We settle in, meet our neighbors, they're okay. On the other side of our duplex lives an Ohio couple. Husband, Ray Breseiani is an insurance salesman. Two doors away, George Goethe, a photographer for the *Sarasota Herald-Tribune*. The big adjustment is getting used to having so many people so close.

Our first Christmas together is in Bradenton. Who'd have guessed? On a trip exploring rural roads, I cut a few short-needle pines, bring them back for us and the neighbors. We miss my grandma's turkey and ham dinner, and I promise to make it next year.

Then comes a letter. Or, I should say, *the* letter. The one that begins with "Greetings...." It's my old Uncle Sam. Yep, my draft notice. A shock my generation knows well. The Vietnam War is raging. I'm not in college, and there's nothing stopping me from serving. Married or not, I'm fair game.

When I share it with my wife, her face goes pale, tears flow. I arrange with work to go for my physical. No part of the bus trip to Miami or standing around naked half the day is much fun.

Turns out, the steel pin in my left ankle, from when the car hit my horse, is a disqualifier. That accident set many changes into motion. I am rejected, given 4-F status, the same as someone blind or quadriplegic. On one hand, I'll admit relief. On the other, I have deep disappointment. My grandfather, my dad and my older brother enlisted. My turn now, but it's not to be.

Dad was in the US Army Air Corps, 340th Fighter Squadron. He served in the Pacific during WWII, saw action in New Guinea's "Thunderbolt Valley," the Philippines and Borneo. Wounded twice, he returned to the fight after treatment in Australia.

Dad seldom spoke of his service. When I was little, we'd watch the documentary show *Victory at Sea*. He told me he fought in the Philippine invasion. After months of island hopping from New Guinea, he landed in Leyte, October 20, 1944. His 30th birthday. He fought in the battle for Leyte and witnessed the Battle of the Leyte Gulf, the largest sea and air battle in history. He said it was unforgettable. I couldn't imagine. I thought if my day came, I'd serve. Now, I've failed them. For over fifty years I have carried the guilt.

My father, "Jack" Cathcart in the Philippines during WWII, holding a bow and arrows and wearing a bolo knife he traded for parachute silk with the natives.

CHAPTER 40:
New Surroundings, Fitting In

J anuary 1968, Ed and I cross to Bimini one more time in his boat. We take fishing poles and bring back dolphin and grouper along with our snakes. Despite our strained relations at times, these are among the best of the best times of my life.

Distance from South Florida changes things. The trips to Bimini with Ed grow less frequent and more uncomfortable. Our expectations diverge. He's more hit and run, leave, and return the same day. I prefer to explore, stay over, enjoy the trip. Overtaken by temptation, I buy a boat. Sure, it's foolish. I'm young. Bimini trips with our neighbor Ray or guys from work help with expenses, but there's more fishing than snake hunting. My wife tries, but boating is not her thing. Homelife suffers.

I find peace exploring the woods and swamps. It's different on the West Coast, snakes are not so abundant as in South Florida. Before long I locate most of the local reptile species, learn their habitats. A few are rarities, new to me, for one, the Crowned Snake, *Tantilla relicta*. Our FPL crew, maintaining lines in a rear easement, stops for lunch in a stranger's backyard. As if by magic, out of a wooded lot crawls a Florida Pine Snake, *Pituophis melanoleucus mugitus*. It's a stunning creature. Tan and brown saddles over a white. My first, I recognize it from Conant's *Field Guide*. I've no sack with me, tying the neck and armholes of my tee-shirt suffices. The guys laugh, make fun. It doesn't faze me. On their best day, I'd be bored to tears.

Black fossils turn up while walking ditch banks, old quarries, and streams,

The *UNWIND*, the author's 23-foot Spicklemire Islander, (foreground) tied up in Bimini, 1968.

fascinating fragments of bone from extinct animals. As a naturalist, I'm never disappointed. If no snakes, there are fossils, plants, or butterflies. Inland creeks and rivers run clear and shallow in the dry season. In the sand or hollows of bedrock, shark's teeth as big as the palm of my hand, Mammoth, and Mastodon molars. Glyptodont body armor. Horse and tapir teeth, whale, and manatee bones. Unknown creatures, my friend Prof. Lew Ober in Miami helps name.

People interested in reptiles tend to find one another. Two older guys, I guess in their late 40s, seek me out. Russell and Ben hunt rattlesnakes for a hobby. They know the rattler's habits and habitats in Central Florida's backwoods well. "We dig gopher burrows," Russell says. "We never gas them." Pouring gasoline down gopher burrows to flush out snakes is a common but destructive practice.

"We dig them," says Ben. "Some run 20 to 30 feet, takes us all day."

They come bearing a few Red Ratsnakes and a coachwhip for which they only want a few dollars. I ask if they find anything else. "Indigos," Russell says. "We dug out a fat one this morning. We don't keep them though." He adds, before I can ask, "We don't keep Gopher Tortoises or Gopher Frogs either." All are becoming endangered.

"What do you do with the Diamondbacks?" They never offered them to me.

"Sell them to Ross Allen," Russell replies. At other times he claimed they sold the snakes to Ray Singleton, a notorious Tampa snakeman. I met Singleton a time or two and found him to be difficult. His place was a mess, too many animals in too small an area. The stench was awful. He had dirty clothes, a filthy mouth and stank from catching, keeping, and deodorizing skunks.

Russell and Ben would show up in the evening or weekends without a phone call and sell me a few snakes, cheap. They would often offer to take me hunting, but then we never did.

In nearby Parrish, a man named Ross Socolof runs a fish farm. I show up one day at his farm on Moccasin Wallow Road to find him standing knee-deep in one of his fishponds with a dip net in his hands. "Damn African Clawed Frogs are eating all the guppies!" He grumbles as he dips three-inch-long clawed frog tadpoles with every pass of the net and drops them into a bucket of brine. He dips for five minutes more, swearing all the while, before asking me who I am and what I want.

"I'll catch them for you," I offer, "If I can keep them."

"There's thousands of them," he says, and keeps dipping.

He gets out, I introduce myself. He takes me on a tour of the farm. Ross has hundreds of ponds, and sheds with cement tanks, all filled with an incredible array of tropical fish. When I inquire if he ever gets in any reptiles or amphibians, he tells me, "Not on purpose. Not anymore. I made a lot of money on the clawed frogs, pet shops bought tens of thousands, until some escaped, bred, and spread everywhere. I'm going to be forced to lime half of my ponds."

We find a tank with a few Surinam Toads, *Pipa pipa*, another aquatic marvel. These bizarre animals look like a dried, submerged leaf. Flat, angular, and weirdest of all, they bear live young from eggs embedded in the back skin of the female frog. In another tank are two baby Matamata Turtles, *Chelus fimbriata*. I go crazy for them. He sells them and the toads to me, cheap. "Call me if you get any more of these. I'll buy them," I implore him. He never does call, but I show up every few weeks and half the time he has something I can't live without. He's a great man, passionate about his work, an adventurer and pioneer in the exotic, freshwater fish business. I like and admire him.

Lane Southerland, a local reptile enthusiast who lives in Bradenton with his uncle, finds out about me and reaches out. We become fast friends, have fun collecting snakes around southern Florida for a couple of years, until he joins the Navy. On a trip to Clewiston, Lane is riding on the hood along a cattle trail. He shouts, "Coachwhip." I speed up, the truck goes through a dip, and sends him flying. When I hit the brakes, he lands hard in the dirt, right on his tailbone. I jump out, run to him. He's unhurt, crawling on all-fours. I fall to the ground, convulsing with laughter. Yeah, it's great to have someone local to share my reptile interest.

CHAPTER 41:
Decisions and Dilemmas

My venomous snake fascination started in high school. I read library books, and papers bought from Ralph Curtis, but literature is scarce. I write to herpetologist Edward H. Taylor, at the University of Kansas. He's worked in the Philippines, SE Asia, Mexico, and Central America on many reptiles and amphibians. Of special interest are the pit vipers. He writes back! His publications, out of print for years, are rare. I ask if he knows of sources for his titles. He shocks me by loaning his personal copies. Margins bear notes, revisions, and references. Technical, difficult, but I devour and return them with a handwritten letter of thanks and more questions.

Accounts of tropical pit vipers by Ditmars and Clifford Pope fuel my interest in Asian *Trimeresurus* and New World *Bothrops*. I yearn to explore, find them myself.

Costa Rica has 22 species of venomous snakes, more than any other country in the Americas. My Costa Rican friend Louie shares my passion. He visits there, staying with relatives, collects reptiles. Lucky guy! He's met Major Herschel H. Flowers, a researcher who is doing antivenom work, and tells me I should reach out to him. I do, hoping to develop a source for specimens, but it's not something the major is willing or able to do.

He's a specialist in serology and venoms, assigned to Costa Rica from the US Army Medical Research Lab in Fort Knox, Kentucky. His task is to produce a series of antivenins for New World snake toxins. He enjoys corresponding with those interested in his field.

Early in 1968, he writes: "You're welcome to visit, take as many snakes as you want. Give me a hand in the lab." *Is he sincere or calling my bluff?*

Excited but nervous, I post a return letter, taking the chance he's serious, ask a few "What if" questions. "Whenever you wish to come is okay, but this project is wrapping up in August. I could use help with that phase."

I'm incredulous. *Me,* help *him?* Well, there's my answer. Now what? To be honest, I have no idea.

What about my wife? How can I leave her again? Or get time off to go? My opportunity is becoming a dilemma. I have a few months to think it through before telling anyone.

I have a reptile shipment from Colombia to pick up in Miami. I call Ed to see if he'd want to make a quick Bahamas trip. "How's Bimini sound this weekend? I'll bring my boat."

"Nah, can't, I'm overloaded." *Since when is that an excuse?* "Why don't you stop by and show me what's in the consignment?"

Something's up. He has zero interest in Colombian animals these days. He must have a fresh scheme up his sleeve.

Baby boa constrictors come in, along with Garden Boas and vine snakes. A few *Spilotes,* spectacular but challenging to keep, none of which I ordered. The promised Emerald Tree Boas are not included. Yet another reason I'm glad to be quitting the import business. I stop at Ed's house. He doesn't mention the shipment—as I figured.

"C'mon on back." He leads me to his air-conditioned reptile room. "Are you up for Haiti? Jacques has 10 Ford's Boas and no plans of coming to Miami." *I knew there was something!* "I can't get away, any chance you could?"

He makes things sound so simple. Haiti isn't a drive around the block. "I don't know Ed, getting time off now's difficult. Besides, I have no money for travel."

Ed works for FPL, same as me, but in the office. He knows I'm not kidding but persists in sugarcoating it. "It's a shame to miss those Ford's. I'll pay for your trip and split the returns. I'd hate for Jacques to let them go to someone else."

Who else? We have Haiti sewn up, but it makes sense. As for splitting the profits. Like last time? Doggone it, Haiti is amazing. Am I being sucked into this? Crap!

"I'll sleep on it." My mind reels on the five-hour drive home. Costa Rica— and now Haiti?

To only fetch the Ford's Boas, regardless if Ed pays the airfare, I don't see how I can justify it. Since my first Haitian trip, plenty of people have asked for specimens. If I collect on my own, I could make out okay.

My wife is neither happy nor on board with a Haiti venture. She scoffs at Ed's offer. "You're going to split the profits? Like last time?" *It was kind of a drawn-out affair.*

Her reaction is predictable, so no problem so far. She isn't being difficult, she's afraid. Afraid of being alone. Afraid we will lose more money.

After dinner I explain the plan, laying it out in black and white. "I'll quit reptiles altogether if we don't make a profit. Regardless, we'll start looking for a house to buy." She knows the first part is BS, but the second wins the day. She agrees. *Why am I disappointed?*

What of Costa Rica? Can't think now. I send a note to Major Flowers. "Working on arranging the time." *(I'm not.)* "It looks good." *(It doesn't.)* I have told no one. Not Ed, not my spouse, not a soul.

I phone Ed. "I should have my ass kicked, but I'll go. I'll be there Saturday and leave Sunday for Haiti."

"Great, I'll contact Jacques."

CHAPTER 42:
Haiti, Single-Handed

I've entered the *Twilight Zone* this last Sunday of April 1968. As if through a time warp. Few could believe this world exists. I have returned by myself in the next chapter of my life's journey. What can I expect? Only God knows the answer. My hopes are for success, a safe trip, but adrenaline is coursing. I'm young, eager, and thirst for adventure.

Familiar with the drill, I push through the crowds to the terminal's curbside. Jacques is waiting. "You came alone? How long are you staying?"

I throw my gear in the back. "Six days. Gonna head up North."

"Wonderful. I'll keep the snakes until you return. There's 12 now."

"Great." Ed sent $250 cash for ten, $25 each. Hard to imagine we pay 15¢ for boas in Limbe. The Fords are rare and valuable, and Jacques knows it.

No sightseeing. We drive into the city, paying scant attention to the squalor, poverty, and filth. In the middle of the chaos, we find Pierre-Paul. "Remember me?"

He beams. "*Koulèv moun!* Snake man!" We embrace.

Still dapper, with shiny shoes, ready for any opportunity chance might bring his way. Jacques speaks in French, outlining my plans. He listens, saying, "*Wi. Dakò. Wi*" between nods. I make eye contact. A grin spreads across his face. Yeah, he's excited.

Pierre-Paul will meet me in the morning with a taxi, we'll go to the Interior Ministry for travel papers then to Hertz for a car. A few blocks on, Jacques pulls over to the curb in front of the Hôtel Henri, an old church converted to a hotel.

A flight of granite steps leads to heavy, double doors carved of mahogany. At the desk, a man in khaki pants and a white shirt greets us in French.

"Captain, meet my friend Dennis from Florida."

We shake hands. He has a firm grip. "Welcome to Haiti." His English surprises me.

With the hotel arranged, Jacques leaves, taking the extra suitcases and a change of clothes for my trip home. We'll call him when we return to the city.

The vaulted ceiling in the cavernous church magnifies the smallest sound. Inside walls are partitions of gray-painted plywood, not reaching the floor. *Like stalls in an airport restroom.* Each 8 x 12-foot cubicle has a cot, table, and wooden chair. A shared bathroom has a shower and toilet. "We lock up at 9 pm. For late entry, knock on the outside door of my room." He points to a rear corner. Believe me, I won't be on the streets of Port-au-Prince after dark.

A worldly man, Captain François learned English in Florida. In the Haitian air corps, he got jet training in Pensacola. Haiti has three military branches. Cuba its chief external adversary. He's proud of his service. Haiti's jet force never materialized. He flew transport aircraft and P51 Mustangs. Nostalgia colors his voice with sadness for the pitiful condition of Haiti's armed forces. His kind demeanor is comforting, his love of Haiti obvious, his martial decorum explains the spartan conditions at Hôtel Henri.

We stand in the vestibule overlooking the city. "So, what brings you to Port-au-Prince?"

"Snakes—*Koulèv*." He looks surprised, eyes wide, head cocked right, nodding.

"What do you do with them?"

"Study, sell a few to zoos for our expenses."

"When I was in flight school in Pensacola, I saw a rattlesnake on the base. It was big." His arms are fully outstretched. "They killed it."

"The snakes in Haiti aren't venomous," I mention. His blank expression says he's not convinced.

The captain directs me to a nearby Chinese restaurant. Spaghetti, their main dish, is hot and tasty, safe to eat. I'm learning to understand the country and its people. I steel myself against the sights and smells of the Port-au-Prince street. The only white person in a sea of black faces. Having every eye on me no longer feels strange.

Muddy village between Pont-Sondé and Gonaïves.

Rhino Iguana habitat

CHAPTER 43:
Northbound

The smell of charcoal smoke is heavy in the morning air. The primary cooking fuel in a city of 400,000. We load the gear in the taxi and ride to Hertz. At the interior ministry, travel papers to Cap-Haïtien again come in an envelope with a wax seal. With Pierre-Paul as copilot, we cross the first checkpoint without incident.

An hour beyond Port-au-Prince, trouble. Soldiers with guns. A row of men, hands up, lean on a bus as others check their pockets. The ground is strewn with their belongings.

This isn't good. "What's happening?"

"Police. They're looking for someone."

I slow to a crawl, keep moving, stay far left. They stare as we pass but make no move to impede us. After that, the road is open to the Artibonite River.

Approaching the Pont-Sondé checkpoint, we brace for a hassle. The pole gate is up. We prepare to stop when a guard motions to continue. Relieved, we steer with caution between vendors over the crowded bridge.

We continue, passing the Africa-looking dry plains and I quip, "This is the place we saw the boys with the iguana last trip." We make the distance to Gonaïves in record time, where we pick up a few bananas and oranges from a roadside vendor, before turning inland towards the mountains. The terrain changes from dry to more tropical, with palms and tall broadleaf trees. The road winding, rocky. In rugged terrain beyond Ennery, the wheel tugs to one side. We change a flat and continue to Plaisance for repairs.

A savory fragrance wafts from an outdoor market by the tire repair stand. Pierre-Paul wanders over while they work and buys a fried pastry with a flaky crust. It looks delicious. Haiti's cuisine has deep roots in French and African cultures, and food is tasty.

"What is that you're eating?"

"*Pâté.*"

"It smells great." A woman dips more from hot grease on a charcoal fire. "What's in it?"

"Goat paste." I'm hungry, but not *that* hungry. It's not something I'm ready to try, so I opt for a ripe papaya.

In Limbe midafternoon, we pause in our usual spot. In minutes, a few people gather. I hear the familiar words *blanc* and *Koulèv moun* in conversations as the crowd grows. I take a moment to absorb the surreal scene. Men in ragged clothes, many shirtless, glossy black skins tight over muscles. Eyes bright, faces smiling, they're eager, happy to see us, chattering with excitement. Pierre-Paul doesn't need instructions, he asks the whereabouts of Felix.

"Felix moved to a mountain village, far off the road." Alarm in his voice.

"Damn! Ask if someone can get word to him." Felix is by far Limbe's best snake hunter. It's frustrating not to speak their language. "Tell them we'll be back tomorrow morning and buy any healthy snakes." I flash back to the last trip and add, "No tarantulas."

We're confident they'll spread our message. We leave for Cap-Haïtien and a warm welcome at the Roi Christophe. Without asking, they offer a second room. It's custom. We shower and meet on the pool veranda to enjoy cool fruit juice and await dinner. Then I remember our travel permit. The red-wax-sealed envelope is in the car.

CHAPTER 44:

Tuesday in Limbe

Tuesday breakfast begins with *jus papaye*, a wonderful concoction of papaya juice and milk. Local coffee, warm French bread and poached eggs follow. It ends with a sumptuous fruit and cheese platter. The office of the minister is not open, so we tour the town. Pierre-Paul is a tourist in his own country. The last trip was so hasty, we saw little.

Once hailed as "Paris of the Antilles," Cap-Haïtien is a shadow of its former glory. It sprawls on the slopes of the Massif du Nord, Northern Mountains that parallel the coast. A quaint seaside city steeped in antiquity and history. Many buildings from the French colonial period line narrow cobblestone streets. The imposing Notre Dame Cathedral dates to the 1600s. Christopher Columbus established La Navidad here, the first New World settlement in 1492. He returned from Europe to find it destroyed the following year.

We circle by the minister's office with our papers. Friendly, they say nothing of being late. We suppose the "must deliver within 24 hours" rule is a myth.

A crowd awaits in Limbe. Large and growing, it's surprising. Several men have boas tied to sticks, others have burlap sacks, two kids with gourds. I can't expect Pierre-Paul to help with the snakes. To untie, stow them, and pay is tough, so I make him paymaster. The result is a dramatic elevation of his status in the eyes of the villagers. I swear he's standing taller as he counts coins into outstretched hands.

Ten curious onlookers for every collector press in to not miss a thing. Pierre-Paul contends with a mob of his own, barking orders to stand back.

We're losing control. A man from the throng steps up, helps move the crush back, and earns a tip for his valued good deed.

I dump a sack in the road. As the pile of snakes untangles, one slips free to escape. People scatter, shout, and scream. God, it's a glorious sight! Poetic justice. Pierre-Paul keeps count as I pull out boas and pays as I bag them. We have over a dozen when we finish. Two boys, I'd guess are 12, bring their gourds. Halfway expecting a tarantula to pop out, I remove the grass stopper with care. Instead, out zips a *Hypsirhynchus ferox*. The other holds a large, green *Uromacer oxyrhynchus* and a smaller *Uromacer frenatus*—the Haitian Brown Vine Snake. What a morning!

But no Felix. What a shame. He is a skilled hunter. We leave, promising to return in a few hours, and drive west towards Port-de-Paix. On the way, a village on the wide river, where trees are lush, looks good for snakes. People ignore our attempts to persuade them to collect. Storm clouds form, so we turn towards Limbe.

Only gone an hour, pouring when we arrive back, we wait it out. The car is hot and steamy, so we run for the thatched-roofed shelter where a few older men sit on a log. The rain sets in, but we stay. When the sun sinks low and we're sure no one will come, we return to Cap-Haïtien. Today was great despite having but a single round of buying.

At the hotel, I inspect and re-bag the specimens, shower and meet for dinner, *Pwason boukannen*—grilled fish, served with *pikliz*—a spicy pickled vegetable relish. Delightful. Pierre-Paul sits quietly, looks satisfied, reflective. I have a sense of being right where I belong.

CHAPTER 45:
Vodou Wednesday

The morning starts rainy; we delay. We arrive, park in our usual spot, no one is waiting. I brought Pierre-Paul a pair of cheap sneakers from Florida. His fancy shoes will be no excuse for avoiding mud. We walk among stick-walled, thatched-roofed huts. The village poor, but clean. There's scant evidence of how people make a living.

An entourage of boys call *blanc, blanc, blanc.* When I'm looking away, there'll be a gentle touch on my arm. My guess is they want to know how white skin feels. I try to understand their life and culture—they are equally curious about me.

A few houses display dishes with fruit, bread, and meat in front. I see patterns drawn on the ground with cornflower. "What is this, Pierre-Paul?"

"Vodou."

"What? Voodoo? Are you serious? Do you believe in that stuff?"

"No."

I'm not convinced. To whom or what are these offerings? Interesting, but creepy.

People gather by the car for the show to begin. Hunters trickle in with boas tied to vines. The two gourd-boys who came yesterday arrive with a small, yellow-striped, black *Leimadophis parvifrons.* Then we're done. No one else comes forward.

Things take a strange turn. While we wait, our entourage remains. Unless we leave, they stay as though mesmerized. A lad of four is my shadow, taking my every step.

Palm thatched roofs on stick and wattle and daub houses, Limbe, Haiti

"What's your name?" I'm aware he doesn't understand. I pat him on the head in a friendly gesture, his coarse hair wooly, reddish from poor nutrition.

A screech comes from within the crowd. A woman, the mother? is shouting, cursing, near frothing at the mouth. She rushes up and grabs the boy's arm, snatches him hard. I'm taken aback. *What's this?*

Pierre-Paul steps forward. Hand on my shoulder, he looks into my eyes. His voice is stern. "Never touch a child's head or compliment their features! It brings evil."

"What? How?" Offended, I scowl.

"If you call attention to an adorable child, the vampires may attack them." He is serious.

"This is crazy talk." I'm dismissive, and wave him aside, stomp off, clench my teeth.

"No." He follows. "If they hear your compliments, they will cut him, make him ugly."

"Bullshit. I don't buy this hocus-pocus." The woman continues scourging, the remaining crowd scatters. "Let's get out of here."

We speed off. Not hiding my anger, I careen towards Cap-Haïtien, rocks flying, decrying their narrow-minded superstitious ways. After a few miles I cool off, aware we must focus on why we came. But I'm upset. Can't return today. Six snakes are all we can show for a day's work. Pierre-Paul, dumbfounded, hasn't seen me angry.

CHAPTER 46:
The Save

Thursday morning before daylight, I check the specimens for the return. There is less than I'd hoped. Soiled sacks washed last night are damp. I spread them on the back seat. No rain! The sun, coming up over Cap-Haïtien, cuts through the foliage with blinding light. Raindrop bejeweled leaves twinkle. Our final Roi Christophe breakfast is a hearty dish called *Mayi Moulen*, or mashed corn. It doesn't sound appetizing, but it's great. Cooked, coarse cornmeal comparable to oatmeal, but spicy with garlic and cilantro. Sliced avocado and fried plantains on top—yummy!

We avoid talk of yesterday's drama while we eat, and on the 20-mile drive to Limbe. Rains have eroded gullies across the road. The going is slow and bumpy. At 10 am, no one's waiting, I worry aloud. "That crazy woman has ruined our good rapport." At least she's nowhere in sight.

An older man under the palm-thatched shelter says collectors will come. That's a relief. We head south along the river, swollen from heavy rains, to kill time. I walk a wooded hillside while Pierre-Paul watches the car. After, we drive around, then park in the shade of a massive Breadfruit Tree. Past noon we return, a few people are waiting.

Two have boas, nice ones, we bag them and pay. Our catch is off with our difficulties and without Felix…. The men say others are coming. Over the next hour, one more. We prepare to move on when we see a group approaching. What now?

As they draw near, I can tell they're carrying sacks. "Hey, it's our friend!"

When he gets close, I go to him, shake his hand. "Felix! Man, I'm glad you're here." He doesn't understand my words, but knows my meaning.

"When I heard Zye Ble was here, I knew it was you." He tells Pierre-Paul. "I live in the mountains; it takes a few hours to walk to Limbe."

His burlap sacks hold 20-plus snakes. As usual, each is in perfect condition. He produces a small gourd out of which pops an *Epicrates gracilis*, the coveted Vine Boa. I've yet to learn the value of this superb rarity, as Ed kept the specimen we obtained on our last trip. I tell Felix he's an excellent collector and pay him a whole US dollar like the last time.

An hour ago, I was ready to leave. Now I wish there was more time. Pierre-Paul explains we must head back. We promise to return. It might be months. Felix says he will watch for us. After saying goodbyes, we start towards Port-au-Prince with a sizeable collection, including several rarer snakes.

I ask Pierre-Paul, "What does *Zye Ble* mean?"

"Blue Eyes."

"That's better than *blanc* or *Koulèv moun*, I suppose."

Pierre-Paul laughs. "*Zye Ble blanc.*"

At Plaisance we stop for a bite. It's getting late as we continue out of the mountains.

We arrive in Gonaïves after dark. The somber city sets us on edge. Same hotel as the last trip, everything out of the car. In the morning, we leave without incident. I watch for anyone with iguanas as we pass the *bomas* going towards the Artibonite River, but see none.

"Next visit we must ask at a village."

We cross the crowded bridge, roll to a stop at the Pont-Sondé checkpoint. The gate pole blocks the road. We're apprehensive. The heavy-set guard isn't here. A different one asks for papers. He looks in the windows, sees the sacks piled on the rear seat. He speaks with Pierre-Paul. I overhear, *"Koulèv."*

He hands back our identifications, signals to raise the pole. *"Pase."* He waves us to pass.

After dropping the specimens and supplies at the hotel, we go to Hertz. No issues, so we call Jacques for a ride. I pay Pierre-Paul, plus a hefty tip, and thank him. He cuts me short. "I'd come for free."

Choked up, I tell him. "If you want to visit the US, I will help you."

"Someday." He sounds less than convincing. A plane ticket costs many month's wages.

Without him, we could do nothing. I wish for him to know he's appreciated.

Jacques arrives with the Ford's Boas, now 13. I have money from Ed for 10 and pay for the others myself. They might bring me some needed cash. If not, I'll keep them. We'll see. With the unexpected *Epicrates gracilis,* it should be an interesting homecoming.

CHAPTER 47:
Holding the Cards

Back in the real world, Ed picks me up at the Miami Internatioal Airport. I'd told him on the phone that'd I'd gotten the Ford's. He's eager to see them. As typical, no problems at Immigration, Customs, or Agriculture. While he drives home, I tell of my experiences. Ed seems to be half paying attention, he's seen it all before, I know his mind is on the specimens and nothing else.

He's ecstatic over the *Epicrates fordii*. They are outstanding, smaller, different in every way from the *striatus*. First time on the collector market where Caribbean reptiles are rare.

While Ed's euphoric, I seize the opportunity. "What are your plans for the Ford's?"

Ed's a shrewd businessman. He replies, "People have spoken for most. They're waiting for them." *He must think I want a few.*

"Oh yeah? What are you asking for them?" Ed balks, mumbles. My gut tells me he's unwilling to reveal his dealings. I remind him, "I've got an investment in this venture, too. Besides having to pull in favors for time off work. I'm depending on the sales, and I need to know what my share will be."

I sense he's trying to figure a way to stall. "How's this?" I suggest. "Pay me a flat fee, then sell them for whatever you can, and not split with me."

He likes my idea. "Okay. I paid $25 each so I'll ante up $25 for your part."

"So, tell me, what are you proposing to ask for them?"

"I'd like to double it. I'm thinking $100, but not positive."

A hundred bucks is a princely sum in 1968. Over a week's wages for me.

Still, collectors with means will pay up for rare snakes.

"So, you earn $50, and I make $25 for my work? I guess I'll sell the other three myself."

Ed flies angry, snaps back. "You'd never have gone to Haiti if it weren't for me."

He is right. Despite that, it's an unfair statement, and he knows it. He's quick to change his tune. "Okay, $50 per snake for the ten, and $75 each for the other three. I'll raise the price and they'll pony up if they want them."

I agree. A decent offer. $725 for my part of the *fordii*.

I pull out the *Hypsirhynchus*. Ed's face lights up and he reverts to herp enthusiast. This is the Ed I respect as a friend and mentor. "You know, most colubrid snakes do not carry the value of boids or venomous species."

"Yeah, I'm aware. Why don't you keep those and the *Leimadophis* to learn how they adapt to captivity? I don't need them."

"Yes, thanks." Ed bags the snake and puts it aside.

We go through the 40 regular Haitian Boas. I pick 10 for myself. The rest I offer to Ed.

"I gave you a fair shake on the Ford's and paid part of the trip expense. You should give them to me." *Damn, he's serious. It makes sense, at least for him. Points for being ballsy.* I take five more and gift him the others.

I've saved the *Epicrates gracilis* for last. Ed's jaw drops. It's only the second one he has seen. He takes the serpent to examine every detail of its pattern and bizarre shape. We are both aware this jewel is something special. Ed falls silent.

"Well?"

"Where did you find it?"

"Same as last time, Felix in Limbe. I made a fuss over him, hoping to inspire someone else. I paid a buck."

Ed laughs. "Wow! A whole dollar? That's big money in Haiti."

"What do you reckon it'll be worth?" I watch for any subtle reaction.

He replies without hesitation. "A hundred easy, two, if it thrives, who knows? Looks like a male. If it is, I'd like to keep it with the first one, try to breed them."

It's good having Ed's respect. He is, despite any issues, an outstanding herpetologist. We agree, Ed will hold the specimen and try to breed them, then later assess interest before setting a price. I must trust him. I'd prefer cash, but with this rare snake's value unknown, this arrangement is best. Ed agrees.

We shake, it's a done deal. I drive home with $300, less than half of what he owes me, but confident he'll deliver on the balance. After two weeks, he does.

Everything is copacetic on our side of the duplex. My wife is glad to see me. The neighbors give her the willies. I get a detailed account of life while I was away, but few questions of my Haiti exploits. Typical. I'm used to it now, it doesn't matter. The important thing is she's okay, happy with the cash. The success has restored a degree of her confidence in me.

CHAPTER 48:
Big Decisions

I seek, explore. No longer content to read of adventures, I live them. Even a coin has two sides. As a husband, and working for an electric utility, I must fulfill the obligations of both. It's not without conflict. The expeditions are for me, my calling, who I am. My occupation is for survival, for family, and for the life we love. Marriage is central or should be. Not sure, so I struggle. I owe my greatest effort to the extent I am able. The challenge is being all three people.

Time to step up, keep promises. I won a recent bid to become an apprentice lineman, a path to journeyman, and higher pay. My wife took a job with the hospital. With our joint income, a house hunt begins. Bradenton is growing, plenty are available, but crammed into developments, in rows on treeless lots. Raised in the country, I find the thought unbearable.

One day I stumble upon a half-acre corner lot, wooded with oaks and Cabbage Palms. Overgrown with weeds and trees, beside an old shell pit, which reminds me of the abandoned rock pits back in Lauderdale. The seller, a contractor, offers a package to include constructing a house. We accept. My wife loves it. She is as happy as I have seen her. Life has blessed us. I try to be the dedicated husband she wants. We long for the same things. Happiness, security, a sense of normality, and the hope to build a family. But reconciling home, work and my need for exploration leave me conflicted.

No one knows Costa Rica is calling. Time is getting short, forcing me to make a move. It's not right to keep Major Flowers guessing, nor my wife to wait until the last minute to spring this. I gather the courage to broach the topic.

"There's something I, uh, we need to talk about." I'm nervous, don't want to blow it.

Her brows draw together. Eyes plead. It pierces my heart. "About what?"

"Nothing serious. A special opportunity to visit Costa Rica. I know my timing is terrible."

"What do you mean? When? Who's going?"

She's full of questions—this is good. I try my best to explain, and to my absolute shock and surprise, she agrees. Were the house plans the balm I needed? If so, it wasn't my intention. Did my recent position help, or her job with new friends? Whatever the reason, I'm relieved. I want to avoid hurt feelings or causing her worry.

The dread was more painful than convincing her. Who knew? Now to arrange the 90 days I calculate needing. It won't be easy. I put together a presentation for my supervisor. Letters, maps, documents—things that might give the trip gravity and bolster my case.

The answer is swift. "No. I can't okay a three-month leave of absence. There's protocol. The union and regional supervision must be onboard. I don't see any way."

To interrupt apprenticeship training is significant, unprecedented except for military service. Things are not looking positive. The company warns me. "If we approve, it will cause a gap in your seniority."

The IBEW balks, taking the focus off me and onto contract bylaws. They grant me unpaid leave with no interruption in tenure. My coworkers look at me as a short-timer. None of them believe I'll be back. They think I have lost my mind.

I contact Major Flowers and set a departure date, July 5, 1968.

Air travel is $200 round trip, on two different airlines, several layovers. Board is free at the major's compound. I won't need much cash. The chief concern is paying bills when the paychecks stop. I take home $500 per month at FPL, so there's a potential $1,500 in missed wages to consider. From reptile sales, many from Haiti and Bimini, I have saved $2,000. Ed agrees to buy part of my collection when I tell him of my upcoming travels. He wants snakes from Costa Rica; I am making no promises. Together, this will net another $1,000 easily. More than enough to offset lost pay and expenses.

Yes, I should save the extra money for our many needs when we move. But that's not before December. If my bride is on board, I'm satisfied.

My fight for furlough takes a toll. With everything now set, I'm filled with doubts and guilt. Is my dream journey a fool's errand? A selfish waste of time and wealth? The scope is huge. Up to three months, thousands of miles, leaving others behind to fill my place. I'm torn, but realize this trip is the next natural step in my life's saga.

Until I leave, I dote on my wife. We enjoy life together, walk the property, imagine our home, make plans. I persuade my apprentice instructor to arrange Saturday classes from twice a month to every week, to speed the schedule. Life is exciting. Part of me hates leaving.

I've reduced my collection and lined up help to care for what's left. House construction is set. I'm as prepared as possible. Packed, traveling light, Fourth of July morning, I leave for Miami. My wife puts on her brave face. We've seldom spent over a week apart. Now we're saying goodbye for the rest of the summer. Never easy. This time departing is heart-rending.

Basiliscus vittatus in the jungle along the shore of Lago Xolotlán, Managua, Nicaragua

CHAPTER 49:
Central American History—A Crash Course

Despite having traveled in Mexico, Haiti, and Bimini, I face my boldest venture. Months in Central America, out of touch with home, a test of will, stamina, and our marriage. I do not take the dangers lightly.

No passport is needed to visit Costa Rica in 1968. Pan Am flights stop in multiple countries on the way to San José. To leverage this perk, I plan overnight stops in Guatemala and El Salvador. Two nights each in Honduras and Nicaragua. Naïve regarding Central America and its politics, I'm in for a harsh, first-hand look.

In Guatemala City, a hotel near the American Embassy costs a few dollars. After ditching my suitcases, my next thought is food, then to explore. A walk along the wide boulevards and narrow lanes, past ornate colonial public buildings, and cathedrals, leaves me breathless. Not just from their splendor, but from the 4,990-foot altitude. Pervasive military, with armed soldiers on sidewalks, armored vehicles in the streets seems strange. Concrete-filled oil drums stand in front of banks and hotels. A man in a café is reading a *Miami Herald*. I introduce myself, ask, "Why the army presence?"

He's articulate, with an accent. "Security has been this way a while. With President Johnson coming, things have tightened."

"Oh, when is that?"

"The 8th. You don't know?"

That was embarrassing. A month away from being 20, politics and the president's travels aren't on my radar.

A state of civil war has existed for years, since 1960. Insurgents control a sizable part of the countryside. Attacks in Guatemala City are not frequent but happen. Despite this, I travel up to Antigua by bus, the old capital when Central America was a single country. An enjoyable day. I explore ruins, sample local foods, listen to folk music played on an amazing, huge, wooden marimba. Life presents as normal, at least on the surface. There is much to learn.

On August 28, 1968, FAR *(Fuerzas Armadas Rebeldes)* guerillas will try to kidnap the US Ambassador to Guatemala, John Gordon Mein. Instead, they'll shoot him and his aides dead in the street when he runs to escape. The tragedy strikes between the American Embassy and the Hotel San Carlos where I'm staying.

⁓

Tegucigalpa's turmoil makes Guatemala seem calm. President Lyndon Johnson will visit Honduras in two days on his epic Central America tour. Protestors block roads on the taxi ride to town. Carlos Roberto Reina (future *Presidente*) leads banner-carrying FENAGH members. Lopez Arellano seized control in a 1963 coup. Now he's struggling to hold power. War is imminent amid rising tensions with San Salvador. Placards covering buildings and phone poles protest illegal Salvadoran Immigration. The country is under a general strike.

I check into a downtown hotel. The crush of protestors leaves me bewildered. Late afternoon, I don't stray far and find a bistro for dinner. *Milanesa de Res* is a treat. Thin-sliced, pounded, bread-crumbed beef, seasoned with cilantro, fried, and served with lime. Street violence erupts on the street out front. People running, screaming, shouting. A few duck into the restaurant. Everyone jumps to their feet. Masked men armed with sticks chase the crowd past amid flying rocks and bottles, shouts, and chants. It isn't long before military police push them back the other way. Confusion reigns as the drama unfolds. I never learn what's happening. When it quiets, I hurry the three blocks back to my room.

At dawn, I want to flee the city. On the mile walk to a transit terminal, crowds gather. Through the chaos, the bus detours around roadblocks of tires ablaze. Past the town center, it's peaceful. The ride bumpy, crowded with Indians carrying everything they own. Over an hour the ancient bus labors up the steep mountain grade to reach scenic Valle de Ángeles.

Uncrowded, no protesters, no graffiti. In an open-air diner, I enjoy *pupusas*. Imagine a fat tortilla filled with quesillo cheese, beans, or shredded meat with salsa. Scrumptious. Shops sell wood carvings and paintings. I enjoy a delightful day far from yesterday's wild scene. My flight departs in the morning, so I catch a late afternoon bus back to Tegucigalpa's pandemonium.

࿊

It'd be a lie if I said I'm not relieved to be safely aboard the plane to El Salvador. I liked Honduras, the parts outside of Tegu. But the feeling was of being near a puddle of gasoline when everyone is carrying matches. At Ilopango International Airport, passengers get frisked as we deplane. Here we go. After passing Immigration, the reason becomes obvious.

President Lyndon B. Johnson arrived yesterday, here for a summit with the presidents of five major Central American countries. I've caught up to him but have seen the effects of his tour for days.

I taxi to a hotel near Centenario Park in downtown San Salvador. Modern and bustling, more so than Guatemala or Honduras. I walk over to Alameda Juan Pablo II, where President Johnson's motorcade will pass. Throngs of people wave Salvadoran and US flags. Protestors arrive, carrying banners, chanting "Johnson *Asesino,*" (murderer) and anti-Vietnam War slogans. Others read, "Yankee Go Home." At least the noisy protests stay peaceful.

It's exciting, but just the same, confusing, not knowing the reasons for the demonstrations. The throng on the sidewalk is cheering, jeering, and shouting. Thunderous cries echo in waves as the motorcade approaches.

I climb a building's steps for a better view, glimpse President Johnson as he passes. The man standing next to me in a business suit asks, "You're American, right?"

"Pardon?" Surprised by hearing English, I reply, "Yes, I am." At six-feet-two with sandy hair and blue eyes, it's not a wild guess.

"So, what do you think?"

"Of the protest?"

"And Johnson, his visit."

I hate to show my ignorance by admitting I know little. "I'm sure he's trying to help."

"Of course. What choice does he have?"

I fake it, clueless to what he is referring to. The Vietnam War? Civil wars flaring in neighboring countries? Other issues of which I am even less aware? "What's your opinion?"

"The situation is getting worse; something has to change. Everyone knows FPL *(Fuerzas Populares de Liberación Farabundo Martí)* backs the protesters. They fool no one. The communists are spoiling for war with the government. They've got the students fired up, their usual tactics."

The guy's English is excellent. "You from El Salvador?"

"Honduras. This will end in revolution." He's angry. "Are you with the Mil Group?"

"Mil Group?" Wasn't sure I heard him over the ruckus.

"I thought you might be with the US military mission. We don't see many tourists."

"Oh, sorry, no. Not a tourist either. Passing through to Costa Rica."

"Poor timing." He grins, shakes his head.

"Yeah, ain't that the truth."

Turns out he was right. Within months, a brief war breaks out with Honduras. Conditions continue to deteriorate with the murder of Catholic priests and other atrocities. Full-blown civil war erupts in 1979, lasting over twelve years. An umbrella group, the FMLN, *(Farabundo Martí National Liberation Front)* forms in 1980. They prosecute the war until 1992 and remain a political force today.

El Salvador, in ways unsettling, is my most interesting stopover in the long run. It's not every day we can witness history. I spend the night, and by the time I leave, the president has departed for Nicaragua, and the tightened security has returned to normal. *Pupusas* from a stand outside the airport make my best meal here.

꿍

I'm relieved to arrive in Managua, away from El Salvador's intensity. President Johnson visited yesterday for a brief visit with Presidente Anastasio Somoza Debayle. Crowds have dispersed. What I find is a quaint, colonial city immersed in a lush tropical forest on the shore of Lago Xolotlán, the smaller of two massive lakes, in the shadow of twin volcanic peaks, one active. This country, the size of New York State, has 19 volcanoes.

Despite the outward calm, Nicaragua smolders—a volcano ready to explode. The Somoza family, rulers since the 1930s, face mounting opposition. Chief adversary, Carlos Fonseca, leads the FSLN *(Sandinista National Liberation Front)*. A communist-led rebellion is imminent. Green uniformed troops and political posters bode of hard times to come.

The short flight from San Salvador leaves a full day for exploration. I check into a downtown hotel and wander to the jungle-cloaked lakefront. Wildlife abounds within view of the buildings. I see basilisk lizards, birds of every kind, and butterflies. High in a *Ceiba* tree, a Coendou, prehensile-tailed porcupine. Parrots, macaws, and monkeys. I wander deeper, as more treasures show themselves, and emerge at an abandoned quarry, now a garbage dump. Around the margins I search for reptiles, finding a few small snakes, *Rhadinaea* and *Ninia* and several geckos, but keep none. Trash pickers, scruffy people gleaning useful bits, notice me. I slip back into the woods.

The highlight of my day is a lakeside market with baskets of rainbow-hued cichlids. Bull Sharks inhabit larger neighboring Lago Cocibolca. Hungry for a fish dinner near my hotel, I settle for *nacatamal,* a banana-leaf-wrapped corn tamale stuffed with pork.

Storm clouds are roiling above the lake and Volcán Apoyeque. Rain falls with darkness. The courtyard comes alive with unfamiliar squeaks, bonks, and whistles of treefrogs. A surprising variety of species right in the city. I rest, mind and body, prepare for my next stop: Costa Rica. My trip up to now has been more akin to a living lesson in international affairs. I'm weary of the political atmosphere in the countries I have visited. What awaits me, I am not sure, but it can't happen fast enough.

꒰�___꒱

Aboard the flight, I sit beside a guy who looks American. "You going to San José?"

"Panama. I work in the Canal Zone," he says with a friendly smile.

That sounds so exotic to me. Imagine working and living there. "It must be fascinating."

"It's a slice of America. We have everything."

CHAPTER 50:
Costa Rica: Meeting the Major

Am I in a movie? As we approach our destination, the cabin breaks into the song: "Do You Know the Way to San Jose?" A refreshing change from the somber atmosphere in other Central American countries. Joyful people coming home. It must be a wonderful place.

Juan Santamaria International Airport is in Alajuela. Clean, tropical, bustling. No visible military or police, political posters, or banners. The mood is friendly. The usual cadres of taxi drivers and wannabe porters surround me. I repeat "*No, gracias*" while heading to the curb where an army Jeep awaits. The driver, wearing green fatigues, is Major Flowers.

"Welcome to Costa Rica." He extends his hand. Genial, the same as in his letters.

"It's great to be here. Thanks for inviting me. I can't tell you what this opportunity means to me."

"Save it till you find out how much work I have for you." He chuckles, smiles. "You hungry?" Before I can reply. "There's a place on the road. I don't cook, and my housekeeper is off today."

The Huevo Grande is an egg-shaped fried chicken stand. While he orders, I wander to a bridge across a deep gorge. Wonder what might live on the jungle cloaked canyon sides? I try to imagine, can't wait for a chance to search.

We chat, get to know one another, while enjoying lunch in the cool mountain breeze. "Thanks, Major."

"Call me Herschel." (I never did.)

"This is a special spot for me."

"Oh? How so?"

"I'm sure you'll hear the story before you leave." He laughs without elaborating.

A quick trip through the mountains to rural Santa Rosa. A small neighborhood of houses with red tile roofs around a wooded park. His home is on a large corner lot.

"Welcome home." We pull through a black iron gate, never closed. A white-painted brick-and-stucco wall overgrown by Bougainvillea, ablaze in crimson blooms. "The house is here; snake room and lab over there." He points to two buildings connected by a breezeway.

The courtyard of the acre-sized compound is part clay-and-gravel parking lot, the rest is a lawn with trees and landscaping. A brightly painted antique ox cart sits in the grass. Strewn throughout the garden are large, natural boulders.

"It's an old villa from the coffee plantation era. Perfect for me, with privacy and the space I need."

The sprawling building has a long corridor. A plain but cozy room with a bed, chest of drawers, wardrobe, and table is mine. There's one bathroom and rooms for Maria, the housekeeper, and the major's helper, Guillermo.

He shows me a spacious kitchen, cement counter and sink dyed red, polished smooth. He opens the refrigerator. "Help yourself." I see a pitcher of water and many bottles of beer, little else. "Maria takes care of cleaning, washing clothes and cooking. On her days off we're on our own."

He points to a gallon jug of white vinegar on the counter. "I drink a small glass each day to keep my blood on the acid side. Prevents all sorts of bad things and can interfere with haemotoxic venoms in an accidental bite."

Who am I to argue with one of the world's leading toxicologists?

Major Flowers has exercise quarters with a bench and weights. He's 35, fit, and on active duty in the US Army. Across from the kitchen, a storage closet. Through a breezeway, the laboratory. The lab is spartan and spotless, equipped for the task at hand.

Next to that, the snake room. Heaven to me. It's immaculate, shelves floor to ceiling, wood boxes and glass-fronted cages of various sizes. Each holds one or more venomous snakes. I stop for a closer look at a coral. "*Micrurus nigrocinctus*, the most common one here. Kills many people." A sobering bit of information that brings focus to the purpose of this facility.

I have the kid in a candy store feeling. Excited by the opportunity to study and work with species I've only seen in books. It's beyond my wildest expectations. The major gives me full reign of the collection. My task is to help maintain it during my stay.

That evening my friend Louis Porras stops by before leaving for Miami. He stays here occasionally during his collecting trips. A native Costa Rican, he is visiting with relatives in San José. It was he who put me in touch with Major Flowers. Without his introduction…who knows?

We talk. Louie tells me of life at the compound and tips on the country and living with the major. "A colorful character." Pressed for details, he says, "You'll see," then chuckles.

CHAPTER 51:
Beginning of the End

My Costa Rica trip begins at the end of Major Flowers' four-year tour assignment. This coming Saturday, July 13th, the major will take part in an award ceremony, commemorating the hand-over of his antivenom program to the Costa Rican Ministry of Health and University of Costa Rica.

The major is a toxicologist and venom specialist. His mission is to develop snakebite antiserums. No other country in the Americas has more types of venomous serpents than Costa Rica, a country smaller than the state of West Virginia. The population suffers an astonishing average of 3,000 venomous snakebites per year, 10 percent fatal. Most of the rest end with the loss of a limb or other severe disabilities.

Conducting venom research at the US Army Medical Research Laboratory in Fort Knox, Kentucky, a 1963 visit by Dr. Antonio Peña, began a long association with Costa Rica. Dr. Peña, director of the San Juan de Dios Hospital in San José, proposed a cooperative program to develop snake antiserum in his country. The US Army, with more involvement in Central America, saw the value in such a program. With support from US Ambassador Raymond Telles to work out diplomatic arrangements, the major began his assignment in November 1964.

His laboratory established, collaborating with Costa Rican scientists he set up the program from top to bottom. He ventures into jungles to collect venomous snakes and establishes a network of collecting stations. Despite being in the US Army Veterinary Corps, they often call him to treat human victims.

Army Veterinarian Lauded for Snakebite Antivenom Research in Costa Rica

Mid-November marks the first anniversary of an era in Costa Rica when the venomous bushmaster, fer-de-lance and other poisonous snakes scarcely dare raise their heads lest they be captured for science by a U.S. Army veterinarian.

Capt Herschel H. Flowers, VC, is a veteran capturer and "milker" of the reptiles for their venom. The practice of snake-milking is age-old, dating to aboriginal warrior use and even as a tourist attraction at Florida snake "farms" for many years.

Capt Flowers extracts the venom into sterile containers and uses it to produce antivenom serums to combat the serious snake problem in Costa Rica, a cause of governmental concern.

A recent dispatch to the U.S. Department of State from the American Embassy at San Jose, capital of the Central American country, praised the effective antivenom production work of Capt Flowers. He was assigned to Costa Rica by the Army Medical Research Laboratory, Fort Knox, Ky., at the request of Costa Rican authorities and with the support and interest of U.S. Ambassador Raymond Telles.

Capt Flowers was commended jointly by the Embassy and the Assistance for International Development (AID) Mission in Costa Rica for the antivenom project development; also for instructing Costa Rican medical personnel in antisnakebite procedures and first aid.

Typically North American is his reaction when advised of the laudatory message to high levels. Handwritten just after his name on the message distributed through the Departments of State, Army and cognizant agencies is the notation: "WOW!"

The current research and development program began in February 1964, with the Fort Knox laboratory and the University of Costa Rica School of Medicine pooling resources.

Capt Flowers, engaged for more than four years in an Army research project on snakebites, visited Costa Rica to discuss mutual problems with personnel of the Ministry of Public Health and the National University of Costa Rica.

From these informal talks came a Joint Costa Rica Ministry of Public Health/U.S. Army Medical Service Research Project on Poisonous Snakes, effected through an exchange of diplomatic notes in October 1964.

Capt Flowers arrived in Costa Rica Nov. 15, 1964, to start the program. Extraction of venom from the snakes abounding in the thickly wooded tropical coastal areas and uplands, processing the venom, the immunization of horses used in antivenom production and serum collection, separation and testing are among his duties. He also instructs indigenous medical personnel in new surgical procedures related to chemotherapeutic agents.

Laboratory spaces are provided by the University of Costa Rica School of Medicine. The University also processes the collected horse serum, transforming it into antivenom.

Latest reports are that antivenom production began on a commercial basis last month. Injection of 15 horses, donated by Costa Rican ranchers, began last April.

In this tropical land, where five major families of poisonous snakes are native, it is estimated that there are approximately 1,500 snakebite cases annually. A third of these result in permanent or partial disability to a limb. The mortality rate (1962 statistics) is about 32 out of approximately 10,000 "deaths from all causes," with many suspected of going unreported as death-by-snakebite in the remote areas.

Until recently facilities for producing antivenom serums did not exist in Costa Rica and the techniques of chemotherapy of snakebite victims were virtually unknown.

In addition to the bushmaster (Lachesis mutus), largest poisonous snake in the New World, and fer-de-lance (Bothrops atrops), there are the Central American rattlesnake (Crotalus), the coral (Micrurus) and a sea snake (Hydrophidae).

Through the efforts of Capt Flowers and his colleagues, optimism has risen regarding the use of EDTA (ethylene-diaminetetraacetic acid) as an effective neutralizer of the venom of the bushmaster, fer-de-lance and related species. Preliminary results of chemotherapeutic and surgical techniques in 13 hospital cases have been encouraging.

The chemical EDTA is believed to be effective against certain venoms because it chelates, or binds, the metallic ion molecularly structured in venom enzymes. Thus it neutralizes the enzyme, making harmless or at least partially ineffectual, the venom in a snakebite.

While snake hunting in the jungles of remote Osa Peninsula, accessible only by launch or aircraft, Capt Flowers won the gratitude of the timber workers by teaching courses in snakebite treatment and general first aid.

An official of OSA Productos Forestales, S.A., expressed appreciation for Capt Flowers' work by letter to the U.S. Ambassador at Costa Rica. He credited the saving of at least one life to the first aid knowledge Capt Flowers had imparted to timber workers. In the Osa mountains, he taught several of the lumbermen how to catch live snakes for lab work at the University.

A native of Orlando, Fla., Capt Flowers entered the Army early in 1961 and began working with venoms six months later at the research laboratory, Fort Knox. The laboratory subsequently produced an antivenom serum effective against North American coral snakes.

Article from
Army R&D Newsmagazine,
November 1965 outlining
the work of Maj. Flowers
in Costa Rica.
(Courtesy: Army R&D
Newsmagazine,
now under Army AL&T)

The Vet Strikes Back

COL J. J. Caulfield

Deadly fer-de-lance shows its fangs as MAJ Flowers prepares to extract venom.

Article describing
Maj. Flowers
antivenom project, from
Army Digest
Vol. 23 #2 2/1968.
(Courtesy of Army Digest)

For the first time, the campesinos of Costa Rica face a future which need not be cut short by a snakebite, thanks to the work directed by MAJ Hershel H. Flowers who has 150 snakes in his home near San Jose, Costa Rica, and handles thousands more each year.

MAJ Flowers is technical director of a serum program that will save the lives of thousands of people in Costa Rica and Central America. He is the first man to develop a serum that is polyvalent, that is, potent against all poisonous snakes found in Central America except for the coral snake. And for that, too, he has developed a cure.

Before availability of the serum, an estimated 200-300 persons annually have died of snake bites. Some survivors have lost a foot, leg, hand or arm, and have had to spend weeks in a hospital and receive countless skin grafts.

With the assistance of the U.S. Agency for International Development, and the University of Costa Rica, the 33-year old veterinarian officer plans to produce this year over 10,000 bottles of anti-venom serum for distribution to every hospital, school, police station and pueblo in the country. Every Costa Rican will be close enough to the serum to reach it in time to be saved.

At least once a week MAJ Flowers is called to treat snakebite. The Guardia Civil brings him to the

In the research reported here the investigators adhered to the "Principles of Laboratory Animal Care" as established by the National Academy of Science National Research Council.

airport where a Cessna from the Ministry of Internal Security flies him to the airstrip nearest the victim. If not too many hours have elapsed, MAJ Flowers can save him. However, it is often more than distance that prevents a victim from reaching help in time. Many superstitious folk believe that once a person is snakebitten he cannot touch water. Hence if he reaches a brook, he will either give up or walk miles to a bridge, thus losing precious time. Some also believe that if a snakebitten person sees a pregnant woman, he will die regardless of help.

Snakes Needed. As he dispels these myths and counsels them on snakebite treatment, the major also tells the campesinos that he needs

snakes for research, that his organization is willing to pay for them. In the depressed pueblo of Penshurst over 1,000 snakes were caught last year. The $3,000 paid for the snakes represented a lot of money which supported many families.

"Helping these people is a vital job that must be done," MAJ Flowers states, "and handling snakes is just a part of it. It is not even dangerous if you know what you're doing."

The doctor adds that he "is not in love with snakes or is not some kind of weirdo snake-charmer." He does respect snakes though, because one wrong or slow move could be disastrous. After handling several thousand snakes, he has been bitten only once, by a cobra. "Only once is one too many," he says. "In this business, Zero Defects really counts."

Production of the serum has now entered the clinical evaluation stage. The first 1,000 ampules have been distributed. Producing the antitoxin is an elaborate process requiring the cooperation and resources of many. It is made from the venom of fer de lance, bushmaster and rattlesnake families.

The Major extracts the venom from what he believes is the world's largest collection of bushmasters, the biggest venomous snake in the Western Hemisphere.

Serum Made. The collected venom is then injected in horses in the

Among the Costa Rican Indian population in the Talamanca Mountains and beyond, he's saved many lives, winning support, and admiration. Many times, he's flown by small plane to remote villages to treat snakebite victims.

At a ceremony planned for the 13th, Major Flowers is to receive top awards from the US and Costa Rica. For the occasion, he'll deliver a bilingual address. His command of Spanish, despite lessons, remains limited. A neighbor, retired Santa Rosa schoolteacher Corina Rodríguez López, taught him what he knows. She's older, with the patience needed for a reluctant student. He's nervous over the speech, more so than his other remaining duties.

With a day of intensive training, I settle into a routine as a lab assistant, and maintain the snake colony while the major concentrates on his speech and administrative duties.

To the mission's ceremonial hand-over, Major Flowers wears his dress uniform with gold oak leaf. With clean jeans and shirt, my best clothes, I feel out of place. The auditorium of the College of Physicians and Surgeons brims with US Army officials, Costa Rican dignitaries, doctors, professors, and the public. The major receives the US Legion of Merit Award, presented with medal, ribbon and certificate by four-star general Robert W. Porter Jr., Commander-in-Chief of the US Southern Command. They present this award for "Exceptionally Meritorious Conduct in the Performance of Outstanding Services and Achievements." The major earned his for service to the US military and the people of Costa Rica.

On behalf of the people and government of Costa Rica, Doctor Alvaro Aguilar Peralta, Minister of Public Health, presents the Certificate of Commendation, his country's highest civilian honor.

The major delivers an impassioned address in English. [Copied below from the major's notes, contributed by the Flowers family.] In it, he expounds on his life in Costa Rica and his fondness for the people. He outlines his work, and the cooperation between UCR and the US Army.

Major Flowers in a Speech: How Costa Rica Rallied for Antiserum

Mr. Minister, General and Mrs. Porter, Friends, and Colleagues:
At a time like this, words are inadequate to describe one's emotions and feeling of gratitude.

I thank you Mr. Minister and you, General Porter from the bottom of my heart for the very great tributes you both have bestowed upon me this morning. I accept them with humility, but I do not accept them entirely for myself. Our success in the antiserum program is due to the combined efforts of many Costa Ricans and Americans. We have received assistance from all classes of people. The Clachar family has donated all the horses needed for this program, campesinos unwilling to accept pay have donated snakes, throughout the country other dedicated persons without compensation have established snake collection centers so vital to this program. The Minister and my fellow colleagues have worked tirelessly to achieve this success. Therefore, I am able to accept this honor only in the same spirit of togetherness which has been the keystone in the success of this vital program.

Let me remind you this morning that the first objective of this program is to place throughout Costa Rica sufficient quantity of antiserum to where there will be no one more than two hours away from adequate treatment. This antiserum is to be placed there free of charge. This antiserum is now in all parts of Costa Rica. Thousands of people who never before had this security now realize that snakebite death is a thing of the past. Clinical results have demonstrated this fact, where in the past an estimated 10% of all victims that entered the hospital died, and others who were bitten lost limbs, none have died that have been treated early with the Costa Rican antiserum. Three years ago, a coral snake bite meant sure death. Today there are no deaths. This antiserum which was the second ever produced is a typical result of the cooperation realized in this program. Doña Lolita Clachar donated the horses that were used, Costa Rican collected coral snakes, my colleagues produced the serum and Costa Ricans reaped the benefits. In two years, there have been no deaths. In my opinion there will be no more.

The employees of this program have always agreed with me that this is a program of Costa Ricans for Costa Ricans. I appreciate the fact that they have let me become a part of it.

I thank all of you for honoring me by coming here this morning, and I can assure you if God wills that I return from Vietnam, I will return to Costa Rica. And to my colleagues, may God continue to bless and strengthen your dedication in providing all people with this life saving antiserum.

Then he repeats his speech in Spanish. Sra. Rodríguez, his elderly language tutor, sits in the front row, beaming with pride, cheeks wet with tears. When the applause fades, he motions her to the stage then stands behind her while she makes a speech on his behalf, saying the things that he cannot, speaking to the

Major Flowers receives Legion of Merit Award from four-star
general Robert W. Porter Jr. (Photo: Col. Herschel H. Flowers family archives)

Señora Rodríquez prepares to deliver statement on the major's behalf at the
dignitary-studded award ceremony.
(Photo: Col. Herschel H. Flowers family archives)

The President of the United States of America, authorized by Act of Congress, July 20, 1942, has awarded the Legion of Merit to

MAJOR HERSCHEL H. FLOWERS, UNITED STATES ARMY

for exceptionally meritorious conduct in the performance of outstanding services

Major Herschel H. Flowers, Veterinary Corps, distinguished himself by outstanding meritorious service from November 1964 to June 1968. During this period, in conjunction with his Costa Rican counterparts, Major Flowers helped develop highly effective anti-serums against the severely toxic poisons of the most venomous snakes of Central and South America. Through the use of these anti-serums many lives are now being saved which would have been previously lost. Incapacitating after-effects of poisonous snake bite have also been greatly reduced by use of the anti-serums. In addition to his medical research and development work, Major Flowers was always mindful of the needs of the local community and, within his capability, provided medical assistance to those in need. He played a major role in initiating other civic action projects in Costa Rica, notably a highly successful community development project with the Talamanca Indian Tribe of Eastern Costa Rica. By his persistence, tact, enthusiasm and many other commendable professional and personal attributes, Major Flowers exemplified the finest traditions of the military service and his accomplishments have greatly enhanced the image of the United States Government, the United States Army, and the United States Army Medical Department. His cooperation and work with members of the Costa Rican professional community and his fine rapport with the citizens of Costa Rica have been an outstanding example of international exchange and understanding and have helped strengthen the already close bonds of friendship between the United States and Costa Rica.

Copy of Major Herschel H. Flowers Legion of Merit Award.
(Photo: Col. Herschel H. Flowers family archives)

people of Costa Rica on whom the gravity of this moment is not lost. [Corina Rodríguez López's speech contributed by the Flowers family.]

Lopez: How Major Flowers Waged War Against Poisonous Snakes

Major Herschel Flowers came to my little school to study Spanish. He entered my home like the sun enters a poor room and gilds it on the inside.

He came in a dress uniform and since he is so tall and has the martial bearing of an officer and the grace of a gentleman, next to him I felt very small.

It was neither the uniform, nor his stature, nor his panache that impressed me; but the magnetic current that was established between my mind and his.

We began to chat in my modest classroom, which he illuminated with his presence, and soon after he told me: "You are going to be my mother in Costa Rica."

The vowels of the word mama came out of his mouth like distant and sad music: like the evocation of his absent mother to whom he pays homage.

I soon learned that then Captain and now Major Herschel Flowers was coming on a sacred mission.

He came to my blue and upright mountains to wage a war to the death against the poisonous snakes that swarm in the undergrowth and destroy the lives of our peasants. He came to develop a program of anti-snakebite serums.

And the fact is that he has carried out his work with resounding success, and today no one dies in Costa Rica from a snake bite, except for negligence.

The Major combed the mountains of Costa Rica. His small plane, carried and brought by the storms, furrowed the national sky, even at the risk of his life.

His high boots forded the rivers and in the most remote places left footprints in the valleys that he crossed.

The inclement rain swept away the boot prints. The clouds erased the plane's trail, and the wind carried the echo of his voice across the cliffs and crags; but the traces that his strong and generous hands left on the soul of the Costa Rican people will not be erased even by death.

Captain Flowers, now a major in the US Army, will go down in history as a benefactor of Costa Rica, even as he goes to Vietnam to carry out the orders of his army.

The children he saved will raise their prayers to heaven so that God will keep and protect him, and the prayers of their mothers will build an impregnable wall to stop the bullets.

The peasants, when depositing their seeds in the black bowels of Earth, will think of him. The farmers, when opening the furrow, will remember him. The axmen when cutting down the trees, will evoke his handsome and gallant figure.

The Minister of Public Health of Costa Rica, Dr. Alvaro Aguilar Peralta and General Robert W. Porter, Commander-in-Chief of the Armed Forces of the United States Southern Command, did well by decorating Major Flowers in a joint ceremony to recognize the merits of a man of science and a military officer. May God make you more worthy each day of the high positions you hold.

Costa Rica has known, throughout its length and breadth, the work of the Major in his laboratory: on the football field of Santa Rosa de Santo Domingo, in the school of this town and, in Talamanca where he lived with workers.

Major Herschel Flowers lived with and for the humble. He sat at their table and shared with them joys and sorrows.

He knows that without workers no country can have an army. He knows that strength comes from below and that, if the column formed by the peasants falls, the social architecture will inevitably collapse.

The Major will leave soon for Vietnam, leaving an immense void in our country, our true affection and, upon his return, we will all be at the airport to give him a welcoming embrace and never let him go.

— *Corina Rodríguez López*

I struggle to understand her words in my limited grasp of Spanish, but the emotions come through loud and clear. I bite my lower lip to distract, but when I glance around me, not a dry eye can be found. Who is this man of whom she speaks so lovingly? How has he earned such devotion? I witness the close of a glorious chapter. For now, the major remains in charge.

CHAPTER 52:
An Extracting Business

How often snakes can be milked varies widely with many factors, including size, species, and health. Daily we milk those that are ready. "Milking" is a colloquial term for the simple but dangerous procedure of extracting venom. Selected snakes we remove in sequence by species to a holding pen. The handler pins the snake's head with a special stick, using due care to minimize the risk of injury—to the snake! The sticks or "hooks" vary in size and shape and are custom-made to suit.

With the snake immobilized, he grips the sides of the neck close behind the jaws, index finger atop the head. An assistant may hold the body of larger specimens. If working solo, tucking it under his arm for support keeps them calm, protecting valuable snakes from trauma.

To extract toxins, we use a tapered beaker, separate vessels for different species, with a latex membrane stretched over the top. With a gentle touch to its mouth, the snake bites, fangs extended, expelling venom. Sometimes massaging cheek glands increases output, though it risks injury. The major does most of the milking. He's training me. It requires concentration, though is not as difficult as it might sound.

Each snake gets inspected for health issues. While out, I clean and disinfect cages, fill water dishes, and note dates and accession numbers in a logbook. It's efficient, and we can process 10 to 20 snakes in an hour.

Work is in near silence, each concentrating on the task at hand, avoiding distractions.

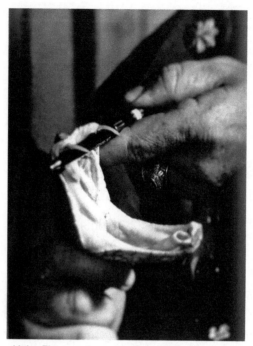

Major Flowers shows fangs of a large Terciopelo.
(Photo: Col. Herschel H. Flowers family archives)

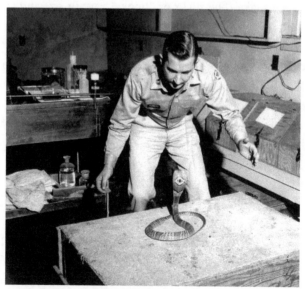

In 1963 (then Captain) Flowers prepares to capture a cobra
in his Ft. Knox, Kentucky lab.
(Photo: Col. Herschel H. Flowers family archives)

We transfer collected venom, one species per, to refrigerated ampoules, which we deliver to the University of Costa Rica (UCR) School of Medicine lab for processing. The total extractions it takes to produce a gram of refined, freeze-dried venom varies. Terciopelos and other large pit vipers yield the greatest volume. Corals could take dozens of extractions to make a single gram.

Outside of Santa Rosa, the major keeps what is no doubt the healthiest herd of horses in the country. Fifteen animals, donated by the Clachar family. The major is a horse lover and gentle handler. The horses enjoy his visits and gallop to the corral when we arrive. He brings treats, and each gets a health inspection on every visit. Blood samples sent to the laboratory for dilution tests keep track of their level of antibodies.

To maintain a high titer, during my visit, eight horses receive injections of tiny amounts of haemotoxic pit-viper venom. Two others only receive neurotoxic coral snake venom. Done at regular intervals, it stimulates antibody production. Calculated to avoid harm or discomfort, he injects a blend of several venoms. Each with unique characteristics, the aim is to develop a polyvalent antiserum. This affords protection from a wide variety of crotalid snakes. Critical when the exact species causing envenomation is unknown.

On schedule, we draw blood for the actual manufacture of the antivenom. We use sterilized and sealed five-gallon glass jugs containing stabilizing agents. The equines do not mind the extraction and eat sweet feed from a bucket during the phlebotomy. The volume taken varies based on the horse's weight and other factors. Well-loved, our horses give more than typical, because of their excellent physical condition.

We take the blood on ice without delay to the laboratory. Technicians separate the antibodies to generate antiserum. The horses save hundreds of lives.

CHAPTER 53:
The End of My Rope

My first week in Costa Rica flies. Post ceremonies, things return to a version of normal, work is nonstop, no field collecting yet. Today, while the major tends the horses, I'll search a ravine behind the farm. Steep, 100-foot walls cloaked in trees and vines tower over a hidden river. A ledge 25 feet below looks perfect for snakes. I'll rappel to it, should be easy.

A rope, fetched from the horse barn, tied to a tree, tossed over the cliff, disappears into dense vegetation. Looped to form a sling for support, I lower myself over the precipice. Dangling above the chasm, I panic.

This isn't working. I hang on for dear life. The stable is too far for anyone to see me. No one knows where I am or is concerned. I'm on my own.

Lineman's work climbing poles gave me muscular arms and helps in coping with heights and daunting situations. This sure qualifies. After a minute, I laugh. I'm five feet over the edge. I'll climb up. I have no choice.

I take a vice-like grip, let the tether slip from around my hips, and dangle, arms supporting my body. Pressed against the rocky bluff, I pull with all my strength, reach over the top. My boots scrape for a toehold, knocking small stones loose as I scramble to haul myself upward. I draw a deep breath, heave until I can swing a leg over the rim. With a final good grasp and tug, I roll to safety.

I collapse against the tree, whisper a prayer of thanks. Lucky, foolish, I coil the cord, walk to the barn. Blood stains my shirt from scratches on my arms and chest. The major sees me. "What happened? You take a spill?"

"Yeah."

CHAPTER 54:
Collecting Stations

S kills polished by daily handling of venomous snakes earn the major's confidence. His techniques differ from what I knew. For one, free handing select species without a stick. Tropical Rattlesnakes, *Crotalus durissus durissus*, and Bushmasters, *Lachesis muta stenophrys*, he claims, act threatening, but are timid, seldom bite. With thousands handled, he's learned their characteristics. In his presence, I try, but I'm not comfortable taking the risk.

Road trip! Music to my ears. We load a stack of empty snake boxes and leave to visit established collecting stations, starting in Guanacaste Province. Most are near farms, coffee plantations, and forestry activities.

Dry forest dominates Costa Rica's northwest. A feature is *Enterolobium cyclocarpum* the massive Guanacaste trees. Quarter-acre canopies give shade for cattle. Choice habitat for Tropical Rattlesnakes also known as Cascabel. Campesinos have no irrational fear of snakes, surprising considering the frequency of bites, and catch them without harm. Such collections are essential to the antiserum program.

Our first stop is in Liberia, where a man maintains a network of snake collectors. He gathers what the farm hands collect, keeping them in heavy wooden boxes. Major Flowers opens one. Several large Cascabels come to attention, rattling inside cloth sacks. A second takes my breath when opened. Two Bushmasters, a four-footer and another over six feet. Lively, fresh-caught specimens, the largest, deadliest New World serpent. We load them and leave empty cases.

In 1968, traditional ox carts could still be seen
on Costa Rica's mountain roads.

Cloud forest shrouded mountains along Cost Rica's Cordillera Central.

The author holding a large Bushmaster, in the Santa Rosa villa garden,
collected in N.W. Costa Rica, July 1968.

Snake collecting stations work as branches of the laboratory. Workers who run the stations and most collectors are volunteers and refuse compensation. A minority of people bringing snakes get paid cash, every accession, paid or not, gets logged. They ship the dangerous venomous snakes in strong crates to San José by bus or train. Guillermo brings them to the compound in Santa Rosa. It's an efficient setup. The major likes to visit field operations unannounced, to assure they uphold standards.

We leave for the Nicoya Peninsula through dry country with ranches, cowboys, and cattle. Near the coast is mountain wilderness with Capuchin Monkeys, peccaries, Coatis, and parrots. I'm in awe. In the fishing village of Potrero, we take a late lunch with a stunning view of the Pacific Ocean. We have *ceviche*. It's fresh-caught, raw marlin marinated with lime, cilantro, tomato, chilies, and onion. My first, I love it! The main dish is tasty fried corvina with plantains and rice. An outstanding meal enjoyed to a spectacular sunset.

"I've seen Yellow-bellied Sea Snakes here. *Pelamis platurus* sometimes washes up on the beach." I'd love to see one, the only sea snake found in the Western Hemisphere.

Our splendid day continues. Turning towards Liberia, we find a six-foot boa, and many Cat-eyed Snakes. I keep several neonate Cascabels small for the lab but perfect for me. Surprise of the evening is *Bothrops ophryomegas*. A species, the size and pattern of a Pygmy Rattlesnake needed for the antivenom program. We collect four more within a few miles.

We stay at a tiny hotel and get started at dawn. The Iglesia Inmaculada Concepción de María is new. Massive and unusual, white painted, its modern design looks out of place in Latin America.

With no time to waste, we head east to a cattle ranch near Arenal. One box with a few large rattlesnakes awaits. In the nearby town of Tabacón, we pick up a case of Cascabels, and another with several robust Terciopelos. Volcán Arenal looms close, a giant pyramid on the horizon, an ominous, smoking sentinel. Next stop is Fortuna, at a police-run collecting station.

Jewels come to mind when we open the first snake box. *Bothrops schlegelii*, mossy green with reddish spots to solid brick red and vivid lemon yellow. The local name is *Vibora de Pestañas*, Eyelash Viper. Their supraocular scales resemble eyelashes. Small, stout, arboreal, this species is the one most often encountered by coffee pickers. Despite being timid and reluctant to bite, many pickers are bitten, by them, most often on their fingers.

Another box holds a batch of Terciopelos. The last one has thick-bodied, 14-inch, velvety-looking snakes with colors of dark and light chocolate. A russet dorsal stripe, and large, triangular heads, with an upturned snouts. *Bothrops nasuta,* the Hog-nosed Viper.

We invite the police chief to dinner and stay the night at a hotel the major knows. The trip home, along the Cordillera Central, passes volcanic peaks: Cerro Chato, Cerro Congo, Volcán Poas, Volcán Barva, and Volcán Irazú. Horses and colorful oxcarts share the mountain road. Verdant cloud forest, trees laden with epiphytes, waterfalls, brilliant butterflies. The *neblina* cool on our skin, the scent of virgin jungle, fresh. Costa Rica is a paradise.

∽

At the lab, we catalog the snakes from the trip. What a collection! How I wish they were going home with me. Few herpetologists have had such a privilege. A photo of me in the garden holding the huge Bushmaster becomes a treasured memento. A snake of legend. Raymond L. Ditmars once gifted a Bushmaster's fang to President Theodore Roosevelt, for his son Archie, after his visit to the Bronx Zoo in 1911. "By George! That Bushmaster must have been a big snake," Roosevelt commented in his letter of thanks to Ditmars. Indeed, they are.

Despite our TLC, venom harvesting exacts a toll on a snake's health. Many species are hard to get, so keeping them alive and healthy is important. We care for our charges to the best of our ability. Shipments of mice from UCR are food for the stock. We're vigilant. Mice often kill or injure passive snakes. Most eat with gusto and take dead rodents, limiting danger. Force-feeding is done routinely with valued specimens which resist eating. Not something we relish. Difficult and dangerous for us and the snakes.

When animals perish, we record losses. Most we preserve for later educational use. Our preferred method is to freeze them for university students to process. We keep the heads of a few larger species, preserving them in formalin. Though important, it's my least favorite part of the job.

"Do you ever release any of the snakes if their health declines?" Weak snakes produce little.

"We do, but we don't mention it. Not a popular idea."

He admits to releasing failing snakes, rare ones mostly, in hopes they'll survive in natural areas far from people. I respect that.

CHAPTER 55:
Volcano

The major feels the pressure. His control of the antivenin initiative is ending, but much work remains. Monumental tasks only he can do. Create training manuals for the Costa Rican team for snake colony upkeep and details for venom extraction. Outline every aspect of the horse farm's operating procedures and maintenance. Finish logbooks and audit records.

We leave for the major's retreat. A Swiss-style chalet high in the Talamanca Mountains near Copey. We drive south on a rocky road, far into the mountain cloud forest, a wooded property with a spectacular vista of mountain peaks and valleys to the east. He plans to retire here and comes up to escape. Now he seeks solitude to work on his special projects.

A stream in the front yard has Rainbow Trout, long ago introduced to Costa Rica. Active year-round, they grow to a massive size. Enamored of the brook, he wanted a pond for fishing and swimming, despite the chilly water. On the slope below his house, he constructed a 10-foot-high earthen dike, to form a quarter-acre reservoir. The dam failed when it filled, resulting in flood damage to his neighbor's land. He smoothed over the relationship and rebuilt a version reinforced with steel and concrete.

It's an idyllic workplace. No close neighbors, zero traffic. An evening fire against the chill mountain air. In the serenity, he shows incredible determination. I help by merging notebooks from the various collecting posts to a ledger sheet. Fascinating. I can't believe the number of specimens generated over the past few years! Many species I have not yet seen.

Misty jungles near the major's Talamanca Mountains retreat outside of Copey.

Volcán Arenal, active since July 1968.

While the major works on his guidebooks and monolog, I explore the bush. Few snakes, many frogs, and colorful birds. A splendid place. I see why he loves it so. We grill out with meat, plenty of fresh vegetables, and a good supply of beer. Spring water for me.

Monday, July 29, 10 days after visiting the collecting stations, the phone rings. I continue working until the major calls out. "Volcán Arenal has erupted."

"Wow, we were there last week!"

He's not concerned. "When I first came here in 1964, Volcán Irazú was in eruption, and it ejected ash a foot thick. Black snow. It was a mess. I doubt this eruption is as bad."

Tuesday, back in Santa Rosa, we learn how deadly the eruption was. Arenal and Tabacón towns were devastated by lava. Pyroclastic flows rained death. Ninety-two people perish. A terrible human toll and a national tragedy that remains front-page news for weeks.

Urgent inquires go out to the stations in the Northwest. Days later, he hears from the ranch near Arenal. Not destroyed, but it won't be operational for a long while. The volcano wiped Tabacón out. It cripples facilities in nearby towns, a colossal blow to the mission.

The region is in complete turmoil. A return to normal will be generational. When the antivenom program changes hands, managing these indispensable stations passes to a fresh team. Timing couldn't be worse.

CHAPTER 56:
Panama

Two weeks of program transfer meetings at UCR have the major in a funk, drinking more. The major carries a heavy burden. Preparing to leave Costa Rica for his next assignment, he has many personal issues to attend to. Along with completing the program transfer, he has much on his mind. Extraction lab operations fall to me and Guillermo. I've grown proficient in handling the snakes. He's confident in my ability to take care of the entire regimen. Each evening he checks our work, the venoms, the records, the specimens, and drafts orders for the following day. I know I'm needed and consider it an honor to be of help.

I care for specimens, extract venom, aid in attending the horse herd. We receive and inventory shipments from collecting stations in distant parts of the country. Not work, it's a privilege. A dream come true. How great doing something of value involving reptiles. It took Major Flowers many years of study and dedicated research to achieve his position. I respect him for his accomplishments and for the man he is. Apart from his formal training and military discipline, he's a regular guy who lives a life I admire.

Word the major is a trained veterinarian got out after his arrival. It wasn't long before village folks came with sick dogs, cats, and parrots. A good neighbor, he accommodates. Odds are Santa Rosa's pets are the healthiest in Costa Rica. He has none of his own.

⌒

With the pending handover, visiting collecting stations has fallen by the wayside. The Península de Osa, San Vito, Sarapiqui and a dozen more in regions with diverse terrain and different snake species. I don't complain, but he understands my frustration. Unbeknownst to me, he arranges an expedition I will remember for a lifetime. Over dinner prepared by Maria, he lays out his plan.

"A Morsink family friend owns a banana plantation in Limón Province, in an unbroken tract of lowland tropical forest that stretches from Colombia to Guatemala along the Caribbean coast." My hair stands on end. "I'll take you to Turrialba, and we'll meet the police captain who runs the collecting site. Jenny and Bert will join you, and go by train to Limón, before heading south to Vesta."

Jennifer, 17, and Bernard, 13, are the younger sister and brother of his fiancée, Corinne. I'm beyond excited. "I don't know what to say. Thank you, this will be outstanding!"

At every opportunity, the major visits snakebite victims in hospitals, field clinics, or morgues. He aids in treatment, studies symptoms and effects of venomous bites and therapies. The first week of August, days before the Limón trip, he receives a call. "There's a coral snake victim in the Canal Zone. They need my help. Want to come?"

"To Panama? Sure!"

No time to lose. The major packs several vials of anti-coral serum on ice. We grab an overnight bag and head to SJO where an olive drab US military C-47 awaits. The flight's an hour and a half to Howard Air Force Base. We race through Panama City to Fort Clayton, United States Southern Command headquarters. Four-star General Robert W. Porter Jr., Commander-in-Chief of the USSC, meets us. The brief first meeting is with full protocol. After that, they drop any semblance of formality. To my surprise, the general remembers me from the Legion of Merit ceremony and shakes my hand.

The unfortunate snakebite victim dies before we arrive. The snake that killed her, cut into pieces in a pail, is *Micrurus nigrocinctus*. At four feet, the largest of the corals and deadly. The major observes the autopsy, I decline the invitation. It takes several hours. Meanwhile, I have free rein and wander at will.

Rudyard Kipling could not have imagined a more tropical setting or buildings of a more fitting style for a military base. Building 95 Quadrangle with three-storied headquarters and barracks, built in the 1930s, has red-tiled roofs and generous overhangs. Palms sway, surrounding the well-maintained grass parade ground.

In the verdant, wet Pacific lowlands, lizards abound, as do birds not seen in Costa Rica's mountains. To escape the heat, I find the library. An aid to the general offers a tour of the Panama Canal's Miraflores Locks. I jump at the chance. Nearby, the trip is fun and interesting. My first impression is how narrow they are. A ship making passage has only inches of space on either side.

When finished at the hospital, we retire to guest quarters. In the evening we dine with General Porter. Theirs is a personal and cordial relationship. Top brass enjoy trout fishing at the major's chalet in the Talamanca Mountains. On this trip, I gain enormous respect for the major. The Army considers his work crucial. He holds special autonomy. They afford full support within the capacity of the Army to help his project.

We breakfast in the officers' mess. "Let's go to the firing range. I need to stay qualified while we're here."

They allow me to fire an M16 automatic rifle. It's exciting, but stirs feelings of guilt for not serving, though not by choice. Aside from General Porter at dinner, no one inquires about my military service. A tender subject.

"Do you wish to call home?" My jaw drops. Embarrassed, I have not given it a thought. "If so, we can phone for free."

"I guess. I mean, sure, thanks." At headquarters across the green, I pencil my number on a slip of paper. In a few moments, I hear: "Mr. Cathcart, go to booth three."

I step in, pick up the receiver. My wife is on the line. A month since I left, I struggle to find words. "Hey, how are you? I'm in Panama."

"Panama? What are you doing there?"

"Long story. We're on our way back to Costa Rica. Are you okay? I've missed you."

"Everything is fine. I miss you, too. When are you coming home?"

"A few more weeks. Been working hard on the program. It's amazing here. Any news on the house?"

"They were to pour the foundation last week, but we've had lots of rain."

A loud click. "Hello? Hello?" The call cuts off. We both know things are okay. Glad I called. I wish it were my idea. I suppose I've been in a place where nothing else exists.

CHAPTER 57:
Turrialba

Sunday, we prepare for the Limón trip. I feel guilty leaving with so much work to do. The major reassures me. "You'll just be in my way. Only kidding. Don't worry, I have things to do in town. Guillermo can handle the lab."

A borrowed rucksack holds clothes, sacks, flashlight, and personal items. "You shouldn't need much, you'll be staying with friends." With my snake stick, I'm ready. Monday morning, August 5, we head out.

We're bound for the wet eastern slopes of the Cordillera Central, or central volcanic belt. Descending on a ribbon of asphalt and gravel hung tenuously on dizzying cliffs, we race through foggy, deep canyons above dramatic white-water rapids of the Río Reventazón. White-knuckled, stomach-churning switchbacks, swerving on wet pavement around boulders from frequent landslides. I see bromeliads, orchids, aroids. As the altitude decreases, *Rhipsalis* cactus hangs in cascades. Bizarre window-leaved *Monstera friedrichsthalii* grows in profusion. Graceful palms thrust through the forest canopy. *Cecropia* trees flash silver.

We reach the police post outside of Turrialba. "Dennis, meet Captain Rojas. We call him El Capitán."

The chief is enormous. His thick black mustache hangs to his square jaw. Bushy eyebrows shade his dark eyes, peering from meaty slits. His broad-shouldered, narrow-waisted build, that of a wrestler, brings instant trepidation. His craggy features and tanned skin speak of many years of working outdoors. He shakes my hand with a bone-crunching grip. "*Bienvenidos.*"

Despite his hard exterior, his demeanor is pleasant, not what I expected. He doesn't speak English nor I much more than a few words of Spanish. Our bond is the snakes.

In the station, padlocked snake boxes line a wall. The major lifts the first lid with his stick. Hairs on my arms bristle. Terciopelos! Two big ones, not in sacks. They make a run for it, sliding onto the precinct floor. This species kills more Costa Ricans than any other. Large, aggressive, vital for the antivenom project. We wrangle them back into the box.

A second holds several Eyelash Vipers, the lovely common color phase resembling moss and lichens. It's their camouflage that leads to so many bites among coffee pickers. Another sizable, thick-bodied snake I don't recognize. "*Bothrops picadoi*," Major Flowers explains, "you're seeing a rare species here. At most, we get a few each year."

Its short, stocky build reminds me of a Cottonmouth. Coarse, prominent scales have a dark chocolate zigzag dorsal pattern over lighter brown. Its massive head is as big as my fist. Similar specimens in another box are *Bothrops numifera*, Costa Ricans call them "*Mano de Piedra*" or Fist of Stone. Much feared, ill-tempered with a dangerous bite. Thick-bodied, shorter than the related *picadoi*, but no less deadly.

There's a case with a few handsome *Bothrops nasuta*, Hog-nosed Vipers, and two small, delicate snakes new to me. They are vivid green with coarse black speckled scales, heads oversized for their slender bodies. "*Bothrops nigroviridis*. We don't see these often." The major's voice belies his delight.

A last box has *Micrurus nigrocinctus*, one in each sack. The largest of the coral snakes, reaching four feet, is cannibalistic. This is the species that killed the woman in Panama. Assets to the program, producing a high volume of venom that will save lives.

After tallying and logging the specimens, we ride in Capitán Rojas' pickup to a restaurant for traditional *Gallo Pinto*, a rice and beans dish with *churrasco*, a thin steak. Simple and delicious. El Capitán outlines plans to take me into the mountains tomorrow, at the behest of the major. I can't wait to get into the jungle. An hour before dark, we drive a dirt road to a mountain stream for an evening of hunting.

We carry flashlights, collecting sacks and sticks. El Capitán has a pair of sturdy tongs. They're homemade, from a piece of pipe fitted with a trigger grip and jaws to pick up most venomous snakes without risk or harm.

Above the gurgle and splash of the creek, I hear: "Dennis, here's something for you."

An 18-inch snake with black alternating bands lies at the water's edge. When picked up, it flattens its neck and inflates its body. The skin between the scales shows through red—it looks as if it's glowing. The amazing color change startles predators.

"Oh my gosh, a *Leimadophis taeniurus juvenalis*." My first. Rare in captivity, I pop it into a sack. We find others near the water, right where we should expect these frog eaters.

"Locals call it *Serpiente de Fuego*." Fire Snake.

Capitán Rojas calls out. An Elephant Beetle, *Megasoma elephas*, fills his hand. It has tan elytra or wing covers and a long, stout, forked black horn. A spectacular highlight of the trip. He sets it back on a rotted log.

We pass a scruffy-looking, skinny boa constrictor, then find a Terciopelo. The young, three-footer may grow to over six feet. Velvety, with a cryptic pattern in shades of cream and brown. Spaniards called them "*Barba Amarilla*," Yellow Beard, for the yellowish sides of their head and lower jaw. It tenses up, pulling its body into kinks. The major collects it for the lab, bags it and hands it to me. "Don't let it bump your legs." He needn't worry.

A downpour cuts the trip short. We return to the precinct. A room has cots we can use. After rain stops, noisy cries of "Chack, Chack, Chack" lead me to Red-eyed Treefrogs, calling from a branch. *Agalychnis callidryas,* three inches, skinny, green with blue thighs and orange hands and feet. Their bulging red eyes are fantastic. Tadpoles form in eggs laid on leaf undersides, falling into the water when they hatch. A delightful end to a great evening.

CHAPTER 58:

Swallowed by the Forest

The major departs to San José at sunrise with the boxes of snakes. Tomorrow, I'll meet Jenny and Bert at the train station for the trip to Limón. Today El Capitán is taking me snake hunting. I'm nervous about communication, or lack of it.

Tires hum on the rough roadway, winding upward through the magnificent rainforest. My head on a swivel, trying to miss nothing. Windows open, I hear parrots, see a kaleidoscope of butterflies, feel the sun's heat and cool mountain mist. The scent of wet forest stirs my blood. The mean altitude is 2,000 feet, warm, humid, with frequent rains. East 15 miles, the cone of stratovolcano Turrialba soars 11,000 feet into the clouds. We spot something. El Capitán stops, I jump out. A Hoffmann's Two-toed Sloth, *Choloepus hoffmanni*, the larger, rarer of two Costa Rican species. Unusual finding one on the ground. These creatures can't walk, must crawl along on their bellies with legs splayed.

"*Es un Perezoso.*" Its colloquial name, meaning lazy.

I lift it by the scruff of the neck. The captain snaps a photo. One angry, unhappy critter. It struggles, emitting a startling high-pitched, shrieking moan. I set him free, safe, off the roadside. An unexpected, exciting find.

We drive on to a pull-off and leave the truck. It has a police insignia, so no theft worries! The captain calls on the radio before we go. I'm guessing to let them know where he is. With sacks, our sticks, and machetes, we climb uphill on a narrow trail.

We abandon the path, descend into a *quebrada* (a ravine) among forest giants. *Ceiba pentandra*, trees with blade-like buttresses, forming sinuous, wood-walled canyons where Bushmasters lurk. A quick search, digging in leaf litter with my hook, finds none, only an *Imantodes cenchoa*, Blunt-headed Tree Snake. Cryptic, its blotched brown and white pattern blends with dried leaves. Pencil slender, 30 inches, with an oversized head and eyes. Though rear-fanged, their mild venom is harmless to humans. It also occurs in Mexico, but this is my first find of this delightful species. In another chamber formed by the roots, an angry tarantula appears.

In primary forest never cut or altered, we slip and slide descending the slope. The captain, behind me, clears his throat for attention. "*Amigo, mira. Cuidado, esta palma es peligrosa.* Be careful, this palm is dangerous."

He points to a slender *Bactris* palm with long, black, needle-sharp spines covering its trunk. Then he points to my machete, wagging his finger. The message plain. "Don't hack this." I suppose it might send a spine fragment into my eyes. Friendly advice. He has warned me not to cut *Dieffenbachia* as the sap may damage eyesight.

Despite traveling to Mexico and Haiti, I have more to learn about jungles. Unnecessary hacking at things gets on El Capitán's nerves. Nodding my understanding, I take a step and slip. Out of reflex, I grab the barbed palm. The spikes impale my fingers with searing pain. The captain shakes his head. His eyes say, "What an idiot."

Author holding sloth he rescued crossing road in mountains of Turrialba.

Bactris palm with dangerous spines.
Bromeliad growing on trunk is *Racinaea venusta*.

⌒

While I pull out needles, El Capitán investigates a rocky outcrop. I lose sight, continue downslope. There's no trail, the forest is open, leaves ankle-deep. An enormous tree lays fallen, upslope, canopy full of dying bromeliads and orchids abruptly robbed of sunlight. I step towards its base to climb the angled trunk.

Without warning, I disappear into a hole. Well below the surface, I land on my butt in a dark, creepy place. Sheer terror! I try to stand but can't. I can't see out, can't see light. It's as if the ground swallowed, then sealed itself over me.

Sand and leaves in my hair, down my shirt and pants. I hunker in the Stygian gloom, my thoughts jumbled, heart racing.

Darkness is complete, it's dank, musty. The silence is deafening. I can't sit up with the low ceiling. Disoriented, I fight panic, dread. Then, a thin crack of dim light. Driven without thinking, I crawl on my hands and knees, pushing through unseen dangling roots. Ten feet, 15 feet, not sure. Then I squeeze, claw through moist soil, tangled roots, and leaves out the narrow opening. Choked, blinded, I struggle to escape from the cave or wherever I am. I scramble out, jump to my feet, gasping quick breaths, strip off my debris-filled shirt, wipe my eyes, my face, spit dirt.

What the hell? I back off to take stock. When the giant tree toppled, its huge flat root system lifted, creating a cavernous space beneath. It formed a false floor in the forest. Lucky me to fall through. I have the machete, but not my snake hook. I go around to the top. It's amazing. Nothing looks amiss. It swallowed me and sealed up, leaving no more trace than a nail pulled out of a tire. My collecting stick lies beside a slight depression. Stepping tentatively I retrieve it, climb off and step away, trying to make sense of what happened. It gives me the willies thinking of what may have been in there, unseen in the damp dimness. Without that crack of light? I shudder to think.

⌇

El Capitán, well downslope, misses the drama. No way I can explain. A sudden movement, reveals a Great Curassow, *Crax rubra*. Pheasant-sized, brown, with a black neck and tail, and a feathery crest, as it fades into the undergrowth.

At the bottom of the *quebrada*, a stream tumbles between banks of ferns. It's steep, rocky, rushing—more of an extended waterfall. In the deep shade, exposed rocks grow cushions of mosses. *Heliconius* butterflies hover. A serene and idyllic spot. I wade in to wash.

"*Hay muchos Terciopelos aquí.*" El Capitán, animated, parts the vegetation. I cross to the other side. He whispers, "Dennis, *ven aca*. Come here."

Snakes are deaf. I chuckle under my breath. Between the foliage lies a small Terciopelo in a neat coil. He looks at me, smiling with excitement. With his tongs, he picks the snake up and drops it in an open sack I'm holding. We find two more while following the stream to a spot where it disappears into a culvert. We clamber up the steep embankment to the roadside.

"Dennis, Dennis, *mira, mira.*" I run, and he's looking skyward, pointing. A brilliant emerald bird flies the gap between trees over the roadway. "*Quetzal.*"

A Resplendent Quetzal, *Pharomachrus mocinno,* national bird of Guatemala. Spectacular, iridescent green with a red breast and yard-long tail. It swoops across, calling *"Keeow Kowee,"* repeated several times, then fades from view into the mist.

We walk the road downhill, counterintuitive to the direction I'd guess the pickup should be. An exquisite place, with unseen parrots squawking in the trees, the fragrance of *Datura.*

El Capitán points. "*Tucán Verde.*" An Emerald Toucanet, *Aulacorhynchus prasinus,* a bird I recognize from my time at the Blue Ribbon Pet Farm, a joy to find flying wild.

We arrive at a bodega and parked in front is the police pickup. "How did the truck get here?" I ask aloud in English, not expecting an answer.

My guess is the call El Capitán made was to have it moved. I'm relieved, tired from the trek. A few miles climb back up the mountain road is nothing I was looking forward to doing. We have a lunch of empanadas and fruit and drive back to the station.

CHAPTER 59:
Road Collecting Turrialba

The captain has afternoon duties to attend—after his siesta. I love the slower pace of life in Latin America. Start early, work late, but enjoy a delightful midday break. I use my free time exploring a rill in the woods behind the police station, rich in wildlife. Most dramatic are the poison dart frogs, *Dendrobates auratus*. Camouflaged, I detect one by a slight movement. Under two inches, living jewels, black and fluorescent green, the first I have seen. I don't collect as I'm unsure of how to keep them alive until we get back to San José.

Another exceptional, delicate creature is the Casque-headed Lizard, *Corytophanes cristatus*. I regret not taking it for my friend, Lew Ober. The single snake I keep is a False Terciopelo—*Xenodon rabdocephalus*—it fools me for a few moments. Evening we leave for a quick dinner and a road collecting trip. My heart races with anticipation.

We follow the same route as this morning, there's little traffic, the roadway is in decent condition. A light, steady rain is falling. Steam, with its familiar smell, rises from the asphalt still warm from the sun. We haven't gone far when we see an *Imantodes*. I bag it, we move on, and discover a Cloudy Snail-eating Snake, *Sibon nebulatus*, new to me. A stunning specimen, dark gray, black-banded, with narrower, pink bands. First of several tonight.

The next hour I'm in and out of the truck like a jack-in-the-box. We catch a few *Leimadophis* and a small, feisty Terciopelo. Cat-eyed Snakes, *Leptodeira septentrionalis*, are common. Brown with black saddles, venomous looking with vertical pupils, they're harmless. Of no value to us, we set them off the road. Then the find of the night.

El Capitán exclaims. "*Es una Coral Gargantilla.*" The name means choker, or necklace.

I'm not sure. Could be a Gargantilla, *Micrurus mipartitus*. A coral snake that lacks the yellow bands of most familiar species. What a stunner! Black body encircled with red rings. I slip my hook under the tiny creature and drop it in a sack.

Then he says, "*No es una Gargantilla.*"

"What is it?" He doesn't need English to understand my question.

"*No se.*" He shrugs.

I learn the identity from Major Flowers on my return to Santa Rosa. *Urotheca euryzona*, known as the Halloween Snake. "People bring these in thinking they're a coral."

A splendid night of collecting. I lay my clothes out to dry, sort and pack my specimens. El Capitán will send them over to the lab within a week. It's a relief not having to take them on to Limón. In the morning we meet the train and locate Jenny and Bert. Two bright, enthusiastic young folks. They share the same small bag for the trip. Both speak excellent English, Dutch, and Spanish. Despite a privileged lifestyle, they are regular teens. Curious about everything American, and both eager for a wilderness journey.

CHAPTER 60:
The Jungle Train

I thank El Capitán for his gracious hospitality. We embrace, I board. No roads connect Turrialba to the coast. Travel to Limón on the Caribbean is by rail or plane. The trip is a rare, unforgettable experience, for a fare of five colones, 60¢ US. Work on the narrow-gauge railway started in 1871. Mountains, jungles, rivers, and swamps stood in its path. Completed in 1890, it's said thousands of workers—4,000 by some accounts, died in its construction. Descendants of Italian railroad workers later settled in San Vito de Java. Many Jamaican laborers hired to clear the right of way stayed as labor on banana plantations being carved into jungle along the Caribbean coast.

We roll out of Turrialba, black smoke billowing from the old diesel locomotive. Pulling six cars: two wooden passenger cars with hard, well-worn, wood seats, two boxcars, one flatcar, and a livestock car with Brahman cattle shipped from Guanacaste. At stops, vendors ply the train selling refreshments through windows that stay open unless it rains. Fruit juices and *Pejibaye*, the fruit of spiny *Bactris gasipaes* palms, *Mamoncillo*, and ripe bananas. Others vend tamales wrapped in banana leaves.

Spectacular scenery along steep canyons supporting a tiny ribbon of steel. Through jungles, where cascades of vibrant *Tibouchina* and *Heliconia* decorate the slopes. The constant click-clack, click-clack masks the calls of plentiful parrots and macaws. I catch fleeting glimpses of orchid flowers and multicolored birds. Riders throw food scraps to spider monkeys and Capuchins waiting in trees by the track.

Jungle rivers and rapids along the rail descent towards the coast.

Capuchin monkey along railway, eastern side of the Cordillera Central.

Reaching Costa Rica's eastern lowlands.

Rocking and swaying gently, each time the train reaches full speed, 20 miles per hour, it slows. We stop at pastel-painted villages with dirt streets, any cluster of thatched-roof huts, and each farm, from the mountains down across the coastal plain. Passengers board with produce, a chicken, dog, or pig. I get off to stretch my legs among houses on stilts while a crew offloads logs for a sawmill near the coast. Wide-eyed children watch my every step.

The 100-mile trip takes nine hours. One of my best spent days. The train's passage keeps the rampant vegetation at bay. In places, leaving a green tunnel. Trestles over jungle rivers and mountain gorges are breathtaking. No place for those fearful of heights. Along the Río Reventazón, opposite a wall of greenery, is a 200-foot drop to the river. Save for the metal-on-metal squeal of the track, and the smell of diesel smoke, it's easy to imagine we'd taken wing.

Frequent delays from landslides, treefalls, and routine maintenance plague the eastern route. Derailments are common on the aging rails. At such low speeds, damage is rare to people or equipment. Our only delay comes when crossing the Río Madre de Dios. A crew replacing a section of worn track stops us mid-trestle for a half hour. The pilings shudder from crashing waters roiling below, making passengers nervous. Our view is spectacular. Whitewater rapids through the rusted iron of the ancient bridge.

The train arrives in Puerto Limón late afternoon, end of the line. The only hotel is on the beach. With earthquake-damaged pipes, water is on only for an hour, morning and evening. We take two rooms, plain but comfortable, overlooking the Caribbean. Tired from our journey, we rest.

Refreshed and hungry after sundown. The tantalizing aroma of spices and seafood invites us to a seaside restaurant. The menu of the day is fresh-caught snapper fried whole in oil with cilantro and peppers. Served with traditional *casado,* a platter of rice, beans, avocado, sautéed plantain, and a spicy tomato salad. Sumptuous, elegant in its simplicity, we leave satisfied.

Costa Rica's tropical lowlands, wild and primitive, are uncrowded, mysterious. A dream to visit. I am here under the bluest of skies. It is all I imagined and more. Tomorrow I head south, to explore deeper into the wilderness. I can't wait.

CHAPTER 61:
The Banana Kingdom

Dramatic views unfold as we skirt the coast on our southbound journey. Enchanting, a place of dreams. Caribbean beaches of silver and black backed by tall Coconut Palms. We rumble across aging wooden trestles. Over creeks and estuaries, smelling of low tide, lined with Red Mangroves where American Crocodiles, *Crocodylus acutus*, bask. Our train, never fast, stops at each hacienda and fishing village. Boys with baskets held high, hawk coconuts with tops cut for drinking, melon slices, papaya, empanadas, and other tropical delights through open windows.

We detrain beyond the Río Estrella trestle, at the tiny seaside settlement of Penshurst, the site of one of the major's first and most productive collecting stations. Our ride to Vesta is on a stake-bed banana truck. Not a town, but a huge plantation. I hold on for dear life, standing in the back, tossed from side to side as the driver speeds along the potholed dirt road through the trackless jungle.

A steel suspension bridge marks the road's end. It supports a covered conveyor belt spanning the shallow river. Built to move a steady stream of boxed bananas, rain, or shine. Atop is a narrow wooden walkway that looks a complete afterthought to its design.

"How's your balance? There are no railings," The truck driver cautions as he carries Jenny and Bert's suitcase. I follow. Plantation owner, Mr. Taylor, welcomes us to his home for our week's stay. A quintessential tropical bungalow with wide porches and white painted corrugated metal roof to reflect the sun.

Ample rooms for family and visitors and a genteel atmosphere. Daily rains keep a cistern full. A diesel generator provides electricity.

Countless acres of banana plants surround the farmhouse. Planted atop tall rows of black soil separated by ditches. Stout bamboo poles prop up the heavy-laden plants. The fruit, dressed in blue plastic film to protect from blemishes, not pests, looks surreal.

A monorail network threads the maze of banana fields, its chain riding on rusted rollers. There's a rhythmic, clink-clink, clink-clink, clink-clink heard throughout the farm. It carries stalks hung on hooks, bound for the processing shed. Washed and treated with insecticide, they're cut into hands for boxing. Cardboard boxes hold 40 pounds of bananas. Sent across the river by conveyor, then trucked to the train. At Puerto Limón, ships take them to the world. The many steps need a large workforce.

CHAPTER 62:
Exploring the Río Estrella

After a plantation tour, I scan the vine-tangled riverbank. A Plumed Basilisk, *Basiliscus plumifrons*, basks on a log. Prehistoric looking, 30 inches, bright green with blue spots and yellow eyes. A casque on its head and a dorsal crest to the tip of its black-ringed tail. I watch in amazement as it jumps in and runs atop the water on hind legs to the other shore. Enormous feet, long toes, and speed allow it to run across the water's surface. Hence the name *Jesucristo* or Jesus Christ Lizard.

For dinner we meet at a massive, split log dining table. Food is abundant, fried fish, fresh vegetables, and rice, served farm-style in bowls. Mr. Taylor tells the family's history. "We're third generation, from American settlers. They helped build the railroad, received a land grant to open the Caribbean lowlands."

The Mrs. asks, "What brings you to Costa Rica?"

"Reptiles, my life's interest." They're aware I live and work with Major Flowers. The Morsink family are friends. Corinne helped arrange the trip.

My private bedroom has a cot and hooks for an optional hammock. "Make yourself at home." In the evening I visit with Mr. Taylor and enjoy their library with books on Central American natural history, politics, and agriculture.

At breakfast, there's news a workman killed a five-foot Terciopelo. I follow Mr. Taylor out to a shed. The man leads us to the snake. He's dispatched it with a shovel, tossed it into the bush. What a shame, but this is too often the unfortunate fate of most snakes found on farms. Rodents attracted to the barn and bannana residue, it's a natural place for snakes as well.

Farm outbuildings are an excellent place for reptiles. I flip tin and old lumber, find many of two common fossorial (burrowing) species. *Geophis*, a small, dark gray burrowing species. Then, *Ninia sebae*, colorful, tiny, reddish, with a yellow-banded black head.

After lunch, exploring an abandoned warehouse overgrown with weeds under a discarded door, I discover a *Loxocemus bicolor*. Known as the New World Python or Sunbeam Snake, its gray-brown scales are iridescent. Muscular with a pointed, upturned snout. Another exciting first.

Joyful shouts lead me to a river swimming hole. Farm boys splash in the crystal water. Swift and cool, it looks inviting in the tropical afternoon heat. A huge rock is a diving platform. I pull off my boots and shirt, empty my pockets and dive in, reinforcing my vision of paradise.

∾

Jenny and Bert are eager to explore and jump at the chance to come with me on a hike. Jennifer is tall and athletic, with dark hair and Dutch olive skin. Bert is slim and high energy, with sandy hair. He could be my little brother. Thursday, we cross by dugout, and journey upstream towards a vast tract of virgin forest. Butterflies in their thousands congregate on the riverbank, wings folded. They draw minerals from the mud and take wing at our approach, a kaleidoscope of colors in the morning sunlight.

A tumbling stream flows from a jungle ravine. We enter the shady interior. Hiking is easy with sparse undergrowth. Massive trunks are columns supporting the green roof of nature's cathedral. Shafts of light pierce the canopy and recall sun through stained glass windows. A damp carpet of colorful leaves is spongy underfoot. A subtle, sweet smell of decay hangs in the air.

Eyes adjusting to the dimness, I detect movement. Strawberry Poison-dart Frogs, *Dendrobates pumilio*. Red and black icons of the Costa Rican jungle. Under an inch, tiny but fearless, they venture out in daylight. Vivid colors signal their deadly toxin. Amerindians use their secretions on blowgun darts and arrowheads. As a group, they're called poison arrow or dart frogs.

I cup one in my hand. The diminutive creature sits in my palm, calm, his throat pulsing. Hard to believe this creature's skin secretion is among the most toxic substances known. Despite this, handling the frogs with unbroken skin isn't dangerous—if I don't rub my eyes!

Swimming in the clear Río Estrella near Vesta.

The kids, fascinated, handle one with due care. I'll return before we leave to collect a few.

The rainforest is alive with animals. Agoutis and Pacas, rabbit-sized relatives of Guinea Pigs, scurry in the undergrowth. Geoffroy's Spider Monkeys move in silence high in the trees. Red Howlers call in the distance. Colorful trogons and toucanets hop branch to branch, sampling ripe fruit. The songs of unseen birds and whir of insects add a constant resonance. Tiny Costa Rica has over 900 bird species, nigh as many as the entire US.

What's missing are snakes. Impatient, I dig through palm logs—cut, stacked, and abandoned long ago. I pick them up by the end and toss them aside. The first few are so rotted they break open. With my snake stick, I comb through the rotten wood, finding nothing. Then a sudden blazing sting—Ants! On my arms and up both legs of my jeans, stinging in unison. I slap and brush, run from the log pile, they're relentless. In desperation I drop my pants to sweep ants from my legs, now covered in welts.

"*Saca pantalones*," Jenny calls out, as she and her brother laugh from a safe distance. "Take off your pants" is a common term for these vicious ants.

My run-in with the ferocious devils will not be my last. I felt nothing until they spread over me from top to bottom.

"Look, look!" Bert points to a troupe of Squirrel Monkeys passing overhead.

We follow, enjoying their antics for a few minutes. A large male watches our every move until they scamper off into the treetops. I continue picking off ants.

The creek we followed in should be over the next ridge. But no. "Let's find the logs. We'll backtrack from there." We turn around but can't locate it.

"Are we lost?" Jennifer asks.

While obvious, I'm loath to admit it. "No, disoriented. I'll figure it out."

With the sky obscured except for patches here and there, I struggle to get a sense of the direction we need to travel. The forest grows over a series of low ridges, many with streams between, any of which should lead to the river. We hike across several until we come to a larger one and follow. Sounds simple, but we wandered aimlessly a few hours.

The sun is setting as we emerge on the rocky banks of the Río Estrella. Twilight doesn't linger in the tropics, and we've no flashlight. A short way along, a familiar landmark signals we're near, but it's dark by the time we reach the bungalow.

Weary from our hike, glad to be home, Roberto asks if I'd care to go crocodile hunting. He's a worker who enjoys practicing his English with me. I hate to witness killing them, but seeing crocs in the wild is a great opportunity. "Sure." A quick bite and out the door.

"Where are we going?" On the way south, we saw crocodiles in brackish estuaries.

"El río." We take the path towards the swimming spot. One guy carries a motorcycle battery, another a headlamp with a cord attached. We move out onto the rocky ledge we dove from yesterday. The men hook up the light, and the beam shows a pair of glowing red eyes.

"Holy cow! I didn't know there were crocs in here."

"Only at night."

How is that possible? While watching the croc in the light's glare, I don't notice another fellow with a gun. Boom! I near jump off the rock.

"What the hell?"

A twelve-gauge shotgun with buckshot. He missed. Any others are now long gone. The boys go upstream to hunt, and I ramble back to the house, tired, ears ringing.

CHAPTER 63:
Cheating Death

Roberto is excited. He comes for me while I'm drinking coffee. Speaking in mixed English, "Come. *Por favor*," he slips out the back door.

"I guess they got a croc last night." I excuse myself and hurry behind him.

Near the riverside, he stops and points to the ground. A thick, glossy black snake lies between tufts of grass. I grab the four-footer without hesitation. "A Mussurana!"

"*Zopilota*." Roberto gives me the local name. *Clelia clelia* is their technical epithet.

I hold it out to show him. He jumps back, uncomfortable around snakes. "*No es venenosa*. Not venomous." He keeps his distance.

It's a prize that inspires me to hurry out to hunt. I wolf down breakfast and leave to hike up the Estrella. Collecting seems better on the forest edge, perhaps because things are easier to see. I don't ask Jenny and Bert. They're in teenage heaven listing to the Taylors' excellent collection of American and British music. Strains of "Love is Blue," by Paul Mauriat stream from the stereo as I step through the doorway.

Camera in hand, a few sacks, and snake hook, I'm ready for a successful day. As I start upriver, Bert and Jenny shout, "Wait for us."

I'm surprised they wish to join me after yesterday's fiasco. But they're energetic and enjoy the outdoors. I welcome their company. A glorious morning starts with a breathtaking flock of Scarlet Macaws. Huge, noisy, vivid red, blue, and yellow, a signature of the New World tropics. Not far along,

212

a tree full of Collared Aracari. A colorful toucan with a serrated bill, red rump, and yellow belly crossed with black and red bands. Often killed as pests on banana plantations. Waterbirds abound, hawks, and clouds of butterflies.

A bright green *Oxybelis fulgidus* vine snake, stands out in shrubs by the water's edge. The diameter of a pencil, a yard long with a narrow, triangular head that tapers to an elongated point. Their resemblance to *Uromacer*, found in Haiti, is uncanny. Picked up, it takes a threatening pose with mouth agape, revealing a black interior. A mild venom is for stunning their lizard prey. I return it to the bush.

In the first mile, five or six juvenile Jesucristo lizards race across the water surface before I notice them. It's easy to run them down in the open, rocky riverbed, and I take two pairs.

We happen upon a ribbon of a waterfall spilling into a serene fern-filled gully. Bert points out an iridescent violet hummingbird attracted by *Heliconia rostrata*. In the shade of tree ferns, the ground is crawling with living jewels— tiny dart frogs. I spot an *Anolis aquaticus* as it jumps from a branch to hide in the stream. A funny blunt head and white stripe on the upper jaw and sides, with brown bands and spots. I nab three specimens for my friend Lew Ober.

We trek for an hour on the smooth stones, enjoying the sights, but not finding much. We reach a curve where the river passes cliffs. There's no shoreline. It's too swift and wide to cross with safety. The 50-foot bluff extends 200 yards. I am sure I can get past with an easy climb. Bert is ready, but Jenny doesn't want to try. The plantation is a two-mile straight shot, so no worries. We take photos and part ways.

As they head south, I shout, "Meet you at the farm. Be careful."

I change film, stash the exposed roll in my shirt pocket, tie a plastic bag over my camera. My route picked before climbing, I move fast, no path, but clambering is effortless. At a place where it's a vertical wall, I inch along a narrow ledge. I'm not worried. The worst outcome, I'd fall a few yards into the water.

Somewhere halfway across, a boulder protruding from the cliff blocks my way. To go past, I grip it with a bear hug. It dislodges. The half-ton rock takes me crashing to the river in a split second, knocking the air from my lungs. Call it fate or karma, on the 10-foot ride to the rocky bottom, I end up on top. The huge stone pins my camera, its strap wrapped around my wrist. Trapped, disoriented but adrenaline pumping, I pull against the leather thong until it snaps.

Photo of author with Jenny and Bert Morsink along the Río Estrella, only moments before a near-death experience.

I break the surface with a giant gasp for air and fight the churning torrent. In blue jeans and boots, and a machete on my belt, swimming is nigh impossible. Angels are watching. The current sweeps me to the shallows 100 yards downstream. I crawl out onto the opposite shore, bruised, scratched, exhausted. I've once again cheated death.

After I catch my breath, I take stock of the ordeal I survived. That it didn't trap a foot or hand is a miracle. When I hit the water, the rock was on top of me, but I escape being pinned.

To my amazement, I have my snake stick but lost the canister of exposed film. I turn towards the farm and find it floating in rocks at the edge. My first 35mm camera, bought for this trip, is now beneath a boulder on the bottom of Río Estrella. How can I complain? I'm alive.

CHAPTER 64:
Vanishing Eden

Saturday, I awake to the smell of smoke. Mr. Taylor is drinking coffee. "Wow! What's burning?" I pour a cup and sit.

"They're clearing a few hundred hectares near Concepción for bananas."

"Your property?"

"No, I wish it were. Flat country, perfect for production."

"I'd like to see. I'll bet they're stirring up plenty of animals."

"I'm sure they are. Most forest they cut months ago. Now that it's dry, they are burning."

"How far is it? Any chance I could walk?"

"Doubt it. Eight miles on the north side of the Estrella. Tell you what, you could ask Roberto to drive you."

After breakfast, I gather sacks, snake stick, and a bottle of water. Roberto, in the dipping shed, is happy to take me. Gets him out of cleaning vats and he can practice his English.

We head towards the fires, the sun a hazy yellow glow in gray skies. A rutted track cut by bulldozers turns towards the river. We follow it to the riverbank then wade across. Waist deep in the middle, it's a struggle keeping our footing on rounded stones in the roiling current. We slog ashore soaked, but dry out some on the half-mile trek to the worksite. We come to a crew burning brush, logs, and stumps pushed into huge piles. Diesel fuel starter billows acrid, black smoke. Broken roots protrude from muddy black earth where trees once stood. Such a sad sight.

Devastation complete, I see little possibility of finding snakes. Roberto asks a workman if he's seen any. "*Hay muchas aqui.* There are many." He sweeps his arm in an arc. "*Sígueme.* Follow me."

We approach a burning pile, and on the wet soil, he points to a dead Terciopelo. "*Lo maté hace una hora.* I killed him an hour ago."

"Ask if it's okay if we search for more?"

"*Sí señor, sea mi invitado.* Yes sir, be my guest."

I walk off to inspect clumps of brush and stray logs and in minutes find a Hog-nosed Viper. "*Cuidado amigo, esta es venenosa.*" I need not say it twice.

I trudge through mud with renewed energy. Under bark on drier ground, I turn up several small, colorful, Red-bellied Snakes. *Rhadinaea decorata* has a Florida relative, the Yellow-lipped Snake. They're interesting, but not something to keep. I hold them to release in a safer place. One I don't recognize right off is a non-venomous Ebony Keelback. *Chironius grandisquamis*, my first. Five feet, with a slim, triangular, black body.

"Hey Bob, can you carry a few of these sacks? Nothing dangerous."

"Bob? Who is Bob?"

"Sorry. Roberto is 'Robert' in English. 'Bob' is the diminutive."

He smiles. "*Soy Bob.* I am Bob." I'm surprised he had not heard this before now.

Still, he doesn't want to tote the snakes. That's okay. We turn up a few more, not rare, or special, until, by a fallen log, he spots two *Bothrops numifera*. "*Mano de Piedra. Cuidado!*"

Thick bodied with enormous heads, they look fierce but stay coiled. I bag them without resistance. We follow the Estrella back for easier walking on the rocky shoreline. Roberto must be my good luck charm because I catch a second Mussurana.

This is my best day of snake collecting in Costa Rica by far. We cross to the truck, washing our muddy boots on the way, and reach the farm at lunchtime. *Olla de Carne*, a hearty soup of beef, yucca, plantains, and vegetables with a side of rice. I love it. I thank Mr. Taylor and Bob for a marvelous morning. Jenny and Bert are sorry they didn't come, but I assure them it was no fun walking for miles in the black, slippery mud.

Sunday, I search the outbuildings, turning over the same wood and tin. I release the Red Bellies, keeping one. Later, I tell Mr. Taylor I hated seeing so much destruction.

"A generation ago, ours was the only farm. My grandfather cleared this land by hand. North of the river was all forest when I was a kid. Now everything west of here is protected."

I visit the boxing shed and make a container for carrying the snakes, out of banana boxes. The family gathers for a barbecued chicken dinner. It recalls Sundays at home in Davie.

～

Monday is our last exploring day. I bring three glass milk bottles to the jungle, put damp leaf litter and six Strawberry Frogs in each. The snake specimens made this trip successful. A priceless experience. The dart frogs set our journey apart. They survive travel back to San José, then Florida, without a single loss. The New York Zoological Society receives a few which noted wildlife photographer Saul Friess photographs.

Early Tuesday we leave by banana truck to Penshurst, catch the train to Limón. From there we fly Sansa to Alajuela. The old DC-3 is the same basic plane as the C-47 the major and I flew to Panama, but not as nice. Jump-seats accommodate the few passengers. Pallets of produce and fresh seafood secured with nets and straps are the real payload. We take off from a beach airstrip of packed sand. Despite the expanding banana and coffee plantations, logging, and development, I can still see why the national motto of Costa Rica is "*Pura Vida*" the pure life. It would be a shame if this would one day all change.

CHAPTER 65:
Continuing Education

The major is an enigma, intense, detailed, results-driven, has an air of confidence but good humor. Laughter relieves the stress of the dangerous work. His fiancée, Corinne, is a lovely, lively personality. She and the major are a perfect match. Her parents own the Hotel Royal Dutch in San José. We visit often. I'm welcomed, treated like family, put at ease. Sometimes, the lovebirds take off together, leaving Guillermo and me to find our way home. That means buses and much walking.

On weekends, he enjoys grilling. Neighbors visit. Evenings, he'll have a beer while sitting on the veranda of the villa. We watch bats swoop for insects in the darkening skies, and he tells stories of his colorful life.

"My interest in snakes and venoms started as a teenager. I researched at the University of Georgia." *(He earned his doctorate in veterinary medicine there in 1956.)* "I joined the army in 1961. Six months later, I began working with venoms."

He is a published, respected expert in his field. His work at the US Army Medical Research Laboratory in Fort Knox resulted in the first US-produced anti-coral serum. While there, he sustained a cobra bite. He nearly died, spent weeks hospitalized.

In fact, it was his second cobra bite. How tough is he? After his second bite, he had a necktie made of cobra skin and wore it on his off-duty time. "A newspaper ran an article about it," he tells me.

I say, "Reminds me of 'Who Do You Love?' the old Bo Diddley tune."

The major, holding boa constrictor, with US Ambassador Raymond Zeller in Penshurst, ca 1965. (Photo: Col. Herschel H. Flowers family archives)

We both have a good laugh.

"You know my next assignment is Vietnam."

"Yeah. Are you setting up a lab there?"

"Probably. There are available antiserums that I'll be testing. It's a war theater, I have another pet project."

"What's that?"

"I call it 'snake psychosis.' Soldiers in Vietnam suffer few venomous snakebites, but many have an irrational fear of snakes. The enemy is quick to take advantage." The major cracks open another beer. "When I first arrived in Costa Rica, it was much the same. There were many bites, but superstitions kept rural *campesinos* and Indians from getting treatment. There's a belief, if a victim sees a pregnant woman, he will die regardless of any help he receives."

"Man, that's crazy. How do you convince them?"

"It's difficult. Another more common belief is that if a victim touches water, he will die. If a stream blocks their way to get help, they may walk miles to find a bridge or log to cross. Many die."

What he says next almost knocks me out of my chair. "Hear me out. Why don't you join up, go through basic training, I'll have you assigned as my aide and lab assistant?"

My head is swimming. It's tempting, but not insignificant to contemplate. I fumble for words. "I…I'd have to talk it over with my wife. And," I swallow hard, "there's the thing with my ankle. The 4-F designation. How'd we get past that?"

"General Porter took a shine to you. He'd help. His opinion carries weight."

I feel flush. He's serious. I don't know what to think. I promise to consider it.

⌒

It wasn't always shoptalk. Older than me by 15 years, he dropped the occasional pearl of wisdom, or at least his view of life. Asked if his remaining single into middle age is because of his work with snakes, he has a quick reply. "I can look at a snake and tell exactly what he is going to do. In most respects, snakes are quite open in their actions. But a woman, she's something else, and frankly much more dangerous."

One evening he gives me the story of the bridge by the Huevo Grande. Not everything, the gist of it. Corinne later fills in details. I'll preface by saying the major enjoys his beer. Rarely does he stop at his limit. He handles it well. Most of the time.

A year before my visit, he tossed common sense aside. After drinking heavily, inebriated, he drove towards San José. Heavy-footed, accelerator flat on the floorboard, he careened along steep mountain roads, somehow avoiding flying into space. At breakneck speed he approached, careening onto the bridge. The Jeep slid, tumbled, smashed into the guardrail, catapulted twice, stopped. It was a twisted metal heap leaking gasoline and burnt oil fumes.

Witnesses at the Huevo Grande screamed and believed no one could survive. They pulled his battered body from the wreckage, shocked to see he was still alive.

The major lay in a coma, had many broken bones, spent weeks in the hospital, and months convalescing. By the time I arrived, he'd recovered. According to local lore, a miracle. He admits not remembering much. Corinne is a little sensitive over his drinking. He agreed to rein it in. He may have slowed, but sure didn't give it up altogether.

We're watching the sunset. "How 'bout a beer?" He's on his second one.

I never drank. I'm still underage. My father wasn't a drinker, nor the boys I ran with growing up in Davie. "What the heck, today's my birthday, why not?"

"It's your birthday? How old, 24?" He's teasing or doesn't remember.

"Twenty."

"This calls for a celebration. Let's go bowling."

Into the Jeep and we're off to Alajuela, the major, me, and Guillermo. We meet two other guys at the alley, rent shoes, and start a game. The beer flows. Men being men, I'm "the kid," despite my being bigger than any of them. They egg me on to imbibe. My first is rough. The rest go down easy.

The bowling alley is spinning. I excuse myself, stumble to the men's room, and end up in a stall hugging the commode. I heave for who knows how long. It must have been a while.

Someone bangs on the door. "You all right, keed?" in a heavy accent.

"No." I groan.

The next I know I'm in my bed back at the villa, in jeans and boots. How I got here, the drive home, or other details I can't remember. My thoughts on drinking? It could go without saying, I don't yet see the attraction.

CHAPTER 66:
End of An Era

The antiserum program transition to the Costa Rican Ministry of Health is in full swing. The snake colony moves from the villa to facilities at UCR. A slow and detailed process. We focus on keeping operations running during the transfer. Documentation and training involve many individuals. The major must relinquish control to a fresh team. A one-man show until now, it's an unpleasant task for him. This project, his passion, culminates his life's work. No part is without significance. I try being helpful, stay out of the way. While in charge, he continues to teach and instruct. It's his nature.

The snake room is empty. Only specimens I'm taking and those that the major is donating to the University of Florida and Ross Allen, remain.

In the kitchen for coffee, imagine my surprise when I see a tri-colored snake emerging from the sink drain. I grab it behind its head, keep a steady, gentle pull to coax it out. Muscular, it continues to draw itself downward.

Guillermo comes in and sees me struggling. "*Déjalo ir.*" Let it go.

"What? No, I don't want to lose it."

He insists, I refuse. It pulls free and disappears into the orifice. I'm defeated, disappointed. Guillermo goes outside, calls me. The snake dangles out of a pipe stub where the sink drains into a gutter Turns out to be a Double-banded False Coral Snake, a red, black, and yellow banded, *Erythrolamprus bizona*. A species with mild venom, harmless to humans.

Major Flowers is Santa Rosa's local hero. Word of his pending departure spreads. Afternoons and weekends his neighbors reach out, stop by, a few bring small gifts or food. He spends time and visits with them. To show his appreciation, he hosts a neighborhood barbecue the last Saturday I'm there, with thick American-style steaks, plenty of beer.

As someone savors a mouthful, I hear the major quip. "Couldn't bear to waste those horses." Hearty laughter fills the garden.

Despite the merriment, sadness looms over the gathering. Neighbors and guests sense the end of an era.

Major Flowers, in bush hat, going over details of lab turnover with team leaders.
(Photo: Col. Herschel H. Flowers family archives)

CHAPTER 67:
A World in Turmoil

Thursday, August 29, is the day I'll fly home. Wednesday I'll be packing. Tuesday evening, the major, Guillermo and I meet the Morsink family at the Hotel Royal Dutch for dinner. I guess it's my sendoff. No one says. Afterward, they suggest a movie. *To Sir, With Love* with Sidney Poitier is playing. Subtitled in Spanish. Such times make Costa Rica homey and familiar. I will miss it.

☙

Wednesday, I ready my reptiles for shipment to Miami. Aside from those I collected, I'm allowed any specimens I want. I chose juvenile or small-sized snakes from as many species as possible. No corals, they are difficult to keep and of great importance to the program. We plan for their arrival at Miami air cargo the day after I return.

The major receives frequent military informational briefs. News items that might involve military readiness, happenings around the globe. This year, 1968, has seen much conflict at home and abroad. North Korea seized USS *Pueblo*. Vietnam saw the Tet Offensive. Racial tensions are at a boiling point. Johnson drops out of the presidential campaign; men are burning draft cards. April 4, James Earl Ray assassinates Martin Luther King in Memphis. The country erupts in flames. Peace marches in the streets, *Hair* opens on Broadway. Then in June, Sirhan Sirhan kills Robert Kennedy in Los Angeles.

Since I left on this trip, Johnson visited Central America. The Soviet Union invaded Czechoslovakia. On August 28, we're in the snake room when a Jeep arrives. The major goes outside to speak. When he comes back, his face is expressionless, brow furrowed.

"They've killed John Gordon Mein. Shot him dead in the street."

"Who's that?"

"The American Ambassador to Guatemala." He slips through the breezeway into the house, reappears buttoning a clean fatigue shirt, wearing his cap. "I gotta run for a few hours."

It's evening before he returns. "So, what happened?"

"FAR guerillas ambushed Mein and his entourage in Guatemala City, near the US embassy. Troops across Latin America are on alert."

Violence at the Democratic National Convention keeps the Guatemala news out of the American press.

His Serum Later Saves Own Life

Major Herschel H. Flowers

A small Central American country, about the size of West Virginia has, for the past several years, seen and benefited from the untiring work of a dedicated American Army major. Major Herschel H. Flowers, a veterinarian, generally attired in his Army fatigues, has endeared himself to the people of Costa Rica through his development of an effective anti-snake serum — and his willingness to aid any victim of the many poisonous snakes that make their home in Costa Rica.

In fact, Costa Rica has one of the largest concentrations of poisonous snakes, with approximately 3,000 snake-bite victims each year, therefore, Major Flower's lectures and television appearances helped alert the people to the dangers and dispelled some of the superstitions surrounding snake-bite victims. The United States Legion of Merit Medal was recently awarded the Major, in addition to a commendation by Dr. Alvaro Aguilar Peralta, Minister of Public Health of Costa Rica. The serum program is a combined effort, and in addition to the U.S. Army's leading authority on poisonous snakes, Major Flowers, the sponsors were US Aid, the Costa Rican Ministry of Health and the University of Costa Rica.

The remarkable anti-venom serum developed is effective against all types of snake bites, except the coral snakes. And right at this moment, Major Flowers is glad he patiently pursued this new serum, because it just helped save his life.

An Orlandoan, and the son of Reverend and Mrs. Jefferson Flowers of Magnolia Homes, Major Flowers was visiting his parents prior to an assignment in Viet Nam. The Major had brought several specimens to give to Ross Allen's Reptile Farm, and was transferring a deadly fer-de-lance, when struck on a finger.

Had the Major's own serum been available immediately, it would have been better, but it was jetted in from Chicago's Brookfield Zoo, as soon as possible.

Major Flowers is steadily improving at the Orlando Naval Base Hospital, but I suspect his stay in Orlando is extending much longer than his original leave.

The senior Flowers are very well known in this area. In addition to Reverend Flowers's duties as pastor of the Bethany Baptist Church, on Clarcona Road, he has taught school at the Lockhart Junior High School, for many years, I know everyone in this area sends their best wishes to Major Flowers and wishes him continued success in his service to mankind.

Article detailing Major Herschel H. Flowers' near death from a Terciopelo bite in Orlando, Florida, 1968. (Article without provenance from: Col. Herschel H. Flowers family archives)

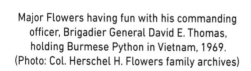

Major Flowers having fun with his commanding officer, Brigadier General David E. Thomas, holding Burmese Python in Vietnam, 1969. (Photo: Col. Herschel H. Flowers family archives)

CHAPTER 68:
Leaving the Land of Pura Vida

The morning starts before daylight. I take a quick bite of toast and coffee, then load my gear and the boxes of snakes and other reptiles. After dropping me off, the major will ship them from air cargo. More than time has passed since my arrival. I've enjoyed a wealth of consequential experiences. My role in this project, albeit minor, is a tremendous honor. During the nonstop adventure, I met incredible characters, traveled to Panama, made many friends, saw history being made. Survived my first hangover. This life's journey exceeded every expectation. I must go now. My other life awaits.

In the vernacular of the times, it's been a trip. Costa Rica was home for two months. Goodbye is painful. The major and I have bonded.

⁓

We embrace at the airport, not knowing we'd never meet again. The major plans to prepare for Vietnam deployment at his parents' home in Orlando. With roots in Costa Rica, leaving will be tough. In Orlando, while transferring a collection of his snakes to Ross Allen, a small Terciopelo bites his left hand. After developing the latest in anti-crotalid antiserum, he has none on hand to use for his own bite. The common Wyeth Laboratory anti-crotalid antiserum is available and administered. With gums bleeding, he checks into a local hospital, then checks out when he feels they handle his bite poorly. Antiserum he developed is sent by jet from Brookfield Zoo in Chicago. It saves his life.

His reaction to the bite was swift and near-fatal and delays his departure to Vietnam a few months. It took nine operations, including sewing his finger to his stomach to save it.

Once home, I talk over joining his project. My proposal does not go over well. The major has not forgotten his offer and contacts General Porter to intervene on my behalf. Despite his influence, letters from my orthopedic surgeon, and proof of being a lineman for the power company, it's not to be. The draft board's 4-F designation, because of a steel pin in my ankle from the horse accident, stands.

The antivenom program becomes the *Instituto Clodomiro Picado* in 1970. They continue to provide snakebite antiserum throughout the Americas. Its value to the world is incalculable. A legacy to the pioneering effort of Major Herschel H. Flowers.

Five months after departing Costa Rica, the major begins his Vietnam tour. Stationed in Long Binh, he travels throughout Vietnam. Among his duties are evaluation and testing of antiserums and surveying the impact of venomous snakes on US troops in theater. He institutes an intensive troop training and education program. The journal, *Military Medicine*, published his findings of in-country research after his tour ended. ("The Psychological Importance of Snakes to the Combat Soldier" - Volume 138, Issue 3, March 1973 - Herschel H. Flowers, VC, USA, Ret., Frederick G.)

Not limited to medical duties, Major Flowers received the Purple Heart for wounds sustained in action. He earned the Bronze Star with V device for Heroism in Ground Combat. In addition, he earned a second Bronze Star with

Article from Army Digest, ca 1969, in Biên Hòa, Vietnam. (Col. Herschel H. Flowers family archives)

Snakes Alive If you have ever seen a man who is thoroughly wrapped up in his work, it's the snake doctor for the 44th Medical Brigade at Bien Hoa, Vietnam. Major Herschel H. Flowers is one of the foremost authorities on venomous snakes in the U S. Army. As a staff veterinarian for the preventive medicine unit, he is responsible for the study and prevention of animal-carried diseases, but a major portion of his work is concerned with testing snakebite antiserums and studying the overall snake problem in Vietnam.

ARMY DIGEST

Major Flowers with his "Snake Doctor" Jeep and members of the 20th Preventative Medicine Unit in Vietnam, January 1970. (Col. Herschel H. Flowers family archives)

Oak Leaf Cluster for Meritorious Achievement in Ground Operations Against Hostile Forces. By any standards, he's an American hero.

∽

We kept in touch for a while until destiny took us in different directions. True to the prayers invoked by Sra. Rodríguez, despite wounds suffered in battle, the major's life was spared. He retired from service after his Vietnam tours and returned to Costa Rica. Corrine and the major married in 1972 and started a veterinary clinic. Later they farmed Rainbow Trout, high in the mountains he loved. Also true to the promise of Sra. Rodríguez, the Costa Ricans embraced him and did not let him go. The major and his wife Corrine had two sons, Herschel Jr., and Wayne. Sadly, he died at the young age of 45 in 1978, losing a long battle with a chronic illness. When he passed, he was buried in his adopted country, leaving many to grieve and mourn his passing.

Looking back, it's over 50 years since my sojourn at the venom lab. Though brief, my time with the major remains a vivid memory. I have been fortunate to know many extraordinary men in my lifetime. Few had a greater influence on me, or earned my respect, more than Major Herschel H. Flowers. In my heart, I know he enjoys an eternal home in glory.

Major Flowers' Bronze Star award, with V Device, for heroism in ground combat, Vietnam, July 1969. (Col. Herschel H. Flowers family archives)

Major Flowers' Purple Heart military decoration, for Wounds Received in Action, Vietnam, July 1969. Awarded January 1970. (Col. Herschel H. Flowers family archives)

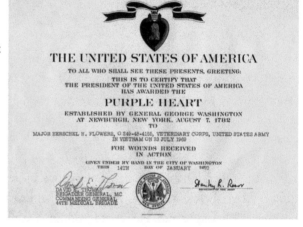

Loving memorial to the major's passing
from Alfredo E. Piza, Costa Rica, 1978.
(Article without provenance from: Col. Herschel H. Flowers family archives)

Herschel Flowers, Beloved 'Snake Man' Dies Here

By Yehudi Monestel

DR. HERSCHEL Flowers, Costa Rica's beloved "Snake Man", died in San José Monday after a long illness. He was 45.

A veterinarian with the rank of Major from the U.S. Army, Flowers helped put Costa Rica on the map as the country which produces the most powerful snakebite serum in tropical America.

Born in Georgia in 1933, Flowers graduated from the University of Georgia in 1956, and joined the Army in 1961, where he became involved in medical investigations using animals at Fort Knox.

HIS long relationship with snakes, which dated back to his childhood, was soon discovered, and Flowers was commissioned to work on the development of a liquid snakebite serum for the Army. His first contact with Costa Rica came in 1963, when Dr. Antonio Peña, then director of San José's San Juan de Dios Hospital, visited the Fort Knox laboratories and proposed a cooperative to continue the serum work in Costa Rica.

The Army decided to send Flowers to Costa Rica to start the program, but before he could make the trip, the soldier-vet had to spend 67 days in a military hospital. While "milking" a cobra for its venom for liquid serum, he was bitten

on the hand and was near death for many weeks.

From 1964 to 1968, Flowers participated in the serum studies taking place here. He traveled to the jungles hunting for poisonous snakes, and his fame as a snake-trapper spread around the world.

IT ALSO gained him the coveted respect of Costa Rica's Indians, who revered him from the day he saved the lives of the mother and daughter of a Talamanca region, and the story of the tall, blond man spread like wildfire through the Indian villages from Amubri to Cabekar.

The "snake man's" efforts meant that Indians no longer needed to expect certain death from poisonous snakebites, and it started a whole new way of life for them.

At that time Costa Rica averaged some 3,000 cases of snakebite a year with a high mortality rate. From one end of the country to the other, whenever anyone was bitten by a snake, Flowers was summoned — and he went.

Once he saved the life of a woman bitten by a coral snake with the only anti-coral serum in the country, before the serum was being produced here. Today, Costa Rica is among the few countries in the world where anti-coral serum is produced, thanks to Herschel Flowers and a

small group of local men.

IN 1968 Flowers was sent to Vietnam. Before taking off, he flew to Florida accompanied by 13 bushmasters, a gift to the University of Florida.

Terrified customs agents in Miami refused to unload the grisly cargo, and Flowers intervened — only to be bitten in the finger. Within minutes he was near death once more, vomiting blood, his finger almost "dead" from necrosis.

He was taken to the hospital and from there, semi-conscious from the poison, he telephoned a zoologist in Chicago to whom he had sent some of the powdered serum from Costa Rica, asking that some be sent back to him. The serum was flown in by jet, and it saved his life.

Five months and nine operations (to save his finger) later, Flowers was in Vietnam, where he spent the first seven months in charge of 2,200 "soldier dogs" trained to sniff out the enemy at a distance of 500 meters.

BUT it wasn't long before he found himself involved with snakes again, after noting that the "snake psychosis" exhibited by the GI's was almost worse than the fear of the enemy.

With a few cobras and a python, Flowers moved

from camp to camp, educating the men with short lectures, helping to ease their fear of snakes. But war being what it is, Flowers was wounded in combat, and later was dispatched with the Purple Heart and Distinguished Service Medal.

He returned to Costa Rica in 1972 and opened a veterinary clinic which immediately became popular with his old and new friends and fans. In 1977 he decided to try his hand

at raising rainbow trout, and was enormously successful at his Copey de Dota fish farm, where he spent most of his time.

FLOWERS was buried

in Copey Tuesday. He is survived by his former wife, Corinne, their two children, Harvey, 8, and Wayne, 18 months, his mother and brother.

COSTA RICA'S Snake Man, Herschel Flowers. –Photo courtesy La Nación.

Obituary article from The Tico Times
detailing Major Flowers' life, his work in Costa Rica and untimely death.
(Article reprinted courtesy of Tico Times www.ticotimes.net.
From Col. Herschel H. Flowers family archives)

Jack Facente Remembers Major Flowers in Vietnam. Talking Snakes.

Author's note: It's a small world indeed. While reaching out to the real characters in this book, my friend Jack Facente commented that he had met with Major Herschel Flowers while serving in Vietnam. Here is his story:

While serving a tour of duty in Vietnam with the US Army, during 1969 and 1970, my interests in snakes and venoms often led to stories enjoyed by my platoon brothers. My friend, and great 1st Lieutenant Phil Haurus, was also a snake buff, and especially enjoyed my stories. Being deployed as a crawler tractor operator to clear jungles for the First Air Calvary, my sitting atop a Caterpillar D7E came to a screeching halt when my civilian communications experience was uncovered. They reassigned me to be the new Commo Chief of the 557 Engineer Battalion. This afforded me a golden opportunity to make calls back to the states when at base camp via radio/land lines. It also allowed me to contact Major Herschel Flowers in Long Binh. He was visiting camps, doing snake lectures, to dispel fears and rumors associated with snakes in combat zones. I tried to join his unit before being deployed—to no avail. I did finally manage to hitch a ride on a Huey (a common mode of travel) headed to Long Binh from my base in Phuc Vinh, with hopes to meet Major Flowers. I was certain my prior employment with Bill Haast, in addition to my friendship with Louis Porras, would be my ticket in when I caught up with him. Our visit was brief, ending with a bite to eat and some great whiskey for dessert. I could tell he loved his whiskey—he even shared it with his Jeep driver! I had heard many stories about him through Louis and while in his presence, could tell they were all true. We spent the time conversing about snakes and venoms along with his work in Costa Rica where he pioneered early antivenom work. I will always look up to Major Flowers. I remember him as a down-to-earth, regular guy, despite his rank and accomplishments. And, how he took time to meet a Spec 5 soldier with similar interests in the middle of a war zone.

Jack Facente in Phuc Vinh, Vietnam, 1970. (Courtesy of Jack Facente)

CHAPTER 69:
Grand Cayman

My heart heavy, but energized, more eager than ever to follow my destiny. Maybe after a brief break. I'm drained, ready to get home, dreading my British West Indies stop. I'd never have arranged it if I knew how complicated life might be when leaving Costa Rica. A million things whirling in my mind, I deplane in George Town, Grand Cayman, for a 24-hour layover.

A few fishermen and divers visit. It will be years before offshore banking, tax shelters, gambling, resorts, and cruise ships arrive. They've neither radio nor television in 1968.

After passing Immigration, I catch a taxi, a 1940s Chevrolet. "Any cheap place to stay?"

"The Beach Club, $10 per night, with breakfast and dinner." There are five hotels.

I've come here to see the Blue Rock Iguana, *Cyclura lewisi*. Rarest of the insular iguanas, on the brink of extinction. Fewer than 30 survive, endemic to Grand Cayman. It will take a miracle, but I want to try. At the inn, I inquire, "Do you know of a naturalist named Ira Thompson, the Iguana Man?"

He doesn't or won't bother to say. I ask around. No one claims to hear of him. How is it nobody knows such a famous guy on this tiny island?

Too late to go inland, so I head to the docks and shore. The waters are alive with colorful corals and fish. *I wish I had a dive mask.* I don't have short pants, much less a swimsuit. Dinner is at 6: grilled dolphin, topped with peppery onions and vinegar. A side of pigeon peas and rice. Dang, it's delicious.

I finish in time to watch the sunset. Bone tired, I crash.

In the morning, over coffee and toast, I plan my day. Only hours to spend, to view an iguana, or at least part of the 22-mile-long island, I should hire a taxi. Several drivers in the shade of a Tropical Almond decline taking me on a tour. I guess they prefer to take an occasional fare on a 15-minute airport ride.

I quiz a driver sitting in his old sedan. "Half-day, ten bucks."

Robbery, but I have no choice. The lanky, sixtyish Black man wears a Hawaiian shirt, a felt fedora, and gray flannel trousers.

"Where to?"

"Show me whatever you can. I have to catch the LACSA flight this afternoon." We head south along the rocky shore. Past town—nothing but bush. How sparse the vegetation looks after Costa Rica's jungles.

"Ever seen an iguana?"

"All de time, mon."

"I thought they were rare."

"Who say dat?"

"Okay, great, let's go!" He drives out to the perimeter road.

We drive east, where traces of civilization are few. At an abandoned, ramshackle house he waits while I flip loose tin. Only a few geckoes and *Leiocephalus varius*, the Cayman Island Curly Tail Lizard.

Near Gun Bay, at the far eastern end of the island, an iguana. "Stop, stop!"

It sits in grass off the roadside. Young, without the characteristic blue that develops with age, but unmistakable. Thirty inches, gray with light black bands on the body, darker on the tail. The driver strains to pick it out. I point. *Has he ever seen one?* Could be I'm cynical.

We continue the Queen's Highway and discover a flock of Grand Cayman Parrots. *Amazona leucocephala caymanensis* are noisy and entertaining. What charming birds. Green with a bright red throat and white forehead. We pause to watch their comical antics. They're eating Seagrapes, holding them with their feet while they peel off the skin to reach the pulp. No more iguanas, but the single sighting makes the trip worthwhile.

We stop by the hotel while I pick up my stuff. He drops me at the airport. "This was fun. Too bad I'm not staying longer." I hand him another five dollars.

"Every hallelujah gat amen." He never cracks a smile.

Shame I didn't meet Ira. Alas, there's a big, wondrous world with so many exciting places calling, "Come see me." By evening I'm in Miami.

CHAPTER 70:

Home of Our Own

I phone my wife from Miami Baggage Claim. I haven't heard her voice in over a month. Since Panama. She sounds happy, I'm relieved. I'm impatient to get home but the animals arrive tomorrow, so I must wait. Ed picks me up, stops for a burger and fries. I miss American food. Too tired to be much company, I turn in early.

Eager to check out the Costa Rican reptiles, he takes me to LACSA cargo in the morning. No one at APHIS wants to inspect them. Free to go. Delighted to find they've arrived in excellent condition. Dart frogs included. Ed desires something of everything. I'll decide later. It's satisfying having specimens of the caliber he'd want. I gather my hard-won bounty and head for Bradenton. A quick stop at Lew Ober's to leave his lizards, then on the road.

Author in his reptile room,
Bradenton, Florida, fall 1968.
(Photo: George Goethe)

235

It's a joyous reunion. Being apart helps us reset priorities. We hunger for a return to our normal routine. My absence from the first week of July to the beginning of September was tough on her. She's managed, done well, I am proud of her and say so. Ours, however bizarre, is the life we chose. This is her moment. I've finished mine. I resolve to apply myself to mutual interests. Walls are up for our new home. I can't wait to see it.

Things return a familiar routine. Our neighbor George Goethe thinks my Costa Rican adventures are worthy of a story. He's a newspaper photographer and one Saturday when I'm washing reptile cages in my backyard he asks, "Mind if I take a few photos?"

I'm transferring a cobra to a holding container. I tell him, "Sure. Be my guest."

George arranges for staff writer Wayne Harris to conduct an interview and write an article for the *Sarasota Herald Tribune*. It's published in late fall of 1968.

My newfound notoriety earns modest respect and credibility from my supervisors and coworkers. Speaker requests follow, adding to the demos on local venomous snakes I already do for the Boy Scouts and other groups. It's fun. The Manatee County sheriff wants to refer nuisance snake calls to me. Enjoyable for a while, it gets old fast. Calls for snakes in carports or porches

Cottonmouth milking demonstration by author. (Photo: George Goethe)

Author handling an Egyptian cobra, Bradenton, Florida, fall 1968. (Photo: George Goethe)

Area Snake Expert Says Danger Far Greater With Bee Handling

By WAYNE HARRIS
Herald-Tribune Staff Writer

Did you know the bees which buzz innocuously around your flowerbeds are potentially as dangerous as a rattlesnake in the nearby woods? If not, cheer up for almost everyone else is in the same boat.

That's the word from Dennis Cathcart, a sparetime herpetologist who lives with his wife a short distance southwest of Bradenton and who says most persons know very little about snakes, and what they do know probably is incorrect.

Cathcart, a young man who thinks its safer to handle snakes than the power lines of his daily chores, also has some startling views on popular methods of snakebite treatment.

Cathcart, who earns his living mending lines for Florida Power & Light Co., has been gathering information on snakes and reptiles "since I was old enough to pick one up."

His search for specimens has taken him as far away as the jungles of Central America. He maintains contacts with fellow herpetologists all over the world.

A great deal of misinformation on snakes comes from writers, and movie producers, Cathcart explains.

"Since the general public knows little or nothing about snakes," he says, "many people have made easy money capitalizing on its fear. Snakes simply aren't that dangerous, in the jungle or out of it, but these people sensationalize to sell a movie or publish a book."

"The jungle is the most peaceful place I've ever been. I feel much safer there than I would in a large city at night."

Cathcart says the danger from snakes in Florida has been exaggerated, too. More people die annually from bee stings and other poisonous insect bites than from the combined bites of all six types of venomous snakes in Florida, he said.

"All snakes, including the ones in Florida, are generally timid and docile," he says. "And if the victim is treated with antivenom within a reasonable amount of time (usually several hours), the chances for recovery are virtually 100 per cent."

Victims of water moccasin bites, he points out, have a 50-50 chance of survival without any treatment at all. This doesn't mean, however, that snakebites are not painful or that they should be taken lightly. But, says Cathcart, often what is not done for the victim is better than what is done for him.

"Most first-aid manuals (including one put out by the state of Florida on rattlesnake bites) are replete with measures that should never be used," he says. "Tourniquets, suction kits, and incisions around the area of the snakebite succeed only in increasing the victim's pain and throwing him deeper into shock."

Proper treatment involves the injection of the proper antivenom and supportive medicines, elevation of the affected limb, and light, unconstrictive bandaging, he maintains.

Cathcart attempts to correct what he considers the surfeit of misinformation on snakes by delivering three-hour lectures to Boy Scouts and other interested organizations. In addition to contributing to the science of herpetology in general by furnishing specimens he receives to the proper universities and research institutes, also on a non-profit basis.

Though he has handled thousands of snakes, Cathcart's own collection numbers around 20 and remains constant. It includes two cobras, one specimen each of the six types of venomous Florida snakes, and a "real" camelion (like the Florida lizard erroneously labelled camelion, the genuine variety is harmless; it exists only in Africa, though, hard

Herpetologist Dennis Cathcart ... displaying 'real' camelion

to get all over the world.)

But his "pride and joy" is a venomous eyelash viper, which he captured in the jungles of Costa Rica. The eyelash viper is one of 20 vipers belonging to Cathcart's favorite genus, bothrops.

Security procedures for the snakes are as tight as in any state penitentiary. The reptiles are kept in sturdy wooden cases and ventilation holes covered with two layers of screen, one inside and one out. All feeding and handling of the reptiles is done solely by Cathcart behind a locked door.

Cathcart advises against snake collecting by amateurs, however. "For one thing," he points out, "it's against the law unless the collector is licensed, as I am, by the state of Florida."

Sarasota Herald Tribune article by Wayne Harris, about author's reptile interest. (With permission: © *Sarasota Herald Tribune*-USA TODAY NETWORK)

spread to Sarasota County. Thank God this happened before cell phones! It's rare to find a snake, and when I do it's a racer or a ratsnake, never venomous.

Our move cannot come quick enough. Tired of only a wall between neighbors. One morning before work, something else makes us impatient for change. Thieves stole my truck. I left the keys in the ignition. Everyone does. Auto theft is rare here, but it's gone. I call the sheriff. Two weeks pass, they find it in the woods beat to hell. Joyriders scratched and dented the fenders, took everything they could. The truck's a mess. We need another vehicle; I put my beloved Bronco up for sale.

By Halloween, the roof is on, interior walls up, we're installing wiring and plumbing. Time drags, waiting for drywall and plasterwork. I paint and clean, do what I can to help. With the yard graded, we chain-link fence the property and do basic landscaping. We move into our completed house right before Christmas 1968.

Nothing beats the satisfying feeling of owning our first home. At 20 years old, the $18,000 cost—including the lot—is a daunting responsibility, but we've never been happier.

CHAPTER 71:
Convoluted Connections of The Reptile World

Gordon Johnston, a herpetoculturist extraordinaire, takes joy in every facet of the hobby. He loves field collecting and the culture of keeping specimens. He trades with fellow herpers across the US and around the world. When a package arrives in the mail from Gordy, it's Christmas. Inside, smaller boxes, each with a single snake in a tiny sack. Out may pop a colorful Sand Boa, or a baby cobra. Like Forrest Gump's box of chocolates, I never know what I'll get. It's a thrill, and without fail, more than expected. A note enclosed gives interesting bits of information on the snake's origins and other details.

Dick Bartlett and I get together in the spring of 1969. He and Gordy hailed from Springfield, Massachusetts. They'd collect snakes, turtles, salamanders—two peas in a pod, lifelong best buddies. I'm not sure how Gordy ended up in New Jersey. Dick moved on to Miami. He traveled in much the same circle of people as I did, but we never crossed paths.

After Dick migrated to St. Petersburg, Gordy told him of our trades. Dick reached out. For reasons long forgotten, I brushed off his contact. Lucky for me, the ice thawed. Dick, with his soon-to-be-wife Patti, and I became fast friends. The next several years we were nigh inseparable. Dick called me "Dentist," I tagged him "Black Bart, Dik Dik" or "Bart Dicklet." Patti, slight in physical stature, got dubbed "Number Eight." We revel in joyous collecting forays to the Everglades and wilds of Central Florida.

The same year, 1969, I meet Alabama reptile collector Tommy Yarbrough while visiting the Tarpon Zoo. It's not so much a zoo as a wild animal dealer.

Owned by Mike Tsalikis of *National Geographic* fame, and run by Trudy Jerkins, it's a hub for the animal trade. Tommy is there buying large Green Anacondas when I come looking for venomous snakes. We strike up a conversation, and I invite him to Bradenton. "Next trip," he says, "I'm on my way back home." He and his wife MaryAnn run the Yarbrough Snake Ranch, a small zoo in Eastaboga. Both work a school circuit doing wild animal and snake shows. Such exhibitions are familiar to most every elementary kid in the South. Along with Yo-Yo professionals, roping and shooting.

A genuine good ol' boy with a deep Southern drawl, Tommy is as country as they come. But a smart businessman and knowledgeable herpetologist. A more authentic, likable guy I couldn't hope to meet. Our friendship grows when a few times a year he stops by while in Florida to buy reptiles. A fearless, cheerful guy, we make many fun collecting trips.

A sweet Southern belle with nerves of steel, MaryAnn is masterful at handling venomous snakes. She cares for the zoo animals by herself when Tommy travels. My favorite memory is of her fabulous peach fried pies. Tommy brings a batch to Florida when he comes. They're the best I ever tasted.

Tommy Yarbrough, the happy animal lover, collector, and showman. One of those rare people that everyone likes, a good ol' boy with infectious humor and a permanent smile. (Photo courtesy of Yarbrough family and Maddie Prickett, Eastaboga, Alabama)

Tommy Yarbrough with a boa constrictor
he bought for his show circuit.
Note his rattlesnake skin belt, with a
resin-cast, neonate rattler belt buckle.
(Photo courtesy of Yarbrough family and
Maddie Prickett, Eastaboga, Alabama)

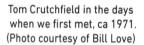

Tom Crutchfield in the days
when we first met, ca 1971.
(Photo courtesy of Bill Love)

Tamiami Trail going west
from Miami,
ca early 1960s.
(Photo: State Archives of
Florida/Liddle)

CHAPTER 72:
Karma in the Everglades

Tommy and I left yesterday, collected our way to South Florida. This morning we made the rounds of Miami animal dealers, buying exotic snakes for his shows. Crossing the Everglades returning to Bradenton, 20 miles west on US 41, in a blink, life changes course for us.

The highway, known as Tamiami Trail, is a narrow two-lane road. A row of old Australian Pines stands between the roadway and a deep canal. "Holy crap! Tommy, I just saw a crash."

"I saw it too. Let's go," Tommy says, and holds on to the dash as I speed towards the accident scene. There's zero traffic. In front of Frog City, a tourist spot where one could buy a plate of fried frogs' legs, a cheap shell souvenir, or take a photo in front of a giant Sausage Tree, are two mangled cars that had hit head-on. A few people rush out as we stop and run to the closest vehicle, a battered Volkswagen. Two men inside are knocked out, bloody.

Gas and oil are leaking. We fear the car could catch fire. I jerk open the sprung passenger door and pull an injured man from the wreckage. Tommy frees the driver. I check the rear seat to see if anyone is there, when I notice a bulging, torn-open sack on the floorboard. The skin of an enormous snake is showing!

I shout, "Look, Tommy!" pointing to the ripped bag.

He peers in from the other side. "Good God, it's an African Rock Python!"

People swarm over the other car, a Cadillac, to aid the injured. Tommy and I must make a crucial decision. What if someone sees these sacks of snakes?

The last thing we need is the Samaritan's panicking. Under the cover of confusion, we gather and move the specimens to our van without attracting attention. The glove compartment is open, a 45-caliber handgun lies in full view. I slip it under my shirt and stash it beneath my driver's seat. Strangers bring blankets to lie over the victims to prevent shock. The passenger, a bloody mess who I thought may be dead, is moaning. I speak to him, but he's incoherent.

On a scrap of paper, I write. "I have your snakes and your pistol. Call me, I will return them." To the bottom, I add my name and phone number and stuff it in his pants pocket.

There's plenty of help now and our truck is blocking the road, so we leave, even before the police or ambulance arrive.

"What are the odds? Talk about perfect timing!" Tommy says, then he makes the "Do-de-do-do, Do-de-do-do" notes of the *Twilight Zone* jingle.

I laugh, then say, "Ain't that the truth. Can you imagine if that big python had crawled out of the torn sack? It boggles my mind."

༼ঌ⁀ঌ༽

More than a month passes with no word. *Did the poor guy lose the note?* Six weeks later, I receive a call. "I'm Tommy Crutchfield, calling regarding the crash on Tamiami Trail."

"My God," I say, "I feared the worst when I didn't hear from you. So glad you called."

I tell him what Tommy Yarbrough and I did after seeing the wreck and finding the snakes, and ask how he and his friend are doing.

"Thank you so much. We're reptile collectors and were returning to Ft. Myers from a buying trip to Miami. I was in the hospital for quite a while. The gearshift knob came off and the shifter pierced my abdomen. It was ugly. My friend Ron Ramsey is okay, banged up." We agree to a future meeting when they are both doing better, and he gives me his contact info.

Ron Ramsey was the driver. He's one of those affable types everyone likes. Gigantic snakes are his specialty, and the python belongs to him. He keeps his charges in huge walk-in, zoo-style enclosures, with ample room to crawl around and grow.

In due course, I deliver the specimens and gun to their grateful owners. We become friendly, but our friendship stops at our common reptile interests.

Tommy Crutchfield is starting a business when I am getting away from the commercial end. It's my pleasure to share contacts and sources. He's an interesting guy, used to work for Ross Allen, but we run in disparate circles of friends and have separate interests. During the next few years, when our paths cross, things get interesting. That momentary quirk of fate carries long-ranging consequences.

Roadside kitsch at Frog City.
(John Margolies Roadside America photograph archive (1972-2008),
Library of Congress, Prints and Photographs Division)

CHAPTER 73:

Meanwhile, in the Bahamas - Bimini Tarantula

My apprenticeship into journeyman lineman with FPL will soon be complete. The dangerous work suits me. At every opportunity, I head to Bimini in the *UNWIND*, my 23-foot Spicklemire Islander with a MerCruiser inboard/outboard. She sleeps four. Inviting coworkers along helps pay for trips and keeps me in good graces. We fish, and when possible, I slip off to spend a day collecting on the South Island. The guys think I'm nuts. Nothing's new.

I remind them, being flippant, "You're on *my* boat in the Bahamas."

I feel blessed having Bimini a few hours away. My wife sees it as a curse, for the same reasons. Truth told—I'm gone more than I should be.

Ed Chapman sold his 17-foot Cobia and I take him across for a change. He likes my larger, safer craft. We set out to search for the snakes we want. By the old tarpaper shack is an oil drum half full of rainwater. It takes two to check. One to tip it while the other looks. I push against the barrel. Ed's on his knees in position in case something's under it.

Reflexively, he lunges to grasp a Bimini Racer, notices a tarantula, but can't stop. He grabs both, and in a continuous motion, tries to fling the spider from his hand. The snake flies, boomerang-style, as the tarantula sinks its fangs into his index finger.

"Kee-rist! Damn thing got me." He slings the enormous arachnid into the bush.

No one we know has experienced a tarantula bite. They aren't deadly, but we can't say what the effects might be. Two drops of blood form a half-inch apart where the fangs entered.

"Does it hurt?"

"Stings—stronger than a wasp." Ed shakes his hand. "Dammit."

In the next hour, the digit swells to sausage proportions, but stops hurting. It's my sacred duty to make fun for the rest of the afternoon. "Show me that technique for tossing the snake and holding the tarantula. It was great."

Western shore of North Bimini, Bahamas, ca 1969.

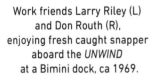

Work friends Larry Riley (L) and Don Routh (R), enjoying fresh caught snapper aboard the *UNWIND* at a Bimini dock, ca 1969.

CHAPTER 74:
Nassau

What explorer wouldn't love the Bahamas? Seven hundred islands, the majority uninhabited, a hint of what Florida must have been like a century ago. It's intoxicating, I must explore. It's early 1969, "The Age of Aquarius," and all I can think about is what reptiles live on New Providence Island and beyond. There's the Bahamian Boa, *Epicrates striatus strigilatus*, black, with brighter white than Bimini's *fosteri*. But what else? I must know.

Adventure comes cheap. Miami to Nassau is $30 on Eastern Airlines. Still, over a day's pay. On the taxi ride to town, I ask the driver. "Any reasonable places to stay?" He drops me at the Delancey Guest House, a rundown but charming inn, enveloped in trees and palms.

A single cubicle with a twin bed is $4 per night. None are vacant. Shared rooms, men and women kept apart, have several cots. At $1, it suits me fine. Most guests are young people from Europe. As the sole American, I'm a novelty.

A Canadian guy asks me about visiting Florida. I tell him tourist stuff: magnificent beaches, crystal springs, orange groves. No Disney World or related attractions yet. As my friend Stephen Littlefield says, "Before the rat infestation."

"I want to visit, but alligators scare me. From what I hear, the Seminole Indians never signed a peace treaty."

I can't believe my ears! I debunk his perceived notions. As I prattle on, I realize he's pulling my leg. He got one over on me. The next day we're chatting, and I comment on his home country. "Jeez, how do you live up there in the ice and snow with seals and polar bears?"

I touched a nerve. He argues how splendid, safe, and modern Canada is, going on and on, until he notices my smirky smile. Wow! The look on his face when he knows I got payback. It's good fun. The two nights I stay, we enjoy swapping travel stories.

During the day, I probe the bush outside of town. There are four anole species native here, and a difficult to catch *Ameiva auberi thoracica.* These colorful back-striped, gray lizards, have a rosy snout and blue tail. They bask on paths or roadsides and dart for cover at any approach. I vow to take a few for Professor Ober before I leave.

The Bahamian Racer, *Alsophis vudii vudii,* is common here. A relative of those from Bimini. Their colors range from reddish and black-spotted to beige and freckled. An uncommon form has stripes. Another is light tan with deep brown bands.

Nassau's two boas are of most interest. I flip stones until my fingers are raw, search along stone walls, under debris, in and around abandoned structures. No sign after two days in Nassau. They're either rare, or I haven't learned their favored habitat. Next, I follow a lead given to me by Ed.

CHAPTER 75:
The Monastery

Fox Hill Village bears the name of Samuel Fox, a freed slave, born in Africa. He founded the settlement, among the oldest in the Bahamas, with a grant of 23 acres of land in 1801. Here on a lofty bluff today stands the imposing St. Augustine Monastery and College. Benedictine monks who have taken vows of chastity, poverty, and obedience, make and sell bread and ice cream to Nassau's hotels. The abbey overlooks a tract of natural forest.

I visit, seeking approval to explore and camp on the monastery's bushland. Ed Chapman came here, along with Jack Facente, and found several nice boas on monastery land. "Check in and ask for Brother Ignatius," Ed told me before I left. "He treated us well and directed us to where we found the *Epicrates*."

The sound of the iron knocker on the heavy wooden portal echoes in the corridor. My heart beats faster, feet shuffle. A Black monk in a tan cassock opens the door. "Welcome to St. Augustine's. How may I help you?" His pleasant demeanor banishes any trepidation.

"Yes sir, I am here studying reptiles, hoping for permission to search on church property. I want to camp there if possible." I point to the dense woods below the hill. "I'm hoping to meet with Brother Ignatius."

"I'm Brother Gregory." He extends his hand, we shake. "I'm sorry to say, Brother Ignatius is on leave." I stand with a blank stare, unsure of what to say next. "Be so kind as to wait here," he says, as he closes the massive door with a thud.

When the brother returns, he tells me, "The Monsignor said, 'You may explore the grounds, but we cannot allow camping.' Please follow me."

St. Augustine's Monastery at
Fox Hill, Nassau, Bahamas
ca 1969

The walls are a yard thick, with 20-foot ceilings. It resembles a castle. He stops at a cubicle, inside are twin beds. "We invite you to stay here if you wish."

"Oh my gosh, you folks are incredible. Thank you so much, I appreciate this. I'll bring my things from the Delancey Guest House if that's okay?"

"Of course. I can find someone to give you a lift to town. I don't drive."

He gets a radio, plugs it in, and bath towels. Wide-eyed, slack-jawed, I follow him into a hallway that leads to a breezeway. Through another set of enormous doors, beside a Coke machine, is a parlor with a sofa, table, television, and a few comfortable chairs.

"This is our rec room. Kitchen's there. Use the refrigerator if you have something to keep cool. There's a pitcher of chilled water, help yourself."

He explains when mealtimes are. "You're welcome to dine with us. Our food is simple."

"Gosh, how can I thank you for your kindness?"

"Our mission is to serve."

As he shows me outside, we pass a shrine to the Virgin Mary. Brother Gregory makes the sign of the cross. *"In nomine Patris et Filii et Spiritus Sancti."*

At the rear of the monastery, along a driveway, I glance over a knee-high stone barrier. Ten feet below in dried leaves is an *Alsophis.*

"Wow, Brother Gregory, look!" I wave for him to come. "This is a good omen."

"We have many snakes here. Sometimes we see a boa atop the Coke machine."

I'm sure he is joking.

"Brother Paul will drive you to the Delancey for your things. You should know, he has taken a vow of silence."

Conversation is one-sided on our trip. Brother Paul chortles if I say something amusing. His face is expressive, smiling, widening his eyes, cocking his eyebrows. He's a likable guy. We arrive back as the monks gather for supper. I join them. They wear cassocks and repeat prayers in English and Latin before eating. The food tastes excellent, a fish and vegetable stew, and loaves of fresh bread. That explains the tantalizing aromas that flood the abbey. I'm surprised that several drink wine, which they offer to me. I stick with water. Most dine in silence. Others ask, "Where's home? What do you want with snakes?" Their kindness is disarming, welcoming.

In the morning after coffee, bread, and fruit, I survey the extensive expanse of native trees and a small wetland. Despite a thorough search, no snakes. The wall along the monastery is the most productive spot. Here I find the coveted banded *Alsophis*.

⌒

St. Augustine's is a godsend. During the next few years, they welcome me back. It serves as my home base even as I branch out to other islands.

One evening comes a knock on my door. "Dennis, come quick to the kitchen."

Several monks are standing by the refrigerator. On top is a four-foot-long boa. "Wow, what a beaut!" I pick it up, hold it at a distance for them to examine.

Another time Brother Gregory invites me to the lounge, where a box sat before him on the table. "These are from Father Jerome. He designed this monastery. Most know of him as the Hermit Monk of Cat Island. His Christian name is the Right Reverend Monsignor John Cyril Hawes."

He built a stone church atop 207-foot Mount Alvernia, the highest peak in the Bahamas. He lived his last years in its modest hermitage, until his passing in 1956. The box holds old photos, letters, postcards, and newspaper clippings. Mementos of the good-humored, eccentric man of God. He was fond of illustrating his messages to the Fox Hill mission with cartoons. A gifted artist and architect, he drew elaborate cathedrals on the stationery margins. Most sketches were tongue-in-cheek, with fanciful side chambers for mothers-in-law or crying babies. Others were serious, masterful works of art in miniature.

A special letter Brother Gregory saved for last. It tells of Father Jerome finding an enormous boa in his Cat Island home. He illustrated it with a caricature of himself pulling the snake by the tail. It looked to be an exaggerated 15-footer. Typical of his humorous and informative reports of his solitary life. I am honored to have seen these treasured relics.

Monasteries are not without drama. I'm in the rec room when an alarm sounds. A monk bursts in, wheezing, out of breath, having run uphill from the campus. He shouts between gasps for air, eyes wild in shock. "Two armed bandits! They took the tuition money!" He's leaning over, hands on his knees. "At gunpoint!"

We rush outside, a brother calls out, "I'll get a car," and disappears into the darkness. Three of us jump in and pursue the bandit's sedan as it careens along an access road through the thicket. Far behind, we glimpse its taillights as it turns onto a busy roadway. By the time we reach the intersection, they're long gone. The police arrive, take statements from witnesses, pick up the chase.

It's among Nassau's most notorious robberies. They struck at the end of fall registration for St. Augustine's College—since 1945, a high school for students from across the Bahamian archipelago. The bandits escaped with a year's worth of tuition fees, many thousands of dollars. So sad to witness. So unfair to a mission set up to serve. The case remains unsolved.

CHAPTER 76:
Eleuthera

Mailboat travel is a Bahamian tradition. Rusted freighters to ferries, they serve every inhabited isle and cay on island-time schedules. If saving cash trumps speed and comfort, or for those who crave the taste of adventure, mailboats are the way to go.

The MV *Air Swift* makes the Nassau to Spanish Wells route three days a week. The 110-foot former USS *SC-1340* is a retired US submarine chaser, refitted post-WWII as an island freighter. Loaded with supplies, cargo, and a few Eleutherans, we leave for the 50-mile voyage. On a bench in front of the wheelhouse, I enjoy a breezy trip over turquoise waters.

In Spanish Wells, I catch the ferry to Gene's Bay, northern Eleuthera, another world. It's rural, few people visit, it lacks hotels and other amenities. Inland, chicken farms, and row crops, fruit trees, and pineapples. In all appearances like perfect reptile habitat.

As usual, I have no plan or knowledge of what to expect. On a country trail, at an old stone house with a roof fallen in, I begin my search. From inside the ruins, I hear, "Ya lookin' for somethin' eh?" The voice has a heavy accent, not the same as in Nassau—reminds me of Scottish.

He's an older European-looking man with leathery skin. He wears black trousers, white shirt, and black, broad-brimmed hat.

"Hello, I'm from Florida, searching for reptiles." I step out. "Didn't mean to trespass."

"I thought ya tief." He stares into my eyes, doesn't smile—then emits a good-natured laugh. "Yinna find noting here. Chicken snakes be by de sinkhole."

"And where is that?"

"Come." The man walks towards a farmhouse, stepping high in the weeds.

Behind the building, he points to a depression, a sinkhole used as a garbage pit. No doubt it has rats, and ample hiding places. "We burn trash. Sometimes snakes crawl out."

"You don't kill them, do you?"

"Sometimes dey eat chicken."

I take that as a yes. Jump in to peek into an opening obscured by rubbish. Too dark, I should have brought a flashlight. "Is it okay if I look around your property?"

"Don't mind."

A derelict chicken coop with old boards and tin lying scattered looks promising. He watches while I turn them over and find nothing. "Are there more pits or caves?"

"Hoo yes, dey 'erywhere."

Encouraged, I wander off, searching the low, scrubby forest. There are few trees, many thorny shrubs. Well out of sight of the farmhouse, I spot a second sinkhole, this one trash-free. It's waist-deep, 15 feet wide. Clear skies, bright sun heats the interior. It's cooler under a ledge, where pieces of limestone flaked from the ceiling lay in piles. I go through them, moving each piece.

Under the moist, flat stones I find a *Sphaerodactylus nigropunctatus,* a Black-spotted Least Gecko. A two-inch male, light gray, speckled with a tan head and tail. Then a banded female. Marvelous creatures. Under the next layer, a miniature ground boa, *Tropidophis pardalis barbouri.* A little jewel, dark brown with black spots. Ideal habitat. The tiny geckoes are prey for the boas.

With renewed energy, I scout for other sinkholes. I spot an *Alsophis vudii,* the Bahamian Racer, but leave it. Striped *Ameiva auberi thoracica,* energized by the sunlight, dart through the underbrush. A large male Eastern Curly Tail Lizard, *Leiocephalus carinatus virescens,* ducks under a rock. I kneel, flip it, and capture the critter. In the brutal heat of the day, nothing else is stirring. I should return after dusk to check. If I can get a light.

I've drained my canteen. Hungry and thirsty, I wander to the road hoping to catch a ride. A pickup approaches, slows, and stops. The driver is White, dressed as the first guy I met, in the manner of Mennonites. His truck is old, rusted from salt spray. I run to the window. "Thanks for stopping, I'm heading south."

"What're ya doin' out 'ere?" He's moving papers and a thermos from the front seat. "Kin take ya ta Alice Town."

I toss my rucksack in back atop sacks of chicken feed, get in the cab. "You have a poultry farm?"

"Do. In Governor's Harbour."

We pass the point where the island narrows to under 100 yards. A concrete bridge spans a gap where old photos show a limestone arch once stood, long ago destroyed by storms. An 1885 Winslow Homer painting made the feature famous. Gave it the name "Glass Window." Waves pounding the 60-foot cliffs often over wash road and bridge. Injuries and deaths have resulted. Seas calm today, the view spectacular. The Bight of Eleuthera powder blue while the Atlantic is the deepest shade of cobalt. I'm blessed to see this natural wonder.

Huge concrete silos dot the landscape as we head south. The driver tells me, "For crop irrigation on Hatchet Bay Plantation."

We turn towards the seaside village of Alice Town. Support community for the surrounding massive farm. Workers live here. The shipping point for dairy products and vegetables. A tractor pulls a wagon load of pineapples to the wharf. South of the village are poultry and egg farms. Agricultural land surrounded by virgin scrub is perfect for collecting.

The farmer drops me near a ramshackle eatery. "Thank you for the ride."

"Good luck with dem snakes." Friendly fellow.

The restaurant's a shack, the broken sign over the door says "Pa" with the rest of it missing. Despite a rough exterior, the food is outstanding! Fried fish, rice, a fresh green salad. I drink a soda and a glass of water, sit back and enjoy a rest in the cool breeze.

When I pay, I tell the owner, "That was fine eating," then I ask, "Any places to stay around here?"

The owner gives change from a cigar box in colorful Bahamian currency. Dollar bills that feature coral reef scenes, square, and scalloped coins. "A guest house nex' street over. 'Nother, a block on da left." He's pointing.

I find one with a cozy room where curtains blow in the breeze. Bed's clean. Saggy but comfortable.

A village hardware has a "torch." Ten bucks. It might have been worth two. Three D-cell batteries cost another $10. Robbery, but I keep in mind I'm on a remote Out Island. Now I can investigate the woods, sinkholes, and caves after dark—but not tonight—dog-tired.

Hatchet Bay lays claim to the Bahamas' safest harbor. Deep, large enough to shelter many boats or smaller ships, it was once landlocked. Workers cut an 80-foot-wide channel through solid limestone, opening it to Eleuthera Bight. Imagine how terrifying to enter the narrow passage in rough seas. Today a few sailboats bob at anchor. Eastern Curly Tail Lizards soak up the last warm rays of sun on rugged shoreline rocks. Drawn to a deserted sandy beach south of town, unplanned, I strip to my underwear and hurl my body into the crystalline surf. Perched on a rocky promontory, I watch the sunset in complete tranquility. Twilight lingers from a sky glowing orange. I pull on my jeans and head to my room, stopping for a light dinner. Spicy conch fritters with coconut marmalade hit the spot.

Come morning I fill my canteen and trek northbound. By 10 am it swelters. Only sun-loving *Ameiva* stir. I examine twin abandoned silos. Marvels to see, but no snakes. I retreat to a coppice of Gumbo Limbo and Mastic Trees for respite from the heat. While looking for sinkholes, I emerge from the bush on the eastern shore. The island is a scant mile wide at this point. Sticky with sweat, I revel in the ocean breeze and sea scent as waves roll onto pink sands. The waters of the deep Atlantic, turquoise inshore, are inky blue where they meet the sky.

I explore north, hoping to reach Hatchet Bay caves, but fall short. Late afternoon clouds gather, obscure the sundown, speed the twilight. A downpour ensues, soon soaked, with no place to shelter. While grumbling over my luck, I meet a six-foot boa stretched across the trail, bag it and jump for joy.

I plan to revisit the sinkholes I located while I work my way back towards town. Rain stops before I arrive at the first. I scan the edges with my light, descend to search the interior, spot a four-footer emerging from a fissure. I hurry to the next stop.

On the side of a bluff, at ground level, is a crevice 20-feet-wide, 18-inches tall. I examine its length, find a small boa. Spot a larger one, deep inside, out of reach. Dangerous to enter such a low cave with the possibility of getting stuck. I won't risk it, not today.

The last sinkhole produces a pair of boas, tempts me to go back to search for the one I missed. Too far. At the roadway, dragging a bit, I halfway hope for a lift. I come across a dump. The stench of rotting vegetables and garbage draws rats which could attract snakes. I skirt the edge, adding two stout boas to my catch. What a glorious night!

A half-mile from the village, a car approaches. Wet, dirty, with bags full of boas, I wave them on and step off the road as they pass. The guest house sure looks good when I finally arrive. After a shower and a change of clothes I feel refreshed, famished, so I go for a bite. Today's my birthday. A milestone, 21! Alone, but far from lonely. After a successful hunt, I enjoy fried grouper, pigeon peas, and rice. I celebrate with a Beck's beer and reflect on how fortunate I am to be doing what I love. What a splendid evening.

༄

The morning dawns bright, cloudless. A mailboat, due in Hatchet Bay tomorrow, goes south before returning to Nassau. I walk to the Queen's Highway to hitchhike. A grandiose name for a two-lane, potholed track. A Black farmer in a pickup offers a lift. "Where ya headin'?"

"North, for the Spanish Wells ferry." The cab is full, so I climb in the rear. The wind in the truck bed is refreshing on my sunburned skin. Many places I'd like to hunt. Time is not on my side. We drive slowly crossing the Glass Window and I get one more spectacular view. Seventeen miles on, he stops in Lower Bogue, lets me off at Johnson's Grocery.

"Gene's Bay Dock's eight mile nort'. Plenty o' people travel that direction. Someone will take you." I thank him and duck inside to have a soda and snack.

Three guys in the store, near my age, are not locals. "You fellows Americans?"

"Yeah. I'm Ken." He points. "Bill's over there, and Tony."

"Dennis, from Florida." We shake hands. "What brings y'all to Eleuthera?"

"Good question. We flew from New Providence. Kinda disappointed. Don't know what we were expecting. And you? On vacation?"

"No, looking for reptiles. Headed to Nassau now." They ask me to explain the snakes.

"Want to fly back with us? No way we're staying here."

"Man, that's great, thanks." I speak before thinking. Doubts arise.

It takes an hour to make the airstrip on foot, and their older model Piper PA-22.

"Do you know your weight?"

"My guess is 250-260 with my gear. That all right?"

He calculates in his head. "We should be okay."

Snug with four of us aboard. Ken calls Nassau tower to report we're taking off inbound from northern Eleuthera. He taxies as far west as he can, turns, guns the single engine. When he releases the brake, we start a slow roll. Speed builds as we rumble along the rough asphalt. The end of the runway coming up fast. We bounce, lift, and pass over the coppice too close for comfort. As we circle, I see to and beyond the Glass Window, look for places I've been.

Over the engine's roar, I hear Ken. "We're heavier than I thought, it's a little scary."

Well, now it's scary for sure. Why in hell did he say that?

Over Nassau in no time, he radios for landing clearance. We come in hard, bounce several times. The cutoff to the terminal is at hand and he takes an abrupt left turn. We leave the pavement, cross a patch of grass.

"Oh crap. There goes my license," Ken is in a tizzy.

It seems we landed on the taxiway and ran out of tarmac too fast. Not certain. Luckily, there's little traffic. Ken, sweating, swearing, taxies to the designated spot. I take my stuff, thankful to be on the ground. He's surprised no one mentions the less-than-perfect arrival. Not me. Hey, it's the Bahamas.

"Thanks for a memorable ride, Ken." I try to cheer him.

"Man, sorry we landed hard. We were heavy, I was nervous."

"Don't be. I'm a day early and alive. I appreciate it." I glaze over the sheer terror.

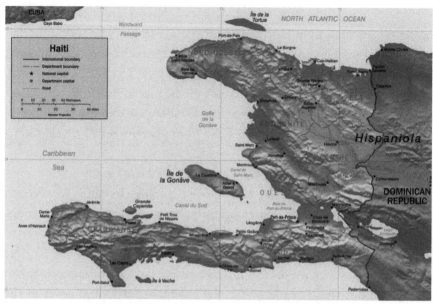

Haiti. United States Central Intelligence Agency. [Washington, D.C.: Central Intelligence
Agency, 1999] Map. https://www.loc.gov/item/99463776/

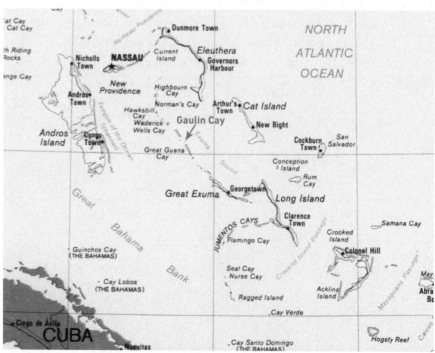

The Bahamas. United States Central Intelligence Agency.
[Washington, D.C.: Central Intelligence Agency, 1986] Map.
https://www.loc.gov/item/2005631594/

PART THREE:
The Real World

Things don't always go as planned. A strike at work opens the door for an extended Haiti trip, followed immediately by a Bahamian sojourn to Andros. We enjoy the glories of snake hunting in Florida and Okeetee, South Carolina with a British herpetologist. Haiti again, this time facing real danger. Exuma is our next target, but things go off the rails and I almost meet my demise. Artful dodgers in Bimini. Strange happenings with an old friend leave us confused on a Glades trip. What's next?

CHAPTER 77:
Strike One

No longer making a business of selling reptiles, it's now an all-consuming hobby. Between Bahamas trips, Haiti, and Mexico, I pursue snakes in Florida for trade. Those few I sell are to trusted collectors to finance travel and buy other specimens.

We still communicate by mail. From overseas, when things go right, it takes weeks for a reply. Often months. Impatience can lead to another letter sent before receiving an answer to the first. The result of out-of-sync communications is confusion. Frustration is the norm.

Many interesting people I know, I met by writing to them. One was Jonathan Leakey in Kenya. His father, Louis Leakey, and mother, Mary, are world-famous paleoanthropologists. He and brother Richard grew up doing field searches for fossilized evidence of early man. In 1960, Jonathan found a fossil jaw that became the type specimen for *Homo habilis*. A find celebrated in anthropologic history.

His interests turned to herpetology, founding a company providing snake venom for pharmaceutical research. Before that, he collected and exported African reptiles. His clients: zoos, serpentariums, private connoisseurs, live in many countries. Lucky for me, I'm on his list.

Jonathan ships Cape Cobras, Egyptian Cobras, and Forest Cobras. I receive Puff Adders, Gabon Vipers, Rhinoceros Vipers, and Green Mambas. Snakes nobody else has, such as: Boomslang, Bush Vipers, and Sand Vipers. He sends Sand Boas, Rock Pythons, Egg-eating Snakes, and Rufous Beaked Snakes.

Odd flat lizards, *Platysaurus,* and wicked spiny Sungazers, *Cordylus giganteus.*

Everyone wants to trade with me to get African and Caribbean herps few others have. My collection grows, quality improves.

Our homelife is harmonious, despite my frequent travels. In September of '69, I and a few friends from FPL head to Bimini. Our excuse is to celebrate my graduation to journeyman lineman. Plenty of beer, reef fishing, and island fun.

October 2, 1969, things fly off the rails. The IBEW strikes Florida Power and Light. I'm unemployed. For how long, no one knows. Picket duty, for no pay, has zero appeal. To take a job elsewhere could mean union fines.

My friend Ed Chapman in Miami works at FPL as a non-unionized supervisor. Now he's forced into maintenance work, and he doesn't like it. At least he's earning a paycheck. I call him. "Any ideas?"

"I wish I did. Working on a crew sucks."

"Welcome to my world. I'd love to go somewhere, make use of this free time."

Two days pass. The phone rings. "Pack your bags, we're going to Haiti."

CHAPTER 78:
A Free Man in Haiti

Most times it takes an act of congress to arrange time off for a trip. Work extra hours, kiss butt, accept the crappy jobs, whatever is necessary to curry favor with the supervisors. Now we have free rein. Well, I do at least. How Ed got a furlough, I couldn't guess. I told the union I had to leave the country and that I'd pay a fine for lost picket duty if required.

My wife is shocked and shaken by a strike none of us expected. She worries. We've been in our house for a year. "How are we going to handle our bills? My salary won't cover everything!"

It's my opening. "Ed called. He wants to do a Haiti run. I have nothing lined up except picketing. I'd rather not travel now, but on the last trip I made good money. What are your thoughts?"

Her face shows surprise. Her brow furrows. "Isn't there something around here? I don't so much mind the Bahamas, but I hate when you go to Haiti."

"I'll be okay. You know we are careful. Besides, what else is there?"

I almost feel guilty—almost. I call on Dick Bartlett to help with the reptiles while I'm gone. It's a huge favor to ask. To make the jaunt from St. Pete. He's a genuine friend.

Nobody knows when the strike will end. If it ends while we're away, we should have a grace period in getting back to work, but we don't know for sure. The plan is for a two week stay, the limit of Ed's permitted absence. We get our tickets, throw our things together, and in a few days we find ourselves, once again, in Port-au-Prince.

We taxi to Hôtel Henri, where Captain François is happy to see me. I introduce Ed. They shake hands, exchange greetings.

I inquire, "We need to locate Pierre-Paul. Have you seen him?"

The captain shakes his head. "Not for some time. I'll ask around."

We leave walking, hoping to spot Pierre-Paul. Not able to speak French or Creole, we can't ask. If his friends see us, they will realize we are looking for him. Nobody comes forward. We eat a plate of spaghetti at a Chinese restaurant and return to prepare for the trip north. It's a sure bet we aren't going anywhere without a translator.

The captain meets us coming up the steps. "No one has seen Pierre-Paul."

Now what? Then, the captain saves the day. He says, "I know a young man. He might work for you. He will come soon."

This is great news, but damn, the last thing we need is to train another interpreter. At first, Pierre-Paul thought he knew everything. Didn't repeat what we told him without changing it. It was a problem until he got experience. After that, he was excellent. "What can we do? Let's talk with him."

Within an hour the young man arrives. "Mr. Dennis, Ed, meet Jean Fritzner Lion. You can call him Fritzner. In Haiti, we go by our middle names, unless they are hyphenated."

"Oh, okay." We shake hands. "Did Captain François explain we are seeking *koulèv*?"

"Yes." His accent and tone are easy to understand, much the same as Pierre-Paul's.

"Are you willing to travel for a week to the North Coast?"

"Yes *mesye*, I will go."

Ed asks, "Have you been to Cap-Haïtien?"

"No *mesye*." He's nervous. It will take time for him to loosen up, relax. We must build trust. Trust is essential.

"Good. We'll instruct you what you must tell people, okay?" He nods. "And you don't need to be formal with us."

We agree on a fee. Fritzner, I'd guess, is 20-ish, hard to say. As Pierre-Paul did, he guides tourists to the markets and wears nicer clothes. Motivated guys can earn a decent living if they learn English and show manners.

We have time to get a car and travel permit and afterward, stop to buy glass bottles of carbonated water in Port-au-Prince. A few cans of food from Miami will help in a tight spot. Fritzner agrees to meet us at the hotel in the morning.

We leave any money not needed for the trip north with the captain, in case of trouble. Robbery is always a possibility, given the extreme poverty, though until now there have been no problems. Our complete faith and reliance please him.

✧

Fritzner meets us early. He's brought a small satchel with his things. As we leave, I tell Ed we had no problem from being late turning in our paperwork in Cap-Haïtien on our last visit. "Great. Let's check out the *Cyclura cornuta* on the way."

The road north has deteriorated. Heavy rains turned potholes into lakes. Too risky to run through in our VW, so we weave in and out around them. Progress is slow. It's approaching noon when we reach the Pont-Sondé checkpoint by the Artibonite River.

Armed men surrounded our vehicle the moment we stop. One has an official insignia on his shirt. Stone-faced, eyes hollow, he places his hand on the roof and gives a command in Creole. We turn to Fritzner.

He's asking for travel documents, wants to open the trunk. Fritzner exits the car.

The other sentries stand on both sides, staring through the windows. After poking through our gear, he slams the hood. Fritzner gets in, the gate rises, I step on the gas.

"What was that?" I speed towards the bridge.

"Tonton Macoute looking for Cubans. Your white skin made them suspicious."

"No nonsense with these guys." I rush over the span, avoiding donkeys and vendors, iron grating clanking, people scattering.

"I saw one time, a Tonton take a black dog from a child. He killed it with a machete."

"Why did he do that, Fritzner?" I check the mirror to see if someone follows.

"Because they're power-hungry assholes," Ed adds his two cents. "Petty tyrants."

Fritzner agrees, "Black dogs are a symbol of resistance. Nobody keeps them, not for years. There still aren't many."

It seems most of the pitiful mongrels we see are brown or white. "Wow, that is bizarre!"

Six months ago, in April, Papa Doc Duvalier instituted an anti-communist campaign to purge Cubans from Haiti. There's bad blood with Castro for aiding Haitian dissidents. Haiti votes with the US to enforce a Cuban trade embargo. Tonton Macoute conducts sporadic sweeps to ferret out any Cuban or communist influence. They put suspects to death, thousands of them. We got lucky.

"Those Tonton are some bad hombres," I opine.

"What it means 'bad hombres'?"

"Bad men."

"*Move moun.*" Fritzner says, as he tries to teach me Creole. Somehow it doesn't carry the same gravitas.

Tonton Macoute with machete in Haiti.
(Photo courtesy of Mack Daniel, www.haiti.fandom.com/wiki/ Tonton_Macoute)

Village in the arid plains north of the Rivière Estber where the Rhino Iguanas live.

Captured Rhino Iguana with toes tied over its back.

CHAPTER 79:
Rhino Iguanas

I try to remember where we saw the *Cyclura* on our last trip. "I'm sure it wasn't far from here. A few more miles? Across the Rivière Estber for sure. I'm thinking it was before the road turns to stones."

We spot the first *bomas*, pull over to ask a group of men if they've seen any iguanas nearby. "There are many. The village with a high fence. Stop there."

A foot trail leads into the thorny brush, so we follow it until it gets too thick, lock up, and walk to the *boma*. Boys playing stickball hide behind a bush as if afraid. We hear "*blanc, blanc*" in their conversation. White skin is a rare sight.

Fritzner goes to a gray-haired fellow sitting by the door of his mud hut and explains we're looking for iguanas. The man is nervous, eyeballing Ed and me, speaks to Fritzner.

"His son catches them to eat, but he's not here."

Encouraged but frustrated, we move on to another village. This time we drive up to the *Euphorbia* fence, follow Fritzner between huts, where he asks a man if he's seen iguanas.

"Come with me." He leads us to his hut and brings out a hefty specimen with legs tied behind its back by twisting tendons of their longest toes together. It's a cruel method, common throughout the world for handling large lizards.

"Will he sell it? Ask him if he can get more." Ed's excited.

Fritzner poses the questions. "He's asking how much we pay."

We offer four quarters. "*Double sa.*" He's demanding two dollars, explaining they are hard to find and harder to capture.

This angers Fritzner. Shouting ensues. "He will accept $1.50." We agree and pay.

Ed has an idea. "We'd love to learn where they live. If he'll take us hunting, we'll buy any iguanas we catch, same price."

He agrees and leaves to bring help. Fritzner doesn't want to go into the field, volunteers to watch the car. They know what we want. We give him a break. While waiting, we have a snack and drink our fill of water.

The old man and his crew lead the way over dried clay-like mud terrain where every bush has thorns. Cacti and *Euphorbias* dot the dry plain. We trek for a half-hour, beyond sight of the *boma*. When a hunter shouts "*Igwan!*" the chase begins.

They're wearing ragged shorts, no shirts, or shoes, but far outdistance us running. When we reach them, they've cornered an iguana. Shouting, machetes flailing, they feverishly hack away at a cluster of cacti. It's amazing someone didn't lose a hand. In moments they've removed the spiny cut stems and probe into a hole. With a blade, they dig until exposing the iguana's tail. One grips it, pulls hard. We fear he'll surely break the tail off, but with the steady pressure, the animal slides out unharmed. Several pairs of sweaty, ebony hands subdue it, pressing it to the ground, avoiding the crushing jaws. A tall fellow grabs the legs, ready to twist its toes.

"Stop." Ed pulls on the man's wrist. "We'll take care of it." He takes control of the struggling lizard. Despite the language barrier, they understand.

The powerful creature has the build of a small dinosaur. A massive head and stout horn on its snout earn it the name Rhinoceros Iguana. Slate gray with a crest of dorsal spines. It's an older male with heavy jowls and dewlap and a padded crown or cap atop its skull. At up to 20 pounds and over four feet long, they are impressive beasts.

We leave to continue our journey, assuring we'll be back in a week to buy what they find. This pleases the men. We consider but decide against leaving our specimens here. It'd be nice not having to contend with them in our cramped VW, but too many things could go wrong. An iguana in hand beats two in the stew pot.

CHAPTER 80:
New Digs

Darkness approaching, we stop in Gonaïves for the night. This city always gives me the feeling we've interrupted something nefarious. We move on at daylight. A few miles beyond Ennery, deep in the mountains where sharp angled rocks chew tires, we suffer our first flat.

While changing the tire, we notice another getting low. It's not far to Plaisance, so we drive on with caution. As they fix the flats, we snack on delicious *pâté*, a fried stuffed pastry. Ours with fruit compote. Fritzner eats the kind that was Pierre-Paul's favorite, filled with "goat paste."

In an hour we arrive in familiar, welcoming Limbe. The small tropical village with a mix of thatched and tin-roofed huts and a few wooden houses looks the same as last year. A single shop sells basic items at the roadside, soap, rice, local foods, clothes, and bottles of potions. A one-room schoolhouse stands back in the trees. Several men recognize us. We have Fritzner ask if anyone has seen Felix. Nobody has. Our best collector, he brings the most, rarest, and healthiest snakes.

A crowd gathers. We announce plans to be here for a few days. People smile, chatter among themselves. We leave energized, bidding goodbye until morning.

Fritzner is quizzical. "Why do you want snakes? Where will you put them?"

"We'll let you hold them." Ed and I laugh. Fritzner doesn't see the humor. His scowl and furrowed brow say he's questioning his coming on this trip. We use his discomfort to poke fun the rest of the way into Cap-Haïtien.

∽

We surrender the envelope with the red-wax seal to the ministry in Cap-Haïtien. They are cordial, say nothing of our being late, and thank us as is customary.

As we walk out, Ed slaps his forehead. "I meant to open the letter to see what it says."

"Next time," I say, as I get in on the passenger side.

To our shock, we find the Roi Christophe closed for painting and renovation.

"Dang, where can we stay now?" I'm disappointed.

Ed pulls to the curb of the cobblestoned street. "I remember when I came with Jacques Durocher, he mentioned Hôtel Mont Joli as another choice."

"Where's that?"

"Don't know." We glance at Fritzner.

"I'll ask a workman for directions," he says, as I get out so he can exit the back seat.

Red roofed white buildings are surrounded by tropical trees and palms, paradise on a Caribbean mountainside. Open porticos, polished quarry tile floors, wooden ceilings—a slice of heaven. There's indoor dining and furniture on a veranda by a spacious pool. A steel drum plays as we unload.

Lanbi an Sòs Kreyòl—conch in creole sauce for dinner is outstanding. It offers delicate flavors new to my unsophisticated palate. Coffee and deserts follow and liquor if we want it. Satisfied, we relax on the deck with a view of lighted boats on the darkened sea.

"Did you see that?" Ed points to the pool. "Look, there it goes again." A large bat skims the water, leaving a long ripple. "Suppose he's drinking or fishing?"

Fritzner, our translator, helping change a flat tire on road north.

CHAPTER 81:
A Tense Start

The bold aroma of Haitian coffee opens our eyes. French bread and mango preserves on silver trays fill the void. Ed and I pass up stewed fish. Three of us, two rooms, breakfast, and dinner, for $8 a day. My mind boggles.

As we reach Limbe, a few men stand in the road, waving. No snakes so far, we're early. We leave them to collect, drive a few miles south to a pleasant place on the river. Women washing clothes drape them on riverside rocks to dry, a group of boys' scatters. "Fritzner, why are they running?" When he gets out, he asks the oldest of them.

"You're the first white men they have seen up close. They fear your magic."

"What magic?" I'm puzzled.

"Every man has magic. Some more than others." Whatever it means, he doesn't explain.

Lunch along the Limbe River. Fritzner sitting on top of car, Ed on side.

Superstitions surround
the Black Witch moth.

The sun brings out lizards. Each stands watch on their own boulder. Rainbow-colored *Leiocephalus personatus,* Haitian Curly Tails. In the riparian forest, a pair of colorful Hispaniolan Trogons are nesting. Haiti's national bird. Once common and widespread, they've become a rare sight. Ed spots a huge dark moth on a tree trunk. Eight-inch wingspan, near-invisible, its cryptic pattern blends with the tree's bark. I look twice before seeing it. Known as a Bat Moth, or Black Witch, *Ascalapha odorata.* We call Fritzner over to see it.

"Kill it, kill it."

"What? Why?"

"*Move chans, sa ki mal.*" He translates. "Bad luck, evil."

"It's a friggin' bug. Not evil. Don't tell me you believe this hocus-pocus stuff!"

"I don't." As we head towards the car, Fritzner excuses himself to have a pee. He turns back. "Whatta ya bet the bastard went to kill the moth."

Ed glances over his shoulder. "Looks that way."

In the village, men with snakes gather. We buy them, including an injured one, to not discourage them. We point out we won't accept any others with injuries. Ed lets it go at the edge of the bush. Someone chops it with a machete. Infuriated, he curses the guy, calls him a "son of a bitch." The words they may not understand, but the anger comes through loud and clear.

Fritzner continues to ask for Felix. Nobody sees him much since he moved to the hills. "What if we offer a reward for finding Felix?"

Ed agrees. "Worth a try."

Fritzner announces. "If anyone finds Felix, we'll pay them a dollar."

No other snakes come in, so we drive east to pass the time hunting. Ed turns a log and beneath is a *Phormictopus cancerides,* the Haitian Giant or Bird-eating Tarantula. He calls me over, nudges it with a twig. The spider jumps out of its hole, front legs waving, its fangs bared. What an impressive creature!

These reddish-brown to purple beasties can reach nine inches across. We have no fear of them, but both of us jump back out of reflex. Fritzner's eyes are as big as saucers.

"Holy crap, he wants to eat us!" It dwarfs the one that nailed Ed in Bimini.

He plans to bring a few specimens home this time, but he forgot to pack the special boxes to transport them. We'll wait until the end to get them in case they're tricky to keep alive.

The afternoon brings a few more snakes before we start for Cap-Haïtien. The first day, expectations aren't high. When the next day ends the same, we worry and wonder. Are the best snake hunting days in Limbe behind us? There seems to be less interest.

On the third morning, the crowd is abuzz. "Felix is coming." A man claims to have walked to his village to tell him we were here. He demands his dollar. Fritzner tells him he'll get it when Felix shows. Three o'clock, Felix arrives. We pay up, thank the finder.

He's holding a gourd. A broad smile lights up his face as he speaks in Creole.

"What's he saying, Fritzner?" I take the container.

"He says 'For you my friend blue eyes', he remembers you."

After pulling the stopper and tipping it—nothing. I can tell something is in there. I jiggle it, and a tiny head peeks out.

"Wow, Ed, an *Epicrates gracilis!*"

He takes the gourd and the snake slithers out the rest of the way. "Fantastic! We want more of these. Where's Fritzner?"

Fritzner is standing back 20 feet. "Not a fan of *koulèv*? Don't worry, they're not venomous, and you won't need to touch them. You have to help us though."

He stands silent, wide-eyed. The past two days doubtless a traumatic experience. Fritzner translates, though I'm sure Felix already got the message. He's beaming and so are we. He has others, big boas. We explain we'll be here for at least several more days. Felix says he'll return tomorrow. It's been a great day.

"And you, Fritzner?"

"I don't like snakes."

"Have you ever seen one before today?"

"Yes, of course." I have doubts. For sure, so far, he hasn't seen anything.

We enjoy a cheerful ride to Cap-Haïtien.

CHAPTER 82:
The Cheat

O ur early arrival leaves time to explore Cap-Haïtien. Though parts are poor, the scenic, colonial-era seaside town has a quaintness. It lacks the gritty, overpopulated intensity of Port-au-Prince. Pastel-colored buildings, cobblestone streets clean by comparison. At a seafront promenade, vendors keep neat displays. They are busy, but not thronged. I wonder whether Fritzner knew such places existed in Haiti. Imagine his life in Port-au-Prince compared with ours at home. As with Pierre-Paul, Ed and I enjoy exposing him to the nicer side of his country.

It's lovely, but where are the tourists? French hotel guests, here when we checked in, have left. We alone remain. No one we know visits Haiti, nor would we if not for the reptiles. Now we have a bond. When here, I must force myself to think of home. Even for a moment. On the expedition, there's no looking back.

After breakfast, we tend specimens, take our time leaving. In Limbe, no sign of Felix, but we're unconcerned. He knows we'll be here a few days more. He might be the sole collector who trusts we'll return. A few come with snakes. One has a serious injury.

Fritzner steps up, makes it clear, "After this, we will buy no more damaged snakes."

Ed cuts the snake loose, tosses it into a mango tree. A woman from a house behind, one of the few houses in the village that is stucco with a tin roof, comes out yelling, wide-eyed, waving her arms.

"She mad." She's ranting, kicking dirt in our direction. It isn't funny, but I snort, crack a smile. A subtle shake of Fritzner's head signals me to cool it.

By day's end, we've accumulated a dozen boas. Not great, but decent, considering no Felix. He's not here again this morning, but no reason to worry. He'll come when he's ready. The fellow with the wounded boa has another tied to a stick.

Ed kneels and unties it. "Look, this guy brought the same one from yesterday." He shows a neck injury and releases it into bushes across the road. His hand is out expecting money. Ed's pissed and turns his back. "We're not buying the same injured snake twice."

Fritzner translates. The man flies angry, yells, curses, grabs Ed by the shoulder. He spins around, points his finger in the guy's face. "You cheated us. We are not paying."

The same woman comes from her house yowling, arms flailing. The cheat is her husband. Other men say she put him up to trying to swindle us. That's no surprise. We're fed up with the drama. Fritzner is nervous, tries to keep the peace.

Ed's had enough. "Tell them, if she doesn't shut up, we'll quit buying snakes."

I'm not sure what Fritzner said, but her fraudster spouse works to calm her, then backs her into the house. Ed sighs, shaking his head. "What a bitch."

The men laugh. It needs no translating.

Ed unties the same injured snake offered yesterday.

Ed launches the snake into the tree, and we refuse to pay.

CHAPTER 83:
Felix Returns

"Felix is coming!" Fritzner reports as word rolls through the crowd that gathered for the mad-woman-sideshow. The circus is in town. Children come running for the main event. Excitement crackles. Up the road, he parades with his entourage. King of the snake hunters.

Guys carry snakes tied to sticks. Boys have gourds. Two heavy sacks, Felix dumps one on the ground. The pack withdraws, then crowds back in like a wave. Oohs and aahs as the pile of serpents untangles. A half dozen boas, the largest we've seen. The other has smaller ones and three *Hypsirhynchus ferox,* the Hog-nosed Racer. Though rare, there's not much demand, but we are glad to have them.

Next, a gourd with *Uromacer frenatus,* the Brown Vine Snake. Then out slips a handsome, yellow-striped, black *Leimadophis parvifrons.*

I tip a second calabash, and nothing stirs. I peek inside, give it a gentle shake, and a tiny Haitian Ground Boa slides into my hand.

"*Tropidophis haetianus,* another new taxon, Ed." It coils tightly around my fingers.

Ed is beaming. The last holds several Rainbow Curly Tails. So they don't escape, he buys the gourd. "No more *Koulèv Baton*?" The local name for *Epicrates gracilis.*

Fritzner translates. "Felix says they live in the mountains near his home."

"Ask if we can drive him partway back." Fritzner's face goes pale, shocked that we'd offer this peasant a ride.

We know Felix is uncomfortable as he and a boy climb into the rear seat. The VW groans with five people and the snakes. We drop him a few miles south and he will walk an hour from here. Asked if he'd want a ride tomorrow from the same place, he says he'll meet us in Limbe. Fritzner's nose is out of joint until we reach the hotel.

CHAPTER 84:
The Spell

What a day! How great to have a shower. We clean up and go to dine. Cool and breezy by the pool, we linger, enjoy a Coke. Fritzner reappears in fresh clothes, shoes shined, and seems over his Felix snit. We treat him as our equal in every way, but he does not extend the same respect to the country folk in Limbe.

Dinner is exceptional. *Griot* is a dish of pork chunks marinated in lime and other citrus, onion, and peppers. Crumbed, fried, it comes out brown with a glaze and tastes out of this world. Served with avocado salad, warm French bread, and papaya juice. Food of the gods!

Satisfied, relaxed when we retire, images flood my mind as we lay in the darkness. Twenty minutes pass, I can't turn off the picture show. "Ed, you asleep?"

"Not yet. Something wrong?"

"Nah. Just thinking. Some week, huh?"

"Yes, it was. Today was crazy. That batshit broad and her lying husband."

"Yeah...I love it, don't you? Not that part, all of it."

"You know what we'll say in 20 years? 'Those were the good ol' days.'"

"Perhaps you're right, before it all ends."

Sleep is deep, peaceful, and welcome.

❧

Ed Chapman removing a boa lashed to a stick.

Locals looking shocked after a boa bites Ed.

After a relaxed breakfast, we tend to the specimens. We gather our dirty sacks and clothes for washing. In town we fuel, check oil and tires, clean out trash, buy a few snacks for our lunch on the road to Limbe. At noon, we arrive at our usual stop. No one is waiting, but a few old fellows are under the thatched shelter, gossiping on their log. They share a jug of *aksan*, a drink of cornmeal and milk, spiked with rum.

Fritzner visits with them. We hang in the shade. A few children join the group, giggling. We hear "*blanc*" in their chatter. A guy brings a boa slung on a strip of bark. We buy it and bide our time. In the next hour, a few others come with snakes as the audience grows.

By midafternoon, 20 onlookers wait as Felix arrives from the south as promised. He has several large boas and two of the exquisite *Epicrates gracilis*. We stand him atop the car when we pay so the watchers can see. A dollar each. This has become a spectacle, but it's our best way to recruit new collectors.

As Ed is untying a hefty boa, it bites his arm. No big deal. One more of hundreds of non-venomous snake bites. It's a solid bite, with profuse bleeding. A gasp comes from the huddle. Everyone steps back. Ed ignores it, bags the snake, wipes the blood with a sack and we load.

There's a commotion, people babbling, craning their necks. "They think you'll die. Will you?" Fritzner's face shows concern, eyes wide, lips parted, brow furrowed.

"What, from a boa bite?" Ed's perplexed.

"They're harmless, Fritzner," I assure him. "They can't hurt anyone."

After the many snakes that men in the village have caught, has none ever gotten bit? If not, it's hard to believe. The crowd stares unblinking, mouths agape. We can smell the fear.

I ask Fritzner to, "Let them know we'll be back in the morning for our last stop." The crowd steps into the road as we drive away, standing there until we are out of sight.

At the hotel, Fritzner examines Ed's arm when he washes it. The outline of both the snake's jaws visible from dozens of tiny tooth punctures. "See, no harm done." He dries with a towel. Nothing more is needed. Fritzner is unconvinced.

At dawn, we breakfast, gather the snakes, an impressive haul, and pack them with our gear in the VW. After checking out, we head for Limbe. A crowd has gathered. The hysterical woman who harassed us yesterday is in the roadway. *Now what?*

People swarm in, trying to glimpse Ed's arm the moment we stop. He holds it up to show everyone he's okay. Fritzner tells them everything that happened last evening to allay their anxiety. The *fanm fou* (crazy woman) dances around to drums only she hears. *Is she drunk?* Her face white with cornflower, wild-eyed, she throws her head back, chanting.

"What the hell is this, Fritzner?"

"She's casting a spell."

"On me or Ed?"

"The three of us." His voice wavers. I sense fear.

"You don't believe in this stuff, do you Fritzner?" Okay, I'm taunting him.

This is ludicrous. How unfortunate the villagers aren't taking it as lightly as me. They give her a wide berth as she whirls and chants, waves her arms, shakes her fingers.

"What's got her upset, Fritzner?"

"The snake bit Ed and he didn't perish."

"I guess his magic is strong then?" I laugh, punch his shoulder.

"It's not funny." His brow furrows, mouth is drawn in a frown, lip poked out.

"She's nuts, Fritzner." I look him in the eyes. "Let's lose this wacko, Ed."

I move 50 yards. The men follow. The crazy woman stays.

Boys in Limbe bring tarantulas in gourds and tied to strings.

A man offers a tarantula in his hat

CHAPTER 85:
Tarantulas

"I forgot to tell them we wanted tarantulas." Ed presses his lips tight. "Dammit."

"We can stay a couple more hours. Let's ask, see if they turn up a few."

Fritzner spreads word we'll buy a dozen tarantulas and he gives them an hour. No one has a watch. Time means little. They trust we're coming back, and that's enough.

We head south, hoping to meet Felix walking down the road to Limbe, but there's no sign of him. A flock of bright green Hispaniolan Parakeets lights in a copse of trees by the river. Distinctive with a white eye ring and red underwing. They chatter and squeak, eating tiny fruits. Ed tells me Jacques snuck a pair into Miami a few years ago. I prefer to see them wild.

"It looks as though the children are the tarantula catchers." A swarm of them meets us with gourds, crowd in tight, as we pull into our shaded stop.

The first has several tarantulas. It's a mess. The spiders fought. Only legs fall out when Ed tips it. When there's a single spider per gourd, they're okay.

A smiling lad hands me a sweaty straw hat, cradling a huge one. "Where are we going to put this?" Ed checks the hairy creature, pays 5¢ for an empty gourd, places the critter in, and pulls a wad of grass for a stopper.

Fritzner explains to those gathered we won't soon return, making sure they understand. A fellow who's a reliable collector steps forward to shake hands. These are decent people, affable, honest, welcoming. More than the money we pay, our visits offer a diversion, we each have our rewards.

Felix knows we are heading out early. He must have nothing. We call, "*Orevwa*," and wave as we leave. Two miles south of Limbe, we meet Felix carrying his sacks.

"Where does he find so many snakes?" Ed says as he steps out. I back the car to where a tree casts a shadow.

No crowds, it's quiet. Felix has a few big boas and another of the precious *Epicrates gracilis*. The boys have gourds with vine snakes and a Hog-nosed Racer. We remind Felix that we are leaving for Port-au-Prince, bid him farewell, shake his hand. I slip him a three-dollar tip. As we drive off, I can't help wondering if we will return.

Burlap sack full of tarantulas.

CHAPTER 86:

The *Loogaroo*

Beyond Plaisance, we pause atop the escarpment before descending to the lowlands. The waterfall that we enjoyed on the last trip is now a mere trickle. We open canned peaches for a snack. Fritzner declares his "Too sweet" but eats them. Children come to pick the metal lids from the dirt road. When Fritzner finishes, he chucks the can into the tall grass on the roadside. Two boys plunge after it. The others have their hands out. I hand mine to one. Ed tosses his and they jump. We laugh, but these kids see the value. They're living in poverty impossible for us to comprehend.

To avoid travel after dark, we overnight in Gonaïves. Our stay is uneventful, but morning finds a flat tire. Déjà vu. "This same thing happened here last year, with Pierre-Paul," I state.

Sure, the roads are terrible, but it's odd. Who knows? We stop on the way out of town where a row of sullen Black men wait in repair shops. Like so many buzzards watching for roadkill.

The road is a series of pond-sized potholes. The swaying motion from weaving in and out, the heat and exhaust fumes, make Fritzner queasy. We dodge people, donkeys, and carts. The going is tedious. Ed watches for the iguana village.

A youngster fetches the man who helped us last. He comes smiling, beckons we follow. In a dirt-floored hut, iguanas lay tied. They're as big as the one we caught on our way north. *Don't they come smaller?* These hefty beasts are valuable but difficult to transport.

A second shack with another the same size has a tiny, dried turtle hanging from a string over the doorway. "Ed, check this out. What do you suppose this means?"

Fritzner answers. "Vodou. It's for the *Loogaroo.*"

"What the hell's a *Loogaroo?*"

"A vampire. If a child drinks baby turtle blood, it turns his blood bitter. A turtle over the door means the *Loogaroo* will pass. It a belief of the country people."

Ed shakes his head. "Just when you think they're the same as us."

"They are. Think about it. It's Passover with an added dash of Haitian hocus-pocus." I look at Fritzner. "Do you believe this stuff?"

"No." He always says that. I'm not convinced.

We cross the Artibonite River to the Pont-Sondé checkpoint. "They say to unload everything from the car." Fritzner is nervous. He picks up on things we don't.

We empty the trunk; the bags are moving. The guard asks, "what's in the sacks?"

Ed picks one up with an iguana inside thrashing. Fritzner tells him "*Igwan*" and that we will eat them. They're skeptical, but let us go. Why is this checkpoint so problematic? At least it's clear sailing to Port-au-Prince.

CHAPTER 87:
Red Mud and Swollen Eyes

We stash the animals in the room provided by Captian François at the Hôtel Henri. The captain is full of questions. "Tell me of your trip to the North Coast." He's glad for the company of Americans, like Ed and me. It's hard for him to imagine why we want snakes. He tells Ed his rattlesnake story from Pensacola. I've heard it.

We plan to make a run up to Furcy to collect a few *Hyla vasta*, the Giant Treefrog, but first we take a much-needed day off to tend our specimens and unwind from the trip. A welcome rest from the intensity of our journey. Fritzner comes in the morning and takes to visit the Iron Market for souvenirs and to buy two sturdy baskets to pack some of the snakes. The Rhinoceros Iguanas are so large that they need most of the suitcase space, we don't have room for everything.

Rain on the way up the mountain turns the serpentine road lethal. We creep along in the blinding deluge and fog, feeling our way around curves and crossing rivers of runoff that wash deep gullies in the mud and gravel surface. Thankfully, the downpour stops before we reach the summit. Our VW slips and slides and skids sideways as we negotiate the narrow trail into the village of Furcy. Deep ruts keep us from hitting the fences, our wheels spin, slinging mud which rains down on the back of the car.

We pull up to our familiar spot, tell Fritzner that he can wait by the car, then we climb between barbed wire strands to descend to the banana grove. Down the muddy slope we go, more sliding than climbing.

In no time, we find the first of the giant frogs. Using caution, we carefully pluck them from between the banana sheaths and deposit them into sacks. Despite our caution, within moments, our noses are burning, eyes watering. We rush to collect our quota and make our way up the slimy slope as our vision fades. At the car, we are coated in red clay from the knees down, eyes watering, tears streaming down our cheeks, noses running like faucets.

"Don't laugh, Fritzner, and whatever you do, don't touch us."

Eyes wide, he backs off. Ed and I struggle to a stream where we wade in and wash our hands, face and trousers. The cloth sacks of frogs look like they are covered in snot, but it's the anuran's toxic foam. Too teary-eyed to drive, we spend a little time hunting in the banana grove and near the stream for herps. A few nice lizards turn up, including an *Amphisbaena*, and some strange beetles.

As if the snakes and spiders hadn't been weird enough, our newbie translator had to witness our masochistic frog hunt. I tell Ed, "This will probably be the last time we'll see Fritzner."

Wood carving of a Vodou scene with a snake.

CHAPTER 88:
Back to the Whirlwind

It's tough to leave our beloved Haiti. Here we're significant, special, larger than at home. Hard to describe, but it's addictive. On our last day, we turn in our car and settle with Fritzner.

"Anytime Zye Ble." He shocks us, we thought he'd be done with us, but we're happy. We thank him for his invaluable help and add a nice tip.

Time crawls. We sort, clean, and pack our specimens. Our collection is massive, the biggest ever. Four suitcases and two baskets, not counting several large wood carvings. I'd found a three-foot-long, heavy, carved wooden plaque depicting a Vodou ceremony with a snake. I had to have it. Ed's not happy.

Our extra clothes we give to Captain François. He'll pass them to those in need. A few tins of fruit, Vienna Sausages, and beans he's glad to have. He remembers eating these things in Florida years ago and considers them a treat. A tradition is opening a tin of black olives for a celebratory taste of civilization after a wild foray. We sit on the steps of the old church-turned-hotel to enjoy them. A successful trip. Our true calling. We are where we belong. We're lucky and know it. Grateful for this opportunity. Nevertheless, it's nice to be going home.

It takes two cabs to bring everything to the airport. We start early and have rehearsed how to explain the snakes, but no one asks. In the departure lounge, we admire a massive mahogany root system carved to depict the Garden of Eden. Adam and Eve are surrounded by animals and plants. By late afternoon, we are in Miami.

❦

"Got any liquor?" The only question at Customs. We make no mention of the reptiles.

We don't know how good we have it. It won't stay this easy forever.

I call my wife from Ed's house; she is well. I promise to hurry home after we split the catch. It can get contentious when both of us want the exceptional specimens. Regardless of who caught or received what, they go into a common lot. The fairest method is to flip a coin for the first pick, then alternate.

I keep a few picks and leave the majority. Ed promises to sell them and split profits. Zoos will get the Rhino Iguanas. I don't know where the rest will go, but Ed's well connected. We part, vowing to stay in touch. Our differences never manifest in the field. Another fruitful trip and enjoyable time.

Lew and Marge Ober invite me to spend the night when I stop by with lizards. Gone over two weeks, I'm eager to see my wife, but it's getting late. I love visiting with these folks. Lew elicits details of the specimens, their habitats, and things we saw in Haiti.

He loves to tell stories from his service in the CBI: China, Burma, India Theater during WWII. Tales filled with humor, of life in China, not of war. He has this trait in common with my dad and neither speaks much of the ugly side of warfare they saw. I love to listen.

A colorful *Anolis hendersoni* delights Lew. It's greenish brown with a bold white lateral stripe and a splash of blue on its head. A strange-looking *Amphisbaena innocens* we collected near Furcy is his favorite. The foot-long creature, pinky finger thick with annulations, or rings, resembles an earthworm. It's not a snake, but a legless, burrowing lizard.

Home! Things are stable. Money is getting tight. My being gone is less of a significant issue these days. Dick's help with the reptile collection is a huge blessing. The few Haitian specimens I give he'll use for trades. He prefers keeping hot (venomous) snakes.

There is no end in sight for the strike. I contact anyone who may want reptiles from Haiti. They sell fast, netting more than $1,000 in the first week: big money in 1969. I prefer not selling reptiles, but circumstances demand I do what's needed to make a living.

CHAPTER 89:
Bahamian Adventures

Austrian herpetologist Erich Sochurek and I trade ratsnakes, kingsnakes, and rattlesnakes for European species. He has a keen interest in Caribbean herps. Before leaving for Haiti, I write. A week after returning, it's past midnight when the phone rings.

"Sell no more to anyone. I will buy them." I struggle to understand his accent. It's Erich, and he wants all of the Haitian snakes Unfortunately, with the mail delays, I've already sold most of the stock that I offered to him.

Ed has the extras, so I contact him in the morning. He wants snakes in the genus *Vipera* in trade instead of cash. Not a problem, at least he still has some of the stock left. I ask him to hold the rest for me.

Before I ship, Erich asks what I have from the Bahamas. Not much, but with FPL still on strike, I make a plan.

Encouraged by sales, my wife agrees. My idea is to pilot my boat to Bimini, then on to the Berry Islands. Next, to Andros before returning to Miami. When I approach Ed, he's skeptical of my grandiose agenda, but offers to watch my truck and trailer for me while I'm gone.

Such a voyage is a longstanding dream. In hopes of one day making the journey, months ago, I installed extra gas tanks. Now, with 100-gallons of capacity it's double what's needed for the longest leg of the trip. As to making the trip solo, Ed can't be off from work, although he'd love to go. Nobody else I know can go, and most I wouldn't ask anyway. I load supplies onboard and start for Miami.

The *UNWIND* docked in Bimini for the first leg of a Bahamian journey.

Four hours across the Gulf Stream is a different world. I tie up in North Bimini. Since I'm by myself, it's easier and safer to use the ferry to reach the South Island. Luck on my side, I catch a ride to the airport. Once in the bush, I go straight for the proven collecting spots. By day's end, I have six *Epicrates* and three *Tropidophis*. I capture a few curly tail lizards for good measure and head back to Alice Town.

As I enjoy Hogfish with pigeon peas and rice at the Red Lion, I want to pinch myself to prove I'm not dreaming. I'm blessed, so beyond lucky, for living the life I love. Gentle rocking, hushed bumps, and squeaks of hulls on docks and the cooling breeze bring on the deepest sleep. Come morning, I stroll to the Compleat Angler for breakfast, then head to the ferryboat. It runs on island time, so I wait on the quay, watching colorful fish swim among discarded conch shells in the limpid water.

I spend the day searching the spots I skipped previously. They are never as productive, but I find four more *Epicrates* and a *Tropidophis*. One under a piece of wood where I collected another yesterday. Bimini is outstanding!

Back on the North Island, I talk with a couple of Bahamian guys who work at the dock. I tell them my idea to visit the Berry Islands and Andros.

"Boy, it niney mile ta Great Harbor. Ya ain't no sea captain." I guess they don't approve.

They think I'm crazy for making the 50-mile solo crossing from Miami. Their comments give me pause. I ask another boater out of Lauderdale what he thinks. His yacht's a 60-footer. "Not without a pilot."

Fuel in Bimini costs $1.25 a gallon, while in Florida it's 35¢. In the Berrys, it could be much higher. Truth told; I'm not prepared. The whole scenario is naïve.

Not giving up, I check on a flight to Great Harbor and find none. There's daily service to Nassau and on Friday and Tuesday connecting flights to Andros. I arrange with the dockmaster to keep the boat. I stay free, since my FPL friends and I fixed up his electric service and do maintenance when we visit. There's a storage shed, set in the shade, with a cool concrete floor where I can put the snakes. My ticket, Bimini through Nassau to Andros and return: $40.

CHAPTER 90:
Andros

The sole passenger on Friday's flight from Nassau to Andros Town. Twenty minutes over the Tongue of the Ocean. I booked my return for Tuesday.

A former logging settlement, population under 50, a few houses, a store, and a dive shop. Tourists are rare. My room is $4 per night. Abandoned buildings, rusted equipment overgrown with weeds, look perfect for snakes, but an afternoon search turns up only a huge scorpion. A German guy running the small restaurant offers advice. "Schnakes? Ja, I droff ein lumper truck. Vould zee zem from time to time. Not zo many here. I'd go north if I vere you."

The vastness overwhelms. 2,300 square miles, more than the other 700 Bahamian Islands put together. A few towns hold most of the 8,000 residents, the rest of the island remains unpopulated. The northern part has higher elevations, which could be better. Nicholls Town is 40 miles up with little between and near-zero traffic.

At a grocery-hardware-post office, I stop for a cold drink and ask the proprietor how I can get to the north end. There's no local transportation. An old Black man buying supplies says, "I give ya ride tamara marnin."

Saturday morning, with my grip, I meet the gent out front. His rusted pickup has a half dozen well-used chainsaws in the back on an oil-soaked sheet of plywood. Every island has a Queen's Highway or King's Highway. The road crosses a newly built bridge over Fresh Creek to Coakley Town and hugs the coast.

"'Ere ya from, New York?"

"Florida. I'm here for reptiles." Silence. "So, you work on chainsaws?"

"Name's Lyle. Yep, fix 'em, sell 'em, any small engines. What you do wit dem snake?"

"Study them. Supply zoos." Eager to hunt, when we reach the Staniard Creek cutoff, I ask, "Think I should stay and search here a while?"

"I'll drop ya. Don' tink dis is what ya want."

He proceeds across swashland or tidal mudflats. The settlement is on a sliver of sand and does not appear as suitable snake habitat. "You could be right."

Lyle has the "I told you so" expression and turns the truck around without speaking. Beyond the new Stafford Creek bridge, the highway curves inland. We rumble along the wash-boarded road, past vast swathes of logged pineyard. Andros has the largest tracts of Bahamas Pine, *Pinus caribaea* var. *bahamensis* in the islands. Rutted trails crisscross the swampy woods, but it doesn't strike me as suitable habitat.

We drive on towards Nicholls Town. Old Lyle tells me he thinks there are more snakes near Andros Town than up here. "I rarely see dem."

The forest changes to thick blackland coppice—mixed tropical broadleaf trees and hardwoods. In places with a tall pine canopy and rock outcrops.

"What do you think of stopping here? It looks interesting."

"Dey's a settlement few mile up, better I drop ya there."

"This is okay, I'll walk from here."

He stops. I get my rucksack. "Ya sure?"

"Yep, positive. I appreciate the ride, Mr. Lyle."

The woods look inviting. Turns out, what's inviting me are mosquitoes that descend in hoards. No repellent. Don't care for it, never have. I have jeans on and slip into a long-sleeve shirt. Wet and swampy, tough for walking, great for skeeters.

Between islands of dense coppice, I run across a pond. Is this a blue hole? Andros is famous for the openings to flooded underground caverns. Most have saltwater below with a lens of fresh water on top. As I approach, a turtle ducks below the surface.

Pseudemys terrapen, one of two Bahamian freshwater turtles. I hunker behind a bush by the water's edge and wait. Tiny *Gambusia hubbsi*, Mosquito Fish, are the only ones I notice. They sure have plenty to eat! Minutes pass, it surfaces. Every detail is visible in the crystal water. A solid black, 10-inch, domed shell, faint stripes on its neck. Inch-long nails on its front feet show it to be a male. The instant he sees me, he's gone.

Ameiva auberi sideroxylon, an abundant, nervous, fast running, sun-loving, blue-tailed, striped lizard. They run, stop, glance around, scratch in the dirt, and dart off in a flash.

Limestone outcrops are prime boa habitat. As I go to look, a large rock iguana slips into a crevice. *Cyclura baelopha*, unique to Andros, is prevalent in the south. I did not expect it this far north. The spectacular, dinosaur-looking creature is three feet long. It is heavy bodied, slate gray with black bands, an orange-headed male with fleshy jowls. When I climb up hoping for a glimpse, an unnoticed female runs under a boulder.

To lose bearings without a compass is easy and dangerous on an island as large as Andros. I work my way east, reassured when I see the roadway. A mile on, I'm drawn to a cluster of buildings at an airstrip. No one's here. I take it as a facility for the lumber company. Not surprised it's deserted on a weekend.

Outside of a building is a Coke machine. A welcome sight after slogging for hours through woodlands. What I find is a broken piece of junk. Bummed until I spot a few inches of a snake's tail sticking out from under it. A four-foot boa. I'd walked miles of forest and perfect habitat to locate my first snake under a soda machine.

I continue, not straying far from the roadside, hoping to catch another ride. Near the cutoff to Mastic Point, a northbound truck stops. "Need a lift?" The driver sounds Canadian.

"Sure, thanks." I'm relieved. I've ten miles to go and couldn't walk it until well after dark. By then, mosquitoes will have drained me dry. "Are you going to Nicholls Town?"

"I am. What brings you out here? You American, eh?"

"Yes, looking for snakes, caught one by the airstrip."

"We have lots of snakes here. What'll you do with them?"

"Study." My standard non-answer. What he says is contrary to what old Mr. Lyle told me. "Where do you see them?"

"They cross the roads after rains and at night." It rings as truthful.

"Where are they mostly?" I expect "Andros Town," since I'm going the opposite way.

"Lots between here and Nicholls Town." Wow, that sounds great! The entire region is now rocky hills. An excellent reason snakes might be more frequent here. If indeed they are.

CHAPTER 91:
Nicholls Town

Nicholls Town streets are unpaved. Its collection of wood houses and shops are painted pink, blue, and white. My thoughts after thanking the driver turn to food. He directs me to Bea's, a small restaurant, a two-minute walk above the shore. The aroma of fish grilling has my mouth watering. My order of grilled snapper arrives. A generous slab, golden brown with grill marks, and side of pigeon peas and rice. Only my taste buds await pleasing. They're not disappointed. Sated, I relax, speak with the owner.

"Superb meal, thanks. You couldn't recommend someplace to stay, could you?"

"Simms Guesthouse, nex' street, two doors pass' the market."

Paradise compared to Andros Town. Founded by escaped American slaves, it's tidy, with a lengthy, pearly beach backed by a limestone bluff. Ocean breezes swish and whistle through Australian Pines. Water a hundred shades of green and blue over grass flats and sand. Offshore, the famous Andros barrier reef. I could get used to this.

A room is $3—with breakfast. Less than Andros Town, and nicer. An hour before sundown, I've not much time to explore. Northside of the village, an old graveyard has a white picket fence around and a view of the Tongue of the Ocean. Across a sand track, rocky terrain shows promise. A brisk sea breeze keeps heat and mosquitoes at bay. Crinkle rock, karst eroded to sharp points atop the bluff, makes for treacherous walking. Inside the tangled coppice in the dim light stands a big Gumbo Limbo with a knothole in the trunk.

A snake! Prodded with a twig, a four-footer slithers out into my hand. The Andros Boa differs from the Bimini form. Brown with white; no black markings. It will become a separate subspecies, *Epicrates striatus fowleri*. The sun slips lower. With a bounce in my step, I head to the inn after a successful day.

Mr. Simms sits outside his guest house enjoying the evening breeze. "Excuse me, any idea how I might arrange getting to Andros Town for my Tuesday flight?"

"I can take you. We should leave by ten."

With that important detail taken care of, I wash up, and walk to a small grocery a block away for a drink and snack. My late lunch still with me. I stroll to the shore, look back over the village to enjoy the sunset, then wander to Simms, turning in for the night.

⌒

Early Sunday, after coffee, corned beef over grits, and bread, I gather my sacks and canteen and walk the beach past town. *Ameiva* and curly tails, active in the morning sun, scamper into Sea Oats. Seagrapes form an impenetrable wall in front of undisturbed coppice. I clamber over rocks and uneven ground and gain entry. Amidst Gumbo Limbo, Mastic, Tamarind, and Poisonwood, sparse undergrowth eases walking.

Before me is a 20-yard-wide, 10-foot-deep sinkhole. It's dry, with trees at the bottom and near-vertical walls. I search for a way to enter. While climbing in to investigate, my foot slips and I bark my shin on jagged limestone. My jeans prevent serious injury, but I'm seeing stars.

I hobble to a rock, pull up my pants leg, and wince at an eight-inch gouge with skin hanging in little curls, blood soaking my sock. Exposed to the air, it stings. I pluck a few loose pieces of skin off, dab it with water from my canteen and a clean sack until bleeding stops. Angry at myself for being careless, I can do nothing but wait for the pain to ease. A black and yellow Bahamian Oriole scolds from a tree. The only other sound is the breeze through trees above the pit. *What a special place.*

Drama over, the hunt continues, with every object seeming to bump or snag my sore shin. Difficult going, and for the next hour, no other reptiles. With the discomfort, my heart isn't in it. I sit often, sweaty, cursing my self-inflicted bad luck. But I don't linger long. Whining mosquitoes spur me to keep moving.

I emerge by the road into a clearing stacked with half-rotted pine logs. Under loose bark a three-inch scorpion, fearsome-looking but not dangerous. One like it, hiding in a canvas tarp, stung my hand when I was a kid. Not something I wish to experience again.

As I pull the pile apart, a tarantula scrambles out. Common on Bimini, it's my first on Andros. Tough work, I'm soaked with sweat, but it keeps my mind off my leg. A few more logs tossed aside; I uncover a young boa. Re-energized, I move every piece, finding three more. A giant boost to my flagging enthusiasm. I find a boulder, sit, rest, reflect, and have a snack.

The forest on the south side is less dense. A fat *Leiocephalus* at a shallow sink darts into a crevice at my approach. The same species as on Bimini, but here they grow larger. A search beneath fallen thatch palm fronds exposes a few tiny *Sphaerodactylus nigropunctatus flavicauda*, Yellow-tailed Geckoes. They are preferred food for young boas and other small snakes. Nearby in a rotted trunk, an Andros Dwarf Ground Boa, *Tropidophis canus androsi*. The run of good luck turns up a second.

Another hour of hard work, turning rocks, logs, digging in leaf litter, yields naught. Feast or famine. I stumble out to the roadway, much further inland, near the intersection of Queen's Highway. It's getting late. I turn back, not wishing to get stuck out here after dark in mosquito heaven. In town I come to the grocery before the guest house, head in for a cold drink.

Three men stand out front drinking beer, laughing. When I step up to enter, a skinny guy in a dirty tee-shirt asks, "Where ya goin'?"

Startled. *Is he going to hustle me?* "I'm here looking for snakes, seen any?"

"Snakes? We don' gat no snakes 'ere."

One of his mates says, "Ya lyin' man, I find lot o' dem in the lumberyard."

That gets my attention. "Where's the lumberyard?"

"On the Main Lumber Road in San Andros, across from the airfield."

That's the airstrip where I found the boa under a Coke machine. As he talks, I chuckle to myself. *Wonder if I should show them what's in the sack?* Inside, I buy a soda, head home.

I shower, check my leg. Looks awful, red, bruised. I wash blood from my pants and sock and change into clean clothes I brought for the flight. I lie back in the sea-scented breeze blowing in the window and rest awhile, cooling off before heading out to eat at Bea's. Conch chowder with white rice and plenty of hot Bahama bread and butter. Doggone good eating.

⌒

Monday morning, I pull on dirty, not yet dry, britches. At breakfast, remembering what the man at the store said, I ask Mr. Simms how to find the Main Lumber Road. "The road out of town becomes Main Lumber Road when it crosses Queen's Highway." He doesn't inquire why I want to know. Sure is a quiet fellow, but seems nice enough.

I hike to where I left off last evening, then continue west, before turning south. The woodland thins and shows signs of a recent fire. Rocky, lower, with fewer broadleaf trees and more pines. Undergrowth is sparse, bright green and the pines show scorched trunks. Several forays into the woods produce no reptiles nor do I find what looks to be suitable habitat. Swampy in places, it'd be great to find a place where the swamp meets a bluff. An ideal combination.

No such luck. Miles on, past noon, finding nothing, I consider turning around, but hate to backtrack. At a clearing where they clean and trim timber to load onto trucks, I find nothing. At the rear of the lot the land rises, upland coppice replaces pines. I'll explore to the top, then across to the Queen's Highway, which I'm guessing is not over a mile or so due east.

Progress is slow through thorny *Caesalpinia bahamensis* and vines that shred my skin. I'm sweat-soaked, so reaching the cooler, more open interior is a relief. While I stand catching my breath, I hear a croaking, laughing, unfamiliar call. It sounds close. I try to move in silence to catch a glimpse. There in a shrub is a pigeon-sized bird with a long, black-barred tail. Gray, with whitish front and russet belly. A Great Lizard Cuckoo, *Coccyzus merlini*.

The biggest trees grow on the highest part of the limestone knoll. The frequency of Poisonwood demands caution. Gumbo Limbo and Mahogany dominate. A few gnarled giants have hollow limbs and cavities in their trunks. It takes an hour to inspect every hollowed-out tree, each notch, fallen log, and solution hole. My find of the trip is a hefty, gravid female boa. This single specimen could make the entire Andros expedition worthwhile. They can produce 50 or more live young! After three others, smaller, turn up, I dub this "snake hill."

I work east, dense coppice thins to open thorn scrub. While struggling through a tangle of vines, I miss stepping on a boa by inches. It tenses its body into kinks, as surprised snakes are wont to do. At six-foot-plus, the largest I have seen in the Bahamas.

The sound of a truck signals proximity to Queen's Highway. My watch, with a broken strap, is in my room. Shadows show midafternoon. At the roadway, laden with my catch, I head towards Nicholls Town, hoping for a ride. No one comes during my six-mile hike back.

At the guesthouse, I'm beat. I clean up, confirm my trip to the airport with Mr. Simms. Nothing to eat since breakfast, my stomach is gnawing at my backbone. Hearty rib soup and Johnnycake at Bea's hits the spot. Belly full, I walk the glorious seashore to lock it into my memory. My leaving brings melancholy, realizing I may never return. There are so many places to explore. But I love it so. On the way back, I snag a cardboard box at the grocery for the specimens. My shin hurts, but I sleep hard, exhausted, satisfied from a long but rewarding day.

∽

Before 10 am Tuesday, we leave for Andros Town. Mr. Simms is quiet, says little. I start. "Nice car." It's a 1963 Chevy Nova station wagon. No response. "Were you born here?"

"Yes." He doesn't glance my way. After a lengthy silence, he continues. "I worked for Owen's Lumber. Bought the B&B when I retired." Well-spoken and dressed, creased slacks, light blue shirt tucked in, shoes shined. Successful, he appears not to have a care.

"Nicholls Town is paradise to me," I say, to which he smiles, nods. At the airstrip, Mr. Simms declines payment for the ride.

"I was coming no matter," he said. Decent fellow.

CHAPTER 92:
Bimini and Home

A Twin Otter arrives, considered among the best small planes ever built. Alone on the flight over, for the return trip, six other passengers board. Rucksack and box stowed. Nobody questions what's in them and I don't tell. After takeoff, viewing the vast extent of cut forest from the airplane window saddens me.

Two hours in Nassau until my Bimini connecting flight. I lunch and plan another round of collecting when we land. By the time we arrive, with the specimens and my shin hurting, I ride the bus and ferry to Alice Town. My boat looks inviting. A first aid kit onboard has Merthiolate and bandages. I doctor my bruised, scratched leg. It stings like hell, but the wound isn't deep, nor infected, so no worries.

After sleeping aboard the *UNWIND*, I'm Miami bound, crossing while the sun is behind me. The solo trips many say are risky, or plain dumb. To me, the voyage is normal and safe. Still, things could happen. Angels are watching.

We never clear Customs when we cross back and forth to Bimini on either end. Does anyone? When we show up, who knows where we've been? Fishing in the Gulf Stream? Out for a cruise? Concerns of narco gangs who might hijack a vessel to smuggle drugs and sink it are years away. No one worries. These are the real good old days.

I call Ed from a payphone at the launch ramp, get lucky, catch him home. He comes in an hour with my truck and trailer. At his house we look over the specimens. The *fowleri* are new to him. He wants a pair.

"They're promised. I haven't forgotten you want those vipers."

"Yeah, you're right. Hey, I sold the Rhino Iguanas and part of the boas. I'll pay you for your half." Now I have a twinge of guilt. Ed's a likable guy, despite his take-no-prisoners business ethic. I trust him. There's little choice. He gives me over $1,000 cash, more than expected and much appreciated. "Strikes still on, I know you need it."

That news is both good and bad. Great, that I didn't miss work with my travels, but he's right, money is in short supply. What he pays me will more than put us on track. "Thanks, man. I'll call when Erich sends the shipment."

Home the same night, beat from the sea crossing and five-hour drive. By not taking the boat the whole way, I'm at least a week early. It surprises and pleases my wife. Mid-December, with her paycheck and what Ed paid, we'll have a merry Christmas. The Haitian, Bimini, and Andros snakes I ship to Erich Sochurek in Austria. Received in excellent condition, he will send his in January.

As the decade ends, Nixon is president. The Vietnam War rages. Protestors fill Washington, DC streets. The Apollo 12 crew returns to Earth from the second manned Moon landing. Hell's Angels kill a fan at a Rolling Stones concert. Peter, Paul, and Mary's "Leaving on a Jet Plane" is on the radio. The Supremes sing on the Ed Sullivan Show. "Someday We'll Be Together," their last-ever performance. It's an interesting time to be alive. The FPL strike settles on December 30, 1969, after 70 days.

CHAPTER 93:
European Treasures

As 1970 arrives, it's back to work, a return to normal, with no travel plans. The expected shipment from Erich Sochurek arrives with an exceptional collection of Mediterranean reptiles. Aesculapian Snakes, *Elaphe longissima*, famed from the caduceus, symbol of medicine. *Elaphe situla* and *quatuorlineata* compare to our own Red and Yellow Ratsnakes. Cat Snakes, *Telescopus fallax*, Transcaucasian Ratsnakes, *Elaphe hohenackeri*, along with other European oddities.

Venomous snakes are most wished for and valuable. *Vipera xanthina xanthina* from Greece and *Vipera ursinii* from France. The Common Adder, *Vipera berus*. Horned Vipers, *Vipera ammodytes*, and the rare Lebetine Viper, *Vipera lebetina*. There's enough to pay Ed for the Haitian snakes and still have plenty to trade and sell a few to defray expenses.

Mediterranean lizards, sought by collectors, include giant Sheltopusik, *Ophisaurus apodus*, a huge form of glass lizard. Huge Algerian Skinks, *Eumeces schneideri algeriensis*, brown with orange bands. The large, (almost two feet!) stunning Ocellated Lizard, *Lacerta lepida*, from Spain. Light emerald green, with a faint, black circular pattern—beautiful!

My favorite, of many jewels, is the Sandfish, *Scincus scincus*. An incredible burrowing lizard from the Sahara Desert. This creature swims through sand like a fish in water. Its snout tapers to a wedge, its lower jaw recessed. Tiny eyes with lids that seal tight. Lovely, white below, tan above with dark tiger bands. My reptile friends line up to get whatever they can of Erich's treasures.

Erich loves salamanders, popular among European fanciers. My source is a Tennessean. He sends striking and oddball species from the Ozarks and Smokey Mountains. They are a challenge to keep alive in Florida's heat, so I repack and ship them without delay. I pack in Styrofoam boxes. Plastic containers of ice secured in place prevent overheating long enough to assure safe arrival in Europe or Japan.

Except for newts and a few frogs and toads, I don't accept amphibians from Erich. He offers an Olm, *Proteus anguinus*, a blind, subterranean salamander from the Dinaric Alps. These creatures are far too sensitive and rare to try keeping. I decline the offer.

Two of thousands of
wooden bridges over
creeks and canals in
Peninsula Florida.
Ratsnake heaven!
(State Archives of
Florida)

Okeelanta, 1964. Jack Facente pulling
a big Yellow Ratsnake from under a
bridge while hanging
from an irrigation pipe.
(Courtesy of Jack Facente)

CHAPTER 94:
The Bridges of Indian River County

The phone rings, and a baritone voice asks, "You up for Vero?"

"Sure." My unhesitating, usual response.

Into the gloom of night, Dick Bartlett and I cross central Florida on Highway 60. Past phosphate mines, cattle ranches, sandy hills, and the Kissimmee Valley, speeding through the darkness towards Vero Beach. We aim to hunt snakes under the bridges of Indian River County.

With winter water temps at 72 degrees, wading is both heaven and hell. I loathe cold, but love snake hunting. Dick and I click. Herpers are that way. We think in unison, as hungry lions stalking an antelope. No discussion as we slip into the canal at opposite ends of a bridge. We wade, or swim to clamber across braces with flashlights or headlamps in search of reptile treasure.

It's an art, catching a snake to wrangle it into a sack while hanging on with one hand, climb to the next piling and repeat. We work in silence, save for the occasional, "Got one" or "Ouch, dammit!" when we get bit. Blissful quiet, only croaking frogs, chirping crickets, the splash of garfish—if you don't count slapping mosquitoes. When a truck rumbles over, thunder sounds, the bridge trembles, dirt rains from the cracks. The experience is hypnotic. Painful, wet, cold, and miserable, but so satisfying.

Countless bridges, no two the same, span Florida's canals and creeks. We skip concrete and those of newer wood that drips irritating creosote. Old wooden ones are perfect. Worn timbers loosen, form crevices where snakes can hide.

When spans are low, we swash between supports, in tea-colored, peat-smelling water, plucking ratsnakes from the beams without climbing. But, this is a rare occurance.

Often the most fruitful are those built inches above the surface. Rich picking for the collector who dares venture where others fear. When flood levels are high enough to touch bridge timbers, to collect we must duck under the dark waters and pop up between each joist to inspect. It's spooky, and more than a little dangerous.

We never know what we'll find: Rusty spikes, or cross braces to crack our noggins. A sticky spider web, a colony of bats, or a wasp nest. Instead of a snake, an angry raccoon, or owl. It takes guts and perhaps a degree of mental instability. At night in floating weeds, add *balls* to the *what-it-takes* part. Not for sissies. To the gutsy and ballsy go the spoils. Reptile collectors understand, others may not.

A chilly evening outside of Vero, and we're having it rough. We're wet, shivering, not catching much. Dick is inspecting a bridge. I trudge into an adjacent swamp, to seek watersnakes and Musk Turtles in the shallows. Aquatic plants limit mobility and visibility.

I step on a submerged alligator. The ten-footer roars, thrashes his head and tail, and launches me into the air. Suddenly, I'm on my back in a swampy morass, headlamp out, in the grip of panic! *Where's the gator?* I scoot backward to escape. The gator splashing, thrashing, and hissing, and my stream of expletives draws Dick's attention. He slogs as fast as possible to reach me through the weedy, knee-deep marsh. When he finds me in one piece, his momentary concern turns to absolute mirth.

Lest I leave the impression that Dick is a heartless S.O.B. without regard for my well-being, let me explain. A good collecting buddy stays within sight or earshot. If his partner gets into a predicament, he's quick to the scene, often to collapse into a heap of convulsing laughter. Only after composing himself does he check to see if his companion needs aid.

Though this may sound cruel, it helps diffuse a tense, dangerous situation and prevents panic or shock. Crisis averted, more times than not, both will join in a hearty laugh. It takes a trusting relationship. In part, to keep the victim from delivering serious harm to his tormentor.

I spring to my feet out of the swamp like the Creature from the Black Lagoon. Drenched, befouled with reeking muck, and cloaked with weeds.

While I fumble to get my light working and wash off mud, Dick wades back towards the bridge, chortling. He spotted two nice Yellow Ratsnakes coiled on the beams before the gator drama.

"Since you're already soaked…." *He wants me to swim out to collect them.*

I decline—not in a cooperative mood. Dick sloshes in, mumbling. He dog-paddles out in pitch darkness and finds footing atop a rotted-off piling. Chest deep in the bayou, he realizes he doesn't have a sack.

"Hey Dennis, toss me a bag, I'm out."

"Sure." I'm in shallows by the abutment, pull a wet sack from my belt. Dip it anew to make it extra soggy, ball it, call out, "Here, catch" and fire a cannon shot straight to his mug.

My headlamp shining in his eyes blinds him. The sodden bag—a thunderbolt he never saw coming—hits Dick full in the face. He tumbles from his perch like a knockdown doll in a carnival game. I sink to my knees, cackling out of control as he flounders and sputters.

"You'll pay." Echoes the bridge troll.

Is his memory too short to remember my brush with the gator? It seemed to bring him such joy only moments ago. A casual observer might think it's all fun and games. I guess they'd be right. If it weren't, we wouldn't expose ourselves to this risky torture.

An October evening after a few hours of bridge collecting, we're soaked, chilled to the bone. From experience, we know to bring dry clothes for the trip home. Parked along Highway 60 out of Vero Beach, I'm stripped out of my wet duds. A car approaches, no place to hide. I try to pull on my dry jeans over my wet legs. No use. I'm standing buck naked in the headlight beams. Thinking fast, I hold my tee-shirt over my face.

Dick erupts in hilarity. "Why did you do that?"

"I didn't want them to know who I was."

Sometimes we return from our collecting jaunts at sunrise and go to work bleary-eyed. We never explain to our coworkers. It's best to leave certain details unsaid.

CHAPTER 95:
South Florida

Road collecting in southern Florida is without equal if conditions are right. Success or failure depends on the season, temperature, and water level. When the weather cools, warm pavement attracts snakes. Rainy evenings, the warmed roads through Everglades are magic.

Watersnakes, ratsnakes, Mudsnakes, other nocturnal species, by dozens or hundreds are easy picking. Snakes that might otherwise be doomed to slaughter by passing vehicles. We keep the choicest specimens and oft times spend hours tossing others off the road to spare them an awful fate. The moment we leave, killing resumes.

Mudsnakes, *Farancia abacura abacura,* are shiny black, to over six feet long. A red venter extends to form triangles on their sides. A specialized diet: *Siren lacertina,* Greater Siren, and *Amphiuma means,* Two-toed Amphiuma, makes them unfit for captivity. These giant aquatic salamanders resemble eels. Sirens have sturdy front legs and external gills. Amphiuma, internal gills, and four vestigial limbs. Mudsnakes manipulate them with a sharp-pointed caudal scale. It's tough to imagine how difficult it must be for a legless creature to eat something so slimy, underwater!

Islands in sawgrass prairies are excellent for collecting. From the levies, few are nearer than a quarter mile. To reach them is challenging. Without an airboat or swamp buggy, trekking in is our only way. Those with willows have little dry earth, are mucky and wet. Those with Bay Trees or hardwoods have higher ground, may have limestone outcrops, solution holes and leaf litter.

Most of my hunting buddies avoid Sawgrass, *Cladium jamaicense,* a razor-edged, skin-slicing sedge. In peaty, swampy prairies, walking is arduous. With each step sinking in muck, leg cramps are a problem. It takes fortitude.

Bayheads and dry hammocks are a treat to explore. Imagine more snakes than we can catch. We grab the best, others escape. Pure adrenaline! Watchful for rattlesnakes and Cottonmouths. Dusky Pygmy Rattlers, *Sistrurus miliarius barbouri*, are abundant. South Florida Kingsnake, *Lampropeltis getula floridana*, is much-sought. Elegant, speckled, white bands outlined with black scales. Tree-borne Yellow Ratsnakes there's no rush to collect. For us, it is hard work, hot, dirty, but always exciting.

Brooks' King, *Lampropeltis getula brooksi,* is a paler form. Found near rock outcrops and along the edges of rocky canals. Excellent *brooksi* habitat is Pine Rocklands in the Big Cypress and extreme southernmost Florida.

Fifteen miles out of Terrytown is a treed island well off the levee. I've often passed it by, today I'll check it. Halfway out, slogging through head-high sawgrass in the knee-deep swamp, I nearly quit. Shoes pull off my feet in the sucking muck. Arms bleeding, I'm pouring sweat when a big horsefly nails me on the temple. But I persist, and reach the hammock, exhausted.

A bolt of fear runs through me. Wild hogs ravage the island. I climb a rubber tree to safety as they grunt, squeal, and root in the earth. There'll be no snakes here. Any creature they catch, they'll eat. *Me included!*

Treed for a half-hour, the Razorbacks leave the ruined isle, splashing through the sawgrass. It goes quiet. Tiny ants stinging me, I'm eager to relinquish my perch. I spot a single Yellow Ratsnake, *Elaphe obsoleta quadrivittata*, opaque in preparation to molt. Their skin, tender in this stage, may tear, causing permanent scars. A common species, I should leave it but take it to avoid being skunked, and make the 20-minute, leg aching slog back to the car. This round the boars win.

In two weeks, the Yellow Ratsnake has shed. It's spectacular, leucistic, white, with faint blotches and normal eyes. My failed foray has turned to gold.

CHAPTER 96:
Cane Fields

US 27 south of Okeechobee near Okeelanta is a choice spot Ed Chapman and I love to hunt. We hike the grassy strip between road and sugarcane, watching for Florida Kings. On the return, we search betwixt Australian Pines that line the road and the canal. Great for indigos, Red Ratsnakes, and Scarlet Kings. We know each board, sheet of metal, and downed sign.

The occasional entrepreneurial collector will salt the area with plywood scraps, roof tin, or carpet remnants. These become fair game for all others that follow.

Farm roads beside canals between cane fields are a kingsnake hotspot. Our technique we call leapfrogging. The first guy gets out, the other drives a quarter-mile and leaves the car. When the original walker reaches it, he'll drive to pick up any snakes his partner has and continue past to park and begin afoot. No need to backtrack. Rocket scientists as we are, we figure no one else has thought of doing this. We keep the strategy to ourselves. Locations of productive tin piles and pump houses are closely guarded secrets.

A target is the exquisite Everglades Ratsnake, *Elaphe obsoleta rossalleni*. Among the world's most vividly colored serpents, a subspecies of the Yellow Rat. Bright orange with subtle longitudinal stripes and a crimson tongue. Yellows are different and vary from gold to tan, with bold striping and occasional faint blotches.

Glades Rats are uncommon. Their favored habitat is the vicinity arouond Lake Okeechobee. A productive location is in the Australian Pines atop the levee.

Jamaican laborers in the field cutting cane by machete in Clewiston.
(State Archives of Florida)

By day we walk beneath the trees and find them coiled and resting on limbs. We climb to collect them. At night they crawl, often on the ground. Catching them is easy.

Between South Bay and Clewiston, along old US 27, is a massive, abandoned building. We speculate it was a feed store, lumber yard, or warehouse. Built on piers, the flooring, interior walls, and other salvageable boards were long since removed. What remains is enough to keep it standing.

It's dangerous walking the floor joists, nails protrude where they salvaged planks. A fall guarantees serious injury. Snakes hide in crevices between wall studs and window casings. Rich hunting grounds above the framework of an office are hard to access. We use a piece of ornate banister as a ladder. Every Florida snake hunter knows this place, but our hunts here never fail. Many an Everglades Ratsnake has come from this venerable ruin.

CHAPTER 97:
Loop Road

Loop Road between Miami and Naples off the Tamiami Trail is the stuff of herper legend. Twenty miles of crushed limestone, graded annually in the dry season. For a while, it's wide and smooth, until, rain, and traffic leave it washboarded and potholed, as rampant vegetation narrows the roadway.

An alligator-filled, roadside canal is rich snake habitat, best hunted afoot. Often, we leapfrog, or one of us may ride on the fender. Driving slowly, the rider can slide off while we're moving. It's a nifty system. The bank grows thick with trees and shrubs, and while we're careful to avoid knocking off the passenger, passing through the occasion bush by accident is a possibility.

Many weekends in our high school years, my buddy Jim Stafford and I collected on the Loop. The 90-miles from Davie took two hours. We'd spend the day. The place for *brooksi* kings, but any South Florida reptile could turn up along the famous route.

In 1965, with my '53 Ford station wagon, instead of sitting, Jim stands on the tailgate for a commanding view. An Everglades Racer, *Coluber constrictor paludicola*, crosses ahead. He calls out, "Snake."

I speed up, close in on the fast species. Jim jumps off before we stop, trips over the strut, lands with arms and legs sprawled and slides up to my window. Face white with road dust, knees tore out of his pants, his pride wounded. I haven't laughed so hard since I hit him in the butt with the car door up in Gulf Hammock.

CHAPTER 98:
Bug Bit

Patti Bartlett and Dick infected me with bug lust in 1970. Beetles and butterflies, my newest obsession, as if I have time to spare. Our collecting trips now have a new dimension and include butterfly nets, kill jars and glassine envelopes. Working with insects, I have a fresh outlook on Florida's country roads. It's great.

The Butterfly Company in Far Rockaway, New York has a color catalog to make any collector drool. Colorful insects, mainly butterflies and beetles, with prices from a dollar to hundreds of dollars. My self-imposed limit is ten bucks, though it often takes great restraint. This new diversion has led to another network of friends with whom to trade and share. Imagine the difficulty before the internet!

Butterflies! Some collected, some traded, in author-made redwood Riker mounts

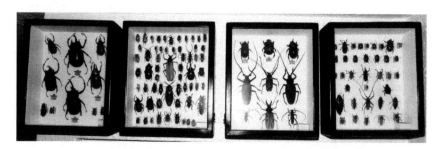

Beetles, traded and collected, mounted on pins in redwood boxes.

My secret weapon then: *The Naturalists Directory.* Scientists, hobbyists, collectors, zoos, and institutions are listed worldwide, along with their interests. Communication by pen and ink. What a thrill to open the mailbox, to find envelopes bordered in red and blue candy stripes. Colorful stamps with birds, reptiles, insects, and flowers, bearing foreign postmarks.

It's all about display. My first were inexpensive cardboard Riker mounts. Flat cases an inch thick with glass fronts, filled with cotton. Butterflies pressed between pane and filler make decorative displays. I thought them tacky for such magnificent creatures and began making my own. I used redwood and made many sizes and shapes. Stained and varnished, they became quality pieces worthy of the best specimens. For beetles, glass-fronted hinged boxes. Homasote backing to hold pins for the coleoptera, their names, dates, and collecting data.

As with any hobby done well, expenses for required equipment, supplies, books, and specimens add up fast. Not least is the time it takes. All this on top of maintaining a reptile collection.

CHAPTER 99:
The Bimini Caper

By 1970, I'm branching out to further islands and my Bimini trips are becoming fewer. Down to one every few months, most times with guys from FPL for fishing.

The phone rings. "Hey, ol' buddy." (It's Ed. I brace myself.) "My boat's in Alice Town with a burned-out starter. Think you could help me?"

"Sure, I guess, what do you need?"

"I have a new starter...."

I cut him short. "Yeah, we can go over. I'll give you a hand, no problem."

"Thing is, I can't get away," he says, with hesitation.

"Bummer. What do you want me to do?"

"Do you suppose you could bring someone and pick it up for me?"

His plan is for me to run over with a friend, change the starter, and deliver his boat to Florida. We have a long and complicated history. Nothing is ever as simple as he makes it sound. I raise an eyebrow, my lips tighten. Still, I agree. "Sure, when?"

I recruit a coworker, Richard Nutter, and leave for Miami. Ed meets us with a set of brushes.

"Nobody has a starter in stock." *Okay, here we go.*

"Wait, I thought you said you *had* a starter?"

"I figured I'd find one easy. Guess I jumped the gun."

"Are you sure these brushes will fit?"

"Oh yes, I'm positive."

The author on a rescue mission to Bimini, piloting the *UNWIND*.

They're the correct ones, all right. But the rest of the story doesn't match.

Richard's an avid fisherman who has cruised to Bimini with me. No way he'd pass up a trip over, no matter how short or for what reason. He can't get enough. Besides, he's a decent mechanic. Either of us could handle something as basic as starter problems.

We arrive, tie up behind Ed's 24-foot inboard/outboard, have a look. The dockmaster comes out.

"What you boys doin'?"

"Sorry, I was coming to explain. We're here to fix Ed's boat and take it to Miami."

"That so? You gat the money?"

"What money?"

"Five hundred bucks fo' my labor and dock rent." He sounds perturbed.

"Um, well, no." I glance at Richard, his palms up, shakes his head, brows scrunched. "Ed didn't mention that."

Of course not. Ed's famous for beguiling me in one way or another. I walk over to the Compleat Angler and pony up $10 for a phone call. "What the hell, Ed? You don't think I should know you owe the guy 500 bucks."

"$500? He said $300 last week."

"Yeah, well, he says $500 now." I spare no sarcasm. "Who's gonna pay that? Not me."

"I don't have it either." *There's a shock. Eye roll.* "Can you sneak it out of there?"

I put my hand over the receiver. "Oh goody, he wants us to steal his boat." Richard's jaw drops.

Over a beer, we concoct a story for the dockmaster. Big-game fishermen and ocean yachters fill the smoky bar. The moneyed crowd from Miami, Lauderdale, and New York. I watch as a Bimini hustler fleeces a wealthy tourist out of $20 on Hemingway's ring toss.

At the dock, I find the master. "Ed's coming in a few days. I misunderstood. He just needs me to make repairs for him."

He looks skeptical. "I hope ya brought another starter. De old one's shot."

"I got brushes."

"The old one's overbard."

"What? How did that happen?"

"I try to fix. Was no good. I toss in the water."

"How long ago?"

"Six, eight days."

"Oh crap. A week in saltwater? Should be in great shape now."

We head to the boat. "Must be more to this story. I sense serious bad blood."

The starter lies on the sandy bottom in 10 feet of crystalline water. I doff shoes and shirt, jump in to retrieve the part. Luck on our side, built-up grease, is enough to protect it from the saltwater. We dismantle, inspect, spray on half a canister of CRC. That's something in the vein of WD-40 we use at the power company, so, free.

The starter is wrapped in rags and set aside to dry, so we walk to the Red Lion to eat. An old haunt that Richard knows from our fishing trips. Ed gave me $50 for expenses. Conch fritters, pigeon peas, and rice are doggone tasty with plenty of beer. Though I never dreamed it possible, the Bimini jaunts are getting tiresome. Meanwhile, Richard is falling in love with the total scene. After sleeping aboard the *UNWIND*, the next morning we start work. Clean and sand the armature and contacts. After installing the replacement brushes, we bolt it on for a trial.

"Ed's frickin' battery's dead. Damn!" The boat's a mess, engine is dirty, rubber dry, cracked. Maintenance isn't his strong suit. Sort of surprising, since he keeps his reptile collection hospital spotless. Mine gets worked between every trip: belts, hoses, oil, grease. No one wants a malfunction at sea.

We approach the dockmaster. "We have it fixed, but Ed's battery is dead. You got a charger we might use?"

He's busy with a paying customer, so we wait. Afterward, he fetches a booster. We hook it up and, while it is charging, we go for a snack. Richard and I must work on Monday. We can't hang around long. With a full charge, we dial to boost and crank it.

I return the charger. "Richard will make a test run. When he gets back, we're heading to Florida. Ed will arrive in a day or two to pay what he owes you and collect his boat."

I flash the high sign. Richard casts off the lines, heads into the harbor, motors through the inlet between North and South Bimini, out of sight... and waits.

After 15 minutes, I tell the dockmaster. "He must have conked out; I'll go tow him back."

Outside the pass, Richard is making slow circles and when I catch up to him, we take off towards Miami. I hear him whooping and hollering as he pumps his fist. His hat is a pair of underwear, and he looks like a goofy pirate as we steer out to sea.

My umpteenth crossing of the northern Straits of Florida. This 5,000-foot-deep trench lies between the Bahamas and Florida, wraps the Keys north of Cuba to the Gulf of Mexico. It never gets old. Never the same twice. Tranquil today, perfect. Sometimes the ocean is smooth as glass. Other times, sudden storms bring heavy rains and gale winds. Seas whip into sharp peaks, spray blows with stinging force. It's terrifying when we dive into a wave, take green water across the prow to crash into the windshield. The boat shudders. I keep bow to the wind, correct bearings after the storm passes. The Gulf Stream sets northward at a relentless 5.5 miles per hour. Any dawdling or temporary course change will alter our landfall. With only a compass, it's always guesswork.

Usual conditions are sea swells that roll like countryside hills. Too large and gentle to affect our small craft, we labor on the upside and speed on the downside. The rise and fall is slow and rhythmic. Flying Fish break from the swell's crest, and sail for hundreds of feet as the water falls away beneath them.

They touch tail to the surface for a boost, fly on until they slip into the waves. We often see Dolphinfish leap in pursuit of their favored prey.

Sailfish leaping or flashing their dorsal fins are a rare sight, treasured memories. Seabirds follow our wake looking for fish snacks turned up in the prop wash. Bottlenose Dolphins ride our bow wave for miles on end. Out of view of land, there's an active, full, vibrant, animal community. Never dull, often harrowing, every crossing is a joyous adventure.

By late afternoon, we're in Miami. Ed brings his trailer. We load the boats and head towards home. Ed knows he owes me big time. Richard's on top of the world. This is a grand experience for him. Within a year, I'll sell the *UNWIND* to Richard, beginning a fresh chapter in both of our lives.

CHAPTER 100:
Okeetee

Englishman Simon Townson, a student of herpetology, arrives for a visit. His dream itinerary worked out by mail begins in the Everglades and South Florida. We hit every hotspot, Loop Road, the sections, Terrytown, Okeechobee. He loves it, the wilderness, the wildlife, the Glades culture. England has nothing to compare!

In a few days, we'll join Dick Bartlett for an excursion to Okeetee. Vast, unspoiled low country, it spans southeast South Carolina and adjacent Georgia. Legendary in the herpetological world. For Simon, a pilgrimage.

In Spring, astonishing numbers of snakes emerge from hibernation. Notably Eastern Chain Kingsnakes, *Lampropeltis getula*. Black and white beauties, common, easy to catch as they soak up the sun on cool spring mornings. Warmed, they hunt, emaciated from their winter fast. They're easy to find in quantity, but the window closes in a few weeks. With summer, the now fat kings become elusive. Diurnal, active before midday heat sends them to cover.

Night walks and road cruising are time-honored collecting methods in Okeetee. It's a herpers' heaven.

Simon, with serious beginner's luck, finds twice the snakes we do. Included is the golden orange phase of Red Ratsnake known as the Okeetee Corn. They're stunning! Two Copperheads turn up in an old stack of logs. We rake a sawdust pile and uncover a choice Scarlet King. Ridge walking by day and swamp trekking by night and driving for miles on narrow country roads. Ridgeland to Pineland, Tarboro to Tillman, and Tillman to Clyo in Georgia.

Dick knows them like his own driveway, no maps needed. He visits Okeetee often. His knowledge and sardonic humor are a tonic. We never tire of hiking, riding, ripping stumps, and flipping tin.

We stay in tiny Ridgeland, South Carolina. Duke's, a local family restaurant, serves Southern food at its best. Melt in your mouth fried chicken, fluffy biscuits, sawmill gravy. The aroma has our stomachs growling from the gravel parking lot. A highlight of every trip. The restaurant's owner is enormous, and he reminds us of Buford Pusser. Remember the Southern sheriff from the *Walking Tall* movie?

Dick never changes. Orders a quarter chicken. For me, a bigger guy, the half chicken is a better fit. Without fail, Dick's is a fat juicy chicken breast. What do I get? Two legs and two thighs, every time. This runs all over me. How can my half-chicken-dinner always the back half? I grumble to Dick, who never sees the issue, and chortles at my obvious displeasure.

One day, the big man himself comes to the table. "How're y'all? How's the food?"

I mention the disparity. How Dick always gets a chicken breast for his quarter chicken dinner and my half is two thighs and legs.

"Is there a problem with that?"

"Well, no. I...I like chicken legs. I like breasts too."

"You could order a breast." He completely misses the point.

What the hell. Did he and Dick conspire to mess with me? As often as we dined there, nothing changed. Dick ate many a breast, and I, none. Not wanting to get tossed into the street, I hold further complaints. The conspiracy theory persists.

Our Okeetee sojourns are welcome respites and sharing allows us a fresh perspective. Snakes not usually given a second glance are novel to Simon. He revels in collecting species he'd known only from books. Southern Ring-necks, *Diadophis punctatus,* deep slate-black with a bright orange collar are pretty and frequent. Desirable additions to his reptile life list.

Southern Hog-nose delight. These charming creatures put on a show worthy of an Oscar. Simon's reaction to seeing his first wild *Heterodon simus* is priceless. He lifts a sheet of roof tin. A blotched brown snake pulls into a coil, flattens its head and neck, hisses loudly. Simon is startled until he recognizes it. The theatrics continue, inflating its body, striking with jaws closed. After a while it rolls over onto its back, mouth open, tongue lolled out, feigning death.

Simon turns it over, and it's quick to resume its belly-up position. After a few minutes, it returns to normal. Their convincing performance too often causes their demise.

Broad-headed Skinks, *Eumeces laticeps,* are striking. The largest lizards in the eastern US. Adults are golden brown. Males develop oversized orange heads with bulging jowls. The impressive, foot-long creatures are a thrilling addition to Simon's list.

While turning tin or rolling a log, no telling what we'll discover. Narrow-mouthed Toad or a Marbled Salamander. A Red Ratsnake, Scarlet King, or a Copperhead. The reptile gods are smiling. We find a significant representation of what this fabled herpers' paradise has to offer.

One should expect juvenile pranks with three guys on a road trip. Good travel rapport is essential. Hysterical cackling follows any stumble or faux pas. We mock Simon's accent. He has a bizarre British sense of humor. Innocuous things can propel him into fits of laughter. Take the word *end,* for example. In England, it's slang for, well, the male member. Dead End signs send him over the edge. Okeetee was a joy, a cherished memory for us and Simon.

We regale Simon with tales of past Okeetee collecting trips. Of the famed herpetologists who have tread these woods. Chief among them, intertwined with its history, is Carl Kauffeld. Curator of reptiles, later director of the Staten Island Zoo for 38 years. Carl's books, *Snakes and Snake Hunting* (1957) and *Snakes: The Keeper and the Kept* (1969) brought the wonders of Okeetee to the world's attention. Since, it has attracted a steady stream of herpetological nobility and its share of rogues and riffraff. Before taking the reins at Staten Island, Carl spent six years under G. Kingsley Noble as assistant curator of herpetology in the American Museum of Natural History. It's notable, Carl never attended college.

Dick visited Okeetee as a teenager in 1954 with his pal Gordy Johnston, and countless times since then. He knew Carl Kauffeld, visited him often at the Staten Island Zoo where they'd talk herps, and once bumped into him while field collecting Okeetee. I can imagine the thrill he must have felt. People who traveled with Dick or he met in Okeetee read like a herp world *Who's Who.* I'm proud to be on the list. Wonderful memories.

One of Dick's joys is photographing treefrogs and recording their calls.

We drive the country back roads, listening for desired calls after sundown. We'll strike out across fields, through pines, homing in on their melodies. Sometimes we find a pond hidden in the woodland where hundreds of anurans are calling. Other times we home in on a single hopeful male.

We've found treefrogs: Gray, Green, Pinewoods, and Barking, along with tiny, Least Grass Frogs and Spring Peepers—all marvelous. Little can compare to the utter silence of the deep forest. Only our footfalls, occasional hoot of an owl, trill of a toad, bark, metallic gronk or whistle of a frog breaks the stillness. A deafening chorus, or a single voice.

"Dick, remember that night off Tarboro we were driving with windows open, and you heard *Hyla gratiosa*?

"No, can't say I recall."

"Yes, you do! We trekked deep into that swampy thicket, skeeters sucking us dry. We located a temporary pool. Found nothing."

"Okay, so?"

"To be clear, Simon, I never did hear them. So, Dick drives on until he sees a side road pulling off at an angle. A mile up he shouts, 'Barkers!' This time I catch the faint sounds. Into the flooded piney woods, we slog through water and red clay. In Summer, heat's oppressive, air's sticky, smelling of turpentine from wet pine needles. Now and then we stop, listen, adjust our heading and trudge on for 20 minutes to emerge onto a paved roadway."

Simon is grinning. "I think I see where you're going."

"Yeah, too bad we didn't." I give Dick a mock glare and continue my story. "What road is this, Dick?" He looks puzzled, says, 'Don't know.' We cross and forge into the timbers. The calling leads to a breeding pool of Barking Treefrogs. He takes a few photos and records their "Donk, Donk, Donk" calls. From a distance, they're reminiscent of a dog's bark. Colorful, two-inches, heavy-bodied with dark-spotted, granular, green skin. A brown-bordered white line encircles the body. What a sight. Worth the trip."

As we leave, I notice muddy footprints. "Boy, this place looks familiar."

"Methinks it's the same pond we walked to off Tarboro Road, Dentist."

"Where were the Barkers the first time? Oh well, stranger things have happened."

Simon laughs as Dick and I trade verbal jabs. He knows how much we love Okeetee and how we enjoy one another's company. Each of us appreciates how lucky we are.

CHAPTER 101:
Lake Mattamuskeet

This trip is amazing for the numbers and the variety of herps seen and collected. More than that, it's an experience that Simon will never forget. Dick and I make sure of that—in a good way. By the Savannah River, near Clyo, Georgia, we stop to rest and snack on Moon Pies and RC Colas we picked up in a filling station, to give Simon a taste of Southern traditional culture. Boiled peanuts are next on our list of experiences. Simon's in seventh heaven, declaring, "If I lived in Florida, I'd be up here every weekend."

I counter his musings. "You say that now, but collecting's not always this good. A coupla years back, we weren't doing so great when Dick suggested, 'Why don't we slip up to Lake Mattamuskeet for Red Pygmies?' Hunting was lousy here. I'd never been to Lake Mattamuskeet, so I agree."

I begin to recount to Simon our adventures on that trip. "The famed hunting spot is in North Carolina, near to Virginia. It's in the low-lying coastal plain dominated by pine woods and swamps. Perfect reptile habitat. We left. The 500-mile trip to Germantown took a full day. In roadside canals and the Pungo River, painted turtles sunned on the banks, on logs and rocks. Dick mentions 'Spotted Turtles live here.' His tidbit of information intensifies my focus. I scanned the shore as he drove, hoping to spot one of these fantastic creatures. Miles passed. We found nothing. My neck is aching from craning it out the window when I ask, 'Have you ever seen Spotteds here?' Dick pulls over by an old tumbledown farmhouse. 'Not so far,' he says with a smirk and twinkle in his eye."

"The old homeplace has a cracked, leaning stone chimney. Dick tells me, 'The cracks are a choice spot for young ratsnakes.'"

Dick takes a bite of Moon Pie. "Oh yeah, I remember that place," he mumbles through crumbs.

"You should, it's where you nearly killed me with that joist," I say with eyebrows scrunched and a mock frown.

"I know not of what you speak," Dick's face contorts in a smug smile.

"Geez, give me a break." I bend over. "Simon, see that crease on top of my head?"

"Uh, well, umm," Simon fumbles for words as he studies my head.

"Just say yes," I prompt him.

"Oh, yep, I see it," Simon confirms with a quizzical look.

I continue my tale. "Inside the old house, most of the walnut floorboards on both levels were missing, leaving only the floor joists. Many shingles had fallen off the roof, and shafts of light illuminated the interior. Things smelled of rot and decay. Then, I noticed a snake coiled on a brick pier support for the floor joists, and I called out, 'Got one.' The nice five-foot Black Ratsnake was my first."

"Outstanding! What else did you find?" Simon asks. He's excited now.

"Well, I'll tell you," I say as I pick up the story. "It was awkward balancing on the joists. Dick climbed to the second level, negotiating the wobbly, half-rotten beams. It was foolish, and he risked grave injury, but what the hey, it's what we do. When he put his weight on a rotted beam, it cracked, and fell. God only knows how he didn't come with it. The beam conked me on the noggin and knocked me to the ground between the joists. I saw stars and was on the brink of passing out. Then I hear Dick's laughter. When he regains composure, he asks, 'You okay Dentist?'"

After the days he's spent with me and Dick, nothing surprises Simon. He's laughing, grinning. "Tell me, what did you discover at the lake?"

"Not a damn thing," I say, shaking my head. Simon rolls his eyes. "After dark, Dick and I drove the causeway, Frying Pan Landing, then the perimeter road along the swampy shore. All of it prime Red Pygmy Rattler habitat. Nada. It was an interesting excursion, but nothing was moving—the same as in Okeetee. Go figure."

Okeetee came to be a joyful destination for many generations of herp enthusiasts. It may yet be to those of whom hadn't known it during its heyday.

For me, not so much. I noted conditions deteriorating during my last trip in 1974. Development and logging claimed more land. Worse, the people who live there became less enamored of herpers. As a group, we were once welcomed for the business we brought to hotels, restaurants, and gas stations. A few who lacked respect for private property spoiled it. They'd destroy things, leave farm gates open. One incident appeared to be the clincher.

Rumor has it, a collector from New York hit a deer, took it back to his hotel room, and butchered it in the bathtub. He kept the choice meat, left a bathtub full of blood, guts, the deer's head and hide. Imagine the horror the maid felt the next day! This caused a huge chilling effect on the locals towards collectors. It was the last straw after many less-spectacular infractions. They rolled up the red carpet and snake hunters became pariahs.

CHAPTER 102:
Simon in Haiti

"Doing the same thing over and over and expecting a different result is the definition of insanity." So, they say. Haiti's different. It's doing something twice and expecting the same result. Simon and I don't need plans. I'm familiar with what works, and what doesn't.

Our flight and arrival uneventful. Airport security has increased. More police and more travelers have their bags inspected. Simon's eyes are wide, seeing the poverty and teeming sea of humanity taxiing to Hôtel Henri.

Captain François greets us with a hearty handshake. "I am happy to see you, Zye Ble."

"Thank you, and likewise. This is my English friend Simon."

"Welcome to Haiti, Simon. Are you here for the *koulèv*?"

"Yes, I am. Nice to meet you." I can tell Simon's impressed with the captain's English.

"How are things with you, Captain?"

"Not so good, Zye Ble. Much tension, no tourists." We step through the massive old church doors for a view of the city. "Police make many arrests. People are afraid. You should be cautious crossing the country."

Excellent advice that carries extra weight coming from the captain.

"In April, the Haitian Coast Guard mutinied, shelled the Presidential Palace. They defected, taking three ships to the US base at Guantanamo to beg asylum. It has stirred anti-Duvalier sentiments."

It's shocking news. I'd heard of the upheaval, but not the details.

While we put our things in our rooms, the captain sends for Fritzner. He meets us on the steps in a half hour. "Zye Ble!" He calls out, hugs me.

"I'd call you brown eyes, but everyone will answer." He likes it when I tease him.

He laughs. "*Zye mawon*, I don't like."

The friendship we built on the last trip is strong. Mutual trust is essential.

Fritzner agrees to meet us in the morning with a taxi. As usual, we leave suitcases, a change of clothes, and cash with the captain for our return. First stop is Hertz to rent a VW, our only choice. We secure a travel permit and pass the first checkpoint without incident. As the countryside becomes more rural, poverty is more pronounced. Shacks line the roads. People wear rags, bear loads on their heads, push carts, pull wagons, or lead livestock. Simon stares in silence.

I do my best to point out interesting sights to Simon, but in the stretch between Port-au-Prince and Pont-Sondé, there is little of beauty or interest. The countryside is bleak, muddy, or dusty, depending on the weather, and by comparison to other places we will see, rather boring. Still, Simon is taken by the people and the poverty, a constant parade of humanity looking ragged, depleted—as listless and dull as the landscape. A scene that is never easy to take in, or to reconcile in our minds. We drive past looking, but not staring, at a loss for words.

Teeming Port-au-Prince street scenes near the Iron Market leave Simon wide-eyed.

Boy on a donkey with straw pack-saddle in Haitian countryside.

CHAPTER 103:
A Deadly Game

Life or death incidents come without warning. On the way, I try explaining the Pont-Sondé checkpoint at the Artibonite River to Simon. "There's been a few problems on previous trips. No worry, stay calm, do what they say. Follow my lead."

We arrive, pull to the pole gate blocking the road. Are the police Tontons? We can't be sure. Not a good sign, yet not surprising.

"Fritzner, we are tourists going to Cap-Haïtien. You know the story."

The guard asks for papers. Others with rifles peer through the windows, aware it's unnerving. That's the idea.

He demands in Creole, "Out of the car."

They check our suitcase, examine a stash of canned food, keep nothing. So far, so good. We put bags inside and climb in the VW. The police and guard huddle. He leans on the door, speaks to Fritzner. "He's saying the roadway is closed. They want us to park on the side street for tonight." The guard points.

"Tonight? It's only noon. No way. Explain we have to surrender our papers in Cap-Haïtien by day's end."

Fritzner's face glows with nervous sweat. He repeats what I said. The guard turns to the police. While we wait, Fritzner strains to listen. "We cannot stay here. These are bad men. We must go."

My mind racing. "Tell them we will pull under those trees over there." A cluster of Breadfruit Trees a few yards beyond the gate. Fritzner hesitates. I repeat: "Tell him."

The guard stands back, raises the barricade. I start the car, drive slowly, staying far right as if I'm preparing to park in the shade. Then take off, pedal to the floor. When they realize we aren't stopping, the men chase on foot, shouting. We're slinging gravel and dust as we fishtail towards the Artibonite River.

Then a loud crack resounds over the other noise.

"Holy crap!" Simon shrieks, terrified. "Did they shoot at us?"

"I don't know, maybe."

Our engine is screaming, metal bridge clanking, the VW bug races across, my hand hard on the horn. People scatter. We hit the gravel roadway flat out, skidding sideways. The car leaps off the ground as we crash through huge, dry potholes. We choke on dust. "Is anyone following us?" I don't remember seeing any vehicles at the checkpoint.

We push as fast as we can. Simon gives a nervous laugh. We're scared, aware we've done something foolish. It isn't a game anymore. I surprise myself by having the presence of mind to point out where we caught Rhino Iguanas. We speed past the mud huts and cactus *bomas* in a cloud of dust. The road, nothing but holes, bounces us out of our seats every few seconds. A white-knuckle ride to and through Gonaïves. Thirty minutes beyond, a tire goes flat. Damn!

We stop and Fritzner points. "Look, a bullet hole."

Sure enough. It's on the rear passenger side fender, above the tire. Is that why it went flat? Not likely, it's been an hour, we've come a long distance.

"Think they were shooting at our tires?" The hole's the diameter of my pinky finger. "With so many people around, I'm surprised they'd take a chance."

"They don't care," Fritzner says.

We change the tire to make a race team pit crew proud, while looking back to see whether anyone is coming. No signs, dust plumes, etc. We're on our way in no time, reach the foothills, drive deep into the Massif Du Nord. Only then do we breathe easier.

"What do you think so far, Simon?" I glance over with a grin.

"The trip is a bit faster than I thought it might be."

"How about you Fritzner, you doing okay?"

I swear he looks a few shades paler after these unprecedented events. He doesn't reply, doubtless trying to figure out how to get away from us.

"That's never happened before today." As if that mattered. No one dares ask how we plan to make it past Pont-Sondé on the way home.

CHAPTER 104:
The North

We stop in Plaisance for tire repair and make Limbe by late afternoon. Early in our rush to escape.

"You won't believe this place, Simon." Black-skinned, shirtless men gather. Fritzner takes the initiative to tell the people we are back to buy snakes. They recognize us. "Tell them we will take whatever they can find. We'll return in the morning."

I wait as he interprets, then add, "Remind them, we won't accept any that are hurt or damaged. No tarantulas." He speaks for a while, answers questions.

"They're asking if you wish to see Felix."

Oh my gosh, in the confusion I've forgotten. Luckily, they remembered. "Yes. A dollar to the person who finds him."

Questions answered, Simon gains an idea of what to expect, and bubbles with excitement as we start for the coast. We reach Cap-Haïtien too late to turn in the travel paper. From experience, the morning will be soon enough. My private worry is if guards at the checkpoint alerted them at the ministry. For certain, I'm disinclined to let the other guys learn of my concern. We make our way to the Hôtel Mont Joli. Simon looks pleased.

"Not too shabby, huh?" I say, with a bit of swagger.

"Not at all. Nearly as nice as the Henri." Simon is back in form.

"You have your usual private room, Fritzner. Is that okay?" He beams.

We're welcomed and shown our rooms. Nothing has changed, it remains a paradise. Dinner is *pwason boukannen*—grilled fish with plantains and rice.

Not fancy, but delicious. Today's been stressful. Exhausted from our adventures, we turn in. I sleep hard.

After breakfast, we stop at the office of the interior minister to surrender the envelope with the red wax seal. "Welcome to Cap-Haïtien." No mention of the roadblock drama.

It's early, and the hunters in Limbe won't be ready. We tour the quaint Caribbean seaside town. Simon takes a few photos. Fritzner and I enjoy the scenery. His face reveals how much he enjoys these trips to the more tranquil north of Haiti.

⟨∽⟩

A large boa tied to a stick welcomes us to Limbe. Simon goes wild, runs over to cut the snake loose. A crowd gathers. The boys croak their familiar "*blanc, blanc.*"

"Wow, look at this!" He holds up the resplendent serpent. His smile shows every tooth.

"Not bad, for your first."

"Time to earn your pay, Fritzner." I slap my hand on his shoulder. "Ask if anybody has seen Felix."

Scene along river near Limbe, northern Haiti.

Ladies doing laundry in the Limbe River.

Women bearing loaded baskets on their heads, Limbe, Haiti. Scenes like this are long gone.

After the initial rush, when no one else comes with snakes, we leave to let them hunt. I drive to a favorite place to explore and kill time. The river where ladies gather to wash clothes and boys play. It's a slice of bucolic Haitian life, peaceful and tranquil. When we return after noon, several men carry snakes on sticks and a few lads hold gourds.

I caution, "Simon, watch the gourds. They may contain tarantulas. We dare not pay for them unless we need more because they'll keep bringing 'em."

"Okay." He takes one, pulls the stopper. A four-foot *Uromacer oxyrhynchus* slides out.

"*Koulèv Vèt*. Green Snake." The young boy says with pride.

Simon grabs it. "These are rear-fanged, aren't they?"

"Yes, but they won't hurt you. They never bite."

The snake's mouth is wide open, threatening. "If you say so." He stuffs it in a sack and shakes the gourd. Two more of the same species emerge.

We untie boas, inspect them, and pay. A boy tugs at Simon's sleeve saying "*blanc, blanc*" holding up a gourd. Inside, a *Leimadophis parvifrons*. Simon is awestruck. "What a handsome snake!"

"They catch few of these, it's your lucky day."

Another has tarantulas. "Fritzner, tell them no more tarantulas."

He does, and despite knowing better, I give him a small token. They are so poor and try to do what they can to earn a pittance.

We linger a while before we leave for Cap-Haïtien. Once more, we ask if someone can find Felix. For me, today was a mediocre day. Simon is over the moon. He's unaware he hasn't seen anything yet.

At the Mont Joli, we clean up and enjoy an evening meal, special even for Fritzner. The foods aren't new to him, but it's the splendid way they've prepared them that make them exceptional. The presentation. The ambiance. Afterward, we sit on the patio with rum concoctions.

"If we're quiet, bats will come to drink." Within a minute, a bat swoops in, skimming the pool surface with its lower jaw.

"Wait, how d'you manage that?"

"What?"

"The bats. How did you know?"

Simon drinks in every detail. The garden, Caribbean view, insects on the wall, smells, and sounds of the tropics. In our hurry, we take for granted the amazing opportunities we enjoy. What few people get to see.

CHAPTER 105:
The Circus

"Wow, look Simon!" A flock of parrots on the road eating fallen fruit. His reactions mirror mine on my first visit. After several Haiti trips, the sights and sounds still bring thrills.

Simon takes in the line of spectators, twice as many today. Men, women, and children lined along the roadway. "Are they waiting for a parade?"

"The circus, and we're the clowns."

We set to work, I cut snakes loose, Simon pays. A man steps up, speaks to Fritzner. "Felix is coming."

"That's fantastic news! Ask if it was he who found him."

He questions him. He shakes his head. "No, it was his friend."

Crowds await our return in Limbe. A few will have snakes.
The rest are here to watch.

336

He knows we offered to pay for someone to locate Felix, and he could have tried to take the money. These folks have nothing, yet they are honest and kind. He deserves a reward, but we're careful not to risk spoiling a system that works. We'll see he gets rewarded. We cultivate the people's trust. It took time to build. In the beginning, when we'd leave for the hotel, they didn't believe we'd return.

First round over, we retire to hunt for a while. The sound of distant drums is not so unusual in Haiti. Today they're pervasive, widespread. "It's Vodou." According to Fritzner.

"Do you believe in that nonsense?"

"No." He hesitates. "Not so much." I'm never convinced.

It sparks a memory. I tell Simon what happened with the crazy woman in Limbe last year. "I sure hope we won't have to cope with her again."

We find a few *Anolis* and Rainbow *Leiocephalus,* and I tell Simon, "It's hard to get anyone to catch these. They break the tails or bring 50 when we want 10."

"I can't imagine." Simon's in awe. "They'll be so jealous at the BHS." He's a member of the prestigious British Herpetological Society. "So, who's this Felix bloke you're seeking?"

"Without doubt, the highest producing snake collector in Haiti," I tell him with a sense of pride. "No one else, so far, has collected *Epicrates gracilis.* We make a big spectacle of paying him a dollar for them, hoping to inspire others. I wish there were 10 more like him."

Late afternoon we return. Simon's astonished at how the crowd has grown. Snake catchers, and those who come to watch the show. He asks, "Is Felix here?"

"Nope." Simon can hear my tone of disappointment.

Several men have boas, three- to five-footers, colors vary from blackish to pale red. Simon's in heaven. Late in the day, still no Felix, we set out for Cap-Haïtien.

At the hotel, we inspect the snakes, then sort and re-bag them. We rinse out soiled sacks—general housekeeping. An impressive hoard. "Imagine having these back in England."

"Wow!" Simon grins, rubs his hands together in delight.

After a tasty meal, Simon catches a few *Hemidactylus brookii haetianus,* Haitian House Geckoes, on the hotel walls. I add few nice hawk moths to my collection. Fritzner looks at us as though we are from another planet.

⌒

Come morning, we check out, load the car for the trip back. On the terrace, over coffee, bread, and fruit, served on fine china, Simon quips. "You know, I will miss this dump."

A good-sized crowd awaits in Limbe. We set to work untying snakes. One guy has a *Hypsirhynchus*, our first from someone other than Felix. Simon can't contain himself. "What a lovely snake. Brown velvet." He holds it with a gentle grip, examines every detail.

A shout goes out. "It's Felix!" They point up the road. He's coming with an entourage. Men and boys carry two sacks, snakes on sticks, gourds. The crowd is electric.

"Felix!" I embrace him.

"Zye Ble." The same cheerful, smiling guy.

"This is Simon."

Some things need no translation. He shakes Simon's hand. "*Bonjou.*"

"Our number one snake hunter." I give the thumbs-up sign. Felix grins. He knows he's the star of our little circus.

We go through Felix's large, burlap coffee sacks first. There are many boas, perfect as usual, in brilliant colors. He has a few *Hypsirhynchus* and *Leimadophis parvifrons,* all choice snakes. Simon is in nirvana counting and rebagging them. Then Felix hands me a gourd.

"Check this out, Simon." People press in with anticipation. I pull the stopper, turn it sideways, gave a gentle shake. An *Epicrates gracilis* peeks out, pulls back.

Simon coaxes the creature out of the calabash with care and holds it as if the crown jewels. "Blimey, what an incredible animal. How slender, it's amazing."

"Any others?" Felix smiles, hands me another gourd. Today's total: three *gracilis.*

It may be the rarest snake in the Caribbean. Three are amazing. For reptiles, our expedition so far could not be better. We pay up. It's a handsome sum for Felix. He's productive enough to make serious cash. Excitement ripples, capturing even Fritzner.

We inquire if Felix wants us to stay over and come again tomorrow morning. Our plans now are to leave for Port-au-Prince.

Fritzner relays his answer. "He says, 'Not enough time.'" It's okay. He trusts us, waited till the last day to bring everything. I thank him. Wish him well. Say I hope to return.

As we load up, I hear Simon. "What the bloody hell is that?" Fritzner's eyes are wide, eyebrows raised.

"That witch of a woman. The one who caused problems last time," I say, shaking my head. Her face is ghost-like, dusted in white cassava flower. "She cast a spell on us last time."

Simon asks, "What did you do to upset her?"

"Nothing. She got angry when we didn't buy a snake from her husband."

"Let's go," Fritzner says, squirming in the back seat, visibly uncomfortable.

"What? You said don't believe in that stuff."

"I don't!" he snaps. He's not fooling me.

As we drive off, Felix shouts in Creole. "I will see you again, Zye Ble."

"What is *Zye Ble?*" Simon asks.

"That's what he calls me. I guess blue eyes are kinda rare here."

I shout back. "*Orevwa*, Felix." Toot the horn and wave.

CHAPTER 106:
The Plan

We rumble along the rocky road, laden with snakes. Our Northern Mountains sojourn a great success by any standard. We found what we'd come for. Simon's on top of the world, having an experience of a lifetime. Fewer problems, flats, and such, than usual. One thing remains unspoken—Pont-Sondé.

How to get past the checkpoint we ran last week? Like a dead fish in the trunk, we can't ignore it forever. I broach the topic. Fritzner is nervous. Simon is having too much fun to fret. They expect me to have a plan.

An alternate route is not an option. The Artibonite bridge at Pont-Sondé is the only crossing. We discuss taking a taxi or bus and hiring someone to drive the car. It could work. No guarantee. Fritzner thinks it's too complex.

"Let's stay in Gonaïves tonight. Tomorrow morning, we'll leave before daylight and hit the checkpoint early. I doubt they'd expect that." Simon and Fritzner agree.

After a fitful night, we leave at 4:30 am, reach the Artibonite as the sky is lightening, turn off the headlights. In the dim light, I see the gate up at Pont-Sondé checkpoint. The metal decking clanks and rattles on the empty bridge. Will it alert the guards? None appear. We go slow, keep rolling, no guard, a little further, a few yards past, then speed off, home free. Our plan worked. I take deep breaths. First time in a week. Neither of the guys knows how anxious I've been. No need to give them more reason to worry.

〜

Captain François provides a storage room for our snakes at the Hôtel Henri. His concern is for the other guests, as the rooms have but a partition between them. Plans are to visit Massif de la Selle tomorrow. Fritzner has the evening off, asks for his pay. I give him half.

The captain is full of questions. "How was your trip?" We tell of our checkpoint ordeal. "You are lucky. That was a foolish move."

"What would you have done?"

"Return to Port-au-Prince." *Hmm, the thought never occurred to me.*

I don't admit that, "We feared for our lives. Needed to escape," I say.

"You were right to be afraid." He doesn't elaborate.

CHAPTER 107:
Pea Soup Fog and Toxic Frogs

We rest at last, enjoying a blissful, worry-free night. Early we leave for the Massif de La Selle and Furcy, first passing the nicer homes and walled compounds of Pétion-Ville. The winding road climbs towards Kenscoff, giving panoramic views across teeming Port-au-Prince, softened by the gauzy haze of charcoal smoke. As we enter the cool pine forest, I give the guys the lowdown on the toxic *Hyla vasta*.

"Don't rub your eyes or nose whatever you do, not with your sleeve or arms. These guys are brutal."

"I can't imagine a treefrog as big as my hand."

"You'll see, my Limey friend." We titter with excitement.

On the crest of the mountains, pea soup fog envelops us. "Everyone wants to live up here. Cool temperature, magnificent view."

"Guess I'll take your word for it." Simon stares out at the nebulous white wall.

"I ordered the fog special, so you'd feel at home."

I glance in the mirror, tap Simon on the shoulder, hold a finger to my lips, point with my thumb to the rear seat. "Looks as though our friend Fritzner enjoyed his evening off, with a little jingle in his pocket." He's dozing, his head flopping as we round each curve.

I watch carefully not to miss the rural road to Furcy hidden in the brume. We creep along the narrow lane in first gear, walking speed between fences.

In the gloom, we lose the main trail. Last time, the fog was light, wispy.

The roadway turns from dirt to grass and grows narrower. It's obvious we're on the wrong path. I hug the steep hillside on my right where the track shrinks until I fear we'll slip off the edge.

"Okay, everyone out."

"Oh, are we here?" Simon's in rare form.

"No. I don't know where we are. You and Fritzner go check what's ahead. It looks as if we're running out of road."

The door won't open against the hill. They crawl out the window, melt into the gloom. When they reappear, Simon states in a matter-of-fact tone: "You're going to fall off the mountain,"

"Izzat so?"

"That's how it looks to me. The trail narrows to a footpath. You can go no farther, not one meter." He studies the wheels. "Do you want to try backing?"

Out my window, only clouds, maybe two inches of grass between the front tire and the abyss. I swear it feels we're slipping. "Okay, I'll try. Watch me."

I cut a tad to the left. Check to be sure I'm in reverse, ease out the clutch. Barely nudge when the wheel slides over the edge. Simon and Fritzner are both yelling, "Stop, stop!" I have a death-grip on the steering wheel, ready to tumble over the cliff. My butt is clenching the seat covers. Now sitting on the frame, the front left tire dangling.

"See if you guys can find help." Afraid to move, I imagine the car slipping.

The fog clearing for a moment shows, indeed, in the mist we've turned onto a foot track. I hear voices. Funny how sound travels in fog. Fritzner shouts to a small group of men, who turn the other direction.

"They fear us." He runs after them, returns with a few fellows. They look over our plight. "They'll get more help and return."

What can we do? We aren't going anyplace unless we rocket-sled into the canyon. It isn't funny, yet the situation is. Who'd believe this crazy mess?

A dozen burly men gather. One ties a stout rope to the rear bumper. "They will pull you back onto the trail. You steer." Fritzner is taking charge.

Transmission in neutral, I hold on, white-knuckled. Despite having the wheel cut left, it slips further over the precipice.

"Stop!" I yell. "This ain't working."

They huddle, split up, half move to the front, climbing between the cliff and the car. They prepare to pick up the VW with me in it. This doesn't look good.

The men grunting, straining, lift the front end, walk it backward far enough to set it on the trail. I'm anxious to get out, can't yet.

"Steer, we'll drag you back." He and Simon grab the rope to help.

A few men push, the rest pull, moving 20 feet to a less dangerous place. Where we sit now is a foot wider than the car. I still can't exit.

"Simon, find a wide place to turn."

He and Fritzner disappear into the fog. They return to report. "There's nothing for at least 100 meters."

"How am I going to drive backward when I can't see shit?" I'm frustrated, nervous.

Fritzner speaks with the men. "They'll push, you steer."

They're pushing, I'm steering as best as I can. Fritzner and the men shout back and forth. We continue, stopping at a spot as wide as the VW is long.

They rest, cheerful at having gotten us to a safe place. I set the brake, leave the car in gear, and jump out, sweating despite the coolness. Where the wheel went over the brink, I'm shocked by how narrow the pathway is. How did we get this far?

"Hey Fritzner, ask the men if they can turn us around here."

"They say 'yes.'"

With me out, they line up on both sides. They lift and push, grunt, and shout, and rotate it a foot or so. More hefting than lifting, to lighten it so it will skid on the wet ground. It takes a hell of a lot of strength and effort. After several times, the car sits crossways on the pathway. The front bumper sticks out over the precipice, the tail end tight against the hillside. Twenty men lifting, pulling, and pushing. Little by little, turning the VW until it's heading downhill.

It takes an hour of hard work. "Fritzner, we must pay them. How much do you think is fair?"

He speaks to the guys. "They say, 'We are Christians. We must help strangers.'"

"I am grateful. Please let me return the favor."

We have $40 between us, $2 for each man. That is over one week's salary. Seventy-five dollars is the average annual income in Haiti. The one we take to be the leader of the group accepts it. They're pleased, and several shake our hands.

⌒

At the bottom, the fog has lifted. Now we can see where we made the wrong turn. A short distance on is the place for *Hyla vasta*. Fritzner wants to walk around, so we lock up. Simon and I climb the barbed wire fence, slipping and sliding downslope into the banana grove. Soaked from dew-laden foliage, Simon is pulling dead banana leaf sheaths and finds his first huge frog. "Crikey, I'm gobsmacked, it's a bleeding monster!"

"Don't touch your face or wipe your hands on your pants, either. It will come back to haunt you."

Soon, foamy white slime from the frogs coats our fingers. Our eyes are watering, noses burning.

"Blimey, these bloody things are lethal."

"Told you so." Laughter echoes through the bananas.

By the time we capture six of the toxic giants and a few nice *Anolis hendersoni*, we've reached our limit of endurance. We clamber up to the fence, our swollen eyes and tear-stained cheeks signs of a successful hunt. Fritzner stares as if we'd been stricken by a weird disease when we emerge onto the road. He keeps his distance.

"There's hotel soap in the VW to wash off the slime." Proud of myself for thinking ahead. Simon asks why we didn't bring rubber gloves. *Damn!*

I reach in my pocket for the keys and draw a quick breath. I've locked them in the car.

"Don't tell me." Simon shakes his head, knows the answer.

"Yep." With my pocketknife, I try to pry the latch on the passenger wing vent. My knife's too small for leverage. As I look for something else to pry with, a crowd gathers. One man has a machete—perfect!

I get his attention, point to the window, then his machete, and make a prying motion. His eyes widen, he smiles, nods. With a kinetic flash, he smashes the glass to smithereens. "Holy crap! I thought he understood I wanted him to pry it open."

He stands there smiling, reaches in, and unlocks the door. Simon stares at me, wide-eyed. "Well, there's a proper cock-up."

Fritzner is rolling his eyes, hangs his head, shaking it. He doesn't need to say that I should have asked him to translate. It's true, I suppose, but none of us saw this coming.

Today we turn in the vehicle. To distract the rental people, we run through puddles, splash the car with mud and daub muck to conceal the bullet hole in the fender. We pluck broken glass from the vent frame and open every window. The rental agent comes out to inspect it, sees the dirt, and erupts into an angry rant. I apologize and explain that the roads are muddy up in Furcy. We keep him distracted. With the passenger door open, he's looking inside, not at the windows.

Rentals are cash in advance. They have no way to add charges after we turn the car in and leave. We walk to the road, get a taxi, and disappear.

Fritzner did excellent, as usual. An effective translator needs more than language skills. He must understand the people's customs. Their taboos, fears, and desires. He read subtle signals we could miss. He got well paid for his services—and earned it. We hope he enjoyed the trip. Without a doubt, it's been an adventure.

CHAPTER 108:
Tan Shoes and Pink Shoelaces

Our last evening in Haiti, Simon and I spend moth and beetle collecting. A row of Royal Palms, bottoms painted white, line the wide Avenue de la République in front of the presidential palace. Their trunks, illuminated by streetlights, attract insects. It makes for easy picking. My kill jar, complete with a cyanide soaked cotton swab, fills with an assortment of colorful and bizarre beetles.

Our activities draw a palace guard's attention. Curious, he wanders over to check. "*Ensèk*." I'd learned the term. Hold up the container.

The guard looks puzzled but makes no move to interfere. Large moths struggle when caught, damaging bright scales on their wings, ruining them as specimens. In anticipation, I brought a hypodermic needle with formalin to kill them. As I walk from tree to tree collecting and injecting them, the guard again comes over to check. I'm sure he wonders what in hell we are doing, but says nothing.

I notice that the guards wear surplus US military uniforms, insignias removed. They wear combat boots tied with pink laces.

"Simon, look at their boots, it's like the old song."

"What song is that?"

"You remember 'Tan Shoes and Pink Shoelaces,' right?"

"No, can't say I do, mate." He misses the whole point.

Our strange final evening in Haiti is fitting, considering how the rest of the trip has gone. We flag a taxi and return to the hotel to pack.

Captain François wishes us safe travels. We thank him for his friendship and accommodation. The airport has more police than usual, but no one asks what's in our suitcases. Our few-hour flight is akin to time travel to the future. In our world, few could imagine the Haiti we know. Or believe such a place exists. But it does. Its indelible mark is stamped on our lives. We may leave Haiti, but Haiti never leaves us.

By the end of 1970, many thousands of repressed, starving Haitians flee to the Bahamas and the US in makeshift boats. Hundreds die trying.

1970 ushered in many changes. National guardsmen kill four Kent State students at a rally. Apollo 13 Moon mission averted disaster. First Boeing 747 flight from New York to London. First Earth Day. US population passes 200 million (Florida 6.79 million). Jimi Hendrix and Janis Joplin die. Simon and Garfunkel's "Bridge Over Troubled Water," Beatles "Let it Be," and Edwin Starr's "War" are number one tunes. Sometimes it's as if it were yesterday when it's a lifetime ago.

CHAPTER 109:
Exuma Fever

My Bahamian love affair started with Bimini in '65. Ed knew my answer before he called that spring day in 1971. "What say to an Exuma trip? Zoos are begging for *Cyclura*."

"Ready when you are." My heart races with anticipation.

Caribbean rock iguanas are rare. Several species hover on the verge of extinction. Habitat destruction takes a huge toll, people, and animals eat them. Concerned zoologists around the world seek to set up breeding colonies. The iguanas survival could depend on it. Before the Endangered Species Act, few protections exist for reptiles.

Exuma Rock Iguanas, *Cyclura figginsi*, are among the rarest. Do they still exist? If so, where? An exploratory trip may provide the answers. "So, when do we leave?"

"Problem is, I can't get away. Could you run over, check things out? If you locate them, we can come back to collect what we need. I'll pay your ticket."

He had me hooked at "Exuma." Of course, I'll go. So what if he wants me to do the footwork? Exploring is my life.

"Sure. When are you thinking? My schedule's open now."

Ed is rarely straightforward. Every plan has a catch. I'm aware, but love collecting the islands so much, it doesn't matter. Ed knows that.

Date set, he gets the ticket as promised and comes up with cash for expenses. We meet at his house to discuss where to begin the search. Unfortunately, information is scarce.

The Exuma archipelago has 365 islands. They extend north/south over 90 miles across the heart of the Bahamas. Great Exuma, the largest, straddles the Tropic of Cancer. A shallow bank extends west to the Tongue of the Ocean. The eastern side of the chain borders the deep Atlantic. Are there still iguanas? To find out, I must explore these mysterious islands.

We agree on Great Guana Cay to start. Rugged, 12-miles long, never over a mile wide. Dense coppice over limestone. A tangle of tropical trees, vines, palms, and cacti. Perfect habitat—not to mention the name!

CHAPTER 110:
Montana

A planned week-long trip begins with a Nassau flight, connecting to Georgetown. Basic needs in a rucksack. I've got boots on, I pack an extra pair of jeans, and a couple of shirts. The things I'm seeking can't be found wearing shorts and sandals. I take a first aid kit, camera, and collecting sacks. My lizard stick is a three-section fiberglass fishing rod with a noose at the end. Excitement surges as we land on an unfamiliar limestone airstrip hewn from dense coppice. Locals call it jungle. The terminal swelters. Tin-roofed, pink clapboard, it opens to meet two flights each week from Nassau. Primitive. I love it.

The archipelago has 3,700 inhabitants scattered in small settlements. By far, most live in Georgetown, on Great Exuma. In the early 1970s, tourism is the occasional sailing yacht and fishermen. A $6 hotel room is home while I ask around for a way to reach Great Guana Cay.

An old man carrying a fresh-caught grouper suggests taking the mail boat. I check. It runs once a week.

I'm getting nowhere in Georgetown. Wednesday morning, I catch a 20-mile delivery truck ride to Rolleville, the northernmost town on Great Exuma, and closest to the Cays.

By any measure, a destitute, Third World looking place. A jumble of a dozen buildings, wood, and cement block roofed with tin. Unpainted or in faded shades of pink and blue. Abandoned rusted cars and rubble line the few unpaved streets. Picturesque poverty.

At a bare-block building with *grocery* painted on the wall, we stop. I thank the driver, go inside for a cold drink. Store shelves offer a meager choice. Bags of flour, rice, and beans, cans of lard, butter, sardines, detergent, soap, and toilet paper. Basics—little else. Cases of sodas, beer, and rum line one wall, piled high. Baskets of fresh vegetables are lined in rows on the cool cement floor. Nothing is refrigerated.

English loyalist Lord Rolle fled America with his slaves in 1783 at the end of the Revolutionary War. When he died in 1842, he left his land to his former captives. Most took the name Rolle and named their town Rolleville in his honor.

Years of isolation ensued. The residents must have married a lot of cousins. As a result, to me, they look like a bunch of twins. I chuckle to myself, thinking, I've never seen such homely people. The few people in the store are friendly, they ask why I came here, offer advice. One of the men introduces me to a tall Black man called Montana, who's in the store buying supplies. I explain my need to get to out to the Cays.

"Sure, I'll take ya ta Great Guana. Twenty dollar a day, plus gas. I gat drop my 'tings in Barraterre first." He has a broom, a bucket, and groceries.

Tiny Barraterre settlement lies on an island of the same name, located in shallow turquoise seas off the northern end of Great Exuma. A former pirate hideout, a fact I will later find fitting, as things progress. Montana's boat is an 18-footer with a center console. A 50-horse kicker can get us anywhere. How did he get such a handsome and expensive craft?

We buy six glass bottles of carbonated water and a bottle of rum—not for me. I fill my canteen from a tap. Crackers and tins of tuna should suffice for our brief trip.

∽

Tide's out. Montana seems oblivious as he churns a muddy path through the grass flats. He ties up to Barraterre dock. I stay aboard while he carries his supplies to a house that sits on a rocky bluff well above the sea, nestled in thick vegetation kept short by constant winds. White painted block, small but neat. Two potcakes, the local name for mutt, bark nonstop. After a while, Montana reappears with his entire family in tow: wife and seven kids. The oldest looks about ten. Montana is smoking a cigar. He herds his clan down to the dock, where they pose for a photo.

Looking northeast in Rolleville, northern tip of Great Exuma, Bahamas.

Montana, the boatman hired by the author to explore the Exuma Cays.

Montana with his wife
and seven children
on dock at Barraterre, Exuma.

A stop off on Bock Cat Cay
proves fruitful.

Passing Big Farmer's Cay
on our way north along
the Exuma Chain.

After a few minutes, we're underway. At once, a great feeling of freedom and relief descends over me as we skip across azure waters. Today I'll resolve the iguana mystery. It's exhilarating. What I live for is not only knowing the answers, it's finding them.

We make for Bock Cat Cay, where a Rolleville resident said Exuma Rock Iguanas once lived, and yet may. Never inhabited, it lies outside of the major chain of Exuma Cays. We circle the island. Limestone cliffs break sections of sandy beach. An interior covered in dense, scrub-thorn coppice looks forbidding, and a tough place to collect. Curious, fat *Leiocephalus carinatus virescens* greet us on a narrow strip of white sand beach, tails curled scorpion-style over their backs. Except for birds, only Bahamian Racers prey on them. Time is short. We see no iguanas, but it holds promise, so we leave to return another day.

We go up the inside, dodging coral reefs across to Norman's Pond Cay. Follow the chain north, passing Young and Darby Islands, Rudder Cut, Cave, and Big Farmer's Cays. Miles of uninhabited shoreline, with black-stained limestone bluffs and ribbons of brilliant silver sand. Their stark splendor, seductive from afar—belying inhospitable, waterless, soilless, thorny interiors. Channels between islands cut through to the deep Atlantic. Surging tidal currents make any passage tricky and fraught with danger.

Seaspray is bracing on my face, tempering the burning tropical sun. My heart races with anticipation when we pull alongside Great Guana Cay at last. We're close enough to catch the fragrance of aromatic vegetation. The evocative scent of seawater on sun-baked rock recalls walks on deserted Florida beaches with my father, who was a beachcomber at heart. I'm eager to go ashore, explore. It's midday and we're low on fuel. Montana insists we stop first at Black Point, the island's only settlement, at the far northern end.

CHAPTER 111:
Black Point

A splintery wooden dock next to a sandy cove extends to deep water. From here the buildings look rundown, abandoned. Montana leaves to buy gas. "I be right back."

Impatient, after 20 minutes in the torrid heat, I look for him. Stagnant air laden with the stench of fish drying in the sun tempers any charm the village might otherwise have. Shade is absent, not a tree nor palm. No electricity. A small generator runs at night to power lights. No cars, so there are no roads beyond town.

Montana's in a local watering hole. A dim, sweltering room with a cement floor, empty except for a few tables and chairs. Inside smells of sweat and beer. Cases of Beck's Beer and Bacardi Rum stacked against a wall. With an open pint of rum, he's feeling no pain. I'm aggravated.

"Let's get going, Montana."

"Wait." He sets his liquor on the plastic table. "I's askin' bout de 'guanas."

True, he is. I sit, drink a Coke. Warm, but wet, bubbles soothing my throat. To my shock, the locals agree. "De no 'guanas on Great Guana Cay— not no more." Once hunted for food, and the island named for them, yet they disappeared long ago. Pigs, dogs, cats, and rats took a toll.

A third inebriated man joins the conversation. "Gaulin Cay gots 'guanas."

"Where's that?" He has my full attention.

"Nex' island north."

"Let's go, Montana." I'm not asking. "We need fuel and it's getting late."

356

"I ain't ready." He sits back. He's a big guy, but so am I. I grab him by his arm. He jerks it away and glowers. I glare back. He gets up and we return to the boat to get the tank. He's cursing, mumbling. I think I've embarrassed him. Tough, I'm paying for his time.

A nearby shed holds a store of gasoline in glass five-gallon water bottles. Montana picks up a 40-pound bottle of gas and pours—without a funnel. Most of it spills on the dirt floor. Fumes permeate the confined space.

He inverts the jug onto the boat tank's opening. Gasoline gushes in until pressure builds up, causing it to spray over our legs every few seconds. Gurgle, gurgle, swoosh—gurgle, gurgle, swoosh. We're spilling most of it. To my horror, the half-drunk Montana has a lit cigarette between his lips. I react in panic, snatch it, and fling it out the door of the shed. My heart stops when a long, glowing ash falls into the gasoline. It could have ended us, but nothing happened. Angels were watching.

The tank holds six gallons. We buy one jug. A lot of it spills. Still, they charge $12. At home, gas is thirty-five cents a gallon!

Gaulin Cay is less than an hour north. A 1,000-yard-long triangle, a few hundred yards wide, separated by a deep channel from the northernmost tip of Great Guana Cay.

On the northwestern side, shallow turquoise sea laps a sand shore stretching in a silver arc half the length of the islet. Coral sand crunches under the hull as Montana beaches. With canteen, collecting pole, camera, and an empty sack, I jump ashore. He reverses the engine to pull free of the beach and motors north. I never see him again.... Ever.

CHAPTER 112:
Gaulin Cay

Reaching iguana habitat is a long-hoped-for moment. In my excitement, I give no thought to Montana, assuming he'll beach the boat or sit at anchor and wait for me. Above the sandy shore, the terrain is rocky, uneven. Solution holes in limestone support bushes, cacti, and thatch palms. No trees. The heat is withering. In my excitement, I pay scarce notice.

A rustling in the bushes, eyes fixed, unblinking—a slight movement. A juvenile Exuma Rock Iguana! Another, then a third. The bush is alive with juveniles and mature females. I reach for my notebook, realize it's in my rucksack on the boat, glance over my shoulder towards the surf. No sign of Montana.

Then I observe a magnificent sight. A grand male *Cyclura* sits perched on a rock with a commanding view over a natural clearing. Three feet long, he's slate gray, heavy-bodied, with broad shoulders. An older male, with a massive head, muscular jowls, and dangling dewlap. Front legs, bowed as a bulldog's, are vivid orange. A row of dorsal spines from the neck to the middle of his stout tail. Rear legs splayed. His head held high in a regal stance. He bobs, puffs up, arches his back in a threatening posture. A threat, not to approach.

Oblivious to his posturing, a female iguana browses on my left. To the right, another male. The lizard-king pays me no mind. He and his kind have ruled this island kingdom for untold millennia. He's warning a potential rival to stay away from his harem.

The other male answers the challenge with a similar assertion. A bout of head bobbing, hissing, and turning to display inflated orange sides ensues. It continues until the interloper flees. Imagine the thrill of seeing this wonderful melodrama played out right before my eyes. Too bad Montana didn't see this. Too bad indeed. He is long gone.

The sky is cloudless, the sun relentless. My shirt soaks with sweat in the oppressive heat, and every few minutes I sip water from my canteen. Back at the seashore after an hour, not finding Montana waiting leaves me puzzled. Though reluctant to interrupt my iguana quest, best I look for him, establish how long we can stay. He's already acting pissy. I don't want to make things worse by ignoring him. Inland a rocky bluff forms an arc around the flat plain. Atop will offer a panoramic view.

Iguanas scurry at my approach. I scarcely notice, focusing on locating the missing Montana. On top is an otherworldly landscape. Crinkle rock— limestone eroded into half-foot high, needle-sharp points. Treacherous to walk on, it can shred the toughest shoes and break under the weight of a person. To cross even a short stretch of this forbidding terrain is a dangerous ordeal. A fall could be lethal.

Waves pound, undercutting the 40-foot east side cliffs. Their thunder heard across the island. Ground shaking underfoot at the precipice. A constant rain of salty mist casts rainbows above the dark Atlantic. I scan the horizon in every direction. No Montana. A sense I'm on a fool's errand sweeps over me. I climb from the bluff, hike to the beach.

Beach on western shore of Gaulin Cay, a true desert island.

I'll bet he's gone to Black Point to finish his drinking. He'll return late in the day. No reason to believe he won't. It makes me angry he'd take off without telling me. True, we have no set plan. My assumption he'd stay close. I mean, why wouldn't he? We have no plans to stick around. With an ounce left, I now ration my last sips of water. How dare he leave me this way? Yet, I feel silly, standing on the shore as though I missed my bus.

With sunset comes the realization: The bastard's not coming—not tonight. Teeth clenched, jaw muscles tight, I hunt for someplace to pass the night. The beach sand is soft, but gathering clouds threaten rain. Towards the North end, the curving bluff comes to the sea. In the twilight, I discover a small cave a few dozen yards from the beach. My home for the evening, little more than an indent in the rock face, gives a sense of shelter. An hour after dark, a drizzle. Good to be in my tiny cavity. *Wait, water!*

I jump out, face skyward, mouth open. A few drops hit my parched lips and tongue. In minutes, it stops. My shirt is barely damp, not enough to squeeze out. I suck on my sleeve to savor even a hint of moisture, but tasting only salt leaves me frustrated.

Dark, I've nothing but time, and my anger festers. Damn Montana! What is he thinking? He'll get a piece of my mind when he comes back. I planned to spend two days in the cays, but not on one island. Not without supplies. I rest against the warm rocks. My thoughts turn to him drunk in Black Point. Does he even remember he brought me out here? Damn him.

My wife was not keen on my taking this trip. "How are you going to make anything?"

Not concerned for my safety, but in fairness, neither was I. "It's exploratory. I'll find the iguanas and we'll return to collect. Then it will pay." Alas.

Cave-riddled karst cliffs on Gaulin Cay. White cliff in background is on Bitter Guana Cay, over a mile distant.

CHAPTER 113:
Castaway

An ordeal follows for which, in every respect, I'm unprepared. It nearly cost my life. The depth of my predicament is not yet manifest. At dawn, I dash through the bush to the seashore, expecting to meet an apologetic Montana. The beach is empty. Frustration and anger take root. *Get a grip, don't let the bastard win.* My head, swimming with the first blush of worry, spurs my search for drinking water.

The cloudless day promises to be sweltering. Yesterday's island paradise now looks menacing. Waterless, no shade. Rocks and thorns. I need a plan. Where to begin? Few travel these isolated waters. A walk on pristine shores to seek useful items yields two old, faded beer cans. Both kept.

In the brush, I find a piece of plastic film. When I lift it, unnoticed water trapped in its folds spills into the sand. *Drat!* Six feet across, brittle from the sun. I spread it over a thick shrub in case of rain. A glance at the cloudless sky leaves me feeling glum.

I clamber the cliff, searching for trapped rainwater. Painful, disappointing, my fingers made raw from clinging to the rock. Sharp limestone cuts the soles of my boots. Who could have imagined so many iguanas! My efforts yield not a single drop.

Fear intensifies with my anger. I wonder, *How long does it take to die from thirst?* My last sip finished in the night. I've drunk nothing for hours. Near the cliff, hidden by brush, a tree grows out of a sinkhole. Could this hold water? Must check!

Eight feet deep, 10 wide. Sheer sides make for a tricky climb to the bottom. Cracks for hand or footholds. It's creepy, full of dead branches and spider webs. Dark after coming from the bright sun. I find no standing water. On one side is a mound of fallen karst.

"Dig a hole." Wait, was that my voice?

First, I break dried limbs off the tree to make room and then scoop up twigs and leaves and pile them over the limestone. With debris tossed aside, pill bugs and millipedes run for cover as I kneel and pull roots out of the way. I dig through moist compost with my hands, finding a wetter mix of soil and sand. With a hole open, I wait. Wait. And wait more. *Come to Papa.* Hoping to see water seep in to fill the void. Though never forming a puddle, mud oozes. Encouraged, I squeeze a double handful to yield a muddy slurry into a waiting beer can. I shake the mud to get the last drop. Repeating the process over and over produces half a can of disgusting, trash-filled, mucky liquid. But hey—water!

A sip comes with dirt and debris. It's brackish. *Yuck! Pour it out.* Instead, I set it aside to let the mud settle. This is an important find, but every fiber of my body still believes Montana will soon return. No way he'd abandon me. *Would he?*

⌇

At the bottom of a sinkhole, I'm out of sight. If anyone were looking, they'd never notice me. I scramble out, run to the beach—no Montana. Has he come, not seen me, and gone? Not knowing leaves me frustrated, annoyed. Scared? Nah, not me.

The wind blew the plastic sheet to the ground. No clouds in the sky, anyhow. The unrelenting sun sparks an idea. No point wasting time on false hope and self-pity. Near the surf I scoop a pit in the soft beach sand by hand, three feet across, half as deep. I place a beer can, top cut off, in the center, then cover it with the brittle plastic and secure the edges with sand. A small rock centered atop forms a funnel shape over the container.

Sun-caused evaporation condensed on the inside of the covering should trickle to the point and drip into the can. *A solar still.* Did I say that aloud?

My mouth is painfully dry. I wash my hands in the surf, slurp in a handful of seawater, swirl it between teeth and cheeks. Feels good. *Don't swallow. Don't swallow.* I spit. *I won't.*

I'm happy, patting myself on the back, smug from my stroke of genius. By gosh, in a few hours, I'll have fresh water. Then sit things out. I leave the solar still and try not to think of it. "A watched pot," they say. It's difficult. At the sinkhole, I sip from the top of my half-full can of mud, certain I won't need this nasty fluid much longer.

Thirst becomes unbearable. Hours crawl. Squeezing ever drier mud, sipping the muddy liquid barely wets my lips. Grit crunches between my teeth. Sweat soaked, my body cries out. *Check the still. Harvest the water.* The relentless sun burns my skin through my long sleeves and jeans, crossing the rocky ground to the shore. To my shock, I find the can empty! Blown sand fills part of the cone, not a drop of water captured. Why? I'm confused, convinced it was my salvation. My spirit is crushed.

My solar still failing is sobering, frightening. How? I was so sure. I fight a wave of panic, my mind racing. No time to waste. I reset the cover, head to the pit. On my knees, I toil without rest, squeezing the precious liquid from the mud. All the while cursing the feckless Montana. Then I shake, swirl, tap, and wait. Only then I tip it to sip between settled sand and floating debris. Each hour's work nets at most an ounce of cloudy liquid. Turbid, filthy, lifesaving water.

Nightfall, exhausted, back pressed against the warm cave wall. The hopelessness of my circumstances weighs on me. Aware, if not for the meager water produced by the pit, I could be dead. I contemplate my few options. To accept I'm in peril runs against my nature, seems absurd. Yet the danger is real. In the darkness, every second of the trip replays, as I search for any hint of what went wrong. A miscommunication? Did Montana think he was to drop me off for two days? Without supplies? Of course not.... But I've no way to know. Why leave me? What's he gaining? He'll be here in the morning. At least, I hope. *Surely.*

I want to stretch out. I'm so uncomfortable trying to sleep in a sitting position. Lying prone is impossible among these sharp rocks. Despite my mind racing, slumber comes until a leg cramp shocks me awake. I stand, straighten, twist, fight, until it subsides. I doze again, the spasm returns. So goes the night.

CHAPTER 114:
Coming to Grips, or Losing Grip?

Ever hopeful for rescue, my third morning starts with a quick beach recon. Shocked by what's not there. That son of a bitch! He'd damn sure better have a good excuse. The dryness in my mouth now constant, my tongue is cardboard, seems I've stopped making saliva. Saltwater rinses give a brief reprieve from discomfort. My muscles sore from cramping and climbing in and out of the sinkhole. I form the word help with seaweed in big letters on the shore, visible to a passing boat or plane. Couldn't hurt if someone came when I was in the pit. The sea air and dried seaweed scent refreshing after the stuffy, grimy pit. For a moment, I feel normal.

Sun scorches the earth from a cloudless sky. Two hours of work produces a half-pint of water. I've discovered filtering it through my shirttail removes sand and debris. Though still muddy tasting, gray, and a tad salty, it's better than yesterday. My biggest fear is not having enough. The earth grows drier the more I remove.

Mud squeezing is intensive, hard work, but time flies. Not as hot here. Far from cool. Shady, at least. Dig, squeeze, refill the hole, wait, repeat. Dig, squeeze, repeat. While waiting for the mud to re-saturate, I rest my back from bending. My hands are cramping, eyes closed, resting, listening. The only sound is my breathing.

And the voice. Montana, is standing on the beach, his boat with the bow in the sand. "Sorry mon, I's gat drunk in Black Point. Don't be mad a me. Here, I brought ya Coke soda."

Cactus studded interior of Gaulin Cay. Iguana habitat.

Waves pound cliffs on eastern side of Gaulin Cay.

Damn, I'd dozed. I jerk awake, look around, unsettled. *That was weird.*

Spiders and bugs stirred up digging make me wonder what invisible things might live in the water. The island lacks mammals, contamination should be minimal. It doesn't matter, my sole focus is staying alive. Can't bother with such trivia.

I'm alone with my thoughts, and the likelihood there will be no rescue becomes real. Fear of the possibility forces me to consider what else I need to survive. Food is one. *Damn, wouldn't those crackers and tuna taste wonderful about now?* The thought of Montana choking on them brings a smile. The asshole. Screw him.

Cacti dot the plain. Iguanas eat them. Are they edible to people? In the afternoon, snaring an iguana is my insurance against starvation. A light fiberglass rod, brought for the purpose, has a stout cord forming a noose at the tip that makes capturing easy. I wish I'd brought fishing line and a hook. I'd have fish to eat. *Yeah, well, you didn't, dumb ass.* I could devour the flesh of the two-pound adult female iguana raw. *As a last resort,* says the disembodied voice. For now, secured in a cloth sack, I stash her in the shade of a rock by the cave. It gives me a degree of security.

Fearful that the mud will dry up, my search for water never ceases. Low tide allows me to walk beyond where the bluff meets the surf. I find a cove, backed by a 30-foot cliff with a cavern facing the beach. A rock-free sandy floor and headroom back 10 feet. I fetch my few possessions. It improves my sense of wellbeing, despite providing no greater survival prospects.

High tide isolates the cave's beach. To come or go requires wading around the base of the cliff, knee-deep. By day it doesn't present a problem. On my first night in the new location, splashing sounds draw me to the surf. By moonlight, I watch the shadowy shapes of large Bull Sharks. A startling sight, thrashing and wallowing only a few feet from shore. With their backs out of the water, they risk stranding, searching for food. *It will not be me!* Through the evening they ply the shallows, leaving an eerie phosphorescent glow. I sit in the dark, listening to their struggle for subsistence. My quest is on hold till morning.

Notwithstanding my predicament, I notice my glorious surroundings. A place of the sort that dwells in my dreams. Under other circumstances, idyllic. Clean air carries a fragrance of islands and sea. It's that elusive scent; salty, aromatic, hinting of strange foliage, soothing. The funk of wet sand and seaweed at the tide line, sunbaked rocks and my sweat.

Nights are pitch black an hour after sundown. Stars shine with intensity. It's perfect silence save for gentle waves and splashing sharks. Restricted by darkness, it sets the stage for profound, introspective reflection. At peace, despite desperate straits and forced isolation. Now able to stretch out on soft sand in the spacious grotto, deep, tranquil slumber comes calling.

Sleep frees me from the torment of thirst. I do not dream of it. Or dream at all now. Do the body and the brain reserve their energy for actual survival? Even awake, thoughts of what might happen next come only if forced. Likewise, any image of home, my wife, my friends, my work. My mind wanders, drifts. Every thought is fleeting. Emotions on hold, I'm not fearful, or even sad. Strange. Only increasing leg and arm cramps disturb a perfect rest.

CHAPTER 115:
Desperation

At first light, I stumble to the surf to rinse my mouth. The sand is damp, evidence of overnight rain. I rush to my abandoned solar still. An inch of rainwater lies atop wind-blown silt trapped in the cone, enough to fill my canteen halfway. I scoop the wet sand into the beer can, shake, tap it on the side. Another couple tablespoons of precious water. I savor a few sips, save the rest and repeat until recovering every drop. A miracle. Angels are watching.

No sign of boats. *Shame I didn't find Montana's body washed up on the beach. At least I'd know where in hell he was.* Despite the heaven-sent H_2O, it's off to the pit to dig and squeeze. The rainwater tastes so good, but insufficient to sustain me for long. I sip, never taking a satisfying mouthful. I long for the refreshing sensation of gulping, swishing water around, splashing across my tongue, swallowing. My thirst never abates.

The mud grows drier, quicker, from my mining activities. The rain did nothing to replenish the supply, a cause for concern. How much more can it yield? Heat near unbearable. Weakness from lack of food or enough water makes my arms and legs heavy. Sweat robs my fluids. Shade is absent except in the hole. After midday, the sun guts every trace of shadow from my west-facing cave. Rocks radiate fever. Though tempting, I shun a cooling swim. My skin is peeling from sunburn, my lower lip cracked, eyes swollen.

My plight grows more difficult, alarming. Worry sets in with a vengeance. I reconsider escape, dismissed early on. To go north is impossible. There are several deep channels, small islets, and two-mile Bitter Guana Cay to cross.

Five miles of hiking and swimming. The biggest obstacle is a mile-wide channel to swim, to reach inhabited Staniel Cay.

The only reasonable possibility is swimming across to Great Guana Cay then walking three miles to Black Point. On the high bluff above the churning passage, the folly of the idea is plain. The channel is two football fields wide at its narrowest point between islands. Powerful rip currents could sweep me far out to sea in shark-infested waters. On the other side, another cliff. Can't swim in boots, no way to hike or climb without them. To enter the water anywhere other than the cliffs would double the distance. In my weakened condition, it's not possible.

Don't make a fatal mistake. I won't.

Dejected, my only sure salvation is the sinkhole. Now a chore to traverse the length of the tiny island. I stumble across the sand and rock, body aching, vision blurry. Sapped of strength. I rest in the leaves before taking to my knees to dig. Lightheaded, mind racing. I sip as I work, forcing myself to save an ounce for overnight.

As I wade in knee-deep surf around the point of the cliff, sunset paints clouds on the far horizon in blazing orange. I watch for sharks on their nightly quest for food. Perched on a rock by my cave I enjoy the evening's spectacle. The momentary distraction a soothing break from the gravity of my circumstances.

High cliffs border channel between Gaulin and Great Guana Cays.

While darkness falls on the fourth night, I can't help but wonder. *Will this sunset be my last?* Thirst's burn is constant. It tempts me to drink the last sips of water. Hunger, relegated to the shadows, doesn't bother me. But thirst, thirst is agonizing, inescapable.

A sense of gloom descends. A need to set things right compels me to pray. Prayers for rescue. For forgiveness. Forgiveness for having brought worry to my wife and friends. *They're worried, aren't they? Do they know I'm missing?* Swept by guilt. *Is this my doing?*

The greatest lesson of my father was self-reliance. Strong of hand and heart, he made me believe in my abilities. There'd been tests. *Might this be such a time?* How we handle hardships not of our own making shows our true caliber, something I'd best contemplate.

CHAPTER 116:
Deliverance

Mentally exhausted, physically weak, I sleep without waking. Night passes into day, the sun's above the bluff before I stir. I awake to laughter. *That damned Montana, laughing his ass off at me.* I open my eyes. Seagulls! I scan the beach and horizon. Nothing has changed. In the darkness I drank the dregs of water, and none remains. Desperate with thirst, there's a buzzing in my ears, my vision is blurry, every muscle aches. I fight panic, and stumble towards the pit.

On my knees, 30 minutes of squeezing mud earn the first sip of stinky, dirty liquid. Enough to dissolve my dry saliva and turn it into a sticky paste. My throat parched. Swallowing is painful. Head throbbing. *How long can I endure?* I linger in the relative cool for another hour, contemplating my only remaining choice. Squeeze out one more precious ounce before climbing up to the heat and cruel, unfiltered sun. My life is ebbing. I've no choice. It's time to kill and eat the captive iguana. Sunday dinner. I try to make light of the grim task.

It takes everything in me to struggle out of the pit. I stumble through the thorny bush towards the shore, freeze at the sight of a small sloop near shore. *A mirage, a hallucination? Oh my God! Run, run, run!* I bolt for the surf, leaping over brush, cacti, and rocks, reach the sand, "Hey, hey!" arms flailing. He's out of earshot. I splash into the water, jumping, yelling, trying to attract attention. It does not divert. I race up the beach, shirt pulled off, waving it in the air, calling.... A dark figure stands. The boat turns. Saved.

An old Black man, alone except for his potcake dog, lowers the sail as he nears shore. I wade out to meet him, babbling incoherently.

"Give me ya hand." He reaches to help.

"Wait, please, a moment to get my stuff." I slosh ashore, run to the cave.

With collecting pole, camera, and sack with the iguana, I rush on pure adrenaline. Stop short to release the big lizard, plunge into the surf. The elderly man helps me aboard the tiny sloop. Pulls hard, not as frail as he looks.

"Ere, take water." He hands me a glass jug, pulls the stopper. I tip it up, swill a pint without stopping. In moments, it spews back up with force. "Drink slow." His voice gentle.

Exhausted, peaked, I lie to rest on the wet hull. It's the last I remember until we reach Black Point late in the afternoon. My head is swimming from dehydration and sun exposure. Body and mind surrender.

☙

I'm much better by morning, having taken plenty of fluids and a light meal. I don't recall last night, where I slept, what I ate. The old fellow must have paid. I have no money. No other boats are in Black Point. We leave again together towards Great Exuma at 7 am. It doesn't occur to me to ask if anyone has seen Montana.

"Thank you, sir, for rescuing me."

"Bout passed. Didn't know any 'ting wrong but didn't see a boat. Thought I'd bes' check." *Really? Maybe if I'd been on fire?* No, no, I'm sincerely grateful.

"Thank God. I was losing sight of tomorrow. I'm Dennis from Florida."

"Stubbs." He reaches out. "Dey call me Pastor Stubbs, circuit preacher."

Did God send him? He explains how he sails between islands, staying a few days at a time, he and his potcake. Seventyish, small of stature, his skin deepest black, wrinkled from the sun. A ragged straw hat never leaves his head.

"Not many boats on de inside. Lot o' dangerous reefs in these waters." His light Bahamian accent musical. We talk little, confusion reigns in my addled mind.

Time passes in slow motion. Carried past islands on gentle breezes, the wild, distant shores beg exploration. Another day. A patchwork of greens and blues, starfish, and conch visible in the seagrass through the crystalline water. The voyage is a serene respite from the intensity of the last four? Five days? The old pastor hums hymns, waves splash the hull. With the breeze in the sails and clunk of the wood boom, I fade, cradled in the sloop's moist, wooden womb.

My savior, Pastor Stubbs, circuit preacher.

As my condition improves, I become uncomfortable. Half sitting, half lying on the bottom, below the boom. My clothes stay wet in the bilge. I bail with a worn coffee can. The preacher stays busy with sailing, sits on the gunwale holding the tiller. Boom tied short, so it won't knock him off when the wind shifts. His faithful potcake close by his side.

Halfway on our 40-mile journey, we beach on Darby Island to let the doggy do his business. Nice to stand up, walk around, stretch. We don't stay long. I'd love to come back to explore this cave-riddled island. Baxter Castle ruins atop the island's highest point are a rumored Nazi submarine supply post from WWII.

CHAPTER 117:
Angels

The sun sets before we reach Rolleville. We tie up in twilight. The preacher takes me to friends, an elderly couple, to await a ride to Georgetown. Word spreads. People gather. They show concern, listen to my story as told by Pastor Stubbs. Still loopy, it's hard to understand their words. My mind drifts. Eager to serve, the kind folks of Rolleville give me water, sodas, and fruit. They feed me warm, tasty food. A bath in bathwater heated on a stove. Everyone says "Mmm, mmm," shaking their heads when hearing of Montana's dirty deeds. I vow revenge for his treachery, but doubt my conviction.

Montana has my wallet, airline ticket, and other belongings. I have no money, no identification. But I have my life!

Saved by angels. *Could there be any uncertainty?* The past week is a blur, unforgettable, yet fading. Traumatic, though strangely exhilarating, having survived. I recover in one of those dilapidated Rolleville shacks while someone washes my filthy clothes and I rest on a bed with clean sheets in a room provided by a stranger. My belly is full, a glass of water by my bedside. Safe.

Humbled by gifts given without hesitation out of kindness by the same people I secretly ridiculed as homely. Now, secluded, my eyes well with tears. Not of gratitude or relief, though I overflow with both. Rather, with profound shame for my narrow-minded ignorance.

With a good night's sleep I'm feeling much better, if still wobbly. Famished from four days of forced fasting, a breakfast of fish and grits hits the spot. I've never tasted finer. The selfless old couple who took me in is full of questions.

"An' ya from bey?" Mrs. Rolle asks.

"Florida, ma'am. I can't thank y'all enough for helping me. I wish I could repay you."

"Hush, child. Pastor Stubbs say Montana done left ya on dat cay. Dat so?"

"Yes, ma'am. He dropped me and disappeared. Never came back."

"Wait till I see him. Bey ain't gat no broughtupsy." She's waving her chubby arms and shaking her head.

Mr. Rolle pours coffee and cuts a slice of Johnnycake. "True, true."

I don't understand all the words but pick up the meaning. It upset them Montana did what he did. Thing is, he's a part of this community. His actions will likely come to naught.

In late morning, a truck with supplies arrives. A local gent arranges a ride for me. I leave the folks in Rolleville with my thanks and a promise to return someday, grateful beyond words.

On the road to Georgetown, the driver asks: "What happen?"

"Wow, long story! Are you familiar with a guy named Montana?"

"No, but word is he left ya with no water."

"That's right." I give him the story.

"What's ya plan? Where can I take ya?" Everybody is so friendly!

"Not sure. I need to get another plane ticket. I lost everything, my ID, cash, clothes. Don't know anyone or how I'll get home."

"Nassau flight was yesterday. It's a few days afore another. I have a friend. He'll help." In Hooper's Bay, outside of Georgetown, we stop at a neat, modern, cement block house. The home of Hullen Darville, a stocky, self-described Conchy Joe. It's a name by which Bahamians of white-British ancestry refer to themselves. The trucker sounds the horn, and he comes out to greet us. Ushers us inside while the truck driver explains what happened. Hullen listens in disbelief. Then takes charge.

"Come." He motions me to follow. "You can stay in here." A nice room with a bed. "Make yourself comfortable." Is this heaven?

The driver leaves before I notice and can thank him for his kindness. Hullen is full of humor, joyful. His wife Adina is his foil, mollifies him when he gets too boisterous. Though not always obvious, they share a great love. Both are angels and want me to know I'm welcome. Their daughter, Charlene, lives at home with four brothers: Kendal, Ramon, Craig, and Dwayne. Hullen's elderly parents live close by.

Thriving on their care and wonderful food, I regain my strength and get my bearings. We enjoy getting acquainted. Hullen is 36 and I'm 22 this spring of 1971. I arrived helpless, disoriented, without my identity, plane tickets, or money. First, they help me call my wife. By now I am days overdue. She's frantic and has pressured Ed to find me. With no idea of where my iguana quest might take me, he had plans to fly over to search, before I called. They faxed my identification to the telephone office in Georgetown and arranged another flight home. I'm set.

Hullen and Adina treat me like family. Not special. It's great. My week-long trip has stretched to two. The Darvilles invite me to return and offer the use of a small boat to navigate the cays on my own.

⚬⚬⚬

A quote by Oscar Wilde might be cliché. Still, it rings so true. "Experience is the hardest kind of teacher. It gives the test first and the lesson afterward."

Life becomes an adventure when our carefully planned destinations get abruptly changed, when we are forced to rethink everything on the fly and in the process find our true strength. From this Exuma experience, realizing I am a survivor tops my list of insights. My ability to cope with dangers and the unexpected saved my life. Luck for sure, or divine intervention, but grit, tenacity and will to survive all helped. Was finding the pit and wet mud—the sole fresh water on the island—pure chance? The vital beer cans and plastic sheet? Minus any single element, the outcome could be different. Still, I beat the odds with life lessons applied, faith and resourcefulness. Never giving up was key. It kept me alive. I'm proud.

As often happens, an adverse or unpleasant experience turns into something positive. My blossoming friendship with Hullen is a direct result of my ordeal. I will make many more trips to his home on Great Exuma during the next several years. Each the result of Montana abandoning me on Gaulin Cay.

This and time temper my vow of revenge. Besides, I never again lay eyes on Montana.

CHAPTER 118:
Fading Back to Normal

A readjustment period follows any sojourn. Unique, personal events happen on each expedition. This, a trial, was far from usual. Who but me could understand what I experienced when the quest turned to ordeal? The excitement, deprivation, thirst, pain, fear, confusion, tranquility, joy, and gratitude. What should I share? What is possible to share?

Any journey can change a man. This passage changed me. Not everyone can tell, but I know. I am stronger, more confident, a better person. I've matured, shed a burden of antipathy. Part of me never will come home. This is a good thing.

Friends and family are glad to see me. It means something hearing them declare their love, worry, and how my returning safe matters to them. Each time I'm asked to recount my story, I skip more details: things too painful or embarrassing. No one digs deep. They can't conceive the tribulation. How is it possible only five days and four nights were so tough? As the saying goes, "You would have to have been there."

Many Exuma trips follow. Despite many wonderful experiences, none equals my first. Facing death on a desert island, I felt more alive than ever. Back home, I again fade into the daily routine, nameless, faceless. I wait, yearn for the next opportunity to return to significance.

CHAPTER 119:
The Exuma Days

Plans for a hoped-for late '71 Haiti trip are on hold since Papa Doc Duvalier—President for Life, died in April. His son Jean-Claude Duvalier took over. For the first time since 1957, the people of Haiti believe they are free of tyranny, but little changes. Confusion and panic reign. Political unrest makes us reconsider an expedition. The words of this old Haitian proverb ring true: "Only when the serpent dies do you know its true length."

Instead, we embark on several successive Exuma trips. On Ed's initial visit, our luggage gets left in Nassau. It's promised for later in the day, so we call on Hullen and Adina at their grocery store in Georgetown. Entrepreneurs, they own a hardware and lumberyard near their home in Hooper's Bay. They welcome Ed. We talk awhile, discuss our plans.

Time flies, and in a while, we borrow Hullen's pickup and drive to the airport to get our bag. The plane has come and gone. Airport's closed. Our suitcase is visible inside the office shared by Out Island Airways and the Customs officer. No one's here. The door is locked.

With my pocketknife, I slip the lock pin. We take our tote and re-lock the door. At the store, we tell the tale. "Man, you guys are crazy." Hullen loves it. He's never one to be timid.

He'd offered his 14-foot Boston Whaler, perfect for our needs. "You can use it if you return it as you found it."

We stay with the Darvilles. In the evening, we enjoy grilled fish served with warm friendship. At dawn, we depart from his dock on Hooper's Bay.

Ed Chapman with a
curly tail lizard
he noosed on
Bock Cat Cay.

Treacherous karst shelves
just below the surface on
Bock Cat Cay

Ed with captured
Cyclura figginsi in front
of our cave on Gaulin Cay.

With provisions to camp, and extra gas, we're set for a few days. The first stop is the enchanting isle of Bock Cat Cay. We collect a few *Leiocephalus carinatus virescens*. What outstanding lizards! They're fat, with tails curled over their backs, and as they display no fear, are easy to noose. After taking loose the first, it has a bloody eye.

I regret the trauma and release it. The same thing happens with the next! How could this be? Having caught many, we'd never injured a lizard by noosing. Now it's two in a row. As I study the apparently injured creature, blood squirts from its eye onto my hand. Mystery solved. It's autohemorrhaging. Though rare among reptiles, the *Phrynosoma*, or horned lizards, do it. So too dwarf boas, *Tropidophis*. A shocking sight, it will startle any predator, but no harm comes from this self-defense tactic. We move on after catching a few more curly tails and an *Alsophis*.

As we leave, we circle the island paradise, scouting other places to investigate on our next trip. Parts of the shore have narrow sandy beaches with thick bush coming to within feet of the sea. Other sections have 10-foot limestone bluffs undercut by wave action. It leaves a mushroom-style profile. Through limpid water, we see Spiny Lobsters tucked cheek to jowl under the overhanging rock. Hundreds of them. We agree to stop on our return to catch a batch for Hullen.

On the voyage north, we resist the temptation to investigate myriad other islands. With our mission focused, we beach on Gaulin Cay in front of the cave where I spent my last nights. Memories flood. With great effort, we pull our boat onto shore, bury the anchor in the sand as extra security. Well prepared with water and food, we're not dependent on anyone.

The grotto has sandy floor space for both of us to sleep. After stashing our supplies out of the afternoon heat, we set out for a quick tour of the isle. The sun is sinking low. Most iguanas are in for the evening. The few remaining on the cliffs to catch the last rays of sunlight, get Ed excited. Tomorrow is soon enough for collecting. We gather driftwood, build a campfire. Without the burden of worry, it's paradise.

We enjoy the island's charm and serenity as the sunset paints the sky. When darkness falls, the fire illuminates the inside of our cavern with a warm glow. As if on cue, to Ed's amazement, the Bull Sharks come to scour the shoreline. We sit fireside, enjoying dinner from our medley of Beanie-Weenies, spaghetti, and canned fruit. It's a spectacular end to a great day.

⁓

With a collecting pole, we capture two pairs of *Cyclura* for the zoo client. Afterward, we explore. Many iguanas bask in the morning sun, browse on fresh vegetation. We count at least 50 in a small part of their habitat. Recent hatchlings a sign of a healthy population. I revel in the experience in a manner not possible on my first unplanned stay.

Striped Exuma Racerunners, *Ameiva auberi obsoleta*, escaped my notice on the original trip. I wonder why? Distracted? We capture a pair for our friend Professor Lew Ober.

Ed gazes into the sinkhole where squeezing mud saved my life. We stand in silence, my mind still trying to grasp the reality of the ordeal. It's fading, becoming a distant dream. If not for finding the well-hidden pit—I'm convinced I would have perished. I'll never know. In our explorations, we never find another sinkhole. Nor another spot with the remotest possibility of water. Angels led me here, without doubt. After a glorious sunset and a good night's rest in the cave, we leave Gaulin Cay.

We motor north to Staniel Cay, a Caribbean paradise for yachtsmen. It lies in turquoise waters several islands up the chain. A popular stopover for those sailing the central Bahamas. We discuss bringing our wives along, check accommodations. There's nothing we can afford.

Lobsters migrate. Lines of them march across the sandy bottom around Bock Cat Cay. Pack side by side under the cliffs. Hullen asked us to pick up any conchs spotted on the grass flats. Scarce near Georgetown, Queen Conchs are still abundant in the cays. Dive masks and a polespear brought to spearfish for things to cook at camp prove perfect for spearing lobsters. Anchored in 10 feet of water beside an undercut cliff, I doff trousers and dive overboard. Only a few feet deep beneath the limestone overhang, I shoot two with each breath, then slide them off the spear in the boat where Ed rings off the tails and tosses the carapace into the sea. In under an hour, we're on our way with dozens.

Grateful, Hullen stashes them in his freezer, and keeps a few for dinner. Despite these delights living in waters near Georgetown, with two businesses to run, he rarely has time to seek lobsters or conch. Our hosts prepare a sumptuous repast. Lobster tail, pigeon peas, and rice, and conch salad. Adina serves *switcha*, a refreshing tart drink made with key limes and sour oranges. We regale Hullen with tales of our excursion. Our iguanas fascinate him.

CHAPTER 120:
Island Life

Treated like family, we're invited to join whatever Hullen and Adina are doing. They put on no airs. Hullen is a genuine character, he sings, dances, enjoys drinking at the Peace and Plenty pub.

Hullen is a happy drinker. One night, a blaring sound startles us awake. He sitting in his pickup truck, tooting the horn to a rhythm only he feels. Then singing at the top of his lungs, he gets out and uses the hood as a bongo. When he steps in the door, Adina is waiting. She clocks him with a cast-iron skillet. Yep, like a scene from a 1950s TV sitcom. Knocked cold, he falls to the floor with a thud.

The next morning Hullen is sporting two black eyes at the breakfast table. No one mentions it. Not the first time, we're told, nor the last. He loves his drinking and fighting over local politics at the pub. It's in his blood. He's a good old island boy at heart.

〰

For several years we visit the Exumas often. Their hospitality knows no end. Though they never ask, we bring gifts. Even with owning a grocery store and hardware, certain items are hard to get. Their daughter appreciates long-play record albums, scarce in the Bahamas. We come bearing peanut butter, a novelty in the British Crown Colony. When we brought American bacon on ice, we were royalty.

We meet Hullen's parents. Their tiny house is crowded with too large furniture. We sit knee to knee while Hullen and his dad sip-sip, their word for island gossip. Senior Mr. Darville is a well-educated man. Imagine my surprise hearing: "No man never walked on no moon." In 1971 or '72, after several lunar landings, nothing sways him. The more we argue, the more adamant he gets.

"You're starting to wex me."

Vex? What did that mean? His demeanor leaves little doubt he's getting annoyed with my impudence. The subject never again comes up between us.

A charming community pastime in Hooper's Bay is watching movies outdoors. No theaters here, not much television. Video cassettes haven't reached the out islands. Sixteen-millimeter films are available out of Nassau. People bring chairs, set up a painted plywood screen. In the cool sea breeze, it's a cut above sitting in a theater. Island life is a powerful lure. *Night of the Generals* with Peter O'Toole, a few years old, and new to them, never looked grander.

Two Darville boys preparing to set up camp at our cave on Gaulin Cay.

A captured Exuma Rock Iguana, *Cyclura figginsi.*

The author and Ed Chapman taping the jaws and legs of a newly caught iguana. (Photo: Linda Chapman)

CHAPTER 121:
The Iguana Quest

Despite the good times with Hullen and his family, (one trip to Gaulin Cay we took two Darville boys and had a great time), the Exuma Rock Iguanas are the reason we come. Caught on demand, mostly for zoos, a few specimens at a time for breeding programs. Ed handles sales and does not sell them to collectors. I'm here for the love of the experience. The cave on Gaulin Cay is a second home. We carry everything we need each trip, and leave behind nothing. It's pristine, desolate, but exquisite in its isolation, and insular beauty. The way we found it is the way we leave it.

Iguanas abound on the arcing bluff, backing the rocky, sandy scrubland. Ed climbs the craggy cliff, stepping with care along a narrow, 10-foot-high ledge. He adjusts the loop on the 12-foot-long collecting pole, extends it towards a female iguana to slip it over her neck.

The noose is well past her snout, he's waving it to and fro. "Ed, what are you doing? You're out six inches too far."

"I forgot my glasses, dammit. I don't have any depth perception." My laughing out loud doesn't help. I direct from the ground. He draws the pole in, slips the snare over the iguana.

Young iguanas are hard to catch because they bite at the cord as if it were a bug. A zoo requested a few juveniles, so we keep trying. When Ed sees one run under a flat rock, he calls me. "You lift, I'll grab." As he drops to a knee, he yells out in pain.

"What the hell, Ed?"

He sits back, holding his leg. A long cactus needle protrudes. With a deep breath, he pulls it out. He grits his teeth, rolls up his pant leg to check. The spine went in under his kneecap. His knee balloons, throbbing for the remainder of our time on the island.

Things can always get worse. On the way to Hooper's Bay, they do. In choppy seas after crossing to the outside, Ed is piloting, standing barefoot. A spare prop bounces from a shelf under the console. A blade near severs one of his toes.

Other pain is self-inflicted. Hullen requests we pick up conchs on our return. We spot a few on a grass flat, drop anchor, strip naked, jump in to retrieve them. As we dry off to dress and search for more, Ed has an idea. "Why get dressed? We're in the middle of nowhere."

It makes sense. After each dive we move the boat and dive again until we have a couple dozen nice, large Queen Conchs. At the north end of Great Exuma, we cross the reefs to deep outside water and enter Georgetown Sound, then anchor to put on our clothes and realize we're sunburned in places the sun rarely shines. It's a miserable night's sleep. Hullen's appreciating the conchs didn't stop him from calling us "idiots."

❧

We run hot and cold on inviting our wives to Exuma. At Hullen and Adina's urging, the day arrives. Neil Young's "Heart of Gold" serves as a place-marker in memory for the spring of '72. We bring a tent, better food than usual, a Coleman lantern, and sleeping bags. It's a slow cruise through the islands to Gaulin Cay so the ladies can take in the gorgeous scenery.

Set up seaside in front of the cave, the girls tidy things, we gather wood. After a gray-streaked, red sunset, we cook dinner and enjoy the fire. The tide comes in, isolating our beach. Bull Sharks on their nightly visit, their backs out of the water, swish a few feet from shore. Their noisy splashing spooks the gals at first. Soon they grow used to it.

During our stay, we cruise north to Staniel Cay, to see the spectacular Thunderball Grotto on an offshore islet. The name comes from the 1965 James Bond movie filmed there. Colorful corals, sea fans, rainbows of fish, and hawksbill turtles populate the fabulous reefs. The wives love it. They never ask about my being marooned.

Our cave and tent
on Gaulin Cay,
Exuma Chain,
Bahamas.

Ed Chapman with his wife
Linda at our cave camp.

A feral goat we shot on
Gaulin Cay.

Repairing Hullen Darville's
Boston Whaler, reef-damaged
during our last trip.

The previous trip we found goats on the pristine island, brought, we suspect, from Great Guana Cay. Competing with goats for sparse vegetation could put the iguanas in peril. Today we killed a rat, no doubt introduced by accident, with the goats. If they establish, their potential damage is immeasurable. Hullen loaned his rifle. Before leaving, we go goat hunting and discover they're damn difficult to shoot. Wary, they seek refuge on high ground where crinkle rock makes walking difficult. We both try shooting, missing every time. In frustration, I fire from the hip at a distant goat without aiming. It tumbles over dead, shot between the horns. We look at each other in disbelief. After it is bled out and gutted, we load the carcass and make way for Georgetown. It tickles Hullen. We enjoy helping keep his freezer packed full.

In a few months, we return and find the Boston Whaler inverted on sawhorses behind his house. Fiberglass repair materials and paint waiting. He's not happy. With the extra weight of our wives and equipment, we scraped bottom, and coral gouged the hull. We grind, sand, patch, and re-glaze the boat—do a good job. We owe him our best effort. Hullen, pleased, forgives all.

With his craft out of service, he tries to help find a rental. Percy Minns runs a dock and rents boats in Georgetown. He and Hullen have history and never got along well. When we're introduced, Percy acts strange, as if intimidated. He refuses to offer a decent deal. They argue, shout, call each other vile names. It's uncomfortable. Other things are likely at play. No boat for us. We stay on Great Exuma, hunt snakes, enjoy the Darvilles, and build priceless memories.

CHAPTER 122:
Tommy Trouble

Peach fried pies. MaryAnn Yarbrough makes the best. Tommy brings a batch when he visits. "How are the men we helped rescue from the crash?" He hasn't met them since the accident, so we drop in to visit Tommy Crutchfield.

Tommy lives with his wife Penny in a trailer in Ft. Myers. It's chock-a-block with reptile specimens and Tommy is happy to show them off. Tommy Crutchfield is from Mariana in the Florida panhandle "Lower Alabama" as many locals call it, and he and Tommy Yarbrough hit it off well. Thankfully, to avoid confusion of being in the company of two Tommys, Tommy Crutchfield agrees to go as Tom.

Snake hunters love to hunt snakes, never tire of it, and look for any excuse to go. Tommy poses an idea. "How 'bout we three plan a collecting trip together to the Glades?"

In late fall of 1971, on the date set, Tommy comes from Alabama. We leave Bradenton with my van to pick up Tom, who invites us in when we arrive. While he's showing off some reptile specimens, a Freddie Hart song comes on their radio. "Turn that up," he shouts to Penny. She does and as the music blares, Tom belts out a chorus of "Easy Lovin'" to her at top of his lungs, right hand on his chest, left hand reaching out to her. Yeah, it's a little embarrassing. Soon, thank God, we're on the road.

I'm 23. Tom, 22, suggests, "Let's buy some beers." I seldom drink and Tommy isn't interested, but Tom persists. I relent, figure, why not? We stop at a package store and Tom comes out with a six-pack. Tommy has a fifth of vodka.

"Whoa, what's that for?" I'm not thrilled to see hard liquor.

"If you're going to drink, get the good stuff." Tommy twists off the top, tips the bottle.

We travel on, Tommy is in the rear. Before we notice, he's downed a third of the vodka. We're uncomfortable with him being tipsy when we hunt a bridge south of LaBelle, but what can we do? Tommy's pushing 40, he's not listening to us. Before long, he's drunk. Only an inch of vodka is left in the bottle when Tom grabs it and tosses it into a canal. Tommy flies mad, yelling, thrashing around in the back seat, slurring his words.

At a traffic light in Immokalee, he jumps out and runs through traffic towards a liquor store. "What the hell, Tommy?" I holler out the window.

"He's gone nuts," Tom yells as he chases after him. I pull off the road.

Tom catches him, tries to calm him, gets him to the van. I make eye contact in the mirror. "Okay Tommy, we're returning to Bradenton."

"No!" He screams. "No, no, no." He's waving his arms, banging on my seatback, scaring us with his crazy behavior. Finally, he cools off, lies back. "I'll be okay," he says, and falls asleep.

Any thoughts of continuing the hunting trip are long gone. We're in a dilemma and know it. As we drive along, discussing options, hell breaks loose. We hear a loud thump. I look in the mirror and Tom turns to look in the back seat. Tommy has a machete and is trying to hit me with it. When he swings it overhand, it hits the headliner of the van—thump! He continues to try, each time hitting the ceiling. I pull over. Tom jumps out, pulls open the side sliding door and Tommy has his head back, mouth open, about to pass out again. Tom grabs the machete from his hand and puts it under the front seat. Tommy is half slumped over, semi-conscious, so we drive on.

Discretely heading north, all's quiet for a while, when suddenly Tommy grabs a dip net we use for turtles, slips it over my head and pulls. Its rim is throttling me. I'm swerving, trying not to wreck, and try to pull off on the shoulder. Tom has one hand on the steering wheel to help me keep control while he grabs the net handle with the other to take it away from Tommy. He's shouting at Tommy to let go. I'm choking, and Tommy is yelling something unintelligible. When Tom wrestles the net from his hands, we jump from the truck, slam the doors, and confront Tommy. His eyes are floating, his head wobbling. Man, he is drunk. He's slurring gibberish, falls over on the seat, out cold.

I state the obvious. "We gotta take him home. He's gone slap-ass crazy."

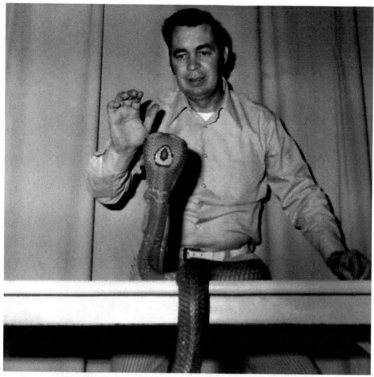

Tommy Yarbrough on his show circuit with a monocled cobra—*Naja kaouthia*.
Snakes and other animals were always handled professionally,
with all due care and caution. The purpose was education, not sensationalism.
(Photo courtesy of Yarbrough family and Maddie Prickett, Eastaboga, Alabama)

Several times on our way north, Tommy awakens, babbles something unintelligible, and passes out again. What's happened to the kind, funny, county bumpkin we knew?

Finally, after we've returned to Bradenton, he's still out. At a loss for what to do, we call MaryAnn. We hate to, but it's the right move. "Oh my God, Tommy's an alcoholic." MaryAnn sounds frantic. "He hasn't taken a drink in years. How did he get hold of alcohol?"

"Um, well, ah, ah." I search for words. "We have to do something. He talks like Donald Duck. We can't understand him."

"They stationed Tommy in Japan when he was in the Navy. He tried hard to learn Japanese. He thinks in Japanese. When he gets drunk, he speaks Japanese."

"So how do we handle him?" I ask sincerely.

"You must bring him home."

Tom Crutchfield holds a cobra which has assumed the position associated with snake-charming acts.

Tom Crutchfield performing a school circuit snake handling demo.
(Photo courtesy of Tom Crutchfield)

That, we soon learn, is much easier said than done. We tell Tommy where we are, and of our plans to take him to Alabama. "No, no, no!" He yells, his face contorted in anguish.

"Look, Tommy, we called MaryAnn." Tears fill his eyes. Tom and I feel like crap.

Still, he refuses to cooperate, so we hatch a plot. We'll hogtie him. We drive to an abandoned shell pit. "Come on, Tommy, let's talk."

He gets out, stands there wobbly, swaying. I grab for his arm, and he pulls back. Tom is built like a small bull and tries to seize him from the other side.

Tommy's no pushover, he's strong and wiry with lightning reflexes from handling snakes and wild animals and isn't going down easy.

"You gonna beat me up?" Tears are welling. "I thought you were my friends."

Holy crap, we can't hurt him. He is our friend, and it's painful to see him this way. We try to reason with him. "Tommy, MaryAnn needs you at home. She's worried sick. Let us take you." He comes around, drops his head, gets in the van.

I take Tommy while Tom follows in Tommy's truck. We leave for Alabama. Fall weather deteriorates on the way north. I find it uncanny when "Rainy Night in Georgia" plays on the radio as we enter Atlanta in the pouring rain. Rain turns to snow, the first I've seen, and I'm driving in it through Atlanta. At this moment, life sucks.

MaryAnn meets us when we arrive in Eastaboga. Her typical sunny, smiling countenance now sad and sullen. She takes Tommy from the van, his head on her shoulder, as she walks him into the house. We bring his things. The mood is somber. She apologizes. We won't hear it. "We bought the liquor." I have a lump in my throat. "We had no idea…."

"I know. Tommy would never buy alcohol on his own. He drank heavily when he left the service. When we married, he swore off for good. He fell off the wagon, once or twice." She wipes tears. "It's been years since he's drank. It only takes one."

We feel like hell, like we'd wrecked their happy home, and drive in silence back to Florida.

❧

A few months later, Tommy calls to apologize. He's his old cheerful self. He tells the same story as MaryAnn. I beg his forgiveness and swear we have learned a lesson.

Next time he visits, Tommy and Tom Crutchfield bond. Tommy's snake-talk circuit is booming. Booked solid with more opportunities for shows than he and MaryAnn can handle. Before long, Tom moves to Alabama to work for Tommy. They stay busy across the state and beyond and build a solid relationship.

When something goes askew, they part ways. My gut tells me Tom took too much control. Tommy never said. Only that, "Things didn't work." It was after a good long run. Tom returns to Ft. Myers, continues a reptile business on his own. He and Tommy remain friends.

We have scant contact after that. Time distanced us. Our interests diverge. One more issue is yet to come involving Tom Crutchfield. It will happen a few years later.

CHAPTER 123:
Is This Where It Ends? Far from It!

An Exuma expedition ends 1971 the way it began. These rapid-fire excursions are made fast and cheap. Get in, collect a few animals for zoo orders, and get out. Don't spend much time. Don't spend much money. It's all made possible with the help of our friend Hullen Darville and his wife Adina in Georgetown. They provide transportation, a place to stay, a boat to reach the out islands—all for free. Bad thing for me is that I thrive on exploring new territory, and though these trips are always exciting, they have become routine. Sure, the first one was anything but routine, but it's ancient history now. Our world is spinning faster. The good and the bad fall quickly by the wayside as we move on to the next adventure.

As 1972 begins, life is back to a version of normal. Living in Florida we're on the edge of the Caribbean and the jumping off point for travel to Latin America. Visitors heading to or returning from trips south come and go. There are many. If people stop by in their travels, and have time, we often go field collecting in Florida, sometimes beyond. If not, we provide a bed and often supply information or loan collecting gear. Travelers may pick up suitcases for specimens when needed or drop off extras. I always have a good supply and no two are ever alike. Fellow collectors visiting our home get treated like family.

Late January Ed and I visit the Exumas. While camping on uninhabited Gaulin Cay, long nights there's nothing to do but tend the fire and watch the sharks. We sit in silence, soaking up just being here. We know how lucky we are to have these opportunities, aware these times will not last forever.

This night our conversation turns to "where to next?" A good Haitian trip, Ed and I agree, is what we need. Now *that* is real adventure. It would do us a world of good. It's been over a year since we visited the mysterious island paradise. After Papa Doc's death, his son, Jean-Claude Duvalier, became president. Things have been too unstable to visit, but now, after some months, we await word from our friend Jacques Durocher, in hope the coast is clear. Meanwhile, I dream and plan, and prepare to grasp any window of opportunity. Another chance to fulfill my destiny.

"American Pie" is on the radio in early February 1972, when the phone rings. I turn it down and answer. It's Ed, with a proposal. I am so ready for an adventure.

Ed cuts right to the chase. "Don Hamper and a his friend, Mike Myers, want to travel to Haiti. Jacques came to town and said it's looking better there now. Might be an excellent opportunity."

I am always wary of Ed's schemes, so I ask, "How so? You know me, Ed. I love Haiti. I'm not keen on traveling with other people, though. Besides, four people and a translator are a lot. Why do you need me?"

"I don't care for the idea of traveling with others much either." *I can believe that.* "Thing is, Don's willing to pay expenses, everything except airfare. We keep an even split of the animals. With you along, we get a bigger stake."

And there it is. Ed always has an angle.

To be continued....

CHAPTER 124:

In *Koulèv*: Adventures of an American Snake Hunter, Book Two

Of course, there's a book two! The adventure continues, starting with a four-man expedition to Haiti. Turmoil stirs the village of Limbe over the discovery of a white snake. A sign from *Danbala*? Do Voodoo spells bring the ambush? What about ending up in a Port-au-Prince jail?

Long-time trading partner, famed Austrian herpetologist Erich Sochurek arrives for an American sojourn. His story of being a German POW in the US during WWII is enthralling and attracts newspaper attention. The Everglades, Florida's Eden, he declares, "Resembles Africa." Adventures abound, including a visit to the dangerous Gator Hook watering hole on Loop Road, hangout of rough and tumble Gladesmen.

Okeetee is next for Erich, with veteran collector Dick Bartlett, while I stay behind to finalize plans for a Mexico expedition. Erich and I head to Mexico, for a month-long series of triumphs and pitfalls with rattlesnakes and beaded lizards, ancient pottery, and a human skull. Then it's drama at the Texas border, resulting in a bus ride home with our truck and our specimens locked in a quarantine yard.

While I'm still feeling deceived by a trusted friend, disaster strikes. A bite from a dangerously venomous snake sends me to the hospital for an extended stay, where I battle to keep my fingers. When my spirits are on the bottom, my employer, FPL, is hit by a strike. I have no income, and an injured hand. Then, while I'm in the depth of despair, I get an offer to go on an assignment that becomes an adventure of a lifetime.

On one of my grandest expeditions, I set out for the southern Bahamas and the Caicos Islands in search of the rarest of island boas on a three-month, non-stop adventure. I survive close calls on reefs with sharks, moray eels and long-spined sea urchins. I meet two famed Bahamian naturalists on Inagua, Island, wade in saline lagoons for miles on thrilling flamingo counts, hog hunts through dense bush and then travel to an abandoned turtle kraal on the north shore to seek my special quarry. After a month that includes fascinating characters, island archaeology, danger, and life lessons, I achieve success in my boa quest, finding the rarest of all Bahamian boas. Next stop: the Caicos Islands. I leave Inagua on a flying garbage truck, making a stop in Haiti on my way.

A final meeting with old friends in Port-au-Prince leads to some dramatic surprises. Off to South Caicos, I witness an airport assassination moments before we escape to the air. A chance encounter on the airplane gives me a free place to stay on an abandoned barge. From this platform I view the daily dramas of island life and death. I meet many unique characters: a sea captain and Stan Brock, famed animal collector and TV star, and I embark on an overnight sailing fiasco. On North Caicos, I find adventure and collecting success, while discovering how local lifestyle has changed little since the first settlers arrived in the 1500s. A rare and valuable striped boa is an unexpected discovery.

My next destination is Little Ambergris Cay. I wrangle a boat ride with a lobster company to spend nine days alone on an uninhabited isle. Solitude-supreme is life affirming. It's my personal paradise until I almost perish in quicksand. When I think my Inagua-Haiti-Caicos sojourn is over, unexpected opportunity takes me to East Caicos, where I find an incredible world of caves and reefs, cacti, and donkeys.

Back in the US, I'm demoralized when I perceive that my doing a favor ends in a shocking betrayal from a well-known herper. Later, I'm off to Mexico with friends Dick Bartlett and Gerald Keown. We search for spectacular rattlesnakes in the moonscapes of Veracruz, and beaded lizards in Colima, all with plenty of good-natured pranks. We experience a night of scary, giant insect encounters and an eerie black-sand beach before heading home to Florida.

Soon our thoughts turn towards exploring the jungles of Venezuela in our first ever visit to mainland South America. Fortuitous meetings with great folks help us cut through government red tape to get our trip going. From the rainforests of the coastal Andes Mountains and Caribbean coast to the llanos, we encounter amazing reptiles, amphibians, mammals, birds, and plants.

The jungle rings with laughter as we slip and slide on the perilous slopes among Fer-de-Lance snakes and scorpions. We walk in the footsteps of famed explorer William Beebe in the high jungle fortress of Rancho Grande before steering south, where we find tegu lizards and Electric Eels and learn about Paradox Frogs and caimans.

Our group heads home, but I stay behind for an adventure-filled excursion to the deep, wet jungles of Guatopo. We find rare orchids, venomous snakes, and strange animals. Our discoveries include species new to science.

Back in Florida, my life takes a dramatic turn. I establish a plant nursery in Bradenton and return to Venezuela to stock our newly built greenhouse benches with botanical riches. We travel to the Lost World, on an epic journey through rainforest, tepuis, crossing rivers and uninhabited wilderness. Close calls require medical attention, but the spectacular beauty of the surroundings is worth all the effort and risks. With two vehicles and eight people, it's five weeks of adventure, an expedition of a lifetime. We explore the jungles of The Abyss along the Brazil frontier, where the Guyana Shield meets the Amazon Basin. We find wild animals and Indians, gold, and rare orchids, and non-stop thrills.

Then in 1976, back in Florida, I begin a new life chapter: forty-plus adventure-packed years as a plant explorer. Oh yes, there are many stories, but those are for another time, and another book.

RECOMMENDED READING

A brief list of books that I enjoyed over the years. Some inspired me and were companions in my youth, others I found later in life. Some entertained me and helped me reconnect with the reptile world after a long absence.

Books about reptiles.

Bartlett, Richard D. and Patricia P. Bartlett – *Reptiles and Amphibians of the Amazon: An Ecotourist's Guide* (2003)

Carr, Archie – *So Excellent a Fishe: A Natural History of Sea Turtles* (1967)

Ditmars, Raymond L. – *Reptiles of North America* (1936)

Ditmars, Raymond L. – *Snakes of the World* (1931)

Murphy, John C., and Tom Crutchfield – *Giant Snakes: A Natural History* (2019)

Pope, Clifford – *The Giant Snakes: Natural History of the Boa Constrictor, the Anaconda, and the Largest Pythons* (1961)

Taylor, Edward H. – *The Serpents of Thailand and Adjacent Waters* (1965)

Books about collecting and studying animals in the wild.

Buck, Frank – *Bring 'Em Back Alive* (1930)

Ditmars, Raymond L. – *Strange Animals I Have Known* (1931)

Ditmars, Raymond L. – *Thrills of a Naturalist's Quest* (1932)

Kauffeld, Carl – *Snakes and Snake Hunting* (1957)

Kauffeld, Carl – *Snakes: The Keeper and the Kept* (1969)

Pope, Clifford – *Snakes Alive: And How They Live* (1937)

Pope, Clifford – *The Reptile World: A Natural History of the Snakes, Lizards, Turtles, and Crocodilians* (1955)

Ryhiner, Peter – *The Wildest Game* (1958)

Books about exploration and adventure.

Bartram, William – *The Travels of William Bartram: Naturalist's Edition* (1958)

Beebe, William – *High Jungle* (1949)

Beebe, William – *Jungle Peace* (1918)

Carr, Archie – *The Windward Road: Adventures of a Naturalist on Remote Caribbean Shores* (1956)

Darwin, Charles – *The Voyage of the Beagle* [abridged] (1989)

Fawcett, Percy – *Exploration Fawcett* (1953)

Grzimek, Bernhard and Michael – *Serengeti Shall Not Die* (1961)

Heyerdahl, Thor – *The Kon-Tiki Expedition* (1948)

Johnson, Osa – *I Married Adventure* (1940)

Sanderson, Ivan T. – *Caribbean Treasure* (1945)

Reptile collectors' biographies, autobiographies, and memoirs.

Bartlett, Richard D. – *In Search of Reptiles & Amphibians* (1988)

Christy, Bryan – *The Lizard King: The True Crimes and Passions of the World's Greatest Reptile Smugglers* (2008)

Eatherley, Dan – *Bushmaster: Raymond Ditmars and the Hunt for the World's Largest Viper* (2015)

Fry, Bryan Grieg – *Venom Doc: The Edgiest, Darkest, Strangest Natural History Memoir Ever* (2016)

James, Jamie – *The Snake Charmer: A Life and Death in Pursuit of Knowledge* (2008)

Lapidus, Richard – *Fun with Snakes: Quirky Stories and Anecdotes of Snakes, Extraterrestrials and Lots of Other Interesting Creatures* (2018)

Lapidus, Richard – *Snake Hunting on the Devil's Highway* (2006)

Love, Bill – *Reptile Odyssey: Adventures of a Herpetologically-Oriented Life* (2017)

Means, D. Bruce, PhD. – *Stalking the Plumed Serpent and Other Adventures in Herpetology* (2008)

Smith, Jennie Erin – *Stolen World: A Tale of Reptiles, Smugglers, and Skullduggery* (2011)

Socolof, Ross – *Confessions of a Tropical Fish Addict* (2014)

Trumbower, Craig – *More Than Snake Hunting* (2013)

Trumbower, Craig – *Even More Than Snake Hunting* (2015)

Weed, Frank – *Adventures of a Snake Hunter: with Frank Weed* (2019)

Weed, Frank – *Gone Snake Hunting* (2010)

GLOSSARY

anti-crotalid
Antiserum effective against crotalid serpents. See: polyvalent antiserum.

antiserum
Blood serum which contains antibodies effective agains a toxin, bacteria or other virulent substance.

antivenin
Blood serum containing antibodies effective against specific animal venoms.

anuran
Amphibians lacking tails. (Frogs and toads)

APHIS
U.S. Department of Agriculture Animal and Plant Health Inspection Service
https://www.aphis.usda.gov/aphis/home/

autohemorrhaging
The defensive emission of blood. Some lizards forcefully eject blood from their eyes, while a few snake species emit blood from the mouth or cloaca.

birdlime
Any of a number of sticky substances used to entrap small birds. For live capture, the substance is manufactured from raw materials which are non-toxic, and can be later safely dissolved with water. The use of birdlime has long been illegal in some countries, and still is.

bodega
A small grocery store.

boma
A word with African roots, for fence, barrier or stockade surrounding a community or livestock.

brackish
Water with slight salinity, such as in an estuary.

Conchy Joe
A white Bahamian, typically of British descent.
https://theculturetrip.com/north-america/caribbean/bahamas/

coppice
Bush, dense shrubland or a group of trees growing closely together.

crotalid
Belonging to the family Crotalidae: snakes with heat sensing pits and moveable fangs. All venomous North and South American snakes except for the corals. Any pit-viper worldwide.

diurnal
Active in daylight hours.

DOR
Dead on the road.

formalin
An aqueous solution of formaldehyde, usually mixed with methyl alcohol, used as a preservative.
https://www.cdc.gov/niosh/npg/npgd0294.html

gourd
Fruit of the calabash tree—*Crescentia cujete*. Dried, it has a hard shell, and when hollowed out are used widely as storage containers for liquids and solids.
https://www.missouribotanicalgarden.org/PlantFinder/PlantFinderDetails.aspx?taxonid=277886&isprofile=0&

gourde
National currency of Haiti

haemotoxic
Any substance, mainly of of biologic origin, that destroys red blood cells. Medical Dictionary for the Health Professions and Nursing. S.v. "Haemotoxic." Retrieved November 28, 2021 from
https://medical-dictionary.thefreedictionary.com/Haemotoxic

Haitian Creole
With French, the official and most widely spoken language of Haiti. A French-based language with a mix of several African languages.
https://omniglot.com/writing/haitiancreole.htm

herp
Abbreviation for herptile. (See herptile)

herper
A reptile and/or amphibian enthusiast. One who studies, collects, keeps, or breeds herptiles

herpetoculturist
A person with a deep or serious interest in reptiles and/or amphibians, to include keeping, and breeding.

herpetologist
A person, typically a biologist or zoologist, who specializes in the study of reptiles and/or amphibians.

herptile
A slang term for reptiles and amphibians.

IBEW
International Brotherhood of Electrical Workers https://www.ibew.org

Johnnycake
In the Bahamas, a flour, sugar, milk, and baking powder bread that is pan baked. https://www.trubahamianfoodtours.com/tru-bahamian-must-eats/bahamian-johnny-cake/

labial
Lip region, for example: labial scales.

machete
A versatile, heavy, long-bladed knife used for cutting brush, cane or as a weapon.

mulatto
Mixed race of African and European descent.

naphtha heater
Flameless, catalytic heaters fueled with naphtha.

neblina
Fog or mist, typically in mountainous areas and cloudforest.

neurotoxic
Poisonous to the nervous system altering its structure or function. Farlex Partner Medical Dictionary. S.v. "neurotoxic." Retrieved November 28 2021 from https://medical-dictionary.thefreedictionary.com/neurotoxic

phlebotomy
Surgically drawing blood or introducing fluids to the bloodstream.

pit-viper
Venomous snakes with loreal "pits" located in front of the eyes, giving the ability to "see" in the infrared region of the spectrum.
https://snakesarelong.blogspot.com/2012/09/snakes-that-can-see-without-eyes.html

polespear
A steel or fiberglass pole with a spear tip on one end and a high-tension rubber band on the other. Used for spearing marine life.
https://apnealogy.com/beginners-pole-spear-guide/

polyvalent antiserum
Antiserum containing antibodies specific for more than one antigen, such as snake venom. Medical Dictionary. S.v. "polyvalent antiserum." Retrieved November 27, 2021 from
https://medical-dictionary.thefreedictionary.com/polyvalent+antiserum

potcake
Mixed breed dog, a mutt. Often a stray.
https://theculturetrip.com/north-america/caribbean/bahamas/

rear-fanged
Opisthoglyphous snakes with enlarged teeth at the back of the jaw. All have some degree of venom, and a few can be deadly, most are considered harmless to humans.

serology
The scientific study of blood serum and its response to pathogens or toxins.

snake psychosis
Pathological phobia or irrational fear of snakes. (The Psychological Importance of Snakes to the Combat Soldier Military Medicine, Vol. 138 #3 March 1973)

supraocular
Located above the eye.

titer
The medically effective concentration of an antibody.

toxicologist
A scientist with an understanding of the medical effects of toxic substances.

venom
Poison, secreted by an animal's glands, that is delivered by spines, fangs, teeth or stingers for defense or to subdue prey.

venomous
An animal that possesses venom.

venter
The belly or underside.

CONVERSION TABLE FOR LATIN NAMES IN TEXT TO CURRENTLY ACCEPTED BINOMIAL

Latin Name in Text	Current (2021) Binomial (if different)
Agkistrodon piscivorus	*Agkistrodon piscivorus conanti*
Alsophis vudii picticeps	*Cubophis vudii picticeps*
Alsophis vudii vudii	*Cubophis vudii vudii*
Ameiva auberi obsoleta	*Pholidoscelis auberi obsoleta*
Ameiva auberi richmondi	*Pholidoscelis auberi richmondi*
Ameiva auberi sideroxylon	*Pholidoscelis auberi sideroxylon*
Ameiva auberi thoracica	*Pholidoscelis auberi thoracica*
Bothrops atrox asper	*Bothrops asper*
Bothrops nasuta	*Porthidium nasutum*
Bothrops nigroviridis	*Bothriechis nigroviridis*
Bothrops numifera	*Metlapilcoatlus nummifer*
Bothrops ophryomegas	*Porthidium ophryomegas*
Bothrops picadoi	*Atropoides picadoi*
Bothrops schlegelii	*Bothriechis schlegelii*
Corallus hortulanus	*Corallus hortulana*
Cordylus giganteus	*Smaug giganteus*
Crotalus durissus durissus	*Crotalus simus simus*
Cyclura baelopha	*Cyclura cychlura cychlura*
Drymarchon corais couperi	*Drymarchon couperi*
Elaphe guttata	*Pantherophis guttatus*
Elaphe hohenackeri	*Zamenis hohenackeri*
Elaphe longissima	*Zamenis longissimus*
Elaphe obsoleta quadrivittata	*Pantherophis alleghaniensis*
Elaphe obsoleta rossalleni	*Pantherophis alleghaniensis*
Elaphe situla	*Zamenis situla*
Epicrates fordii	*Chilabothrus fordii*
Epicrates gracilis	*Chilabothrus gracilis*
Epicrates striatus fosteri	*Chilabothrus strigilatus fosteri*
Epicrates striatus fowleri	*Chilabothrus strigilatus fowleri*

Epicrates striatus striatus	*Chilabothrus striatus striatus*
Epicrates striatus strigilatus	*Chilabothrus strigilatus strigilatus*
Eumeces laticeps	*Plestiodon laticeps*
Eumeces schneideri algeriensis	*Eumeces algeriensis*
Hemidactylus brookii haitianus	*Hemidactylus angulatus*
Hyla dominicensis	*Osteopilus dominicensis*
Hyla gratiosa	*Dryophytes gratiosus*
Lacerta lepida	*Timon lepidus*
Lachesis muta stenophrys	*Lachesis stenophrys*
Lampropeltis getula brooksi	*Lampropeltis getula floridana*
Lampropeltis getula floridana	*Lampropeltis getula floridana*
Lampropeltis triangulum doliata	*Lampropeltis elapsoides*
Leimadophis parvifrons	*Hypsirhynchus parvifrons*
Leimadophis taeniurus juvenalis	*Erythrolamprus epinephalus juvenalis*
Natrix cyclopion floridana	*Nerodia floridana*
Natrix sipedon pictiventris	*Nerodia fasciata pictiventris*
Ophisaurus apodus	*Pseudopus apodus*
Pleamis platurus	*Hydrophis platurus*
Pseudemys terrapen	*Trachemys terrapen*
Pseudemys terrapen decorata	*Trachemys decorata*
Tropidophis canus androsi	*Tropidophis curtus*
Tropidophis canus curtus	*Tropidophis curtus*
Tropidophis pardalis barbouri	*Tropidophis curtus*
Typhlops biminiensis	*Cubatyphlops biminiensis*
Urotheca euryzona	*Pliocercus euryzonus*
Vipera lebetina	*Macrovipera lebetinus*
Vipera xanthina xanthina	*Montivipera xanthina xanthina*

Names checked for accuracy courtesy of:
Uetz, P., Freed, P., Aguilar, R. & Hošek, J. (eds.) (2021) The Reptile Database, http://www.reptile-database.org, accessed 11-02-20

TABLE FOR COMMON AND COLLOQUIAL NAMES IN TEXT TO CURRENTLY ACCEPTED BINOMIAL

Common or Colloquial Name in Text	Current Latin Name
Aesculapian Snake	*Zamenis longissimus*
African Clawed Frog	*Xenopus laevis*
African Lion	*Panthera leo*
African Rock Python	*Python sebae*
agouti	*Dasyprocta punctata*
Algerian skink	*Eumeces algeriensis*
alligator	*Alligator mississippiensis*
alligator lizard	*Gerrhonotus infernalis*
Amethystine Python	*Simalia amethistina*
Andros Boa	*Chilabothrus strigilatus fowleri*
Andros Dwarf Ground Boa	*Tropidophis curtus*
Andros Rock Iguana	*Cyclura cychlura cychlura*
Australian Emu	*Dromaius novaehollandiae*
badger	*Taxidea taxus*
Bahamian Boa	*Chilabothrus strigilatus strigilatus*
Bahamian Racer	*Cubophis vudii vudii*
Bahamian freshwater turtle	*Trachemys terrapen*
Baird's Ratsnake	*Pantherophis bairdi*
Barba Amarilla	*Bothrops asper*
Barking Treefrog	*Dryophytes gratiosus*
basilisk lizard	*Basiliscus basiliscus*
beaked snake	*Rhamphiophis oxyrhynchus*
Bearded Dragon	*Pogona vitticeps*
Bimini Blind Snake	*Cubatyphlops biminiensis*
Bimini Boa	*Chilabothrus strigilatus fosteri*
Bimini Ground Boa	*Tropidophis curtus*
Bimini Racer	*Cubophis vudii picticeps*

Bimini Racerunner	*Pholidoscelis auberi richmondi*
Black Racer	*Coluber constrictor priapus*
Black Ratsnake	*Pantherophis alleghaniensis*
Black-headed Python	*Aspidites melanocephalus*
Blue Tongue Skink	*Tiliqua scincoides*
Blue-throated-Sapphire Hummingbird	*Chlorestes eliciae*
Bobcat	*Lynx rufus floridanus*
Boomslang	*Dispholidus typus*
Broad-headed Skink	*Plestiodon laticeps*
Brooks' King	*Lampropeltis getula floridana*
Bull Shark	*Carcharhinus leucas*
Bush Viper	*Atheris squamigera*
Bushmaster	*Lachesis stenophrys*
Cacomistle	*Bassariscus astutus*
Canebrake Rattlesnake	*Crotalus horridus atricaudatus*
Cape Cobra	*Naja nivea*
Capuchin Monkey	*Cebus capucinus*
Cascabel	*Crotalus simus simus*
chicken snake	*Chilabothrus strigilatus fosteri*
Children's Python	*Antaresia childreni*
cichlid	*Amphilophus citrinellus*
Coatimundi	*Nasua nasua*
Coatimundi (Mexico)	*Nasua narica*
Coendou	*Coendou mexicanus*
Collared Aracari	*Pteroglossus torquatus*
Copperhead	*Agkistrodon contortrix contortrix*
Cottonmouth	*Agkistrodon piscivorus conanti*
Coyote	*Canis latrans*
Desert Iguana	*Dipsosaurus dorsalis*
Diamond Python	*Morelia spilota spilota*
Dominican Treefrog	*Osteopilus dominicensis*
Egg-eating Snake	*Dasypeltis scabra*

Egyptian Cobra	*Naja haje*
Emerald Tree Boa	*Corallus caninus*
European Ratsnake	*Zamenis situla*
Everglades Ratsnake	*Pantherophis alleghaniensis*
Exuma Racerunner	*Pholidoscelis auberi obsoleta*
Eyelash Viper	*Bothriechis schlegelii*
Fire Snake	*Erythrolamprus epinephalus juvenalis*
Florida Banded Watersnake	*Nerodia fasciata pictiventris*
Ford's Boa	*Chilabothrus fordii*
Frilled Lizard	*Chlamydosaurus kingii*
Gabon Viper	*Bitis gabonica*
Varden Tree Boa	*Corallus hortulana*
Geoffroy's Spider Monkey	*Ateles geoffroyi*
glass lizard	*Ophisaurus attenuatus longicaudus*
Gray Ratsnake	*Pantherophis spiloides*
Gray Treefrog	*Dryophytes versicolor*
Great Horned Owl	*Bubo virginianus*
Green Iguana	*Iguana iguana*
Green Jay	*Cyanocorax yncas*
Green Mamba	*Dendroaspis angusticeps*
Green Watersnake	*Nerodia floridana*
Ground Boa	*Tropidophis curtus*
Guacamayo	*Ara macao*
Haitian Boa	*Chilabothrus striatus striatus*
Haitian House Gecko	*Hemidactylus angulatus*
Halloween Snake	*Pliocercus euryzonus*
Hispaniolan Parakeet	*Psittacara chloropterus*
Hispaniolan Trogon	*Priotelus roseigaster*
Hog-nosed Viper	*Porthidium nasutum*
horned lizard	*Phrynosoma*
Horsefly	*Tabanus species*
indigo snake	*Drymarchon couperi*

Jaguar	*Panthera onca*
Kinkajou	*Potos flavus*
Koulèv Baton	*Chilabothrus gracilis*
Least Grass Frog	*Pseudacris ocularis*
Lebetine Viper	*Macrovipera lebetinus*
Leopard Lizard	*Gambelia wislizenii*
Lesser Anteater (Mexico)	*Tamandua mexicana*
leucistic Yellow Ratsnake	*Pantherophis alleghaniensis*
Lindheimer's Ratsnake	*Pantherophis obsoletus*
manatee	*Trichechus manatus*
Maned Wolf	*Chrysocyon brachyurus*
Mano de Piedra	*Metlapilcoatlus nummifer*
Marbled Salamander	*Ambystoma opacum*
marmoset	*Callithrix species*
Maroon-Fronted Parrot	*Rhynchopsitta terrisi*
Mountain Trogon	*Trogon mexicanus*
Musk Turtle	*Sternotherus odoratus*
Narrow-mouthed Toad	*Gastrophryne carolinensis*
Night Monkey	*Aotus trivirgatus*
Nightsnake	*Hypsiglena jani jani*
Nine-banded Armadillo	*Dasypus novemcinctus*
Ocellated Lizard	*Timon lepidus*
Ocelot	*Leopardus pardalis*
opossum	*Didelphis virginiana*
Organ-grinder	*Cebus capucinus*
otter	*Lontra canadensis*
painted turtle	*Chrysemys picta picta*
Pampas Cat	*Leopardus pajeros*
peccary	*Pecari tajacu*
Pinewoods Treefrog	*Dryophytes femoralis*
prawn	*Macrobrachium carcinus*
Prehensile Tailed Porcupine	*Coendou mexicanus*
Puff Adder	*Bitis arietans*

raccoon	Procyon lotor elucus
razorback	Sus scrofa
Red Faced Uakari	Cacajao calvus
Red Pygmy	Sistrurus miliarius miliarius
Red Ratsnake	Pantherophis guttatus
Rhea	Rhea americana
Rhinoceros Viper	Bitis nasicornis
Ringtail Cat	Bassariscus astutus
Roadrunner	Geococcyx californianus
Saki	Pithecia monachus
Sand Boa	Eryx colubrinus
Sand Viper	Cerastes vipera
Scarlet Kingsnake	Lampropeltis elapsoides
Scarlet Macaw	Ara macao
Serpiente de Fuego	Erythrolamprus epinephalus juvenalis
Sheltopusik	Pseudopus apodus
Shingle Back	Tiliqua rugosa
skunk	Mephitis mephitis
South Florida Kingsnake	Lampropeltis getula floridana
Spotted Turtle	Clemmys guttata
Spring Peeper	Pseudacris crucifer
Squirrel Monkey	Saimiri sciureus
Squirrel Monkey (Costa Rica)	Saimiri oerstedii
stingray	Dasyatis americana
Sungazer	Smaug giganteus
Tamandua	Tamandua mexicana
tamarin	Saguinus species
Terciopelo	Bothrops asper
Texas Tarantula	Aphonopelma hentzi
Transcaucasian Ratsnake	Zamenis hohenackeri
Tropical Rattlesnake	Crotalus simus simus
Vermilion Flycatcher	Pyrocephalus rubinus
Víbora de Pestañas	Bothriechis schlegelii

Vine Boa	*Chilabothrus gracilis*
Water Moccasin	*Agkistrodon piscivorus conanti*
White-tailed Tropicbird	*Phaethon lepturus*
wild hog	*Sus scrofa*
Wood Snake	*Tropidophis curtus*
Woolly Monkey	*Lagothrix lagotricha*
Yellow Bellied Sea Snake	*Hydrophis platurus*
Yellow Ratsnake	*Pantherophis alleghaniensis*
Yellowjacket	*Vespula squamosa*

INDEX

This extensive index is arranged by related categories to facilitate its use. Entries not associated with People, Places, Animals, or Plants can be found under the heading of General Index.

戉

ᢙᢙ

Plants

CPSIA information can be obtained
at www.ICGtesting.com
Printed in the USA
BVHW051739070522
636310BV00002B/2